hn Heskett
Reader

A John Heskett Reader

Design, History, Economics

Edited and with an Introduction by
Clive Dilnot

With Contributions by
Sharon Helmer Poggenpohl,
Carlos Teixeira and Tore Kristensen

Bloomsbury Academic
An imprint of Bloomsbury Publishing Plc

B L O O M S B U R Y
LONDON · OXFORD · NEW YORK · NEW DELHI · SYDNEY

Bloomsbury Academic

An imprint of Bloomsbury Publishing Plc

50 Bedford Square
London
WC1B 3DP
UK

1385 Broadway
New York
NY 10018
USA

www.bloomsbury.com

BLOOMSBURY and the Diana logo are trademarks of Bloomsbury Publishing Plc

First published 2016

© Clive Dilnot, 2016

Clive Dilnot has asserted his right under the Copyright, Designs and Patents Act, 1988, to be identified as Author of this work.

No responsibility for loss caused to any individual or organization acting on or refraining from action as a result of the material in this publication can be accepted by Bloomsbury or the author.

British Library Cataloguing-in-Publication Data
A catalogue record for this book is available from the British Library.

ISBN: HB: 978-1-4742-2125-2
PB: 978-1-4742-2126-9
ePDF: 978-1-4742-2128-3
ePub: 978-1-4742-2127-6

Library of Congress Cataloging-in-Publication Data
A catalogue record for this book is available from the Library of Congress.

Every effort has been made to trace copyright holders and to obtain their permission for the use of copyright material. The publisher apologizes for any errors or omissions in the above list and would be grateful if notified of any corrections that should be incorporated in future reprints or editions of this book.

Typeset by Deanta Global Publishing Services, Chennai, India
Printed and bound in India

CONTENTS

Notes on Contributors viii

List of Acronyms x

Introduction *Clive Dilnot* 1

PART ONE Key Themes

Introduction 17

1 What Is Design? 19

2 Commerce or Culture: Industrialization and Design 24

3 Design from the Standpoint of Economics/Economics from the Standpoint of Design 42

PART TWO Design in History and the History of Design

Introduction 59

(A) Designing and Making in the Pre-Industrial World 64

4 Some Lessons of Design History 65

5 Crafts, Commerce, Industry: A Global History of Design: Introduction and Conclusion 74

6 Chinese Design: What Can We Learn from the Past? 83

7 Three Moments in the History of Making: Nomads, Traders, Slaves 89

(B) Designing in the Industrial World 104

  8 The 'American System' and Mass Production 105

  9 Writing the History of Design in the Industrial World:
       An Overview and Two Review Essays 116

 10 The Growth of Industrial Design in Japan 131

(C) Design in Germany 1870–1945 139

 11 Government Policy and German Design 1870–1918 140

 12 The Industrial Applications of Tubular Steel 152

 13 Modernism and Archaism in Design in the Third Reich 159

              PART THREE Design, Business, Economics

Introduction 177

(A) Corporate Design Strategies: Design between Economics
       and Practice *Sharon Helmer Poggenpohl* 181

 14 GM: The Price of Corporate Arrogance 183

 15 Everything Changes, Nothing Alters 189

 16 Design Management in Phillips in the 1980s 195

 17 Teaching an Old Dog New Tricks: How RCA Is Using
       Design as a Strategic Tool 204

 18 Current and Future Demands on Hong Kong
       Designers 215

(B) National Design Policies: John Heskett and
       Design Policy *Carlos Teixeira* 224

 19 National Design Policy and Economic Change 229

 20 Learning from Germany's Integrated Design Policy 233

 21 Design and Industry in China 237

 22 A Design Policy for the UK: Three Suggestions 252

(C) Creating Value by Design: John Heskett's Contribution
to the Business and Economics of Design
Tore Kristensen 268

23 Creative Destruction: The Nature and Consequences of
Change through Design 283

24 Product Integrity 287

25 Cultural Human Factors 293

26 Creating Economic Value by Design 303

PART FOUR Reflections

Introduction 333

27 Past, Present and Future in Design 334

28 Reflections on Design and Hong Kong 340

29 On Writing 346

PART FIVE Last Words

30 Can the Center Hold? 355

Appendix: A first bibliography of John Heskett's published work 359
Index 365

NOTES ON CONTRIBUTORS

Clive Dilnot is currently professor of design studies at the Parsons School of Design and the New School in New York. Educated in Fine Arts and Social Theory, he has taught the history, theory and criticism of art and design in Britain, at Harvard University, in Hong Kong and at the School of the Art Institute of Chicago, where he was also director of design initiatives. He has written extensively in these areas. Recent publications include *Ethics? Design?* (Archeworks, Chicago 2005) and the essay for Chris Killip: *Pirelli Work* (Steidl, London 2006; second edn. 2015). He is the editor of *Design History Economics: A John Heskett Reader (2016) and John Heskett's Design and the Creation of Value (2016)* and is working on a four-volume series of essays under the overall title *Thinking Design: On History; On Ethics; On Knowledge: On Configuration* (forthcoming). Current concerns focus on the role of design capabilities in terms of understanding how we can contend with the implications of the anthropocene as the horizon and medium of our world.

Tore Kristensen is professor of strategic design at Copenhagen Business School. He is educated in business, has a PhD in product development and taught cross-disciplinary marketing and design. His research concerns strategic design, economic analyses of design, experimental methods and transformation economy. He has also been active in assessments works, committees and international research projects. Recent publications include 'Is Product/Brand Familiarity a Moderator of the Country of Origin Cue in Consumer Choice? One More Look' in *Transnational Marketing Journal*, October 2014 with Gorm Gabrielsen and Eugene Jaffe; 'Whose design is it anyway? Priming designer and shifting preferences' with Judy Zaichkowsky and Gorm Gabrielsen, *International Journal of Marketing Research*, Vol. 52, No. 1 (2010); 'The Micro- and Macro-levels of Co-creation: How Transformations Change preferences in Open Source Business Resource' with T. Kristensen in *Open Source Business Resource* (2009): s. 25–9; 'How Valuable is a Well-Crafted Design and Name Brand?: Recognition and Willingness to Pay' with T. Kristensen, G. Gabrielsen and J. Zaichkowsky in *Journal of Consumer Behaviour*, Vol. 11, No. 1 (2012): s. 44–55. Currently, he is co-editing a work on Trans-visuality, a work covering global visual design expressions.

Sharon Helmer Poggenpohl has taught in notable design programmes: The Hong Kong Polytechnic University, the Institute of Design at the Illinois Institute of Technology in Chicago and the Rhode Island School of Design. Her focus over a long career has been postgraduate design education, both master and PhD, as well as design research. Taking a human-centred position with regard to design, she teaches to help students humanize technology, to learn to work creatively and collaboratively with each other and to prepare them to contribute to building a body of design knowledge. She was a colleague of John Heskett for fifteen years at two institutions. For twenty-six years, she edited and published the international scholarly journal *Visible Language*. She co-edited with Keiichi Sato Design Integrations, Research and Collaboration (Intellect Books, 2009). Currently, she is working on a book tentatively titled *Design Theory-to-go*, while teaching occasionally in Hong Kong.

Carlos Teixeira was recently appointed to a position in the Institute of Design at Illinois Institute of Technology. Until 2015 he was an associate professor in Strategic Design and Management at the School of Design Strategies at Parsons The New School for Design. He has a PhD in design from the Institute of Design, Illinois Institute of Technology. His expertise is revealing the operational logics that guide design practice. His academic research and teaching centres on the application of such logics to processes of open innovation. Carlos Teixeira was a doctoral student of John Heskett from 1998 to 2002 at the Institute of Design, which resulted in his doctoral dissertation 'Design Knowledge and Business Opportunities' in 2002. Under Heskett's supervision and intellectual influence, Teixeira collaborated with Paola Bertola, PhD, currently associate professor at the Politecnico di Milano, but in 2001 a visiting scholar at the Institute of Design, resulting in an article titled 'Design as a Knowledge Agent: How Design as a Knowledge Process is Embedded into Organizations to Foster Innovation,' published in the journal *Design Studies* in 2003.

LIST OF ACRONYMS

ERCO	German Lighting Company
I.D.	International Design (bimonthly design journal)
ID	Institute of Design, Illinois Institute of Technology, Chicago
IDSA	Industrial Designers Society of America
IIT	Illinois Institute of Technology
IJD	International Journal of Design
LSE	London School of Economics
METU	Middle East Technical University, Ankara
MIT	Massachusetts Institute of Technology
OBM	Own Brand Management
ODM	Original Design Manufacturing
OEM	Original Equipment Manufacture
OSM	Original Strategy Management
RCA	Radio Corporation of America
RCA	Royal College of Art
SME	Small Medium Enterprise

Introduction

Clive Dilnot

John Heskett, who died in February 2014, was one of the first serious historians of design in Britain and latterly one of the first economists of design. Between the late 1970s and 2010, he made a series of important contributions to the history of design, to the study of design policy and latterly to the theoretical and applied articulation of the economic value created by design, first in the United Kingdom, then in the United States and, in the last decade of his life, in Hong Kong.

I

Born in Coventry in 1937, his father a merchant seaman, he took a degree in economics, politics and history from the London School of Economics (LSE) in 1960. After a variety of jobs in the UK and Australia in 1967, he secured a lectureship in social and economic history in the Department of History of Art and Design at Coventry Polytechnic.* This was at a moment when art and design education, elevated after 1964 to degree status, was beginning to consider what constituted the necessary historical and theoretical background for studies in the field. While fine art was able to appropriate the long tradition of art history and criticism, no such histories or traditions were available for design. Essentially, much of this history had to be written – and on the social, economic and political components of design almost wholly so. With his background in economic and social history, Heskett was well positioned to begin this work. In the early 1970s he became part of the emerging first generation of historians of design.

It is difficult now to recover the context of this moment. In terms of Britain, there is a work to be written of the institutional and pedagogical developments of the period – and of John Heskett's roles within this.

---

*Reading #29, 'On Writing,' contains some autobiographical paragraphs that flesh out in interesting ways the details of Heskett's early work in Britain.

Thought in wider terms, and seen retrospectively from a position where design education is undertaken more and more within university contexts, the difficulty is to understand, in both its virtues and vices, the mentality of the 'art school' approach to art and design education, especially at a time when some of the traditional approaches were breaking down, both professionally and institutionally (stand-alone and art-dominated institutions becoming merged into the (then) polytechnic sector and hence, if slowly, into a university discipline). If there was still very little graduate study in design at that time in the UK (save at the Royal College of Art (RCA)), the shift to teaching design as a degree-level subject was not coincidentally linked to the growing professional self-awareness of the design profession. However loosely applied, consistent government support for design since the Second World War had begun to suggest roles for design that considerably went beyond the subaltern and 'applied-art' mentalities of the 1930s and 1940s. While many of the older attitudes persisted – indeed have ever been entirely eradicated (nor perhaps should they be) – a certain confidence in the field meant that design began to demand, even if equivocally, its 'own' study and pedagogy. 'Design History' and the formation of the Design History Society (1977) are the UK markers of this.

But an immediate question that presented itself to those teaching in the art schools was from where did the scholarship and understanding that could underpin such studies come from – especially in a context where there was all but no research funding and indeed, institutionally, at that date a continuing *opposition* to research and where publication was not only *not* demanded but also not necessarily even wanted?

If these were not already sufficient problems to contend with, there was, at the same time, little assistance to be had from the disciplines to which one might look for support – history, and particularly social and economic history; art history and the history of the decorative arts; anthropology and archaeology. History, for example, was at that point an emphatically text-based activity. Art history and the decorative arts wished to have nothing to do with design.

There was Pevsner of course – a far too easily criticized figure – and eccentricities like Geidion's *Mechanization Takes Command* of 1948. There was also, around 1974, the surprisingly successful publication of Victor Papenek's *Design for the Real World*, but as the diversity of these authors and texts reveal, they were like small islands in a much larger uncharted ocean of practice – in both its historical and operational, and, especially at this date, its strategic and policy, aspects.

The change, such as it was in the 1970s, came about through a number of catalysts. One was the growing importance of the image fuelled by factors such as the development of cheap colour printing and the switch to photographically based advertising. The commercial mechanisms of style, youth culture and 'consumption' forced a new attention on the visual realm and on products in general. Along with the rise to visibility of design as a professional activity in its own right (no longer simply 'applied art'), these developments contributed to an atmosphere in which it was possible to *begin* to treat design and its history with some seriousness. Nonetheless, even as attitudes changed, the resources for creating the serious study of design other than from the models of art history were pitifully thin. They had to be made from scratch and to be successful, that is, to truly engage with the complex actualities of design, they had to be constructed on a different basis.

II

In 1974 *The Times Literary Supplement* published two articles on the state of art history, Joseph Rykwert's 'Art as Things Seen' (whose thrust was precisely to ask about and, to a degree, test the limits of art historical inquiry) and T. J. Clark's much more famous 'The Conditions of Artistic Creation.' Clark nailed his political, and to a degree his methodological, colours to the mast with a quotation from Georg Lukács', 'Reification and the Consciousness of the Proletariat' (1922).

> And yet, as the really important historians of the nineteenth century such as Riegl, Dilthey and Dvorak could not fail to notice, the essence of history lies precisely in the changes undergone by those structural forms which are the focal points of man's interaction with environment at any given moment and which determine the objective nature of both his inner and outer life. But this only becomes objectively possible (and hence can only be adequately comprehended) when the individuality, the uniqueness of an epoch or a historical figure, etc., is grounded in character of these structural forms, when it is discovered and exhibited in them and through them. (*History and Class Consciousness*, p. 153)

Clark's fascination, however, was really only with the first part of the quotation: the identification of art historians as 'real' historians, worrying away, as he puts it, at the central questions – the nature of representation, the structure of artistic production, the processes of social and cultural change. It is this model of the questioning art-historian – who by the depth of the questions he asks becomes de facto a historian per se – that provided for Clark the force of Lukács' quote and the hint of model desperately needed by an art history then slipping into genteel irrelevance. In the process, however, the second, substantive half of the proposition is all but ignored.

But it is just here that the difference between art history and design history becomes sharply evident. For anyone looking at Lukács' quotation through the lens of design, what leaps out is less the 'roll-call of names' that so fascinated Clark, more the extraordinary statement that Lukács offers us – that the *essence of history lies precisely in the changes undergone by those structural forms which are the focal points of man's interaction with environment at any given moment and which determine the objective nature of both his inner and outer life.*

For design this proposition is immediately and powerfully suggestive. 'Structural forms' that are 'the focal points of man's interaction with his environment' immediately connote those configurations (Simon's 'search for good designs') through which we engage and mediate the world. If in his article Clark all but eschews any discussion of Lukács' proposition, the turn that historians of design like Heskett began to take in the 1970s was that *in effect* (not literally – few design historians, Heskett included, read Lukács at this time) they began to take this proposition, or something very like it, very seriously indeed.

In so doing they were understanding that in industrial society the 'structural forms which are the focal points of man's interaction with environment at any given moment and which determine the objective nature of both his inner and outer life' are, inescapably, designed things.

- They are the 'focal points' of history because they are the mediations of industrialization vis-à-vis the modes of production that largely determine them, and the subjects to whom, nominally at least, they are addressed.

- They represent 'the essence' of our times because the 'structural forms' that 'determine the objective nature of [man's] inner and outer life' increasingly centre on products in the widest sense of this term.

- It is in and through the changes to these 'structural forms' that we can grasp at once the objective and subjective essence of our history and it is in turn through this history – and perhaps in some ways only through this history – that we can begin to understand the continuum and variations of past, present and future.

On this basis, therefore, the history of design opens onto a different kind of history. This is not simply a history of (a minor) professional activity but even when conducted as that it contains, at least in potential, a wider revelatory moment.

For all the limitations now ascribed to him, in the 1930s Pevsner had already in large part recognized this. *Pioneers of Modern Design* contains something of this insight. Post-War, and especially in the late 1950s and early 1960s, it is recognized again, most evidently, in Britain, in the writings of Reyner Banham (coming from architecture and architectural history) and, in a different, but in a way no less significant register, the paintings and projects – *and* the writings one should note – of the artist Richard Hamilton. If 'Pop' had a natural gravitation to industrial and consumer products, this was only intensified by the widening and democratic ethos of the 1960s and by the increasing visibility of design, not least educationally, where if the old primacy of the fine arts was not unseated, the former at least began to take a seat at the same table.

By the 1970s and1980s, therefore, there begins to be a conviction that a historically grounded study of design had something that it could possibly reveal, *not least to design itself*, then as now notoriously, in the main, an unreflective practice. At the same time it was early recognized (though never in the end sufficiently) that if design offered 'truths' they were of a singularly messy character, that there is no purity in design; that even as one foot seeks autonomy, and even a degree of critical distance, the other is always stuck in commerce or in power. But it was also this involvement with the messiness of life that was part of its appeal – and not least (here hearkening back, if ambiguously, to Morris and Co.) a reason for its political interest. The emancipatory role of products in relieving domestic drudgery was at that point a lived experience, not simply a taken-for-granted ubiquity. The notion of art and design for the masses was not *simply* commodification (though it was not *not* commodification). Design history in this moment (a least in its best forms) attempted to straddle these incommensurable truths.

III

All this has seemed a very long digression away from the life and work of John Heskett, but it is not, because it was out of these conditions and mentalities, even at first in inchoate form, that Heskett began to work as a historian of design in the early 1970s. In 1977, he moved to Sheffield Polytechnic and there began to write seriously on the history of industrial design. His first book, *Industrial Design*, appeared in 1980 and was instantly successful. It provided one of the first accounts of industrial design, seen not as a succession of product forms, but as responses to changes in production methods and the organization of capitalism. Written in his characteristic accessible manner, the book broke firmly with earlier ways of seeing design. This was design understood quite outside of the art-and-design paradigm: it was not the 'art-and-industry' relation that interested Heskett, nor any idea of form as simply an expression of a modern telos. The thrust was rather entirely on design in industry, first as an economic and then as a social, phenomenon. In the same way the book did not confine itself to Britain nor only to the period of 'heroic modernism.' Rather, in a brief but authoritative survey, Heskett mapped the different historical forms that designing for industry took as industrial capitalism developed after 1800, offering chapters, for example, on the American system of manufactures in the nineteenth century and giving some weight to developments in Germany, the whole emphasizing, as was recently said, 'design in production as part of a system of thinking about objects in terms of needs, opportunities, cultural context and values'.[1]

Germany had long been an interest of Heskett's and in the late 1970s and 1980s he wrote extensively on German design. His second book (part of planned trilogy that would have continued to present day) was on the history of German design from 1870 to 1918 (1986) and he published further papers on art and design in Nazi Germany, offending many by flatly refusing the identification that 'good design' belonged only and inherently to the opposition to Hitler. As someone who, as a child, was bombed out three times in Coventry, he had little patience with those who, rather than understanding design in the complex contexts of operation, preferred to see it in simplistic (and empty) moral terms. Indeed, although Heskett was part of the first generation of design historians in Britain, he kept his distance from its institutionalized forms (The Design History Society (1977) and its journal (1979)). He was not happy with the continuing underlying art-historical attitudes in design history, or with what he saw as the lack of intellectual and historical ambition; rather, at a time when, particularly in the north of England, de-industrialization was evident on a daily basis – and with it the question of whether, under the double onslaught of Thatcherism and imports competing simultaneously on price and quality, Britain could continue to possess a significant industrial base – Heskett's interests turned increasingly to the questions of design and economics and design policy.

The shift to economics became emphatic when he left the United Kingdom for the United States in 1988, first to work on a project with the Design Management Institute in Boston, and then after 1989, to teach in the graduate programmes in the Institute of Design at Illinois Institute of Technology (IIT) in Chicago. Here, and then, after 2004, in Hong Kong, he undertook teaching and research on the roles of design in production and more widely in the economy as a whole, examining design policy at national levels in the United States, Europe and, increasingly, Asia. In these contexts Heskett was working as an advocate for design and design policy – and as a sharp critic of its absence in both corporate and national governance. This is given expression in much of the journalism that Heskett undertook in the 1990s, particularly for the now defunct magazine *I-D/International Design*.

In 2002, melding this work with his earlier work on industrial design, he published *A Very Short Introduction to Design* (titled in the first instance at the insistence of the marketing department at Oxford University Press, *Toothpicks and Logos: Design in Everyday Life*). This book stood for him as a kind of manifesto of his beliefs in both the civilizing and economic necessity of design in an industrial world. It is this conjunction of seeing design at once in its economic potential for improving product quality and in its wider cultural role that distinguished the work he produced after 1990. Case Studies on contemporary design policy, for example an exhibition at the Science Museum, London on recent German design (1987), and a book-length study of corporate design policy in Phillips (1989) were augmented by a range of journalism, lectures and presentations that explored design in the context of hard economic decision-making and in terms of the possibilities of design policies applied at national and corporate levels.

His move to Hong Kong in 2004 brought this work to a head in the form of applied policy at government level. He chaired task forces for the Hong Kong government and the British Design Council and gradually pulled together his understanding of the role of design in economic development, or as Heskett preferred to title it, 'the economic value of design' (or, as he later authored it, 'the role of design in the creation of value'. These developments are discussed extensively below, but it should be said at the beginning that the word 'value' had for Heskett always a double connotation, at once economic and cultural. He felt his task in these years was to argue for the importance of design, not in any simplistic sense but through understanding its complexities and subtleties as a mode of economic and social agency. In this respect he was one of the first historians to consider in a more formal way the relationship between design and economics, extending it to local considerations of policy and looking at it as at once a potential centre of value, an essential component of strategic initiatives and, to a degree, a potential driver of economic success.

It was precisely this ability to hold together these moments that made Heskett in the 1990s and 2000s a valued consultant and advisor to governments on design policy. He had begun involvement with the UK Design Council before he left Britain. By 1990 he was working for a Japanese consultancy and throughout the next decades he was repeatedly invited to speak and advise at institutional and government level in countries as varied (for example) as Mexico, Chile, Finland, Japan, Taiwan and South Africa.

However, he did not entirely neglect history during this period. A commission that did not, sadly, in the end come to fruition, to 'write a world history of design', produced an extended manuscript, *Craft, Commerce and Industry: A Global History of Design* surveying making in the context of production and exchange from the earliest humans through to the present day. Making use of his very extensive travels, especially but not only, in Asia,[2] the manuscript indeed offers a world history of making and one that does not seek to retrospectively impose 'design' values on aretfacture, but as the title suggests tries to grasp the *longue durée* of pre-industrial production, making and exchange of things. At a time when we are beginning to realize the brevity of the industrial moment, this wider perspective has its force.

As a teacher, speaker and writer about design across four decades, Heskett made a considerable contribution to his audiences' understanding of design. Uniting history with concerns for policy, he kept together two perspectives that his successors on both sides seem to have been unable to achieve. Today, we have policy without history ('design research') and history that eschews concerns for practice. Heskett understood the flow between these moments. In the best sense he had a social-democratic belief in design as an agency of improvement. In a late note he defined design as that capacity which enables us 'to create a world of artifice to meet our needs and give meaning to our lives', and 'to beneficially reshape the world of artifice we have created and inhabit'; all the while acting in itself, as 'a unique characteristic of what defines us as human beings on a par with literature and music'.

At the end of his unpublished book-length ms. *Craft, Commerce and Industry: A History of Design*, he goes further: 'We have in the history of design an astonishingly rich inheritance. What is even more amazing is that with every new-born child the latent potential for similar achievement exists in this incredibly fertile human capability. It is the greatest renewable resource we possess and to acknowledge its creative potential could be the finest legacy we leave for our children and grandchildren.' The risk of bathos in this quotation was calculated. It was the deliberate converse of the fact that looking at design in terms of economics runs the risk of instrumentality. Heskett was aware of this, and on the other side that the approach to the history of designed things that 'innocently' values design often operates merely to the benefit of the antiques trade. The difficulties that a history of design encounters are necessarily of a different nature to those of social history – or art history. The praxiological component; the fact that in design criticism is manifest as affirmation; the necessity to think intervention, all these preclude an approach that differentiates a subject matter from action. To write the history of design is to seek to recover aspects of a capability occluded to itself. One paradox is that, while the impulses that provoked the development of the history of design have faded in the last forty years, objectively the onset of the world-as-artificial has opened again a purpose in the form of the recovery not of the 'value' of design per se but of design as potentially a mode of action in the world, something that has been continually glimpsed, if peripherally, across the industrial period but that is now coming to fuller visibility. The paradox here is that what began in and from industry now finds itself thinking its role at the ending of what we now can see as the (short) industrial period – ending that is, not of course of industry per se, but of the latter as formative in the global economies we are now moving into. The question now to be asked is: What is design in an epoch of the artificial, and what does a history of this capability in this new context have to offer? How does this history help inform our understanding of those structural forms that are today (*pace* Lukács) 'the focal points of man's interaction with environment at any given moment and which determine the objective nature of both his inner and outer life?'

John Heskett's work scarcely touches on these emerging issues. But he was, to repeat, one of the very first historians in his field to both take design seriously as a subject of historical investigation and dare to do what few cultural historians have done, that is, to attempt to think seriously about questions of economic value, both within and without (and by implication beyond) capitalism.

IV

It is a valid criticism of the Reader – and this was made forcefully by one of the reviewers of the draft manuscript – to say that overall the book as it stands, including this introduction, lacks a degree of critical perspective, both in terms of showing how Heskett's work is 'relevant to present and emerging concerns' and to 'offer a stronger critical voice, directing the reader, offering critiques and building on the work Heskett begun'. There is truth to this claim. A discerning reader will notice in a number of the introductory notes to the sections, implicit, sometimes explicit, critical perspectives. But neither this introduction nor the three chapters that introduce the different parts of Part III are *critical* explorations of Heskett's work in the sense delineated above. The reason for this lies in the genesis of the book. I had spoken with John before his death on producing a Reader. His untimely passing and the degree of his illness in the months beforehand made this an impossible project. After he died I took it over, at once as an academic project, but also (this was only a few months after his death in February 2014) as something of a memorial. The aim of the book was to place his work in the public sphere. Indeed, a part of the aim was precisely to stimulate critical debate and discussion – which, to a remarkable extent, design lacks. The reviewer of the ms. was quite right. It is precisely the critical assessment, not just of Heskett's work, but of the fields of design history and design business/economics, that is essential. But this I felt was a separate project to presenting the work. Only with the work back in the public sphere could critical discussion begin. None of this means, of course, that the work evades criticism; far from it. Yet, criticism begins from reading. George Steiner's distinction 'Critic/Reader' applies. The *first* task is to be able to read again the work. It is from that that thought begins.

A note on the selection of the texts

As has already been noted, John Heskett's academic life fell into two distinct periods: his work in England from the late 1960s through to 1989, which focuses on the history of design and particularly the history of industrial design; and his work in America (and then in Hong Kong), from 1989 to 2010, which focuses largely on questions of design policy, design and business and the economics of design. This neat bifurcation does not, in fact, quite hold: Heskett had begun to be interested in questions of design policy and design and business before he left the UK, and from the late 1990s through to around 2006 he was also heavily involved in writing a global history of making. Nonetheless, the distinction is real enough for it to provide the obvious logic for the organization of the Reader.

The Reader thus falls into two main parts, roughly of equal length; the first on history (Part II) and the second on design and business, design policy and design and economics (Part III). Together these account for three-quarters of the texts. They are bracketed in two ways: first, in Part I, by introductions to the three key themes – *design, history* and *economics* – which he explored so assiduously and which were the basis of almost everything he wrote. These themes then reappear at the end of the book in a short series of reflections and last words (Parts IV and V) that mediate on these issues and on the trajectories of his life, work and hopes.

The Reader does not, of course, reproduce everything of interest that he wrote. Although the book is larger than first anticipated by the publisher (they have been generous in their support for this venture), there are necessary limits on the size of the volume. Nonetheless, overall, the book aims, within its limits, to present something of the cohesion and force of Heskett's thinking as at once a historian, a design economist and a design thinker. A quick comparison of the list of contents with the provisional bibliography of his published work published as an appendix to this volume will show that the Reader presents a fair sampling of his work. Outside of the four major books (sections of which are included in the Reader), the pieces included here represent just less than half of his significant published output. The aim has been to be comprehensive in the range of material presented but to put stress on work that is now out of print and difficult to find or was previously unpublished. There is particular emphasis too on articles and the pieces in which Heskett's distinctive voice comes through the otherwise sometimes neutral tone of his writing. The selection deploys range too in other senses. No less than seven of the readings are unpublished and these include extracts from his two most important unpublished manuscripts, the book-length *Crafts, Commerce and Industry: A Global History of Design* and the extended seminar 'Design and the Creation of Value' as well as from two of the government reports (for the Hong Kong government and the UK government respectively) that he authored in the last decade of his life.

In other ways too, the readings are deliberately diverse. They range from extracts of books drafted for wide audiences (*Industrial Design* (1980) (#7) and *Design: A Very Short Introduction* (2002/5) (#1) through to academic seminars, lectures and research notes – for example, the important material on the dialectic of economics and design (#3) and the economic value of design (see especially reading #27). In a different vein altogether are some of the results of his research on design in Germany from 1870 to 1945 (readings #11–13), which are more academic in tone; the fruits of an intensive six-month period spent researching in Germany which is the closest Heskett was able to come to a sustained period of research without teaching responsibilities.

By contrast, and as will become apparent especially in Part III, journalism is also important – especially the series of short essays on design and policy and design and business which Heskett wrote for the now defunct US design magazine *I.D.* in the early 1990s (see many of the readings between #14 and #27). These pieces mark a different kind of public engagement from his books, one sharper and more pointed, even impatient with the failings of policy and attitude that they note.

This emphasis on writings where it possible to hear Heskett's very particular voice and take on things is the reason also for the somewhat unusual reproduction of two book reviews, the only published reviews by Heskett I am aware of (#9). They allow a reader who knows something of the history of design and its methodological debates to hear in these comments a sharp evaluation of contrasting approaches to understanding not only the history of design but industrialization per se.

The Reader ends, deliberately, in Parts IV and V ('Reflections' and 'Last Words') with a series of informal talks, each in its own way reflective at once the past, the future and the capacities of design (#27–#30).

There are, of course, missing items. Word limits sadly allowed the reproduction of only one of Heskett's three major chapters in English on art and design in Nazi Germany.[3] Missing also from this collection are some of the more conventional overview chapters on the contextual history of industrial design, and missing too, with the exception of a couple of extracts noted above, is much of the work on government and institutional reports. These last two omissions are deliberate. The overview chapters, as one would expect, are perfectly competent, but they add relatively little to current knowledge. Excellent in their own way, they are essentially limited to the survey role.[4]

The problems involved in the second have already been referred to in the introduction. By their nature, government and institutional reports demand a certain neutrality of tome and an acute ear for the sensibilities of the institution commissioning the work. They tend, therefore, to the anonymous and the dull. Insights, where they exist, are coded and often neutralized. Blandness is inevitable. Heskett's institutional work, sadly, does not escape these conditions. Especially in the Asian context, the real – critical – insights into the conditions of design and design–business relations in Asia that Heskett developed in more than twenty-five years of travelling to or living in Asia/Hong Kong do not find sufficient echo; only in what is almost the last text in the book (#28) does one get a sense of this.[5]

Missing too from the Reader, edited at a relatively late stage, are Heskett's reflections on the relations of designers and business. These are of two types, schematic and small case studies. The schematic are represented by some of Heskett's journalism in the 1990s which often expresses his double irritation at once with the inability of US companies to see the value of design and of designers to understand their (self-selected) roles within business.[6] The more idiosyncratic, or case studies, and the saddest to cut here to keep the book to manageable length, are on individual designers. Heskett took pleasure, especially in his time in Chicago, in recovering the history of some of the less well-known designers who worked in American industry in the 1920s and 1930s writing, for example, on 'Ivar Jepson: "Mr Sunbeam"' (*I.D.* magazine, 1994) which looks at the career of one of the most unsung and less fashionable of these designers.[7]

Finally, the more complex omissions come from unpublished work. The conditions under which this Reader was put together did not allow a sustained examination of the full archive of Heskett's work. Such exploration as was possible turned up some interesting fragments: readings #6, on the lessons that can be learnt for designing in China today from the study of history, and #29, 'On Writing', were discoveries added to the Reader at a later stage. Other unpublished studies will be published in a second volume, *Design and the Creation of Value*, which will have as its core the extended seminar of the same title, but will include other notes and fragments of Heskett's writing on design and economics. Finally, it is hoped in the longer term to publish the full ms. of *Crafts, Commerce and Industry: A Global History of Design*.

*

I would like to pay tribute to the publishers who have generously allowed us to reproduce work in their copyright and also to those who helped in putting this project together. Here, I want to particularly thank F & W Media, the company that now owns the title rights to *I.D.* magazine. No less than six of the readings come from this source, so their support for this project was essential.

But this project was also dependent on the help of a number of people. The book was assembled quickly, essentially from August 2014 to Spring 2015. It was only possible to do this with considerable assistance. Here, I should like to thank my researchers, Komal Sharma, Mikhail Volf and Qionglu Lei, all students on MA Design Studies at Parsons School of Design, and exemplary and highly professional assistants. The later made a superb contribution to the indexing of the book. Various people gave important and essential advice to the whole project. I would particularly like to mention Christine Tsin, from the School of Design at Hong Kong Polytechnic University, his former assistant and the person who saved the only complete copy of the ms. of *Crafts, Commerce and Industry*; Sharon Helmer Poggenpohl, his ex-colleague from the Institute of Design in Chicago and from Hong Kong, who deftly appraised both the first proposal for the book and a late version of the contents and who has provided a significant introduction to Part III; Suzan Boztepe, a former PhD student of Heskett's at IIT, now a professor at the University of Copenhagen, who gave invaluable advice on the organization of the sections on policy. Finally, Jonathan Woodham, from the University of Brighton, provided a sharp contextual critique of the material and an acute assessment of the value of the work. I am grateful also to two anonymous reviewers of the manuscript for Bloomsbury press – and the strong editorial support for this project from Rebecca Barden, Bloomsbury's acquisitions editor for design.

I have particular thanks to give to Sharon Helmer Poggenpohl, Tore Kristensen, professor at Copenhagen Business School, Carlos Teixeira, an ex-PhD of student of Heskett's, now a professor of design management in Parsons, for their contributions as introductions to and the contextualization of, Heskett's work on design, business and economics.

Finally, my thanks must go to Pamela Heskett, John's widow, without whose support the project would not have been possible.

Notes

1 There is a useful discussion of Heskett's approach to history in Kjetl Fallon's *Design History: Understanding Theory and Method* (London: Bloomsbury, 2010), see especially, pp. 15–19. For Heskett's own approach to understanding Industrial Design, see the chapter 'Industrial Design,' in *Design History: A Students' Handbook*, ed. Hazel Conway (London: Allen and Unwin, 1987) especially, pp. 111–17 (reproduced below within reading #9). For those interested in the genesis, emphases and orientation of *Industrial Design*, there is a typescript of an interview with John Heskett focusing on the book undertaken at the then Middlesex Polytechnic in 1981. It is hoped to make this interview available on the Web in 2016. The sharp and useful observation on Heskett's work quoted above came in an anonymous review of the book proposal for this Reader.

2 Stemming in part from his long over-land journey 'back-packing' his way back from Australia to England in the late 1960s, Heskett had a life-long fascination with observing and recording national idiosyncrasies and characteristics in design. A favourite instance (referred to in reading #25) was the long-time huge advertisement for Marlboro cigarettes in Hong Kong on the way to the old airport, placed, however, on the side of the Hong Kong mortuary in Kowloon.

3   See also 'Art and Design in Nazi Germany,' *History Workshop Journal*,
    no. 6 (1978): 139–53; and 'Design in Inter-war Germany,' in *Designing
    Modernity: The Arts of Reform and Persuasion*, ed. Wendy Kaplan (London
    and New York: Thames and Hudson and the Wolfsonian Foundation,
    1995). In German, see: 'Archaismus und Modernismus im Design im dritten
    Reich,' in ed. B. Hinz et al. (Giessen: Anabas Verlag, 1979), and 'Design und
    Kunsthandwerk unter Faschismus.' *Kunstchronik*, no. 1 (1984).

4   See, for example, 'British Industrial Design since 1945,' in *The Cambridge
    Cultural History of Modern Britain*, Vol. 9, ed. Boris Ford (Cambridge:
    Cambridge University Press, 1989); 'American Design in the 1950s,'
    in *Raymond Loewy*, catalogue of an exhibition jointly organized by
    Internationales Design Zentrum, Berlin, the Stedelijk Museum, Amsterdam
    and the Centre Georges Pompidou, Paris. Prestel Verlag, Munich, 1990;
    'The Emergence of the Industrial Design Profession in the United States,' in
    The Alliance of Art and Industry: Toledo Designs for a Modern America, ed.
    Davira S. Taragin (Toledo: Toledo Museum of Art, 2002).

5   The two main reports are: *Shaping the Future: Design for Hong Kong, Report
    of the Design Education Task Force* (Hong Kong Polytechnic University, 2003)
    and *Design In Asia: Review of National Design Policies and Business Use of
    Design in China, South Korea and Taiwan*, a research report commissioned by
    the Design Council, UK as a contribution to Sir George Cox's report to the UK
    Government on competitiveness in the United Kingdom, 2005. Short extracts
    from these reports are included below. Also under this heading the two books
    Heskett edited for government bodies in Hong Kong: *Design in Hong Kong*
    (Hong Kong Trade Development Council, 2004);
        *Very Hong Kong: A Review of Ten Years of Hong Kong Design since
    the Handover to China*, Hong Kong Design Centre and Hong Kong Trade
    Development Centre.

6   Besides reading #15, whose sub-title, 'Why don't American companies use
    design more intelligently?' sums up the situation as Heskett saw it in the
    1990s, other explorations of this theme are (for example) 'Do designers need
    public endorsement to contribute to a company's values?,' *I.D.* magazine
    September/October, pp. 6–7, and 'Can US designers compete?' *I.D*, November/
    December 1992. Heskett's English language text for a 1994 article 'Trends in
    Amerikanischen Design,' (Special Design Supplement, *Frankfurter Allgemeine
    Zeitung*, 29 November, Frankfurt-am-Main, Germany) is also of interest.

7   For another such figure, see 'The Desire for the New: The Context of Brooks
    Stevens Career,' in *Industrial Strength Design: How Brooks Stevens Shaped
    Your World*, ed. Glenn Adamson (Milwaukee: Milwaukee Art Museum and
    Cambridge, MA: The MIT Press, 2003).

PART I

Key Themes

Introduction to the Readings in Part I

Design, history and economics were the three key themes that John Heskett tackled in his work between the late 1960s and 2010. The texts below offer introductions to how Heskett understood the interaction of these terms.

Design was the subject matter of all of his work from 1967 onwards and the more he pursued it the broader became his understanding. From a professional field in the 1970s and1980s, by the end of his life he was seeing it as a fundamental human capacity. His broadening understanding of design is introduced here, appropriately, by the short chapter from 2002 which opens the successful (and still in print) *Design: A Very Short Introduction*. The question mark in the title of this reading indicates that no definitive answer to this question can – or even perhaps should – be given.

But Heskett was trained as, and for forty years professionally acted as, a historian. The second reading, *Commerce or Culture: Industrialization and Design* opens to history and specifically the history of the industrial epoch and of design's roles in that history – the fundamental subject matter of most of Heskett's work. But precisely because one is dealing with design, and hence necessarily as Heskett says, with the future, then history cannot be simply history per se, antiquarianism, the past thought of as simply 'past,' but rather history as a way of looking at, and holding together, past, present and future; history as understanding, with a normative cast and a view to action. The pairs, 'Commerce or Culture'/'Industrialization and Design', stand for the tensions inescapable in design. The historian's function, Heskett implies, is to be articulate concerning them, to tease out their nature and their implications.

Finally, the seminar extract 'Design considered from Standpoint of Economics/Economics from the Standpoint of Design,' comes from the notes to the extended but unpublished seminar 'Design and the Creation of Value,' given to graduate students in Chicago and Hong Kong from the late 1990s to 2010. The essay stands for the central role that economics and economic thought had in his work. Economics and economic history were after all the general subject matter of Heskett's education at the LSE in the 1950s. They were the underlying theme or content of his historical work across the 1980s and after 1990 they become the increasing focus of his teaching and writing. By the end of his life Heskett is adamant that design cannot be understood without economics – since if nothing else it occurs, professionally at least, only very largely within, and as an integral part of, economic life. But he was equally clear that an economics that could not grasp the contribution of design to the creation of value was inadequate *as* economics. This dialectical play between these positions is caught in this extract.

It should be noted that it is not an accident that this paper formed part of a seminar. If there was a fourth key theme in Heskett's work and life, it was pedagogy: teaching in the high sense of the word, with the necessity of clarity and precision of language that that entails. This sense enters all of his works. Heskett was an academic, but like all those who think about design, he could not but also be concerned with outcomes and by implication with futures. This double concern animates these opening readings. The texts below are, of course, not the only pieces that might be used to illuminate the key themes of his thought, but they are indicative of his life-long struggles to articulate his understandings of 'design, history and economics' across a variety of audiences, from the general public to academics and students, and to create bridges between the study of design and its policy and practice. They provide, therefore, in their diversity a suitable introduction to John Heskett's work and thought.

1

What Is Design?

One of the most curious features of the modern world is the manner in which design has been widely transformed into something banal and inconsequential. In contrast, I want to argue that, if considered seriously and used responsibly, design should be the crucial anvil on which the human environment, in all its detail, is shaped and constructed for the betterment and delight of all.

To suggest that design is a serious matter in that sense, however, is problematic. It runs counter to widespread media coverage assigning it to a lightweight, decorative role of little consequence: fun and entertaining, possibly useful in a marginal manner, maybe profitable in economic sectors dominated by rapid cycles of modishness and redundancy, but of no real substance in basic questions of existence.

Not surprisingly, in the absence of widespread agreement about its significance and value, much confusion surrounds design practice. In some subject areas, authors can assume common ground with readers; in an introduction to architecture or history, for example, although the precise degree of readers' knowledge might vary substantially, a reasonably accurate concept of what constitutes the subject can be relied on. Other subjects, such as nuclear physics, can be so esoteric that no such mutual understanding exists and approaches from first principles become necessary.

Design sits uncomfortably between these two extremes. As a word it is common enough, but it is full of incongruities, has innumerable manifestations and lacks boundaries that give clarity and definition. As a practice, design generates vast quantities of material, much of it ephemeral, only a small proportion of which has enduring quality.

Clearly a substantial body of people exist who know something about design, or are interested in it, but little agreement will probably exist about exactly what is understood by the term. The most obvious reference point

Chapter I of *Design: A Very Short Introduction*. Oxford University Press, Oxford, 2005, pp. 2–11. By kind permission of OUP press.

is fields such as fashion, interiors, packaging or cars, in which concepts of form and style are transient and highly variable, dependent upon levels of individual taste in the absence of any fixed canons. These do indeed constitute a significant part of contemporary design practice and are the subject of much commentary and a substantial proportion of advertising expenditure. Other points of emphasis might be on technical practice or on the crafts. Although substantial, however, these are all facets of an underlying totality and the parts should not be mistaken for the whole.

So how can design be understood in a meaningful, holistic sense? Beyond all the confusion created by the froth and bubble of advertising and publicity, beyond the visual pyrotechnics of virtuoso designers seeking stardom, beyond the pronouncements of design gurus and the snake-oil salesmen of lifestyles, lies a simple truth. Design is one of the basic characteristics of what it is to be human and an essential determinant of the quality of human life. It affects everyone in every detail of every aspect of what they do throughout each day. As such, it matters profoundly. Very few aspects of the material environment are incapable of improvement in some significant way by greater attention being paid to their design. Inadequate lighting, machines that are not user-friendly, badly formatted information, are just a few examples of bad design that create cumulative problems and tensions. It is therefore worth asking: if these things are a necessary part of our existence, why are they often done so badly? There is no simple answer. Cost factors are sometimes advanced in justification, but the margin between doing something well or badly can be exceedingly small, and cost factors can in fact be reduced by appropriate design inputs. The use of the term 'appropriate' however, is an important qualification. The spectrum of capabilities covered by the term 'design' requires that means be carefully adapted to ends. A solution to a practical problem which ignores all aspects of its use can be disastrous, as would, say, medical equipment if it were treated as a vehicle for individual expression of fashionable imagery.

This book is based on a belief that design matters profoundly to us all in innumerable ways and represents an area of huge, underutilized potential in life. It sets out to explore some reasons why this is so and to suggest some possibilities of change. The intention is not to negate any aspect of the spectrum of activity covered by the term 'design', but to extend the spectrum of what is understood by the term; examine the breadth of design practice as it affects everyday life in a diversity of cultures. To do so, however, some ground clearing is necessary to cut through the confusion surrounding the subject.

Discussion of design is complicated by an initial problem presented by the word itself. 'Design' has so many levels of meaning that it is itself a source of confusion. It is rather like the word 'love', the meaning of which radically shifts dependent upon who is using it, to whom it is applied and in what context. Consider, for example, the shifts of meaning when using the word 'design' in English, illustrated by a seemingly nonsensical sentence:

'Design is to design a design to produce a design.'

Yet every use of the word is grammatically correct. The first is a noun indicating a general concept of a field as a whole, as in: 'Design is important to the national economy'. The second is a verb, indicating action or process: 'She is commissioned to design a new kitchen blender'. The third is also a noun, meaning a concept or proposal: 'The design was presented to the client for approval.' The final use is again a noun, indicating a finished product of some kind, the concept made actual: 'The new VW Beetle revives a classic design.'

Further confusion is caused by the wide spectrum of design practice and terminology. Consider, for example, the range of practice included under the rubric of design – to name just a few: craft design, industrial art, commercial art, engineering design, product design, graphic design, fashion design and interactive design. In a weekly series called 'Designer Ireland,' in its Irish Culture section, the Sunday Times of London publishes a brief, well-written analysis of a specific aspect of design. In a six-week period, during August and September 2000, the succession of subjects was: the insignia of the Garda Siochanna, the Irish national police; Louise Kennedy, a fashion designer; the Party Grill stove for outdoor cooking; the packaging for Carrolls Number One, a brand of cigarettes; Costelloe cutlery; and the corporate identity of Ryan Air, a low-cost airline. The range of subjects addressed in the whole series is even more bewildering in its diversity.

To that list can be added activities that appropriate the word 'design' to create an aura of competence, as in: hair design, nail design, floral design and even funeral design. Why not hair engineering, or funeral architecture? Part of the reason why design can be used in this arbitrary manner is that it has never cohered into a unified profession, such as law, medicine or architecture, where a license or similar qualification is required to practice, with standards established and protected by self-regulating institutions, and use of the professional descriptor limited to those who have gained admittance through regulated procedures. Instead, design has splintered into ever-greater subdivisions of practice without any overarching concept or organization, and so can be appropriated by anyone.

Discussion of design on a level that seeks a pattern in such confusion leads in two directions: first, defining generic patterns of activity underlying the proliferation, in order to establish some sense of structure and meaning; secondly, tracing these patterns through history to understand how and why the present confusion exists.

To address the first point: design, stripped to its essence, can be defined as the human capacity to shape and make our environment in ways without precedent in nature, to serve our needs and give meaning to our lives.

Understanding the scale and extent of this capacity can be tested by observing the environment in which anyone may be reading these lines – it might be while browsing in a bookstore, at home, in a library, in an office, on a train and so on. The odds are that almost nothing in that environment will be completely natural – even plants will have been shaped and positioned by human intervention and indeed, their genus may even be a considerable modification of natural forms. The capacity to shape our world has now reached such a pitch that few aspects of the planet are left in pristine condition and on a detailed level, life is entirely conditioned by designed outcomes of one kind or another.

It is perhaps a statement of the obvious, but worth emphasizing, that the forms or structures of the immediate world we inhabit are overwhelmingly the outcome of human design. They are not inevitable or immutable and are open to examination and discussion. Whether executed well or badly (on whatever basis this is judged), designs are not determined by technological processes, social structures or economic systems, or any other objective source. They result from the decisions and choices of human beings. While the influence of context and circumstance may be considerable, the human factor is present in decisions taken at all levels in design practice.

With choice comes responsibility. Choice implies alternatives in how ends can be achieved, for what purposes, and for whose advantage. It means that design is not only about initial decisions or concepts by designers, but also about how these are implemented and by what means we can evaluate their effect or benefit.

The capacity to design, in short, is in innumerable ways at the very core of our existence as a species. No other creatures on the planet have this same capacity. It enables us to construct our habitat in unique ways, without which we would be unable to distinguish civilization from nature. Design matters because, together with language, it is a defining characteristic of what it is to be human, which puts it on a level far beyond the trivial.

This basic capacity can, of course, be manifested in a huge diversity of ways, some of which have become specialized activities in their own right, such as architecture, civil engineering, landscape architecture and fashion design. To give some focus in a short volume, the emphasis here will be on the two and three-dimensional aspects of everyday life – in other words, the objects, communications, environments and systems that surround people at home and at work, at leisure and at prayer, on the streets, in public spaces, and when travelling. Even within this focus, the range is still huge and we need only examine a limited range of examples, rather than attempting a compressed coverage of the whole.

If this human capacity for design is manifested in so many ways, how can we understand this diversity? This brings us back to the second point mentioned above: design's historical development. Design is sometimes explained as a subdivision of art historical narratives emphasizing a neat chronological succession of movements and styles, with new manifestations replacing what went before. The history of design, however, can be described more appropriately as a process of layering, in which new developments are added over time to what already exists. This layering, moreover, is not just a process of accumulation or aggregation, but a dynamic interaction in which each new innovative stage changes the role, significance and function of what survives. For example, innumerable crafts around the world have been widely displaced by industrial manufactures from their central role in cultures and economies, but have also found new roles, such as providing goods for the tourist trade or supplying the particular global market segment known as Arts and Crafts. Rapid developments in computers and information technology are not only creating exciting new possibilities in interactive design, but are also transforming the ways in which products and services are conceived and produced, in ways that supplement, rather than replace the old.

Neither is it possible to describe a process with an essential pattern followed everywhere. There are significant variations in how the process of change occurs in different societies and also in the specific consequences change entails. Whatever the exact details, however, there is a widespread pattern for what existed before to continue in some form. It is this that helps explain much of the dense and complex texture of design, and the varied modes of practice under the rubric that confronts us today. To ancient crafts and forms that survive and adapt, are continually added new competencies and applications. A great deal of confusion in understanding design, therefore, stems from this pattern of historical evolution. What is confusing, however, can also be regarded as a rich and adaptable resource, provided that a framework exists enabling the diversity to be comprehended.

2

Commerce or Culture: Industrialization and Design

Introduction

In an age of change, there are problems in understanding the nature of what is afoot and what the consequences are. For most people, change is resented as a disruption, challenging the rhythms, beliefs and practices of everyday life. To be accepted, change needs to be presented as 'improvement' or 'betterment', or disguised, slipped into our life by small, incremental stages, using forms and metaphors of what is already familiar – 'the iron horse' to describe the locomotive, or the trashcan symbol on a Macintosh computer.

Over the last two centuries, industrialization has wrought massive change across the globe, not just in patterns of life and work, but also in consciousness of ourselves and our world. In its origins, it aroused a deep, instinctive opposition as time-hallowed beliefs and practices were supplanted or marginalized. Today, similar reactions continue to be generated, from the cosmic sweep of Islamic fundamentalism, to the remnants of Australian aboriginal tribes protesting the desecration of traditional ritual sites for mineral extraction.

While echoes of the Industrial Revolution still reverberate, layered upon them is another level of complexity. The technological changes of our own time represent yet another step-change into a further dimension of possibility. In this situation, looking to the past is, paradoxically, the only means available of understanding what this future might be like. It will not help us accurately predict, there are too many unknown and independent variables for that, but it can help us understand some of the problems and dilemmas involved and define the critical issues of human values at stake.

First published as "Commerce or Culture: Industrialization and Design," *American Center for Design Journal*, Vol. 6, no. 1, Chicago, pp. 14–33.

As a comparison with the potential scale of change we face today, this paper will examine examples of change from the historically recent past. Firstly, it will consider the period of early industrialization in Britain, and how positive responses to its potential opened up new opportunities. Secondly, it will discuss the reaction to industrialization in Britain in the nineteenth century, which set the agenda for debate in many countries. Thirdly, the different emphases of the second phase of industrialization in the United States will be discussed.

On a superficial level, two attitudes to industrialization are evident. It has been welcomed, associated with concepts of progress, and seen as an opportunity for social or individual improvement or advancement. In contrast, it has also been resented, regarded as destructive of time-honoured values and social relationships, leading to attempts to restore or recreate these values. Digging even a short depth below that surface, however, reveals complications that reflect the reality and ambivalence of the human situation. For example, the paradox that industrialization might have diffused material benefits, but at the price of concentrating knowledge, power and wealth in a diminishing sector of the population who recognize no other need but their own ambition. On the other hand, another paradox, that the reaction against industrialization, although often reactionary and riddled with nostalgia, has an important message about human and social needs and our relationship with the natural environment.

A short account cannot cover the range of possible permutations and variations opened here, but it can consider, in broad strokes, some key reactions to these changes, and their effects upon design and how design is understood to function in an industrial world.

I

Great Britain was the cradle of the Industrial Revolution, a process that began to take-off around the decade 1770–80. By the mid-nineteenth century this resulted in a degree of trading supremacy and economic power that was feared, resented and emulated across the world, in a way mirrored by similar reactions to the U.S.A. in the early and mid-twentieth century, and by present-day attitudes to Japan.

The price paid in Britain to achieve that world status as a result of industrialization was revealed in 1851. A government census of population revealed that for the first time in any civilization, the number of people living in towns exceeded those living in the countryside. Behind that bland statistic was a wrenching process of upheaval. Within one generation, patterns of life that in essentials had changed but little over the centuries and then for the most part imperceptibly, were totally and irrevocably changed.

Until the Industrial Revolution, most of the population of Britain lived their lives in a small radius from the place they were born, a world circumscribed by how far they could walk, there and back, in one day – a radius of some 13–15 miles. What they lacked in broad world-view, however, they compensated for in depth, by the detail in which they understood their immediate locality. Within that radius, what was needed was produced and made in the locality, by hand, or using simple machinery and tools powered by human, animal or natural sources, using local materials. George Sturt's famous book *The Wheelwrights Shop* gives a vivid insight into craft practices and values. Another English wheelwright, Jubal Merton of Suffolk, also illustrates this relationship with the immediate environment, when he writes of how timber was selected for shafts and felloes, the curved sections that when fitted together, made up a wheel rim:

> ... the wheelwright always chose roadside trees for his fellies. He'd never touch a low-meadow ash because that wouldn't do at all. Of course, ash that grew down by the river was lovely timber to use, but a wheelwright would never use it. He went to the hedges, where the wood was tough and hard. He'd walk through the lanes and note the ashes and when he saw a good one, he'd buy it, cut it down and let it lie in the ditch for a couple of years until the bark fell off. Then it was ready. He also looked for shaft wood. If you look at the ash trees you'll find that many of their boughs grow in the shape of shafts. When my father saw a good shaft shape a-growing, he'd keep his eye on it until it was just the right size to cut and plane. Then he'd have it.[1]

Spotting a shape of the right timber on the bough and patiently waiting for it to grow to the desired size and maturity – the anecdote reveals a balance with the natural environment that we would do well to recreate.

The forms and techniques used by craftsmen were traditional, handed down through generations. Learning was by following accepted practice and absorbing its values by experience, rather than by precept.

> ... sometimes I was allowed to cut out shafts for the tumbrils .... Heaps of times I did a shaft and I'd think, "That's lovely!" Then my father would rub his hand up it and say, "Why, boy, it ain't half done!" He was a first-class wheelwright and was known all over Suffolk, and my grandfather and great-grandfather were the same. They all worked in this same shop and the wagons they made lie about in the farmyards. They ain't used but they can't wear out.[2]

Although change took place slowly, making and shaping were part of the everyday fabric of life. Access to craft skill was, of course, limited to whoever had the wealth to pay, or had the time and ability to shape artefacts themselves. Nevertheless, even with that caveat, products and processes were capable of infinite adaptation to individual people and their needs, in a process they intimately understood, and artefacts were made to last. Like the accumulated wisdom of how to make them, they too were often handed down and used by succeeding generations.

Tradition was respected, because it embodied the accumulated experience of those who had faced the difficult task of survival. Craft culture can be easily romanticized, overlooking the fact that most people lived a short, deprived existence, submitting to the vagaries of nature and brutally oppressive social structures. Famine, plague, natural disaster and human injustice were constant threats. In our prosperous modernity, we forget that for most people throughout history, survival has been a constant fight against precarious circumstances. The crafts embodied practices that had been tried, tested and proven in that struggle, and therefore were not lightly abandoned.

With industrialization, all that began to change. The term, 'revolution' is in some respects a misnomer for this process. In many areas of production there was gradual change and adaptation, utilizing old skills in a new context. Increasingly, however, mechanized production, using artificial power, coal and later electricity, concentrated production into factories, producing standardized goods, distributed over ever larger geographical areas, at costs accessible to greater numbers of people.

There were undoubted benefits from this huge change. Health and life expectancy increased, opportunities for talent and fulfillment were multiplied, new materials, processes and products brought undreamt-of prosperity to great numbers and opened up new worlds to the imagination. There were also disadvantages. Business became increasingly detached from any other values than those it defined as important to its survival. Responsibility to its workers, to society, to the environment generally, did not come within that compass. Those involved in the processes of making became increasingly specialized in function, lacking knowledge of or involvement in the whole process of manufacture, ignorant of how a product was determined or who it was destined for.

As the gulf between maker and user increased and became more abstract, expressed in terms of producer and consumer, so the relationship of people and the objects of everyday life changed. Under industrialization, workers lost any holistic knowledge of processes, and users lost intimate contact with how things were made. As a result, both workers and users were deskilled. People adapted to products and processes that treated them as a mass, and rarely in terms of unique individual or social entities.

A formative figure in providing a framework of ideas that profoundly influenced concepts of modern economics and provided a rationale for the processes of industrialization, was the Scotsman, Adam Smith. His philosophy had three main points: man's basic economic drive was self-interest; the sum total of individual self-interest combined together, represented the social good; and maximum benefit for all would result from governments refraining from interfering in economic processes. The free market place was the arena in which products would be judged by the enlightened self-interest of purchasers. His basic ideas still have many adherents.

In his major work, *The Wealth of Nations*, Smith gave a seminal example of pin production that illustrated the productive power of the new system of manufacture. A worker untrained in the trade and its machines, "could scarce, perhaps, with his utmost industry, make one pin in a day, and certainly could not make twenty."[3] In contrast, a small manufactory equipped with simple machinery and operating on the basis of the division of labour and specialization of task was capable of producing at a level of four thousand, eight hundred pins a day per workman involved in the process. "The division of labour," he concluded, "... occasions, in every art, a proportionable increase of the productive powers of labour."[4]

Several British entrepreneurs in Adam Smith's time provided illustrations of his philosophy. Matthew Boulton of Soho, near Birmingham, commenced construction in 1761 of a water-powered plant to produce buckles and buttons for the fashionable market known then as the 'toy' trade, later venturing into a wide range of metal products for domestic use, such as Sheffield plate tableware and clocks.

Boulton understood that mechanized production enabled manufacture on a larger scale and more cheaply than competitors. He wrote in a letter to the Earl of Warwick: "it is from the extream cheapness that we are enabled to send them to every corner of Europe although in many places they have as good and as cheap Materials as we have, and have Labour Cent P. Cent [100%] cheaper and yet nevertheless by the Super activity of our people and by the many mechanical contrivances, and extensive apparatus wich we are possess'd of, our men are enabled to do from twice to ten times the Work that can be done without the help of such Contrivances, and even Women and children to do more than Men can do without them ... ."[5]

Boulton illustrates some enduring lessons, however, in his understanding that cheapness was not the sole criterion for competiveness. Catering for the various tastes in the markets he supplied, meant he had to adapt to different circumstances, rather than attempting to impose a uniform taste. "Fashion hath much to do in these things, and that of the present age distinguishes itself by adopting the most Elegant ornaments of the most refined Grecian artists, I am satisfied in conforming thereto, and humbly copying their style, and making new combinations of old ornaments without presuming to invent new ones... ."[6] Frequent reports from friends and his travellers abroad about articles in demand supplied valuable information. Models were borrowed from aristocratic friends, and leading artists of the day providing him with drawings and engravings. To provide the necessary range and variations in products, "he set up his own drawing school at Soho and regularly employ some of the leading engravers of the period such as John and Francis Eginton, Peter Rouw and W. Pidgeon. He was from the first essentially design-conscious."[7] He was also convinced that a small, consistent profit on a large quantity of goods for large markets was the only way to sustain a large manufactory.

In his later career, Boulton was involved in two other developments that were critical to the accelerating trajectory of the Industrial Revolution. He joined with the inventor James Watt to begin the serial production of steam engines that provided the motive power for new industrial methods of production across the globe. Secondly, his experience in the metal trades enabled him to develop methods of producing fine, standard coins in large quantities, which was necessary for the rapidly developing monetary economy that was a corollary of industrialization.

His contemporary Josiah Wedgwood, who similarly transformed ceramics production in the late eighteenth century, shared Boulton's belief in an expanding market in which steady profits could be obtained from good quality products made available to a large number of people. He too paid close attention to both form and decoration. In the Experiment Book that catalogued his constant striving for improvement, he wrote of the products of his native Staffordshire: "White Stone Ware was the principal article of manufacture. But this had been made a long time, and the prices were now reduced so low, that the potters could not afford to bestow much expense upon it or to make it so good in any respect as the ware would otherwise admit of. And with regard to Elegance of form, that was an object very little attended to."[8]

In modern terms, Wedgwood wanted to break out of the downward spiral of poor products and price competition and create value added products. To achieve the necessary elegance of form required good modelers and designers to produce prototypes for quantity production. William Hackwood, one of the most skilled in the trade, was engaged in 1769 and other employees were trained in drawing skills, but difficulty in obtaining sufficient competent designers led Wedgwood to lament that he could do with half-a-dozen Hackwoods. From 1776, he began to turn to well-known artists such as John Flaxman, and later Joseph Wright and George Stubbs.[9]

Boulton, Wedgwood and other pioneering entrepreneurs of the late 18th century faced a dilemma. They understood the potential of mechanized methods of production and the role of design in creating new markets. However, new skills were required. Traditional craftsmen were generally unable to adapt to mechanized methods. The need for improved design in products required specialists within the division of labour, capable of adapting to the demands of mass-production. Since no established system of training existed, demand far exceeded the competent people available. Entrepreneurs therefore turned to artists of repute, the only people well-trained in visual techniques, to fill the gap with drawings, sketches and models that could be freely adapted by the draughtsmen and modellers employed in the factories.

It is possible, though it would stretch the facts, to see in this a precursor of modern design consultancies. The point is rather that if, in a time of change, a suitable competency is needed but is in short supply, other skills will be brought into play and adapted for the purpose in hand. The lesson from that early phase of industrialization for designers in the present is that if, like traditional craftsmen, they are unable to adapt and anticipate the competences needed in the current processes of change, they too may find themselves superseded.

II

The application of art to industry originated as a marriage of convenience, the path of which has hardly run smooth. Like an embattled married pair in a D.H.Lawrence novel, desire and loathing have been inextricably mixed. Even advocates of the alliance have had reservations. A writer in the journal Art-Union stated in 1848: '...we do not wish artists to become the servants of manufacturers; we do wish them to be their friends and allies; their partners in educating the people; in improving the tastes, and consequently, the morals, of the community; in developing the intellectual strength and the intellectual resources of the United Empire.'[10] Imperial sentimentality has had its day, but the idea that art, diffused by industry, could improve morality and quality of life, has many forms and still endures.

The optimism of the new age in Britain was revealed with stunning impact in The Great Exhibition of All the Nations in London's Hyde Park, which opened in Joseph Paxton's magnificent Crystal Palace in May, 1851. Half the space was devoted to British products, the other half allocated to the rest of the world - a proportion representing a judicious, if generous, division of influence in British eyes. The exhibition was open until October for 141 days, with the total visitors numbering 6,039,195. The average daily attendance was almost 43,000.[11] Such throngs were only possible with the new railway lines that had proliferated in the 1840s. A tenfold increase of the radius of travel to 150 miles in one day was not uncommon. Day trips to the Great Exhibition were a significant stage in the development of mass travel in Britain.

The products shown at the Great Exhibition are often cited as typical of the age, yet many informed observers such as Richard Redgrave were at pains to point out the contrary: "... such exhibitions ... hardly represent the normal state of manufacture .... The goods are like the gilded cakes in the booths of our country fairs, no longer for use, but to attract customers."[12] In fact, reaction to overwhelming decoration gave new impetus in Britain to measures of reform in design practice, theory and education.

A leading figure in attempting to harness mechanized methods of production to improvements in design was Henry Cole, a civil servant and a prime mover in organizing the 1851 exhibition. Using the pseudonym Felix

Summerley, he designed a tea service for a Society of Arts competition in 1846, winning a silver medal, and in 1847, went on to establish a firm to produce domestic wares, such as ceramics and cutlery, under the title of Summerley's Art Manufactures. The purpose of the firm, according to Cole was:

> ... to revive the good old practice of connecting the best art with familiar objects in daily use. In doing this, Art manufacturers aim to produce in each article superior utility, which is not to be sacrificed to ornament; to select pure forms; to decorate each article with appropriate details relating to its use, and to obtain these details as directly as possible from nature.[13]

The emphasis on the primacy of utility as the basic consideration in a product was echoed by Richard Redgrave, who, like Cole, was heavily involved in government efforts to improve standards of design, and was one of the most consistent advocates of the need to rethink the relationship between art and industry.

If there is one rule more than another which may lead us to a style characteristic of our own age, it is that of making the purpose and utility of our buildings or furniture, and every object and utensil the first consideration; then of selecting the proper materials, by the use of which that utility may be most completely obtained; and, thirdly, ornamenting consistently with the nature of the material chosen, the leading forms arising out of such construction, irrespective of the mere reproduction of the bygone elements and ornamental details of any style.[14]

Cole and Redgrave were influential figures, occupying high positions in the administration of art and design education and major museums. Their belief that industry could produce better products for much of the population had practical influence, as witness the work of Christopher Dresser. His metalware, ceramic and furniture designs for leading manufacturers were of a consistently high standard in concept, utility and aesthetics. He exemplified the possibilities of what could be achieved on the basis of close cooperation between designer and manufacturer.

Yet despite these efforts, ultimately, the impetus for reform petered out. The reasons are complex, but two immediate explanations present themselves. Firstly, the emphasis on art became precious, tending to lofty preaching that industrialists ignored, if they bothered to listen. The South Kensington Museum, (now the Victoria and Albert,) founded from the proceeds of the Great Exhibition to promote the relationship between art and industry, was a treasure-house of decorative arts from across the globe, and the source of learned treatises of value to the antique trade, but, generally, a world apart from the needs of industry. Only recently has the museum's administration sought to revive a sense of the institution's original purpose.

Another reason for the failure of the reformers efforts, however, was the unwillingness of industrialists to acknowledge their arguments. The prevailing economic philosophy of the age was Utilitarianism, and the overwhelming value it engendered, was profit. "The satirist did not exaggerate much when he made the Utilitarian ask, 'What is the use of a nightingale unless roasted? What profit is there in the fragrance of the rose, unless you can distil from it an otto at ten shillings a drop?'"[15]

This arithmetical approach was not confined to business, but became instead applied to every aspect of life – politics, society and culture – all of which could be conveniently regarded as a mirror image of business attitudes and procedures. Theories of industry as an instrument of moral improvement were indeed advocated by some industrialists such as Robert Owen and Titus Salt, but in general played little role in the pursuit of commercial success. For most industrialists, investment in mechanization was to increase personal assets or corporate dividends. Particularly in the production of domestic articles, there was a scramble for greater profit by generating a constant impression of novelty. This led to precisely the indiscriminate combination of decorative forms lifted from all ages and cultures across the world with cheapness and crudeness of execution, that Cole and Redgrave so vehemently criticized. The endemic incapacity to look beyond the tunnel vision perspective of short term profit is often seen as a peculiarly modern affliction of American industry, but it can also be seen as a root explanation for the failure of so many vain attempts, by a succession of governmental bodies, to achieve a fundamental improvement in British design over the last 150 years. The economic philosophy common to both countries, which separates out business concerns from any other concerns in society, and refuses to acknowledge certain values and approaches, may be the problem here, rather than the 'nature' of industrial production or the 'culture' of either society.

There is a great contrast, and also a profound irony, in the way in which nineteenth century opponents of art in industry were far more successful than Cole and his followers in gaining public attention and commitment, but they began with an enormous advantage. Their's was a world of the ideal, in which a conviction of total moral superiority was possible, untrammeled by problems of coming to terms with industry. They were not simply moved by a concern for art, but outraged by the impact of industrialization on the social values of Britain and the physical fabric of the land.

The outcome was a powerful philosophy. Under the banner of art, ideas of joy in work, involving the whole human being through handwork, of the influence of objects and environment on people, were linked to a programme of reform to fundamentally change the direction of how life and work would be organized. The moral potency of art was a central tenet, but only outside the compass of modern industry. The movement proposed changing the whole economic and social basis of society, but had its greatest success in tapping the fears of those British middle class people who regarded industry as a vulgar intrusion and a threat to the social order.

In formulating this critique, the influence of John Ruskin was paramount. In speeches and prose whose Old Testament tones echoed the religious temper of his age, Ruskin indicted economic theory and practice that separated action for personal benefit from consideration of its social consequences. One of his most memorable essays, "*Unto This Last*", opens:

> Among the delusions which at different periods have possessed themselves of the minds of large masses of the human race, perhaps the most curious – certainly the least creditable – is the modem *soi-disant* science of political economy, based on the idea that an advantageous code of social action may be determined irrespectively of the influence of social affection.[16]

Unto This Last was acknowledged by Mahatma Gandhi as a work that transformed his life. Gandhi subsequently advocated the crafts, and especially spinning, as a personal discipline and as a non-violent means of subverting the British Raj in India by countering imports of British mass-produced textiles that undermined the traditional Indian economy. To this day, the Congress Party founded by Gandhi has the symbol of a spinning wheel on its flag and emblems.

Rather than subordinating morality to its ends, Ruskin argued that moral values must be the foundation and justification of social organisms and actions:

> Political economy (the economy of a state, or of citizens) consists simply in the production, preservation and distribution, at fittest time and place, of useful or pleasurable things. The farmer who cuts his hay at the right time; the shipwright who drives his bolts well home in sound wood; the builder who lays good bricks in well-tempered mortar; the housewife who takes care of her furniture in the parlour, and guards against all waste in the kitchen; and the singer who rightly disciplines, and never overstrains her voice: all are political economists in the true and final sense; adding continually to the riches and well-being of the nation to which they belong. But mercantile economy, the economy of "merces" or of "pay," signifies the accumulation, in the hands of individuals, of legal or moral claim upon, or power over, the labour of others; every such claim implying precisely as much poverty or debt on one side, as it implies riches or right on the other. It does not, therefore, necessarily involve an addition to the actual property, or well-being, of the State in which it exists.[17]

Virtue lay in right-doing. Ruskin's condemnation of a system that not only separated cause from effect, but denied responsibility for it, had powerful appeal. Although forceful, however, his social critique never coalesced into a programme for political action. Moreover, his detestation of the forces changing the world around him led him to ignore many positive aspects. Instead, he relied upon romantic visions of the past and the power of art to transform life.

William Morris, who derived many core beliefs from Ruskin, went this further stage and became politically active as a socialist. However, he had little in common with Karl Marx. Rather than looking to the Communist Manifesto and its certainties, he turned instead to the tradition of indigenous, English socialism summed up in the utopian radicalism stemming from John Bunyan and expressed in William Blake's poem, Jerusalem, that became the battle hymn of the British labour movement:

> I will not cease from mental fight,
>   Nor shall my sword sleep in my hand,
> Till we have built Jerusalem,
>   In England's green and pleasant land.

The influence of work on those who produce, the nature of the products, and their influence on those who use them, is a broad seam throughout Morris' life and work.

> ... the chief source of art is man's pleasure in his daily necessary work, which expresses itself and is embodied in that work itself; nothing else can make the common surroundings of life beautiful, and whenever they are beautiful it is a sign that men's work has pleasure in it, however they may suffer otherwise. It is the lack of this pleasure in daily work which has made our towns and habitations sordid and hideous, insults to the beauty to the earth which they disfigure, and all the accessories of life mean, trivial, ugly – in a word, vulgar.[18]

And in another essay:

> It is right and necessary that all men should have work to do which shall be worth doing, and be of itself pleasant to do; and which should be done under such conditions as would make it neither over-wearisome nor over-anxious.[19]

On the plethora of meretricious articles commonly available and the effect on all who produced, sold and used them, he wrote:

> 'It would be an instructive day's work for any one of us who is strong enough to walk through two or three of the principal streets of London on a week-day, and take accurate note of everything in the shop windows which is embarrassing or superfluous to the daily life of a serious man.

He continues:

> But I beg you to think of the enormous mass of men who are occupied with all this miserable trumpery, from the engineers who have had to

make the machines for making them, down to the hapless clerks who sit daylong year after year in the horrible dens wherein the wholesale exchange of them is transacted, and the shopmen who, not daring to call the soul their own, retail them amidst numberless insults which they must not resent, to the idle public which doesn't want them, but buys them to be bored by them and sick to death of them. I am talking of the merely useless things; but there are other matters not merely useless, but actively destructive and poisonous, which command a good price in the market; for instance, adulterated food and drink. Vast is the number of slaves whom competitive Commerce employs in turning out infamies such as these.[20]

Morris' critique is at times still devastatingly relevant. The solution he proposes, however, is less convincing, essentially a romanticized re-creation of the assumed virtues of the mediaeval period. In his Utopian vision of the future, News from Nowhere, he depicted the economic organization of a society founded upon Banded Workshops. A character in the story describes them as places where "folk collect ... to do hand-work in which working together is necessary or convenient; such work is often very pleasant."[21] His reaction to the worst features of his own time are matched with this vision in the opening lines of his poem, "The Earthly Paradise":

Forget six counties overhung with smoke,
Forget the snorting steam and piston stroke,
Forget the spreading of the hideous town;
Think rather of the packhorse on the down,
And the dream of London, small, and white, and clean,
The clear Thames bordered by its gardens green.[22]

In another irony, the debate on art and industry in Britain reached its peak at the time when Britain was losing its dominance in world trade to the rapidly growing economies of Germany and the United States. In the subsequent, lingering decline, the genteel beliefs of the Arts and Crafts movement could play little role other than that of a personal consolation.

The influence of Ruskin, Morris and their followers of the Arts and Crafts movement was particularly strong, however, in Germany, where it split into two trends. On one hand it became part of a mainstream influence in that country that saw industrialization as a positive force for change. Stripped of the insistence on hand-work, it allowed machinery to be incorporated into its thinking, as just another tool capable of being used well for quality production. In organizations such as the German Werkbund and many leading companies it thus became transformed into a concept of industrial quality that was an expression of contemporary German culture. Joy in work became translated into a recognition that taking care of workers could be a means of bridging divisions in the workplace, countering union influence, and valuable in achieving quality products. Such attitudes do much to explain the continuing success of German products in international trade. The second trend continued the emphasis on rural nostalgia and eventually became one of the resentments exploited for political purposes in the rise of the Nazi party to power in the 1920s.

Arts and Crafts ideas were also popular in the United States.[23] Despite differences in the course of development, they also expressed a deep sense of disquiet and doubt about the nature of changes that were fundamentally transforming old certainties for a predominantly middle class following. In the U.S., however, as in Britain, it failed to have any sustained impact on the thrust of change. The reasons are similar: in general it found small response in industrial attitudes that recognized no values but its own. Beyond that similarity, however, the contexts cannot be compared, for a new phase of industrial technology and organization was opening in the United States.

III

The tempo of American industrialization rapidly increased in the late 19th century, but took a significantly different course to Britain. There, most industry remained small-to-medium-scale into the twentieth century, with family ownership or partnerships still widespread. Economic power in the U.S.A., in contrast, was falling into the hands of large enterprises on a scale previously unknown in human history, with ownership separated from management. This dominance fundamentally changed every aspect of life and culture in America and has been a significant influence across the globe in the twentieth century.

The changes in America were greater in scale than in Britain and more compressed in time. In 1790, according to Alfred Chandler, 'only 202,000 of 3,930,000 Americans lived in towns and villages of more than 2,500, and of 2,881,000 workers, 2,069,000 labored on farms.' Manufacturing was a small-scale activity carried on in artisan shops, owned by a master who was typically assisted by one or two journeymen or apprentices who often lived in with the family. 'As Sam Bass Walker wrote of Philadelphia on the eve of the American Revolution: "The core element of the town economy was the one-man shop. Most Philadelphians labored alone, some with a helper or two."[24] It was in this context that the tradition of Yankee ingenuity evolved and flourished.

In 1900 the rural population of the U.S.A. still outnumbered those living in towns and cities with over 2,500 inhabitants, although increasingly farming was for commercial crops. Spearheaded by the expanding railroad system across the continent, the economy rapidly grew and changed in nature, further accelerating in the early twentieth century with the development of electrical technology.[25] In 1914, 30% of US industry was electrified, by 1920 the figure reached 70%.[26] Also in 1920, the urban population of the United States exceeded the rural population for the first time.

Technological change was significant, but so too were changes in business organization. On every level of society, large institutions were imposing their procedures and values, which were very different to those found in a small business economy.

> By 1904, ... about three hundred industrial corporations had won control over more than two fifths of all manufacturing in the country, affecting the operation of about four fifths of the nation's industries.... By 1929, the two hundred largest corporations held 48 per cent of all corporate assets (excluding banks and insurance companies) and 58 per cent of net capital assets such as land, buildings, and machinery.[27]

Thus by 1930, large business units were firmly established as the dominant form in the American economy, with mass-production redefining the manufacturing sector, and a professional management cadre to operate these large organizations supplanting other disciplines. The effects, however, were not only confined to economic organization. As with the Utilitarians in nineteenth century Britain, the new industrial system, its methods, its calculation of value, were justified as a natural evolution on the path of progress and a model for the whole of society. The difference in twentieth century America lay in the power and scale of the mass media, the natural adjuncts of mass production, with a symbiotic relationship of interest and ownership linking the two. The role of the mass media, newspapers and journals, radio, film and television, in conditioning and altering the nature of perception and experience, not in the direction of greater awareness, but to align it with the needs of business is difficult to underestimate. "The advertisement," writes Alan Trachtenberg, "is unique among artworks in that its cardinal premise is falsehood, deceit, its purpose being to conceal the connection between labor and its product in order to persuade consumers to buy this brand. The advertisement suggests the fictive powers of that product, its ability to stand for what it is not."[28]

This was a far cry from belief in the moral power of art to improve life through industry. The idea of the artist as designer decisively influencing modern business organizations has remained a hope of many designers, but has had little credence among businessmen. Instead, at the precise point in the late 1920s when large businesses established control of the economy with new managerial methods, the industrial designer as stylist emerged into the light of day.

Interestingly, the first designer/stylists were also drawn from other spheres of work, those that emphasized spectacle and image, such as advertising and the theatre. The role of designers in this new guise was generally to provide the constant superficial visual changes needed to give an impression of innovation and stimulate sales, with the underlying technology remaining virtually unchanged.

Alfred P. Sloan, the man who built General Motors into one of the most formidable firms in the world, and a prime mover in establishing modem practices of management, was also important in evolving the concept and practice of styling. In his autobiography, he wrote:

> The degree to which styling changes should be made in any one model run presents a particularly delicate problem. The changes in the new model should be so novel and attractive as to create demand for the new value and, so to speak, create a certain amount of dissatisfaction with past models as compared with the new one, and yet the current and old models must still be capable of giving satisfaction to the vast used-car market.... The design must be competitive in its market. Great skill and artistry are needed to fulfill these complex styling requirements.[29]

Artistry was acknowledged, but in a role that was utterly subordinate to marketing needs and the stimulation of sales. In terms of the Art-Union article of 1848 cited earlier, artists had indeed 'become the servants of manufacturers.' For a time, it could be justified by the years of market dominance and great success enjoyed by GM and its numerous imitators. Today, when that dominance has buckled under the combined effect of foreign competition and its own inflexibility in the face of contemporary change, the benefits of hindsight reveal the flaws of the system that Sloan inaugurated.

Despite the material benefits it has undoubtedly provided, acceptance of the mass-production paradigm has never been total. There have always been voices raised against the pattern of work and life it demands. Thoreau, Walt Whitman, Frank Lloyd Wright and Lewis Mumford, the beliefs and practices of the Amish and Shaker communities, are just a few whose contribution has been enduring and influential beyond the boundaries of their own country.

A contemporary example is Wendell Berry, who expresses a sensibility linking him directly with the tradition of opposing a holistic view to mechanization and its values:

> The industrial economy requires the extreme specialization of work – the separation of work from its results – because it subsists upon divisions of interest and must deny the fundamental kinships of producer and consumer; seller and buyer; owner and worker; worker, work, and product; parent material and product; nature and artifice; thoughts, words, and deeds. Divided from those kinships, specialized artists and scientists identify themselves as "observers" or "objective observers" – that is, as outsiders without responsibility or involvement. But the industrialized arts and sciences are false, their division is a lie, for there is no division of results.[30]

Berry's alternative emphasises human values rather than economic imperatives. His vision essentially rests upon reviving ownership of family farms and a property owning democracy, which in his view has been sacrificed to 'specious notions of efficiency or the economics of the so-called free market ... Like a small craft shop, it gives work a quality and a dignity that it Is dangerous, both to the worker and the nation, for human work to go without.'[31] Ruskin and Morris would recognize a fellow spirit in such statements.

Berry gives renewed force to several generations of protest against alienation and abstraction from both sides of the Atlantic, and takes it a stage further to apply it to present day ecological concern:

> No one can make ecological good sense for the planet. Everyone can make ecological good sense locally, if the affection, the scale, the knowledge, the tools, and the skills are right.
>
> The right scale in work gives power to affection. When one works beyond the reach of one's love for the place one is working in, and for the things and creatures one is working with and among, then destruction inevitably results. An adequate local culture, among other things, keeps work within the reach of love.[32]

In the decades in which mass-production has been so dominant, and self-justifyingly depicted as inevitable, such views could perhaps be dismissed as a quaint irrelevance in the onward march of progress. Large organizations and mass concepts applied across the whole spectrum from production to use, however, increasingly seem neither so inevitable, all-powerful, or beneficial. The evolution of flexible technology means that E. F. Schumachers advocacy of 'small is beautiful' becomes realizable and economic. Small-scale, user-oriented production opens up new possibilities for the nature of work, its role and value in our society. Above all it raises questions of human values and how designers can adapt to creatively realize them.

Ruskin, Morris, Berry and the whole tradition they represent are, at one and the same time, so right and so wrong. They are right to emphasize such ideas as the need for creative work and respect for the natural world. They are wrong, I believe, because they specifically identify their philosophy with particular forms of production and organization stemming from the pre-industrial period. They fail to understand or adequately acknowledge that from the beginning of industrialization, men have gained deep pleasure and fulfillment from mastering machines and their processes, sometimes creating out of mechanization forms that are as beautiful as any in history, sometimes creating industrial companies that are successful both in business terms and as a social/cultural expression of all who are a part of them. It would be possible to argue, for example, that the success of many outstanding Japanese companies is founded precisely on applying these values in an industrial context.

In attempting to assess the nature and potential of the changes all around us, we need to avoid nostalgia for a past that has gone, and in some respects, probably never was. We cannot turn the clock back. We can, however, be clear about our philosophy and values and seek opportunities in the process of change to give them new directions, new forms and expression. As Hiroshi Shinohara, design director of Canon said in a personal conversation in 1982, when speaking of the future, "First we must think with the heart, and try to understand what kind of life people want and need, then we must think with the head to provide it." The human concerns of the critique of industrialization survive the particularity of their origins, and their views of the role and responsibility that design has in improving life still has much to offer in shaping our vision of the future.

Notes

1 Jubal Merton, quoted in Blythe, Ronald, *Akenfield*, Hannondsworth, Penguin, 1969, pp. l46–8. George Sturt's famous text is *The Wheelwright's Shop* (Cambridge, Cambridge University Press, 1963).

2 Blythe, *Akenfield*, pp. 146–8.

3 Smith, Adam. *The Wealth of Nations*. Original 1776. This edition, edited by Edwin Canaan, New York, The Modern Library, 1937, p. 4.

4 Smith, *The Wealth of Nations*, p. 5.

5 Robinson, E. 'Eighteenth-Century Commerce and Fashion: Matthew Boulton's Marketing Techniques', *The Economic History Review*, Vol. xvi, No. 1, 1963, p. 43.

6 Robinson, 'Eighteenth-Century Commerce and Fashion,' p. 46.

7 Robinson, 'Eighteenth-Century Commerce and Fashion,' p. 46.

8 Kelly, Alison. *The Story of Wedgwood*, London, Faber & Faber, 1930, revised 1975, p. l5.

9 Kelly, *The Story of Wedgwood*, p. 34.

10 Taylor, William. Cooke. 'Art and Manufacture,' *Art-Union*, 1 March, 1848, quoted in Harvie, C. et al. (eds), *Industrialization & Culture 1830–1914*, London, Macmillan for the Open University Press, 1970.

11 Gibbs-Smith, C. H. *The Great Exhibition of 1851*. London, HMSO, 1964.

12 Redgrave, Richard. *The Manual of Design*, London, Chapman & Hall, 1876, p. 7.

13 Cole, Henry, quoted in Naylor, Gillian. The Arts and Crafts Movement, Studio Vista, London, 1971, p. 17.

14 Redgrave, *The Manual of Design*, p. 35.

15 Saunders, J. J. The Age of Revolution, London, Hutchison & Son, n.d., p. 73.

16 Ruskin, John. *Unto This Last*. Original 1862. This edition, London, Dent Everyman's Library, 1968, p. 115.

17 Ruskin, *Unto this Last*, p. 133.

18 Morris, William. 'The Worker's Share of Art,' in Briggs, Asa (ed.), *William Morris: Selected Writings and Designs*. Harmondsworth, Penguin, 1962, pp. 140–1.

19 Morris, William. 'Art and Socialism: the Aims and Ideals of the English Socialists of Today', in Harvie, Industrialization & Culture, p. 341.

20 Morris, 'Art and Socialism,' p. 342.

21 Morris, William. 'News from Nowhere,' in Briggs, Asa (ed.), *William Morris: Selected Writings and Designs*. Harmondsworth, Penguin, 1962, p. 221.

22 Excerpted in Briggs, Asa (ed.), *William Morris: Selected Writings and Designs*. Hannondsworth, Penguin, 1962, p. 68.

23 See Kaplan, Wendy. *"The Art that is Life": The Arts & Crafts Movement in America, 1875–1920*. Boston, Museum of Fine Arts, 1987.

24 Chandler, Alfred P., Jr. *The Visible Hand: The Managerial Revolution in American Business*. Cambridge, Mass.: The Belknapp Press, 1977, p. 17.

25 Chandler, *The Visible Hand*, p. 230.

26 Hirschhorn, Larry. *Beyond Mechanization: Work and Technology in a Postindustrial Age*. Cambridge, MA: MIT Press, 1986.

27 Trachtenberg, Alan. *The Incorporation of America: Culture and Society in the Gilded Age*. New York, McGraw Hill, 1982, p. 4.

28 Trachtenberg, *The Incorporation of America*, p. 138.

29 Sloan, Alfred P. *My Years with General Motors*. New York, Doubleday, Original 1963, this edition 1990, p. 265.

30 Berry, Wendell. *Home Economics*. San Francisco, North Point Press, 1987, p. 74.

31 Berry, *Home Economics*, pp. 164–5.

32 Berry, Wendell. 'Out of your Car, Off your Horse,' *The Atlantic Monthly*, February, 1991, p. 63.

3

Design from the Standpoint of Economics/Economics from the Standpoint of Design

Note. This text is an extract of two sections (no's 8 and 9) from the extended notes for an unpublished seminar "Design and the Creation of Value" given by Heskett between the late 1990s and 2010 in Chicago and Hong Kong. Other extracts or summaries of the arguments of this seminar (with some small repetition) are given in two of the readings below—#22 "A Design Policy for the UK: Three Suggestions" and #26, "Creating Economic Value by Design." The seminar arose as part of Heskett's attempts to teach graduate design students, especially those involved in product development and innovation, some of the rudiments of economics, not as a quasi-mathematical discipline but via the history and analysis of economic thought. If the "business of design" has been well-accepted for many years, and if schools like the Institute of Design at IIT have developed themselves as outliers of design education where notions of design's contribution to economic value is emphasized and taught with considerable seriousness, the direct relation of design practice to concepts in economic history and theory is still rare.

It was the move to the USA, and in fact to teach at IIT, which gave Heskett the opportunity to develop a more serious engagement with design policy and design and business issues. As his teaching and writing in these areas progressed, often informally—for example the series of columns he wrote on design and business for the now defunct design magazine I.D.—he increasingly felt the need to persuade designers to think also in economic terms; and to make them acquainted with some basic aspects of economic thought, particularly in relation to the question of how design creates value.

"Value" of course is double-edged. If, from the side of economics, at its crudest it is only monetary, seen through the lens of the product considered as a source of value(s) in its own right, then "value" cannot be reduced to

simple monetary value but always exceeds it—this is made clear in some of the readings in Part III(C) below, #23–#26). Indeed, it is the presence in the product of more than economic values that enables it to also to have an economic role.

The question of "design and the creation of value" is thus complex. It cannot be addressed entirely in economic terms, but it cannot be addressed without economics. It is this conundrum—which Heskett recognized as a unique intellectual opportunity—that runs through his work on design and economics and it is this which gives this short extract from Heskett's seminar its interest: design cannot be thought without economics: but in the process economics does not remain inviolate. To be sure, as Heskett himself says in the text below: "To suggest that the fragmented and often ill-defined field of design can usefully augment economic theory, the most powerful and well entrenched of the social sciences might seem overly ambitious, likely to have as much effect as a flea-bite on an elephant." Nonetheless, the relationship is not wholly one-sided. Economics, as the crash of 2007–8 confirmed, is painfully—even obscenely given the consequences of its thought—limited in what it allows itself to think, particularly in its current neo-liberal variants. Economics, if thus necessary (how else do we get a handle on a world that is today effectively made over in its name?) is neither sufficient nor adequate. The dialectic is therefore not absurd. It is not design "and" economics, where the ampersand indicates only separation. The relation is rather one of implication; is internal not external. What design understands about the product offers certain perspectives on economics, just as economics is unsurpassable as a moment in design understanding.

* * * *

Design from the standpoint of economics

(....) All the major fields of economic theory are far more complex and rich in depth and detail than is depicted here. The purpose of the foregoing chapters has been to provide a basic understanding of each in broad terms in order to assess their implications for design.

The greatest problem in considering what economic theory explains about design, specifically or by implication, is in the context of neo-classicism, which in the Anglo-American world dominates both academic and applied economic practice. A frequent criticism of it from other theoretical perspectives focuses on its assumptions regarding the static nature of products and markets. If markets and products are as constant as depicted in Neo-classical theory, this at best reduces design to a trivial activity concerned with minor, superficial differentiation of unchanging commodities, a role, indeed, that it does frequently perform. At worst, it contradicts the whole validity of design.

In contrast, a central assumption of design practice is that every designer is in some manner concerned with the future: this is an innate feature of the discipline. Whether working at drawing boards, in workshops, and increasingly at computers, many designers are concerned with enlarging the boundaries of possibility. Whether expressed in terms of a brochure for publication in one month, a product for production in a year's time, or a system that might take several years, designers' concepts will become the products, communications, environments and systems of the future. The only reason for generating these future concepts is that they will be different and, hopefully, better. Design, in other words, is about envisioning change, a condition not readily embraced by Neo-classical models. Basically, therefore, Neo-classical theory is concerned with explaining what is, and is not fundamentally concerned with what might be.

As soon as the possibility of change is admitted into economic models, however, the perspective shifts and it becomes much easier to relate design to economic theories. For example, the holistic nature of Friedrich List's concepts of the role of state policy in promoting productive powers specifically acknowledges "the art of design" as one of the factors capable of profound influence in improving manufacturing industry.

The continuity of this idea was apparent on several levels by the early years of the twentieth century, following the unification of Germany in 1871 and its rapid industrialization. In terms of policy, the involvement of the German Imperial Government in the applied arts had numerous facets. It provided, for example, a 'Standing Exhibition Commission for German Industry' under the Ministry of the Interior, which included representatives from the Foreign Ministry, the Prussian Ministries of Commerce and Education, and other interested parties. This was responsible for the presentation of official national exhibits at major international exhibitions. Usually, a state official was appointed as commissioner responsible for an exhibition, and direct government funding was provided. Subsidies were also available for exhibitions where a direct state involvement was inappropriate. With Germany's emergence as a major political and industrial power, such events were given high priority in the first decade of the century, as a means of impressing the world outside with the nation's strength and achievement.

In addition to exhibition organization and promotion, an English electrical journal noted in 1907 that commercial attaches were being appointed to German consulates: "It is the duty of these commercial attaches to increase Germany's foreign trade, and these experts of trade and commerce are always in direct communication with all the leading manufacturing and exporting houses of the German Empire, and make frequent trips to Germany for the purpose of personal conference with them."

Another initiative of the Reich government was to appoint Hermann Muthesius, an architect in the employ of the Prussian government, to the post of cultural attaché at the German Embassy in London—apparently at the suggestion of Kaiser Wilhelm II. From 1892–1902 Muthesius reported regularly and wrote widely on developments in British architecture and design. Following his London appointment, he returned to be placed in charge of all applied art education in Prussia and appointed leading reformers to head the major schools within his remit. A constant theme in Muthesius' lectures and essays was the close linkage of cultural, social and economic concerns in terms very close to those used by List.

Another prominent figure in elaborating List's ideas was a liberal politician, Friedrich Naumann, who founded a journal *Die Hilfe*, in 1894, in which he frequently wrote about the applied arts. Most notably, in 1904, he published an important article, 'Art in the Age of the Machine,' which called for industrial methods of production to be used to create new forms expressing the spirit of the time, and the need to positively harness the potential of mechanization.

Quality work and good form were therefore advocated by Naumann as indispensible elements of achieving social unity domestically and international commercial competitiveness. Establishing such standards meant that appreciation of quality must be encouraged in the home market, an aim which could hardly be achieved by oppressing workers, paying them low wages and housing them inadequately. Good wages and working conditions were therefore a necessary precondition. In a book, *Neudeutsche Wirtschaftspolitik*, (New German Economic Policy) published in 1907, Naumann elaborated these ideas. In reviewing the book, Anton Jaumann observed that Germany's competitive position was characterized by possession of few natural resources and dependence on imports of raw materials that had to be paid for by manufactured exports. How could it then survive the intense levels of international competition?

> We must bring goods to the market that only we can manufacture. We cannot in the long run compete in cheap mass-production. Only quality is our deliverance. If we are able to deliver such excellent goods that can be imitated by no other people in the world and if these goods are so excellent that everyone wishes to buy them, then we have a winning hand.[1]

Nothing, concluded Jaumann, injured the commercial reputation of a nation as much as the label, "cheap and nasty." Naumann was also involved in foundation of an association in 1907 to promote design, the Deutscher Werkbund. At its founding meeting in Munich in October, 1907, Fritz Schumacher, a leading architect and designer, gave the opening address and posed the question: why was a new organization necessary? His answer was essentially a restatement of List's ideas as reformulated by Naumann. Art, he said, was not only an aesthetic, but also, a moral power, but both were combined in the most important of powers: economic power. The best creative and commercial spirits of the age should therefore unite to re-establish a harmonious culture. Once again, the unity of national cultural attainment and commercial success in international markets was strongly asserted.

The importance and continuity of the ideas originating with List requires a volume of their own to give an adequate account. It can be argued, however, that the productive powers of Germany, as understood by List, have been an innate factor in enabling Germany to overcome the chain of events it has faced in the last century: a demoralizing defeat in the First World War; a horrendous financial inflation and collapse; the Great Depression; the illusions and ultimate shame of its embrace of fascism; the problems of destruction and loss of territory following the Second World War, and the daunting tasks of reconstruction and reunification that followed.

The example of Germany also played a very important part in the modernization of Japan, where individualism has similarly played a less prominent role in the country's economic progress. Although the direct role of List's ideas in that country requires clarification, the role of state policy in initially establishing design competences and encouraging their application in Japanese industry and commerce has been a remarkable example of how, indeed, a government can encourage the development of productive powers. In the mid-1950s, there existed virtually no formally trained professional designers in Japan. As the result of policies introduced by the Ministry of International Trade and Industry (MITI), it was estimated that the country had 21,000 industrial designers alone by 1992. Their development has been an integral part of the success of Japanese products in international markets in the intervening period. Policies on the Japanese model were introduced in Korea and Taiwan and similarly have played an important role in their economic growth in the late twentieth century.

If List's ideas have been important on a macro-economic level, other schools of theory also have implications for design in micro-economic terms. In this respect, the dynamic view of economics and change advocated by adherents of the Austrian school is particularly valuable. As Ludwig M. Lachman points out, "All economic action is of course concerned with the future, the more or less distant future. But the future is to all of us unknowable, though not unimaginable." As stated previously, design is similarly concerned with the future, and also faces the risks and limitations in the challenge of imagining what is as yet unknowable. The actions involved in design too, as Mises points out, are determined by thought. In shaping these future ideas, moreover, Carl Menger's insistence that the satisfaction of consumers is the primary function of economic activity and Hayek's emphasis on freedom of choice and the possibility of improvement are of enormous significance in ideas of user-centred design, which will be discussed later. Although generally silent about design in specific terms, therefore, the ideas of the Austrian school reverberate with implications that potentially open paths to a broader understanding of what the economic role of design can be.

Institutional theory also provides a contextual richness that similarly offers opportunities for a reconsideration of design's functions. At a general level, it raises important questions on the role of design in society and as generator of the specific forms of a culture. More specifically, theories such those initiated by Coase on transaction costs offer rich possibilities for discussion of how in such fields as information and communications, the role of design can powerfully enhance competitiveness.

The alternatives suggested by attempts to expand Neo-classical theory, particularly New Growth Theory's inclusion of technology as a core factor in understanding how business actually functions, also has intriguing possibilities. Of especial value is the argument that technological knowledge, both coded and tacit, has in-built value from its capacity to derive innovative ideas from practice. This opens the door to a consideration of design also contributing to the processes of generating innovative ideas, (although the balance between coded and tacit knowledge in design may to tilt to the latter). Innovative ideas, of course, are by no means the sole perquisite of designers and, indeed, can originate from a broad constituency. Whatever the source, however, all will need translating into tangible form or definable process, and it is this translation from concept to specificity in terms acceptable to users that is the particular skill and contribution of design.

To summarize these varied possibilities in current trends of economic thinking, three clear areas of concern for designers in the context of production can be stipulated, (these will be discussed in more detail later):

1. Their work must be capable through innovation of contributing to creating new economic value.

2. Given the crucial role assigned to technology in New Growth Theory, an ability to understand technological opportunity and act upon it is required.

3. They must function within institutional structures of various kinds that enable and constrain their endeavors.

More important in the context of innovation and growth, is the role of designers as originators, or contributors to the origins, of totally new products capable of significantly changing existing markets, or even of creating new ones, and therefore of generating new economic value. If a vital role of design, as suggested here, is the translation of technological possibility into specific form, a close harmonization of design and technology is essential.

Concepts of designers being only concerned with superficial visual form completely underestimate the degree to which a working understanding of technology, as a minimum, is necessary to function as a designer. Without the ability at least to have dialogue with, and work in close relationship to, technological specialists, designers will be necessarily confined to the trivialities of what is often called "felt-pen design." To adequately understand technological opportunity therefore requires technological competence.

Design on this level is capable of being involved with the total product concept, not just visual appearance as a last minute additive.

The third strand of economic theory, institutional structures, impinges upon design in innumerable ways, even when design is not specifically considered as an element in their workings. For example, laws, such as those in the U.S. on product liability, or those in Germany on recycling packaging materials, profoundly affect design practice. Other factors, including the general cultural climate of a society, the way design is manifested in public and private institutions, whether and how design is taught at all levels of the educational system, and the immediate context of the firms in which or for which designers work, are just a few of the institutional influences that merit consideration.

Specific attempts to explain design in an economic context have generally emphasized the level of its role in national economies. This focus on the macroeconomic level has produced a number of useful generalities, but few significantly convincing arguments about how design can be effectively applied in the specific context of practice in the business arena. Richard Nelson's stress on activities at the level of the firm as a means of understanding innovation is relevant in this regard.

Since the dominant arena of activity for designers is at the level of the firm, whether working as a directly employed in-house designer or as external consultant, the major emphasis in discussing the role of design will need to be at the level of the firm, or the microeconomic level. A consideration of the functions and processes at this level can reveal some contributions of design to innovation not generally considered in any economic theory.

Economics from the standpoint of design

To suggest that the fragmented and often ill-defined field of design can usefully augment economic theory, the most powerful and well entrenched of the social sciences might seem overly ambitious, likely to have as much effect as a flea-bite on an elephant. Yet, when one moves from the concerns of theory to those of practice and considers the extent of the creation of designs in the world of business and their implementation in everyday life, it must sure be evident that there remain large gaps in economic accounts of how products and services are produced, sold and used. Discussion of these matters can, hopefully as demonstrated by previous chapters, be enhanced by reference to economic theory but their importance also requires consideration of design in its own terms. It also raises many questions of the confusion caused by often radically different emphases in and explanations of the world provided by varied disciplines and their concepts and procedures.

Toilet | **Jonathan Adler**

"I chose to redesign a toilet because even though everybody has one, they're always so dreary. I wanted to create a cheerful toilet. I was inspired by Dior's New Look, with its wasp-waisted silhouettes, from the 40's and 50's. The shape makes it a little cuter; the graphic element makes it fun. There are a number of functional issues that would need to be addressed for this to actually work, but the toilet really is the perfect arena for playfulness."

FIGURE 3.1 *The New York Times Magazine of Sunday, 1 Dec 2002.*

Perhaps the greatest problem in explaining design is its confusion with art. In many publications intended for the general public there is still a tendency for design to be equated with art, which is probably one of the greatest sources of difficulty in developing a better understanding of what design is and what it can achieve.

An example is an article that appeared in the *The New York Times* Magazine of Sunday, 1 Dec. 2002 (Figure 3.1), in which some artists were commissioned to rethink an object of everyday life. Among them was an artist/potter, Jonathon Adler, who applied his creative talents to that essential item, the toilet.

Note the terms to which Adler gives priority: cheerful, cute, fun, playful— all clichés of a society fixated on entertainment, having nothing whatever to do with the essential functions a toilet has to perform, or perhaps it should more accurately be said, the functions we all have to perform on a toilet! He does indeed mention that functional issues need to be addressed, but whether he is competent to do so is unclear—the likelihood of him being able to do so is low. Above all, do we really need something as fundamental as this to be brought within the boundaries of whimsical fashionable and cycles of change? What does Dior's New Look in the field of women's fashion of the post-Second World War period have to do with present day ceramic toilets? If this is the level at which it is being presented in an intelligent newspaper, what hope is there that design will ever be understood in all its complexity, diversity and richness?

Nathan Rosenberg, in examining the problems of technological innovation, shrewdly attributes some of them to what he terms "a frequent preoccupation with what is technologically spectacular rather than economically significant..." A parallel observation is possible about some aspects of design innovation, with in this case the preoccupation being with what is visually spectacular rather than economically significant. Above all, a major objection to this reduction of design to personal whim is that it reduces the complexities of practice to a very simple level, which involves severe distortion of the activity. Basically, the example of the toilet cited above is treated in the following terms (Figure 3.2):

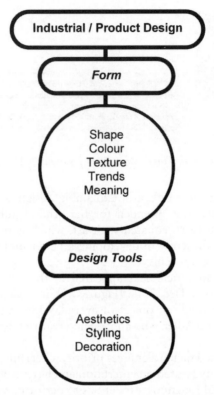

FIGURE 3.2 *Design process simplified.*

The attitudes and approaches manifested in the above exercise ignore several basic facts about design as a form of practice:

- The main arena in which design is practiced is business. There is a tendency for some designers to try to ignore this basic fact of their existence, which is yet another aspect of the problems in giving design credibility, but it will not conveniently disappear.
- As a business activity, design must be judged in terms of contributions to profitability. If it cannot contribute, then it cannot be regarded as of any use in business.
- Business is also a social activity. Both its internal organization and the needs it meets in society depend upon social consciousness and functions. Some business managers educated in the tenets of Neo-classical thinking try to ignore this basic fact of their existence, but it too will not conveniently disappear.
- Making profits is not a self-contained activity determined within a firm but depends upon satisfying customers' needs.

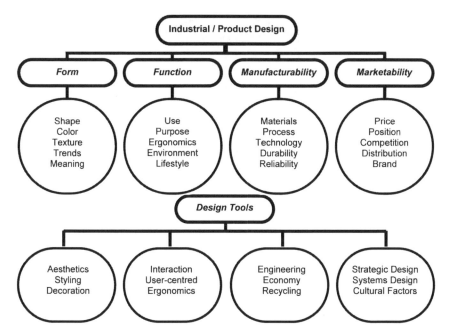

FIGURE 3.3 *Design process complex.*

In contrast with Adler's terms, note the emphasis I am giving here on business, profitability, social activity, and customers' needs. Moreover, design, considered in these terms, is a complex, demanding activity, as depicted in the diagram below (Figure 3.3):

The above does not include every consideration and method needing to be at the command of a designer, or as is often likely, a design team, but it does give some idea of the spectrum of competencies necessary to them to function effectively.

Since the dominant arena of activity for designers is at the level of the firm, whether working as a directly employed in-house designer or as external consultant, a consideration of the functions and processes at this level can reveal some contributions of design to innovation not generally considered in economic theory. As noted earlier, in the context of production (Figure 3.4), at least three major points of emphasis of value-creation need to be taken into account:

1. Through design-led or enabled innovation design makes a contribution to creating and adding new economic value. (cf. The role of designers as originators, or contributors to the origins, of totally new products capable of significantly changing existing markets, or even of creating new ones, and therefore of generating new economic value).

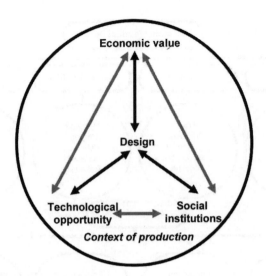

FIGURE 3.4 *The context of production.*

2. Similarly design can assist the ability to grasp technological opportunity and act upon it in ways that can help produce genuine innovations as against technical inventions.

3. Functioning within social and institutional structures of various kinds that enable and constrain their endeavours designers can facilitate the translation of these constraints and social possibilities into value.

In addition, however, if value is determined by customers, as Carl Menger emphasized, then not only the *context of production* needs to be examined, but also the *context of use.* One of the greatest challenges confronting designers is that they have to bridge the constraints and requirements of these two very different contexts.

Also of significance in stimulating innovation and growth is the role of designers as originators, or contributors to the origins, of totally new products capable of significantly changing existing markets, or even of creating new ones, and therefore of generating new economic value. If a vital role of design, as suggested here, is the translation of technological possibility into specific form, a close harmonization of design and technology is essential. [...] To adequately understand technological opportunity therefore requires technological competence. Design on this level is capable of being involved with the total product concept, not just visual appearance as a last minute additive.

The second context in which designers must function, the context of use, requires in contrast a very different set of requirements and constraints (Figure 3.5).

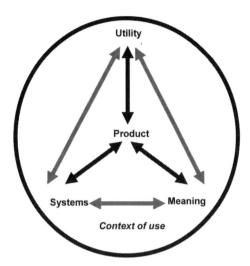

FIGURE 3.5 *The context of use.*

Of fundamental importance in this context is the factor of utility, which in design terms relates to the capability provided for users by a design, or in other words, what it enables them to do. In addition, designs assume meaning and significance in people's lives, which may stem from alignment with the beliefs and symbols current in the outside world, or may be of private significance to particular individuals. A third factor is variations in the systemic nature of the context of use. This can be subdivided into the physical systems, such as the electrical system or TV broadcasting system, and cultural systems, such as patterns of belief and behaviour that are embedded in a pattern of life. These latter often have a profound effect upon how what aspects of utility or meaning people will consider significant (Figure 3.6).

The priorities of production and of use differ radically. In the context of production, the dominant value is profitability, expressed in quantitative terms. In contrast, in the context of use the main emphasis is on values, in terms of satisfaction expressed in qualitative terms.

This distinction between value and values and their relative importance is the cause of enormous confusion in businesses and can frequently be a source of failure. Value is primarily defined in monetary terms. Money is both a measurement of value in markets and a store of value, or wealth. In some parts of the world, the primary expression of value for a firm is its share price and shareholders can often be considered their primary customers. A focus on monetary value, in terms of costs, prices, profits and capital, is a fundamental and unavoidable means of measurement in considering any aspect of business activity, design included. The point, however, is that solely focusing on financial measures or share price can ignore the means by which they are achieved and defined—or how and why they are established, enlarged and maintained. The argument here is that profitability cannot be

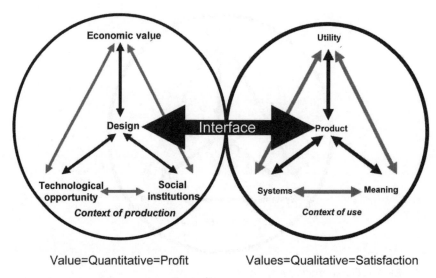

Value=Quantitative=Profit   Values=Qualitative=Satisfaction

FIGURE 3.6 *Production, use and interface.*

understood without examination of these deeper causes, which inevitably involves a consideration of values in a wider sense than the numerical alone.

As a consequence, one of the problems of discussing design in terms of the practices of Neo-classical economic theory is the way the latter has become dependent upon mathematical concepts and methodology. Similar problems also exist with the dominant practices of modern corporate administration and for much the same reasons—management has also become based on quantitative calculation and financial methodologies. This numerical emphasis is widely perceived by designers as a major obstacle to understanding how design functions. Setting aside the irrational aspects of what can often be an exaggerated, defensive reaction, and the deficiencies of some designers in clearly articulating their ideas, there is nevertheless considerable substance in such attitudes.

An illustration of the severity of such problems can be found in David Halberstam's book, *The Reckoning,* which compares the fortunes in the post-Second World War period of the second largest car companies in Japan and the U.S., Nissan and Ford. He describes the conflict at Ford between a new generation of managers armed with powerful statistical tools who gradually took over the firm's management in the 1960s and '70s, and the engineers and designers who lacked any means of quantifying their work. Ford had long been run by one man, its founder, Henry Ford, and the company was indeed in desperate need of effective management systems.

Out of that need grew the immense power of the finance people. A powerful, confident, modern bureaucracy was being installed at the

Ford Motor Company, sure of its skills, sure of its goals. It knew how to take care of itself, to help its own, and at above all how to replenish itself. For there was no easy way to replenish real car men, no graduate school readily turning out designers who were both creative and professional or manufacturing men who could run a happy, efficient factory. People of instinct and creativity, really talented ones, came along only rarely. The great business schools of America could not produce genius or intuition, but they could and did turn out every year a large number of able, ambitious young men and women who were good at management, who knew numbers and systems, and who knew first and foremost how to minimize costs and maximize profits.[2]

Halberstam's explanation of the educational and commercial advantages of what is fact codified knowledge explains in large measure why it was adopted so avidly, and it must be repeated, such abilities were badly needed at Ford. What happened as result, however, was that other disciplines became subordinated to the methodologies of the new generation of managers— they were forced to communicate their work and ideas in ways that were not just inappropriate, but ultimately dysfunctional, to a point where, in the late 1970s, Ford almost went out of business.

The terms Halberstam uses to describe the "real car men"—creativity, talent, genius, intuition—are in fact all aspects of tacit knowledge, which is such an important element in any form of creative practice and most certainly in design. Competence grows from constant experiment on the basis of trial and error, resulting in cumulative experience, which becomes in-built, integral, and not easily rationalized. There are innumerable stories of designers who have completed a project in a manner that satisfies every criterion required by their client, and yet have still woken in the night to do more work on it, because they instinctively know something is not yet complete.

Tacit knowledge can neither be explained in terms of rational decision-making, nor be summarized easily in quantitative terms. If the management of a firm does not have understanding of, and sympathy for, the particular nature and virtues of tacit knowledge, it will inevitably be easy to make designers appear incompetent by demanding conformity to practices alien to design. Under such circumstances, it is hardly surprising that design is often not taken seriously. At the same time, the resentment of designers becomes more comprehensible.

Advocating a greater understanding of tacit knowledge on the part of management should not, of course, absolve designers from extending the boundaries of rational analysis and quantitative explanations that can communicate understanding of their practice. There is much to be done on this level. Without codified basic assumptions and methods, it is difficult to communicate knowledge to successive generations as a starting point. Halberstam's point that there was "no graduate school readily turning out designers who were both creative and professional" is still true to some extent. Design education too often involves each generation metaphorically reinventing the wheel, albeit at a comparatively low skill level. There is much emphasis on "creative" ability, but without technical substance, economic relevance or institutional awareness and it is difficult to conceive of progress in any meaningful sense when small value is placed on the accumulation and codification of collective experience. The result is an inability to cope with new demands resulting from current, widespread change. In particular, when tackling large-scale complex problems of a systemic nature, individual insight and subjective beliefs are often totally inadequate to grasp all the dimensions of the problem being faced. In such instances, methodologies and techniques using logical analysis, quantification and computers are a necessary step in comprehending the nature of the problems involved, providing a platform for creative design solutions at a high level.

The evolution of new approaches in education and methodology are therefore of enormous importance for design. There is a vital need for designers to be more specifically prepared for the decision-making processes involved in complex innovation, combining high-level creativity based on technological competence with business awareness and able to plan how to use a spectrum of design abilities with other disciplines.

Notes

1 Jaumann, A. "Die Wirtschaftliche Bedeutung der Angewandte Kunst," (The Economic Meaning of German Applied Art), *Innen-Dekoration,* 1907.

2 Halberstam, David. *The Reckoning.* New York: William Morrow and Company, Inc., 1986, p. 210.

PART II

Design in History and the History of Design

Introduction to the Readings in Part II

As has already been noted in the introduction, in the first half of his academic life John Heskett was primarily a historian. Indeed, even towards the end of his last decade or so of work, in Chicago and Hong Kong, when he was pursuing most strongly the relation between design and economics and design and business, he was drafting a ms. *Crafts, Commerce and Industry* on the global history of design from earliest times. So history is central to Heskett's project – and he was, after all, as noted in the introduction, one of the first serious historians of design in the United Kingdom. Trained as an economic historian, he never made the mistake of collapsing design into an a-historical entity (which by a miracle is modelled on design as it exists as a professional activity in that precise moment the designer or design scholar gets to work). Heskett was a *historian* of design and was so in three principal registers – the history of designing and making in the pre-industrial world; the history of design and designing in the industrial period; and the history and role of design in Germany from c. 1870 to c. 1945. The readings in Part II are organized on this basis.

The readings in Part II are divided into three sections: (a) the history of pre-industrial design, (b) the history of designing in the industrial period and (c) Heskett's work on design in Germany from c.1870 to c. 1945.

a) Designing and making in the pre-industrial world

The readings begin, chronologically, with some fragments on pre-industrial design, although, as the introduction has already noted, these actually came late in his career. It was only in the late 1990s, when he began the research for the project on the 'global history of design' that he turned to looking in-depth at pre-industrial artefacts. One virtue of this material in his eyes was that it allowed him to break out of the limits of professional design and to begin to explore the history of design both as an integral moment of making (such that in many cases one cannot really speak of a distinct 'design' process) and as an anthropological capacity and capability, that is, one endemic to human life in the wise sense. This sense comes across in the short talk which constitutes reading #4, 'Some lessons of design history,' but it is even more apparent in reading #5, which reproduces the opening and closing sections of his project on the global history of design *Crafts, Commerce and Industry*. Reading #6 then, in turn, takes up the general sense of 'designing in the context of life' through a telling case study of the 'uses' of history for designing today developed via a short but effective study of the history of methods of Chinese cookery. Reading #7 then extends the historical range of the exploration of pre-industrial 'design' through three fragments taken from the *Crafts* ... ms., first on the material culture of nomads, second on the roles of trade in designed goods and third on the craftsmanship of slaves. As noted already, the *Crafts, Commerce and Industry* project remained unfinished at his death. Nonetheless, the issues that the ms. deals with begin to open out, and in that way challenge, some of the norms of our more recent history.

b) Designing in the industrial world

But John Heskett began in the 1970s as a historian of industrial design and of design in the industrial period. This is the *double* subject matter of his first book, *Industrial Design*, published in 1980 and this sense that there were two histories of design at work in this period (a history of a profession or field and a history of a wider practice or capacity) pervades his work, extending into how he conceived of the history of the profession and more generally of the history of design in the industrial epoch as a field of study (see reading #9 (i)). His stance is graphically illustrated in the contrasting book reviews also given in reading #9 where Heskett shows his impatience with those who he regards as myth-makers in the field of design (see #9(ii)), whilst supporting strongly, the more contextual and integrated study of the intertwining of objects, subjects and economy in the industrial period (see #9 (iii)). His own approach is methodologically encapsulated in the extract from *Industrial Design* published below (as reading #8). Indebted neither to art or architectural history (Pevsner) nor to the history of technology (Giedion), this is one of the first histories of design to focus on the context of production.

The chapter from *Industrial Design* looks at the very largest scale of industrial production. (In its largely US focus, it complements reading #2 which looked at parallel developments in industrial production but almost wholly in the context of the British industrial revolution.) In similar vein, the chapter on the growth and developing roles of industrial design in Japan (reading #10) is not simply an account of Japanese designers 'by name' as it were, but rather an exploration of the development of the *structural* role of industrial design in relation to Japanese industry and government policy in the post-war period. This chapter looks forward to, and gives historical perspective on, some of his later work on design policy and design and business relations in Asia.

As a critical commentary on these readings, it might be observed just how ambiguous an entity the history of design in the industrial period is as a field of study. Heskett saw this history in at least two ways: a history of *industrial design* [readings #8, #9 and #10] and as a history of *design[ing]* in the industrial period [largely reading #2 – and also the chapters on the industrial period in the *Craft ... ms*]. This ambiguity carries through the field, but it is also clearly a question of where the history of designing in this period ends and begins. Almost no conventional histories of the period mention design in any significant way (take for example Eric Hobsbawm's magisterial series of books from *Age of Revolution* through *Age of Capital* to *Age of Extremes* – and including also *Industrialization and Empire* on the economic history of the nineteenth century). From the stance of 'history', design is all but irrelevant. Yet, design as a professional activity is brought into being by the Industrial Revolution. That there is 'design' in any professional sense is a consequence of industrialization. For the latter, it is an objective requirement – if it were not it would not exist. Yet from the side of the 'history of design' this relationship is uneasily thought. Economics is almost by definition excluded from history. Very often technologies and modes of production, and even consumption, are not far behind. The 'natural' focus on the quasi-autonomy of the profession, of the story of design's coming-to-be as a quasi-autonomous activity becomes, almost without reflection, a default stance. Heskett was writing at time when these contending impulses were both present (they could not quite be denied) and yet often tacit (How does the history of capitalism fit into the Victoria and Albert museum?) The answer is that, except for superficial consideration, it does not. One consequence of this, however, is that in many ways the history of design[ing] in the industrial period remains underdeveloped. Part, and in fact a very significant part, of why this is so is institutional, in terms of both educational institutions and publishing. The 'history of design' as a pedagogical adjunct to the study of practice 'naturally' focuses on the rise of the profession. Publishing too focuses here. The profession itself, while sometimes welcoming histories of itself, has scant interest in wider issues, while from their side, economic history, economics, even the history of technology (until recently), have evidenced little interest in the history of the intersections of the coming into being of 'designing' (in the modern sense) and wider social and economic histories. All of this plays into what we can feel as the ambiguities and limits of this field, limits that extend quite beyond the remit of Heskett (particularly given the institutions he worked in, especially after 1989 – neither the Institute of Design in IIT in Chicago nor the School of Design in Hong Kong Polytechnic University had the slightest institutional interest in wider historical study).

c) Design in Germany 1870–1945

If the histories of design in industrialization already raise questions of policy and action, it is important to keep in mind that across the 1970s, Heskett was predominantly a researcher in the history of design, specifically in relation to Germany. As noted earlier, he never undertook a PhD. Had he done so, it would have been on German design. The third sub-section of the readings in history deals with his interest in German culture and design. Three texts are offered. The first is a chapter from his 1989 book *German Design 1870–1918* (the first of a planned three volumes – the collapse of the publisher ended the project) which, in an echo of what was just noted above in relation to the work on the rise of design in Japan, focuses on the interaction of design and government policy in the years either side of 1900. The chapter is a relatively early example of Heskett's insistence that in the history of design questions of policy and institution *matter* in terms of how they bear on the forms that design takes both as an activity and in terms of things made. The value of the piece lies in how Heskett shows us, with commendable clarity, how policies on state support for design, on design education and on infrastructural investment in cities – above all, the S-Bahn and U-Bahn urban rail systems in the largest German cities, especially Berlin – bore on both the general practices and particular instances of German design in the period around 1900.

The second piece (#12) is a short chapter on 'the industrial applications of tubular steel'. This deals briefly but concisely with how this characteristic material of the 'modern' 1920s was not only used in iconic designed furniture (the Breuer chair et al.) but in no less significant industrial applications. It is essentially a brief study of how a particular development of the material enabled the re-configuration of a far wider range of products and systems.

Finally, reading #13 is one of three papers he published in English on art and design in Nazi Germany. Heskett spent time in Germany in the late 1970s on a study grant looking at the question of Nazi design. This was at a time when there was considerable social and political ferment, not least around the questions of how the art and design of the Nazi period should be evaluated. Across the 1950s and 1960s, a very simple model had dominated. Obvious in its predictability, it had maintained that all Nazi art and design was 'bad', that is, retrograde, kitsch and anti-modern. It followed that 1933 had marked the end of all 'good' (i.e. modern, progressive, rational) design – whereas the onset of new democratic (West) Germany in 1949 marked the return to the principles of 'good' design. By the 1970s this simplistic view was under challenge. One of Heskett's first published articles, 'Art and Design in Nazi Germany' (*History Workshop Journal* #6, 1978, pp. 139–53) explored in some depth the exhibitions and scholarship that were beginning to challenge the prevailing post-war orthodoxy. His own contribution to the field, originally for a German publication ('Archaismus und Modernismus im Design im dritten Reich' in B. Hinz et al. (eds), Anabas Verlag, Giessen, 1979) was a paper he published in 1980, in *Block* Magazine as 'Modernism and Archaism in Design in the Third Reich'.[1] It is this paper that is reproduced below as reading #13. The chapter comprehensively rethinks the relation of modernity and design in the Third Reich, teasing out a more complex relation to the 'modern' in Nazi ideology and the everyday material practices of the regime.

Note

1   This paper was reprinted in 1990 in *The Nazification of Art*, ed. Brandon Taylor and Wilfried van der Will (Winchester: Winchester press) and then re-presented again, but in a quite different form, in 1995, as 'Design in Inter-war Germany', as an essay for the exhibition catalogue of the opening show of the Wolfsonian Foundation in Miami, *Designing Modernity: The Arts of Reform and Persuasion*. This last version is beautifully illustrated using artefacts from the Wolfsonian collection.

(A)
Designing and Making in the Pre-Industrial World

4

Some Lessons of Design History

What can we learn from history as practitioners of design in today's rapidly changing society? That adaptation is an absolute necessity.

To the extent that a History of Design exists, it is still fragmentary and largely confined to a limited number of countries in the last two centuries, although a welcome trend is its extension back in time to the Renaissance. There is a sharp contrast, however, between the many books published in English on British, German or Scandinavian design while we still lack a satisfactory account of significant work in, for example, Japan or Mexico over the last fifty years, or of many other countries or regions. The innumerable picture books focusing on 'style' in various parts of the world hardly fill the gap. This limited focus is based on an implicit, assumption that design is defined in terms of a relatively recent layer of professional development in a few, mostly Western, locales.

If we are to build a knowledge base for design, which I regard as one of the most important tasks facing education and practice, a crucial element of it should be a history that opens up wider possibilities in geographical, temporal and experiential terms. An important step in that direction would be if we move from thinking of design as a professional discipline localized in space and time, and instead view it as part of a longer process of evolution. To do this, we need to define design in more fundamental terms: as the human ability to shape and make environments that serve practical needs and give meaning to life. Such a generic definition positions the ability to shape and make our world as a fundamental human attribute, opening up the possibility of thinking about the history of this ability in much deeper perspective. It also opens up consideration of the effect of the great changes in human life that have altered the way we live, think and feel, such as the effects of settled cultivation, the growth of cities, and far-flung patterns of

First published as "Some Lessons of Design History" in *Designkompetanse—Utvkling, forskning og undervisning*, ed. Astrid Skjerven, Oslo, 2005, pp. 11–21.

exchange and trade. In other words, a rich tapestry of life and work opens up once this wider understanding is accepted.

Implicit in this suggestion is a belief that understanding of the present, is heavily conditioned by our perceptions of the past. A consequence of the broad definition I am suggesting is that it enables design to be moved out of the shadow of art history, with its emphasis on 'decorative arts' and stylistic factors. The dominant depiction, of art history in terms of a linear evolution of styles and movements in Western countries, with new trends sequentially replacing existing ones, is inadequate to explain design. It may be argued, validly I believe, that this is not what actually took place in the evolution of art, but against that is the fact of its widespread depiction in such terms and the distortion, if so it is, has become widely institutionalized.

Dominant patterns in art history—linear and sequential

Much confusion in understanding design in all its variety is also due to the fact that in contrast to that sequential depiction of art, old tendencies in design, sometimes of great antiquity, still widely exist, even in the most advanced societies, due to the fact that in everyday life, in contrast to the theories of the academy, the new has never entirely replaced the old, but has instead been layered upon it. Some of the earliest and simple means of making and shaping still exist alongside the most advanced contemporary techniques. Design is therefore simultaneously about change, continuity and adaptation.

Patterns in design history—layered and additive

Electronics
Electrical industrialization
Steam-industrialization
Proto-industry
Urban crafts
Rural crafts

In the listing above, a number of fundamental changes are identified in the dominant forms of production that human beings have used to sustain themselves. In support of the layering theory of design history, all still exist in one form or another across the globe, although many have been subject to modification as they continue to evolve. In describing these changes, I want to emphasize how the processes of shaping and making have responded to changed circumstances with very different approaches to what is considered appropriate in different societies.

The early evolution of homo sapiens is the point at which this capacity to shape and make developed in an accelerated scale and scope far beyond the limited range of shapes and forms that characterized early predecessors of the genus homo, although there is still much work to be accomplished before the pattern of evolution in forms can be adequately traced. Nevertheless, there are early indicators of complex functional forms that are sometimes very sophisticated, an example being a barbed bone fishing spear from the Congo Basin, in the region of Katanda / Katanga, dating from between 90–70,000 BC that is on display in the National Museum of Natural History, Washington, D.C. An early hint of decorative form is also evident in hatched geometrical patterns incised on ochre stone and dating from c. 70,000 BC, found at the Biombos caves near the southern tip of Africa and exhibited in The South African Museum, Cape Town. These early examples indicate a latent potential in *homo sapiens* that exploded in an astonishing expansion of forms and patterns from around 30,000 BC.

Nomadic life, the earliest pattern of existence for human beings, imposed restrictions on what could be made and carried. Marshall Sahlins has written that in hunting and gathering life, 'wealth is a burden' and 'mobility and property are in contradiction.'[1] Dependency on available sources of food and water often required rapid movement over substantial distances and artefacts had to be small, light, portable and flexible, adaptable to varied uses. Many of these were made of perishable materials such as skin, wood and bone and so have not survived, although where nomadic patterns of life have continued into the modern age it is still possible to gain hints of what existed in the past. The San or Bushmen of the Kalahari, for example, widely used skin bags to carry possessions or game from the hunt and collected large ostrich eggs for use as water flasks, which were carried in nets of fibre cord. The pattern of adaptation by nomadic groups across every geographical and climatic zones on our planet makes the wealth of examples and adaptations a huge testament to the potential of human creativity, when circumstances require it.

The first patterns of settlement and agriculture that began c. 8000 BC in the arc of hills in northern Mesopotamia, and a little later in the Nile Valley of Egypt, the Indus Valley of the Indian sub-continent, and the great river valleys of China, totally altered the nature of the forms required by human beings to cultivate land and nurture domesticated birds and animals. Living in one place meant that a permanent habitation was required, which allowed an accumulation of material possessions, with a range of specialized tools for repetitive work, and an expanded time-scale for storage of food and seed. Because they did not have to be moved, such forms could be large and heavy in a manner that would have been impossible under nomadic conditions. An example is a finely shaped stone mortar and pestle found in Syria dating from the late 8th millennium BC.[2] It evolved as part of the process of sowing, tending, harvesting and storing, the culmination of which was the conversion of stored grain into flour. Pounding and grinding grain into a form capable of being baked was a repetitive task that required strength and weight in the artifacts used, hence the widespread use of stone implements that had a permanent place in early kitchens. Specialization also became evident early on in the history of pottery, another aspect of settled life. It evolved with crude, hand shaped and sunbaked forms, but even so many sophisticated shapes rapidly emerged, such as earthenware pitchers of a widely found type used for fetching and storing water developed around 5000 BC in the Yangshao culture of the type found at Banpo near Xian.[3] The bulb-like form with tapered base had two lugs to allow ropes to be attached to either side and was cleverly designed to tilt on its side when dropped empty into a stream or a well, allowing the pitcher to fill. Once the water inside reached a certain height the weight of the pitcher would tilt it upright, enabling it to be hoisted out without loss of its contents. Rural crafts such as these are still very widespread in many parts of the globe and present an astonishing spectrum of achievement and continuity.

The next phase of change, the Urban Revolution and growth of cities around 4000 BC, was only possible where a surplus of food was generated by agriculture and brought under the control of small groups of rulers, who could be either priests or kings. Dominance of food supplies created wealth, which was reflected, for example, in stone-lined storage silos found at palace sites of the Minoan civilization in Crete. A terra-cotta storage jar from the Hittite capital of Hattusas in Anatolia,[4] dating from c. 1200 BC had an estimated capacity of 2000 litres volume of grain, root crops, oil or wine.

Wealth and power also required the finest levels of craft skills to create often spectacular objects that proclaimed the status of rulers and aristocrats. The wonderfully crafted articles of the great Mesopotamian urban cultures for the rich and powerful represent new heights of skill in transforming materials such as metals, ceramics and later glass, but the gulf between rich and poor is also evident in thousands of crudely shaped earthenware bowls of identical form and capacity that have been found from Syria to Iran, which are believed to possibly be standard ration-portion bowls for workers on large projects.

A feature even at this early stage was that in terms of status, craftsmen, despite the fine skills of the most talented, were not highly regarded in early urban societies. Illustrations of them and descriptions of their work are rare, but those extant and the fragmentary documentation that exists on their life indicates that the conditions were generally hard and onerous.

A feature of many urban cultures was the growth of organizations, or guilds, to represent the interests of craftsmen, which, in India, for example, become evident by 500 BC. They had varied origins: some, as in Cairo, were established by rulers to ensure taxes could be levied and collected more efficiently; others were established by rulers to control the finest skills for court purposes, as in Mughal India; some had religious origins, such as those associated with the Sufi sects of Islam in southern Persia; others were founded by craftsmen themselves to protect their interests. The history of such bodies varied but the European medieval guilds, which emerged around 1100 AD became a prominent feature of the life and politics of many cities and represent a rare example of control by designers of any kind over their position in society and conditions of work. While some builders later became architects and some, clerks became lawyers, each with highly regarded qualifications and organizations, design never made the transition to professional status.

The power of guilds in many countries began to be eroded by a range of developments in which control of design factors such as product type, shape and pattern were appropriated by other constituents. On one level, from the 1400s in Europe, wealthy customers, rulers, aristocrats and increasingly newly rich merchants, began to demonstrate their wealth and status in terms of conspicuous consumption. The existence of this market provided opportunities for virtuoso craftsmen to cater for this rarified market, in which the demands of customers became the decisive element in what was produced and how. An example is in the field of armour.

In the 12th century in Europe, the rise of feudalism was accompanied by the development of new types of armour for mounted knights that made them the most formidable military force of the age. Early examples indicate very clearly that functional considerations dominated—this being literally a matter of life and death.

By the 14th, the development of gunpowder and its use in firearms create a new situation in which total body armour was no solution—to resist bullets it had to be so heavy that it became ineffective. However, armour not only went on being produced for another three centuries, but became ever more elaborate. The reason laid in the use of armour as court dress, to proclaim the status of rulers, and its use in tournaments, still a major diversion to relieve the boredom of court life. As a consequence, some armourers of the highest skills, such as the Negroli family of Milan, and decorative designers, such as the Parisian goldsmith and print-maker Etienne Delaune, became fashionable 'star' designers of armour, functioning outside the boundaries of guild control.

Another assault on guild power came from a very different direction: the growth in many parts of the world of what is often referred to as 'proto-industry,' which generally took the form of large-scale, serial production on the basis of hand work methods, in which forms were determined by people other than the workers/craftspeople. The scale of such operations could be substantial, and sometimes it was craftsmen who became entrepreneurs, as Indian historian Romila Thapar points out in the evidence of a potter, Saddalaputta, who in the period 200–300AD was said, to own five hundred potter's workshops and 'a large number of boats to distribute his wares to various cities on the Ganges river.'[5] The extent to which division of labour could be a feature of proto-industrial manufacture was illustrated by an account of Father Francois Xavier d'Entrecolles, a Jesuit describing the workshops of Jingdezhen in southern China in the early 18th century. 'It is said that one piece of fired porcelain passes through the hands of seventy workers.'[6] By 800 AD, there was a widespread trade in products such as Indian textiles and Chinese ceramics, with design being removed from the control of craftspeople and increasingly being a matter of negotiation between merchants and customers, with patterns adapted to the cultural tastes of different regions. Chinese porcelain patterns, for example, were markedly different for the Indian markets as against products destined for Persia or the Arab world. The extent of the early trade can be illustrated by the collection of some 13,000 pieces of Chinese porcelain held in the collection of the former Ottoman palace, now the Topkapi Serai Museum, Istanbul. From around 1600, this trade extended to Europe and until around 1800, the manufactures of Asia were dominant factors in shaping European taste and fashion.

The introduction of increasingly powerful mechanized forms of production typical of the Industrial Revolution that began in late eighteenth century Britain signaled further changes. There was a huge increase in scale of production and size of markets, with a further separation of design from making, and image and fashion increasingly being employed as sales tools. A problem for early manufacturers was in finding suitable designers capable of creating forms suitable for manufacture and the new emphasis on marketing, a task for which craft-trained people were generally unsuitable. A solution widely adopted by such leading industrialists as Josiah Wedgwood and Matthew Boulton was for a division of labour within design, with well-known artists being used for what today would be termed concept drawings and draughtsmen within the factories responsible for turning these visual ideas into production specifications. With innovative form being the major criterion for success in many trades increasingly dominated by fashionable concerns, the result of the trend for 'Art in Industry' was, not surprisingly, the increasing separation of decorative concepts from any reference to function. The few designers, Christopher Dresser in late nineteenth century Britain being the most notable, who sought to produce original work appropriate to the new forms of production which could reshape the taste of the market, became ignored in the plethora of styles and counter-styles that dominated the period.

There were, however, many new mechanical industries confronted by problems and functions that could not be conveniently covered in a repertory of decorative forms that pillaged every known culture from the past. An example is the railways that were the major force in transforming societies, linking people and markets and shrinking concepts of space and time. Locomotives, for example, had no precedent and rapidly evolved in the nineteenth century into forms that represent an alternative pole to the decorative trends of the age. Moreover, they also varied in accord with the geographical and climatic conditions through which the railway lines ran, with, for example, American, Indian or Argentinian forms modifying the British models originally imported to reflect the very different terrain and conditions.

The tempo of production was vastly increased with the second phase of industrialization that began in the final years of the nineteenth century with the growth of electrical power and its applications, which greatly stimulated mass production. As it emerged in the early twentieth century in the United States it was on a model in which huge investment was required to produce highly standardized products in vast quantities to be sold at relatively low prices.

Henry Ford's insistence on refusing to change the Model T was a seemingly logical expression of the nature of this form of manufacture. In the early 1920s, however, Alfred P. Sloan, the executive who had welded a number of disparate companies into General Motors, saw beyond the logic of production to the needs of the market. Diversity, not uniformity, was required, but without negating the cost advantages of mass production. Sloan introduced the concept of 'styling,' the use of frequent alterations of superficial forms to convey a sense of innovation that could be exploited in advertising and marketing, while keeping the working elements, such as engines and drive-trains, relatively unchanged over long periods. In other words, for a marginal cost penalty, Sloan gained an enormously important design tool of great power in the market place. There followed the adoption, of similar approaches in almost every sector generating consumer products in large quantities and the rapid percolation of the design techniques and attitudes associated with styling to design schools. It still remains a powerful element in design practice in industry, and not only in the United States.

Another element associated with the rise of large business organizations has been a growth in systemic design practices. By this is meant an increase in the scale of design projects to either encompass all the affairs of large corporations or to encompass projects of considerable size and complexity. Early examples of the former were initially on an ad hoc basis, as with the German company AEG after it appointed Peter Behrens as Artistic Director in 1907, or London Transport under the managerial direction of Frank Pick from 1906 through to 1942. After the Second World War, companies such as Olivetti, IBM and Braun brought design to bear on the full range of their activities that had substantial influence on the concept of corporate identity programmes. One of the most complete systems of this type, however was established by a nationalized organization. British Rail, which evolved a programme of great scope that became a model widely adapted by similar railway groups across Europe.

A current project of enormous scale that is expanding the scope of design methodology is the new Terminal 5 building at London's Heathrow Airport. Din Associates of London are responsible for all user factors involved in arrival and departure. This has nothing to do with detailed design of stores, but with the overall patterns of usability and navigation. To cope with the mass of details this involves has required an expansion of computer techniques used in designing—work on such a scale going far beyond the capabilities of individual designers.

If changes in the past have required adaptation and the evolution of new techniques and approaches in design, what are the changes currently taking place that are likely to bring about similar changes? The shift from electro-mechanical to electronic, technology with the development of information technology, flexible systems of manufacture and global patterns of trade are already having substantial impact. Mass manufacturing is evolving new approaches to meet the demands of globalization and is exploiting new sources of flexibility in concepts such as modular units and platform designs, with more sophisticated forms of styling to adapt to varying circumstances around the world. The dominance of mass manufacturing is in some respects being eroded. However, as flexible manufacturing opens up greater possibilities of profitably catering for smaller scale niche markets more specifically adapted to the needs of users.

Another trend is the need for cooperation across design disciplines as hardware and software become combined and products increasingly demonstrate a capacity for adaptation and embodying knowledge in every aspect of design. More and more design at the present day is requiring of designers' greater knowledge, greater understanding of business and technological aspects, and greater ability to cooperate with other disciplines. The days when design students could be refugees from rigour are limited and those who think it possible to build a career only on playing with visual elements risk being increasingly confined to marginal activities tending to superficial details.

In this very rapid overview of exceedingly broad historical trends over a great span of time it has obviously been necessary to deal in great generalities. To conclude, however, what are the lessons of history? An obvious conclusion is that every age has its characteristic combination of technological and social conditions, which requires a particular approach to design. When the context changes, new design abilities will be required and there will be a period of confusion in which old-established practices will be defended but will generally be incapable of adaptation. What happened to the marvellous skills of the manuscript illuminators in an age when printing was rapidly evolving? What happened to the village wheelwright in an age when automobiles were evolving? What has happened to the armies of female stenographers or shorthand/typists since the introduction of computers? Changes have repeatedly destroyed or marginalized innumerable capabilities and skills. When new technologies emerge, new knowledge and new skills will be required, which is exactly the situation we currently face in design. As in such situations in the past, new abilities will either be adapted from other practices, or will be developed informally and spontaneously by individuals who have the vision and ability to perceive where new opportunities lie.

We are without, any doubt living in an age of enormous change. The lesson of history must therefore be: adapt or be marginalized.

Notes

1 Sahlins, Marshall, *Stone Age Economics,* New York: Aldine de Gruyter, 1972, pp. 10–11.

2 Now in The Metropolitan Museum of Art, New York.

3 The Banpo Village near Xian provides evidence of complex settlement patterns in Neolithic. China. The highlight of the village site is the remains of some 25 houses, with a pottery-making area and burial ground. There is also a small and poorly organized museum which contains, however, some remarkable artifacts—working tools for hunting, fishing and agriculture and some excellent examples of Banpo pottery.

4 On exhibition in The Museum of Archeology, Istanbul.

5 Thapar, Romila, *A History of India, Vol.* 1, Harmondsworth: Penguin, 1966, p. 110.

6 The Letters of Pere d'Entrecolles, translated in Robert Tichane, *Ghing-te-chen: Views of a Porcelain City* (New York: New York State. Institute for Glaze Research, 1983), p. 60. Reference in Robert Finlay, 'The pilgrim art: The culture of porcelain in world history,' *Journal of World History,* Honolulu, Fall 1998.

5

Crafts, Commerce, Industry: A Global History of Design: Introduction and Conclusion

Reading #5 contains the opening section and the concluding paragraphs to the unpublished ms. "Crafts, Commerce, Industry: A Global History of Design," which Heskett drafted between the late 1990s and around 2004. The text is in fact perhaps better read as an attempt at a history of making in which the entanglement of commerce and culture, and production and design, are explored across global history. Reproduced here are the opening and concluding paragraphs to the ms. These short fragments cannot do justice to the scope of the text as a whole but they do in many ways contain the essence of Heskett's underlying vision and understanding of design as a human capacity deeper and more extensive than its merely professional instantiation.

Introduction

Let a man pull himself away from the comfort of the academies and go down into the workshops, to collect information about the arts and set it out in a book which will persuade artisans to read, philosophers to think usefully, and the great to make at last some beneficial use of their authority and wealth ...

Denis Diderot, 1751[1]

I write these words on a computer in my room at home. The table at which I sit was custom-made to accommodate all the ancillary items needed in my work: machines such as modem, printer, scanner and copier, and stacks of documents. Shelves above hold a clutter of objects: computer disks, reference books, books to be read, numerous family photographs, a Braun clock, a head of a Chinese goddess some 1500 years old, a bone-carved Buddhist amulet from Tibet, a small metal model of a bus that carried me as a child to visit my grandparents, and so on.

Two observations emerge from this partial inventory: firstly, all the objects mentioned were designed and made by other human beings at various times, in widely differing contexts using a broad spectrum of materials wrought by very different means: hand techniques, simple mechanized processes or mass production assembly lines. Secondly, while some might potentially have monetary value, it is not the reason they are there. Instead, all have personal meaning, in terms of people, places and experiences with which they are connected. Although this particular array of objects is specific to my life, in innumerable variations other people around the world similarly construct environments great and small that serve their purposes and have meaning for them. The simple point is that objects, communications and spaces of one kind or another are extraordinarily important in people's lives, yet they remain a largely underestimated aspect of our culture. As Mihaly Csikszentmihalyi and Eugene Rochberg-Halton have written: "Psychologists in general have followed the lead of Freud and Jung by ignoring the place of things in the daily commerce of existence." [2] Neither is it only psychologists who have done so.

Such ignorance in a materialistic age in which the role of things becomes more continually more widespread is curious. In 44 AD, the Roman statesman Cicero could write, in contrast, of:

- the obvious fact that it is only the labour of man's hands that places the profits and advantages from inanimate objects at our disposal.
- if mankind did not possess these skills, there would be no healing of the sick, no pleasure for the healthy, no food, no comforts at all. And these are just the things that make a human being's civilized life different from the existence of a beast.[3]

This book is an attempt to explain the evolution of the human capacity to design—the skills of shaping and making objects, communications, environments and systems—that serve our practical needs and gives meaning to our lives. As such, it is one of the fundamental characteristics of what it is to be human, as Cicero was aware, and the root of both great achievements and, increasingly in our age, of acute tensions and threatening dilemmas.

The ability to design initially depends upon a capacity for abstraction, the ability to separate a concept of the essence of something from the reality itself. We also have the capacity to express these abstractions in terms of symbols, such as words or drawings. These symbolic representations might refer to forms in external reality but can in turn take on a reality of their own. In this process of abstraction from life and reference back to it, there is the possibility of change, of altering innumerable aspects of the original concept.

Abstract thought not only enables us to comprehend and record such symbols, therefore, but also to think in terms of them, to envisage modifications and variations, which can lead to contemplating something substantially different, such as new or modified forms that are believed to be better in some respect. "Everyone designs who devises courses of action aimed at changing existing situations into preferred ones," wrote Herbert Simon.[4]

Ideas of possibility thus embody intentionality and are the generative mainspring of the ability to design. His conception of design, however, was of a conceptual process that was common to many professional disciplines. Simon continues:

> The intellectual activity that produces material artefacts is no different fundamentally from the one that prescribes remedies for a sick patient or the one that devises a new sales plan for a company or a social welfare policy for a state. Design, so construed, is the core of all professional training; it is the principal mark that distinguishes the professions from the sciences.[5]

In addition to this general process, however, every discipline has skills and methods specific to it that are essential for it to function practically. In a more specific sense, human beings are equipped with the ability to mould and transform physical reality through the knowledge, tools and processes that constitute technology, enabling concepts to be turned into tangible realities. In other words, from understanding external reality by means of abstraction, through the ability to design in terms of concepts and plans for change, we have the ability to creatively transform external reality to better suit our needs and aspirations. In so doing, we design a world of artifice that imposes human concepts of order and structure in contrast to the unpredictable and untrammelled forces of the natural world.

This underpins another critical factor, which is the difference between processes of change in nature and in human societies. Natural change is random and accidental through processes of evolution, of mutation and survival of the fittest. Human initiated change, in contrast, is capable by design of being rational, deliberate and goal-oriented, which, of course, does not mean it always is so – the role of subjective and emotional factors should never be underestimated. The capacity to design has reached a point, however, where few aspects of life on our planet are totally unaffected by or invulnerable to it. Indeed, it can be argued that the scale and reach of this capacity for transformation is at a stage where the dangers of our collective ability to implement change are far outrunning our ability to comprehend or control its full effects.

The contrast of the world of artifice with the world of nature is not restricted to external reality, but also mirrors a basic dichotomy in all human beings. We are simultaneously the products of both nature and nurture: the inheritors of a vast process of natural evolution reflected in our genetic structure, and of a cultural inheritance embodied in the societies and value systems into which we are born and subsequently live. The natural latent capacity to design in all human beings will depend, in the extent to which it is realized and the form in which this occurs, on the cultural context—the inherited accumulation of tools, forms, procedures, organizations and values of any society, which condition the attitudes and activities of its members as to what is "normal" or "right" and the range of forms considered appropriate for any purpose.

Culture is not immutable, but is also susceptible to change. A characteristic of almost all other species than Homo sapiens in the natural world, whether plants or animals, is they must physically change to adapt to different contexts. In other words, their nature is inseparable from a particular set of conditions. Remove or drastically alter the natural environment of particular flora or fauna and the threat of extinction becomes very real. Human beings, in contrast, respond either to changes in an environment, or to changes of environment, by means of cultural adaptation. They do this on two levels: firstly, by modifying cultural behaviour to acknowledge change; secondly, by radically altering or modifying a physical environment to suit pre-existing cultural values. The influence of culture on the capacity to create an environment of artifice, by design, is the variable separating the condition of human beings from both their own innate natural constitution and the rest of the natural world.

There are many problems in studying how this ability to design has evolved. Above all, since it has been a constant feature of the life of Homo sapiens, its manifestations have evolved in innumerable ways and variations at particular times and places. Attempting to write a history of the whole range of activity grouped under this rubric would be an exceedingly difficult undertaking. Even focusing on a segment of the whole to illustrate the overall pattern of evolution in design—the approach adopted here— involves daunting problems.

The particular focus in this book is on three-dimensional design as used in everyday life, not just in terms of the objects and appliances found in homes, but also at work, in public places, in the forms of transportation in which goods and people are carried and objects used as instruments of status or weapons of war. Reference will be made to other forms of design when necessary or relevant. The intention is to trace how design has evolved from early beginnings in nomadic societies, through the evolution of various phases of craft activity linked to agriculture and settlement, in which handwork has been the dominant factor, into larger-scale commercial organizations, often with a truly global reach in trade, from which emerged modern industrial systems still evolving new variants. It is concerned not only with the utilitarian aspects of such objects but also with their meaning and significance in the lives of the peoples who made and used them, in other words, both how they came to be made and what they meant in use.

The approach will necessarily be broad and synoptic. Within a chronological framework there will be a focus on major themes. The chapters are thus more essays on these themes and how they evolved and developed within a general chronological framework, with considerable overlaps and backtracking, rather than attempting a sequential account of seemingly inevitable progress.

If the capacity to design, the kinds of ends it serves and how it is understood depends upon material, social, political, economic and cultural factors, then these will need to be an integral element of the study of design. A basic difference exists, for example, between human societies at different levels of complexity. As they have evolved from tribal, nomadic units to settled groups in ever-larger agglomerations, so there is a perceptible change of emphasis in the roles of artefacts, from personal use to exchange by barter and gift, to the evolution of markets, the commercialization of production and exchange, and the spread of industrialisation and globalisation

Another level of difference is that between conditions of scarcity or abundance. Use and convenience tend to predominate as criteria in a condition of shortages, but as higher standards of living emerge, even to the point of superfluity, so symbolic meaning, understood in the modern age as fashion and life-style, become primary criteria. The geographical conditions determining the availability of materials or framing possibilities of access and trade are, of course, also important defining elements.

Concluding thoughts

Mass production is not going to disappear, indeed in some important aspects it is moving into what could be called a "super-mass" phase, with some categories of production being organized on a truly global level. As has happened repeatedly in the past, however, new layers of activity are becoming superimposed upon past patterns and in the last quarter of the twentieth century new tendencies have appeared to signal yet another wave of change.

The deepest element in this transformation has been the rapid expansion of electronic technology, bringing change on the same fundamental scale earlier wrought by steam and electrical power. The incredible computing capacity of the silicon chip has made possible a degree of miniaturization in innumerable devices at increasingly lower cost, bringing hitherto undreamed of access to information and computing power. In its early stages, analogous to the concept of the horseless carriage before it evolved into the automobile, the desktop computer took the form of a television screen and a typewriter keyboard with a format dating from 1873, before the more mobile laptop configuration began to take over. It has rapidly evolved into other forms linking various technologies in ever-new combinations and there is clearly still much experiment in search of defining standards. Embedding computer chips in a wide variety of products is still in the early stages but has huge potential, such as chairs or sports shoes that can configure to the dimensions and posture of a user, or clothing that can monitor vital health functions.

One of the most important results of the electronic revolution has been to reduce the monolithic nature of some aspects of mass production. Computerized numerical control of manufacturing machinery means what is made on a production line can be reconfigured in minutes, simply by changing inputs to the computer program instead of having to physically reconstruct the line. Flexible manufacturing is thus becoming an alternative to mass production, enabling markets to be broken down into ever smaller segments with production oriented to the needs of groups and even individuals. Together with information technology enabling close contact to be maintained between producer and user, this creates the possibility of items being made to the specific dimension of particular people rather than them having to conform to standard specifications. The flexibility of both product and on-line information systems can therefore recreate some aspects of older concepts of craft practice, of smaller scale operations and personal interaction typical of pre-industrial methods, with an emphasis on accessibility for greater numbers of people.

Several design approaches to incorporate possibilities of flexibility are already in widespread use, including concepts such as platform products and modular systems, some with deep historical roots. In platform approaches a basic configuration is designed to which additional components can be added to make products appropriate for a specific market. The Ford Motor Company, for example, has reorganized its operations on a global basis, rather than in geographical units all producing their own designs. The global platform concept enables a vehicle in a particular category to be basically designed using components sourced around the world at lowest cost, and then detailed to suit the needs of geographical markets.

The use of modular systems is similar in principle, in that they depend upon a series of standard units and accessories, all compatible that can be configured to the needs of particular customers. Dell attained market leadership in the sale of personal computers by offering modular components that customers could configure to their requirements and order on-line.

Both platform and modular concepts have in common that they are not conceived primarily in terms of the final product, but of a system capable of being adapted to personal needs. Computers and the Internet have opened up possibilities for users to be involved in decisions about what kind of products they want and how they can be adapted to their needs. This tilting of the balance from production-centred approaches to design, as typified in mass production, to more user-centred concepts is likely to increase. A consequence is a change of emphasis in the role of designers from that of creating a final form, to one of acting as an enabler, creating systems that best allow users to take vital decisions. The computer on which these words are written is a good example. Although the physical form is highly standardized, the software allows anyone to configure the machine and adapt how it is used to the most highly personal and individualistic needs. This, with the small scale and low cost in which all this constantly increasing power is concentrated, opens up enormous possibilities, but inevitably, as the economist Joseph Schumpeter observed, innovation on that scale involves a process of Creative Destruction. The new destroys not just product concepts, but invested capital and worker's skills. There is a deadly dance at the heart of capitalism in which design plays a leading role. Apple's iPod is an example. A brilliant exploitation of new miniaturised technology, it also allowed users to download music in terms appropriate to them, with a high degree of personal choice, which places into question many products and procedures in the music industry, who naturally enough wish to avoid seeing their companies rapidly disappear like the stagecoaches between Liverpool and Manchester.

Another aspect of growth is in the scale of many design projects, large, complex networks being conceived as a totality. Designing a hospital in these terms, for example, requires that the needs of users be met on multiple levels— doctors, nurses, technicians, administrators, patients and their visitors— rather than a piecemeal assembly with each aspect considered separately and no-ones' needs adequately met. Transport systems and airports are other examples of such approaches. Just as in the past, new roles have opened up for designers in response to new demands, so designers increasingly need to work in teams with a spectrum of both other specialist designers and other disciplines, with appropriate methodologies to cope with the vast range of information and applications necessary to meet the demands of structuring complex systems. Individual subjectivity is hardly likely to be capable of understanding such patterns of complexity, instead large-scale computer programs and structured knowledge will be a necessary underpinning for creativity. Large-scale projects also imply a move to a more strategic role, in which as much emphasis will be placed on design as a planning process as on the execution in detail of various visual forms. In other words, a new layer will be added to those that already exist, concerned above all with how technology and systems are humanized, configured to better meet the needs of people, while at the same time meeting financial and temporal targets. The layering that has characterized its historical evolution, therefore, is still an emphatic feature of the contemporary design landscape.

We have reached a point where in innumerable ways design determines the environments of the future in all their aspects, playing a primary role in how technology is harnessed for human purposes. History can help us understand how it functions but the choices needing to be made for the future often have no precedent. Design functions overwhelmingly in the arena of business where the major decisions about how and why it is applied are made. Whether this can result in design being used wisely as well as profitably is open to question—the two are often seen as polar opposites but need not necessarily conflict.

If history is one of the major means we have of understanding the present and considering possibilities of what could or should emerge, it is difficult to be sanguine about the future. The evidence is that while our abilities in technology and design have increased exponentially, the purposes to which we apply this vast potential show little advance.

One thing seems to me clear. If we fail to understand that the environment we inhabit is increasingly of human design and accept responsibility for the consequences, the outlook is indeed fraught with danger of our own making. A starting point is to comprehend this ability to design as one of the central capabilities of human existence and a vital determinant of that elusive concept of quality of life.

The objects, the physical evidence that has survived and constitute much of the evidence in the history of design, demonstrate the unbounded creative ability that exists in human beings. From the earliest manifestations of design onwards there is a rich material legacy filled with magnificent achievements and inspiration. This leads to questions about what the legacy of present generations will be to those who follow. In looking at how this human creative capacity called design is being applied in contemporary life and society any conclusions must be more guarded.

We now have an ability to intervene in the most basic aspects of life and the structure of our planet. In terms of how we use this ability, however, we seem to have learned little. Designers have begun to think more systematically in many respects, but the concept of human life being part of an intricate web, with a high degree of interdependence among the component parts, has made little headway. The profligate manner in which finite resources are plundered for short-term financial benefit shows scant concern for the future and designers actively involved these processes are part of the problem.

Neither does the behaviour of human beings one to another provide much reassurance. The number of people killed as a result of deliberate human decisions and actions in the twentieth century has exceeded all great disasters of any kind whether human or natural in the history of the world. As Cicero put it almost two thousand years ago, "there is not a shadow of doubt that man has the power to be the greatest agent both of benefit and of harm towards his fellow-men."

Design in its forms—artefacts, communications, structures and systems—played an instrumental role in these destructive acts. Ironically, the finest contemporary examples of how objects can be consistently designed in superb detail to fit human physical dimensions in order to increase comfort and effectiveness in use are provided by firearms. It is therefore impossible to depict design as an innately benign activity. Instead it is caught in the endemic dilemma of what it is to be human beings: simultaneously creative titans and moral pygmies. We have learnt to control innumerable aspects of our environment and existence, but seem incapable or unwilling to control ourselves. Designers alone, therefore, cannot provide a solution to all the proliferating problems caused by human actions in our time. They could do more, but only if the desire for them to do so exists in societies around the globe.

We have in the history of design an astonishingly rich inheritance. What is even more amazing is that with every new-born child the latent potential for similar achievement exists in this incredibly fertile human capability. It is the greatest renewable resource we possess and to acknowledge its creative potential could be the finest legacy we leave for our children and grandchildren.

References

1 Diderot, Denis, (translated and edited by John Hope Mason and Robert Wokler). "Article on 'Art' from Volume 1 of the Encyclopédie." *Political Writings*. Cambridge: Cambridge University Press, 1992, p. 5.

2 Csikszentmihalyi, Mihaly and Eugene Rochberg-Halton. The Meaning of Things. Cambridge University Press, 1981, p. 25.

3 Cicero. "On Duties (II)", in *Cicero: On the Good Life*. (Translated and Introduced by Michael Grant). London: Penguin Books, 1971, p. 126.

4 Simon, Herbert A. *The Sciences of the Artificial*. Cambridge, MA: The MIT Press, (3rd edition), June 1981, p. 129.

5 Simon, p. 129.

6

Chinese Design: What Can We Learn from the Past?

In all the varied processes of change taking place in China at the present time it is relevant to ask not only what is being gained, but also: what is being lost? The material forms inherited from the past represent the accumulated wisdom of a culture, which developed over a long period of time and was constantly refined to meet the needs of its people and express their sense of identity. With the intense loss of forms and processes and their replacement by substitutes developed in other parts of the world there is inevitably an effect on the structure of values and beliefs that constitute a culture. It is therefore worth asking whether the past can be a continuing source of inspiration in the processes of modernization that are sweeping over China, which also raises questions about the extent to which design is a source of continuity as well as change.

I have to emphasise that I am not an expert on Chinese design history and do not speak or read Chinese, so my observations are restricted to an interpretation of forms that exist in museum collections and publications. In discussing this process, however, it seems to me there are two levels of understanding that are open to us as a result of this process of visual analysis. The first is to represent the forms and materials of the past as being in their construction and expression icons of a culture, a unique representation signalling a quality of "Chineseness". The second is a more subtle quality, of what I would call the underlying principles of design, which are more to do with the consciousness and purpose informing works.

An example is the horseshoe-arm chair typical of the Ming dynasty that has been widely taken as an iconic Chinese form and reproduced in innumerable ways at home and abroad. In formal terms the back and arm support that curves in two dimensions is certainly visually distinctive and

This paper is based on a presentation given at the All-China Design History Symposium held at Shanghai University in December, 2007. It is previously unpublished. The original lecture was fully illustrated. Alas it has not been possible to reproduce these plates.

subtle, but sitting in it brings into play other senses, that reveals it is more than an attractive form. The chair is in fact based upon a very careful and detailed understanding of comfort and posture in seating. The curve of the horseshoe form is beautifully designed to support both the back and the arms of anyone sitting and working in the chair and potentially using it for reading or writing – basically it supports a good posture. The stretcher bar between the front legs parallel to the floor are a foot-rest enabling the underside of the thighs to be raised above the sharp edge of the seat and so avoids a potential source of cramp and discomfort.

It is therefore not just an aesthetic form to be admired as historically, visually distinctive, but embodies notions that today would be included and calculated under the heading of ergonomics, which of course did not exist in the Ming dynasty. What did exist at that time, however, was an understanding the posture of the human body and an emphasis on designing a form appropriate to it.

There are innumerable imitations of Ming chair forms available, but how many of them show any understanding of or respect for these underlying principles? This is part of a widespread phenomenon in which the forms of the past are reproduced in ways that adopt aesthetic superficialities as a route to a quick profit.

The example on which I want to mainly focus is one of the glories of Chinese culture, its cuisine. For me it is one of the best in the world (the other outstanding one is Italian). What I find remarkable about the Chinese approach to food is that relatively simple means are used to produce it, yet the quality at all levels, from the simplest meal to the most elaborate banquet, is generally very high. Another observation is that the Chinese approach to how food is bought, stored, prepared, cooked, presented and eaten represents a very different approach in many fundamental aspects to how these activities are thought of and practised in the rest of the world. The implications of a detailed study of implements used in cooking are very wide-ranging, requiring acknowledgement of regional and ethnic variations and needing to take into account many aspects of Chinese culture, such as the connection between food and health, enabling people to take responsibility for their own well-being instead of being heavily dependent upon a separate profession who "own" medical knowledge.

Historically, a crucial question is: how and why did this pattern of cooking and the values associated with it evolve? Are there underlying principles that can be discerned and if so, are they still capable of being reinterpreted and forming a vital part of the present and future?

Some tentative suggestions about answers to these questions can be provided by examining a series of Chinese cooking stoves found in museum collections around the world. These do not represent a properly organized research project, but result from a random gathering of images that together suggest some preliminary approaches to larger questions. Rather than give specific answers my intention is to suggest possibilities.

What stimulated my interest in this subject of cooking was a small stove that is between five and six thousand years old, produced in the Yangshao culture of the Yellow River region. The stove is crudely made of coarse earthenware, set on small feet, with an opening at the front to insert fuel and with a cooking vessel set in a circular opening on the stove top. Its height measures 10.9cm and with the vessel, 15.8cm.

The use of earthenware as material is inevitable since the stove predates the development of metals. The only other fire-resistant material available would have been stone and carving a shape of this kind would have been extremely difficult. On the other hand the plastic qualities of earthenware for both the stove and the cooking vessel indicate the very remarkable possibilities opened up by the use of the simplest and most widely available ceramic materials. The finish of the stove is crude, with little attempt at smoothness and fingerprints are visible around the front aperture. It suggests an object made by a person for their own use without any attempt to give it a fine finish, but despite this, the form is assured and well-defined and rather than an individual concept, would seem to be an expression of a widely-accepted form within the context of Yangshao culture of what this kind of implement should be and do.

How is it possible to explain the shape of the stove and vessel in relation to their purpose? If design knowledge is embodied in a form, what does this stove tell us? First of all, why is it so small? The size is only capable of burning a small amount of fuel at any one time and if we assume this is a deliberate choice, we have to ask why? One answer might be that in rural areas reliant on gathering wood for fuel from the local environment a process sets in, and it is still widely observable in many parts of the world, where readily available supplies become scarcer and longer journeys are needed to gather fuel. If this explanation has any validity, we would expect to see fuel used carefully and economically, obtaining the maximum value from it for purposes of cooking, and that is precisely what the shape of the stove suggests. The base of the stove flares out towards the top, diffusing the heat upwards. The aperture at the front, in contrast, is wider at the base to allow fuel to be easily inserted, but narrows towards the top, possibly to conserve heat.

Another question concerns the cooking vessel that sits in a circular opening on the top of the stove. The shape is a shallow inverted-cone and this can be explained both in terms of giving stability during the cooking process – the shape fits in the hole tightly instead of just resting on it – and in presenting a greater surface area to the available heat. In other words, fuel efficiency comes into the equation again. The small amount of fuel would, moreover, give a high heat for a short duration with a lower level of residual heat for some time after as the earthenware material retained and diffused heating energy. The partial cover of the top of the vessel could also be explained by a need to conserve heat during the cooking process and possibly could also serve as a support for a steamer to be inserted.

The short cooking time at high heat would also tend to encourage a process of cutting meat and vegetables into small sizes that could be cooked very quickly. It is no accident, it seems to me, that the shape of this 5000-year-old cooking vessel is still the basic inverted-cone shape of the famous Chinese *wok* and this physical evidence from the past suggests this very characteristic approach to cooking has roots deep in Chinese history.

If we ask, therefore, about the underlying principles of this stove, the emphasis appears to be focussed on the efficient use of limited amounts of fuel with methods of cooking adapted to making the most effective use of a limited amount of high heat.

This supposition is supported by comparison with another survival from the Neolithic past, a small stove from the Hemudu culture in the lower Yangtze Valley. It has a different form to the Yangshao example, but there also are some striking similarities. The Hemudu stove is also made of earthenware and is small, but in this case the cooking vessel is supported on three small protruding lugs on the inside surface, that would keep the vessel above the heat to diffuse it more easily. However, the underlying principles remain the same, again emphasizing efficient use of fuel within a limited space.

A further example of how the underlying principles endured, despite changes in materials and contexts, is a cast-iron stove from the Spring and Autumn period, some two-and-a-half thousand years after the early examples discussed previously. Again, however, the basic concept is of a small stove, although now with a chimney to carry away smoke and provide a through draught to keep the fire burning with maximum effectiveness. Again, a container sits in a hole on top of the stove. In other words, there is an improvement in efficiency but the underlying principles differ little from the examples of the Yangshou and Hemudu cultures so long before.

Casting iron was a complex process for the time and therefore the stove must have been produced by some kind of early industrial foundry. China was at the cutting-edge of technological development in the ability to cast a product of this size and complexity (it was to be over a thousand years before Europe learned to cast iron on this scale). An even more complex example of casting on a large scale is the eroded remains of a stove found in Shensi province and now in the Field Museum, Chicago, in which the body of the stove is now lifted above ground level.

In addition to this kind of product, however, there was also evident a long continuity of other types of stoves not so reliant on advanced technology and capable of being built by people in their own homes for their own use. Certainly, during the Han dynasty of between 2200–1800 years ago, such simple forms seems to have predominated, with many museum collections having models from this period of what clearly became a dominant stove type constructed in courtyards from what appear to be brick and earthenware. These vary in size and capacity, yet all still are constructed on the same principles as the cast-iron example from the Spring and Autumn period, with a low aperture into which fuel could be inserted, and a chimney flue at the other end dispersing smoke and providing a through draught to keep the fire burning at maximum intensity.

The raised circular apertures on top of the stoves vary in number, but are still are based on using a limited, confined space to burn fuel and use it effectively, with cooking vessels placed in the apertures to concentrate the heat. The particular interest of the cast-iron example from the Han period is again the way in which the new material is used to construct the same basic structure, with the underlying principles remaining intact.

An important aspect of a functional structure such as a stove, of course, is not only its form but how it is used – and illustrations of this are not as frequently found as the objects themselves. One example, however, is a decorative brick from the Han dynasty, showing the process of cooking. Here another feature of Chinese stoves becomes evident in the height of the working surface, which is generally low enough to allow a cook to easily see into a cooking pot while food is being prepared. Again, there seems to be an innate understanding of what today would be the ergonomics of kitchen design. These traditional Chinese dimensions of stove height are certainly very different to the common ergonomic measures used to define standard heights and dimensions for kitchen units in Western countries, a difference that is vital if culinary traditions are taken into account in designing modern Chinese kitchens.

One final illustration is of a contemporary stove exhibited in late 2007. What is evident after another leap in time of two thousand years is a further shift in technology, this time not only in the materials used to construct the stove but in the fuel source, in this case, gas. It is a very basic appliance, yet the moulded frames to hold the cooking vessels, and the forms of many of the vessels themselves, still present a continuity of the underlying principles.

The examples and interpretations presented here are a preliminary and very personal examination of a few aspects of the history of Chinese cooking. My suggestions of meanings is intended to open up discussion, but obviously, a more detailed research programme would be needed to broaden the scope and examine a much wider range of cooking techniques, vessels and implements, how and why they evolved, and what values they embodied in the wider patterns of Chinese culture.

What can be stated with confidence, however, is that a most remarkable feature of the Chinese tradition of cooking is the way its principles, and even many predominant forms used, continue to be relevant. They have evolved and proven to be efficient and appropriate through long periods of time, while sustaining levels of quality in this most basic and repetitive human need, with their underlying principles capable of sustained evolution and adaptation.

I would also suggest that the characteristics of Chinese cooking are still highly relevant to our modern age. Compare the limited range of implements flexibly used to prepare a Chinese meal to the elaborate specialisation of

Western kitchens, loaded with a wide array of mechanisms and implements that are seldom used. The principles of economy and efficiency are evident in many ways, in the limited number of vessels and implements used and their flexibility of application. Consider, for example, what you need to eat a Chinese meal of the most elaborate kind: basically, a bowl, a small plate, a teacup, chopsticks and a spoon. Compare this with the array of a banquet table in a Western cultural context, similarly laid for an elaborate meal – with different kinds of knives, forks and spoons, numerous glasses, cups and plates, each for a specific purpose. The Chinese principle is a combination of simplicity and flexibility in both preparation and consumption of food that is of high quality; the Western principle is one of specialisation and increasing complexity, with standards of quality in food not always the main emphasis as cultural patterns turn more and more to commercially prepared food. Chinese meals do require more work in preparation, but is it really progress to sacrifice quality for convenience? Which is more appropriate in a world where the stampede towards unnecessary and elaborate over-consumption is an increasing threat to the fabric of our planet?

Design, I have suggested, is both concerned with change and also with continuity. Ransacking the past for easily copied decorative motifs shows little understanding of the cultures of earlier times, and no respect for them. On the other hand, concentrating more on the underlying principles that embody the true characteristics and strengths of past cultures makes it possible to incorporate these into contemporary designs that preserve and adapt the best of what the past has to offer. This, it seems to me, is a valid aspect of contemporary design practice and a worthy task for design historians: changes in forms, styles and materials reflecting social and political influences are certainly important aspects of what we study, but what is also of abiding importance are underlying principles that reflect continuities of defining importance to a culture.

What I am suggesting, therefore, is that design history should be the guardian of these principles. Instead of being a focus of nostalgia for a lost past that probably never existed, it can be a constant means of respecting and incorporating into our present and future lives all that is best in our inheritance. As China regains its rightful position as a leading nation in the world, this is important not just for Chinese people, but for everyone all around the globe. Great nations are respected not only for their economic and military power, but also for the cultural values they embody. The lessons of the continuity of its rich and unique cultural inheritance and its continuing relevance could be the most profound gift China has to offer the world.

7

Three Moments in the Global History of Making: Nomads, Traders, Slaves

The texts below are three extracts from the unpublished ms. "Crafts, Commerce, Industry: A Global History of Design." It is impossible to extract from a text well in excess of 160,000 words three fragments that in a few thousand words represent the range of issues with which the book deals. Any selection will of necessity be arbitrary. The principle used here was that of taking three emphases or moments of persons making and using that may not always be found in usual ways that we think the history of things. Nomads, the question of early trade, the craftsmanship of slaves are three vignettes that offer perspectives on material culture and on designing (in the broad sense)—the first from the perspective of limit and necessity, including the necessity for identity and elaboration, but in the context of ways of life distinguished by impermanent settlement; the second from the perspective of the complex commercial and cultural interactions established through trade (in this instance trade in desired goods occurring in Asia from the earliest times); the third from the standpoint of those who have nothing—slaves—where the preservation and cultivation of skills of making and craftsmanship are not the least effective means of maintaining dignity, and even a modicum of economic standing, in the face of everything in slave societies that must constantly seek to erode both.

(i) Nomads

... The last three chapters have focused upon the emergence of civilizations based on sedentary ways of life, agriculture and urbanization. Across the globe, however, numerous groups persisted in distinct ways of life that for long periods of human history presented a profound, repetitive and destabilizing challenge to civilizations. They lived for the most part on the periphery of geographical areas most suited for agriculture and urbanization, in a relationship that was part dependent and part predatory.

While nomadism was a widespread characteristic of societies living in marginal areas, under that umbrella term there were many variations. It encompassed small tribal groups which in essential aspects represent continuity with ancient foraging ways of life, continually moving from place to place in search of food and water. Other groups, however, where conditions permitted, made a transition to pastoral nomadism. This was an itinerant pattern based on herding large groups of animals, predominantly sheep and less frequently cattle. The capacity to control herds constantly on the move in search of pasture was limited until horses were tamed and methods and equipment for riding evolved to an effective level. Horses, however, transformed pastoral nomadism and the size of groups and their herds became very large.

Other peripheral societies used the sea as their means of communication, as with the Vikings of Scandinavia, who combined agriculture and settlement at home with raids upon vulnerable, richer neighbours. The Polynesian groups who navigated across the island groups of the Pacific can also be included under this category.

For long periods of history this created an uneasy balance between highly differentiated cultural systems. In most cases, close relationships, based on trade, existed between nomads and adjacent agricultural producers and sources of luxury products. The polarity has often been summarized by the terms: barbarism and civilization, inferring a polarity between chaos and order. Such labels are highly biased, however, the extant records of such confrontations being almost wholly written from the point of view of various civilizations. Indeed, the word "barbarian" stems from a Greek term for foreigners, with overtones of a disparaging sense of superiority over uncouth outsiders. Similarly, the Chinese appellation "Xiongnu" for the nomads who appeared in frontier areas of Northwest China can be interpreted as "slave bastard".[1] A consistent feature of many such literary records is that frontier peoples came to represent a kind of alter ego, the enemy at the gate, a symbol of darkness against light, evil against good, by which the cultural self-identity of civilizations could be unequivocally defined in a favourable light.

In contrast, a scholar of Asian nomadic groups, Jaroslav Lebedynsky, comments on them in much more favourable terms:

> The specificity of their cultures, the historical impact of their activities between the great Western, Middle Eastern, Indian and Chinese sedentary areas, justifies them being placed among the principal civilizations of the ancient world.[2]

Lebedynsky's use of the term "civilization" is debatable, since sedentarism and urbanization are widely considered defining components, neither of which the nomads developed to any substantial degree. Describing their way of life as a culture is perhaps more appropriate. This, however, does not disprove his point, which is that the history of over two millennia in Eurasia, the focus of his work, is incomprehensible without including the impact of nomadic groups, which at times was enormous.

The most constant friction between cultures occurred in and around the open plains of Central Asia. If the great civilizations evolved in areas suitable for large-scale cultivation, close to waterways that acted as trade routes, the heart of the vast Eurasian landmass had soils and climate generally unsuitable for the settled agriculture that sustained urban development and centralized states. In fact, its conditions vary considerably, with four highly differentiated geographic zones running in bands north to south across the whole span of Eurasia: from frozen tundra with minimal vegetation; through heavily forested areas, or the taiga; to the steppe, vast open grasslands; and finally, arid semi-desert regions with occasional oases. The steppe region, above all, generated a way of life based on pastoral nomadism on a huge scale.

Describing all the many tribes—thirty-five major groups are described by Lebedynski, with many sub-groupings[3]—constituting the patchwork quilt of steppe societies, and even establishing an outline of how they evolved, is difficult. They were mobile, leaving a light footprint, their oral cultures yielding no written records and a transient life leaving limited tangible remains. Tribes frequently split into small groups that scattered to find grazing in difficult times. Little or nothing might survive of a way of life and what does is inevitably incomplete. Nevertheless, evidence of social customs and craft skills can be reconstructed to some extent from such artefacts as survive, which are often eloquent testimony to the ingenuity of steppe peoples.

Central Asia represented an alternative to agricultural settlement, where people adopted a mobile, semi-nomadic way of life, driving herds in search of fresh pasture, but with settlements as bases at oases, where some crops could be grown. A vigorous expansion of oasis cultures from around 3000 BC typified this kind of coexistence. Contacts with settled areas led to the spread of enhanced metal and transportation technology across the steppe, so that by c.2000 BC, farmer-herders used various alloys, particularly bronze, and carried their possessions in ox-drawn wheeled vehicles.

With the spread of the horse and developments in weaponry c. 1500 BC, differences in wealth opened up, leading to the emergence of a nomadic aristocracy, whose emphasis in material possessions changed, "from a notion of power and status symbolized by weapons and tools, to one in which wealth, accumulated in precious metals and stones, horses, and ornamental art, became its predominant pursuit."[4] Although sheep remained the most numerous animals bred and raised, henceforward the horse had pride of place in the consciousness and values of the steppe tribes. It was domesticated around 3200 BC and first used to pull chariots, a form of transport rapidly adopted in civilizations. While many illustrations of early chariots survive, however, horse riders are less frequently depicted and are generally shown mounted on the animal's rump.[5]

It took a long time for riding to evolve as a skill. Fully developed horse-riding cultures, as indicated by archaeological finds of artefacts such as bridles and bits, did not emerge until sometime around the ninth century BC. From that time, however, the horse became the crucial factor in steppe culture and nomadism eventually superseded every other pattern of life there. Typically, every boy in the steppe tribes learned to ride at an early age and soon acquired the skills of firing a short bow from horseback.

There were, of course, limitations to what could be produced under nomadic conditions and possessions tended to emphasize utility and portability as primary criteria, with decoration integrated into utilitarian function, as in textiles, which were widely produced in colourful patterns. Wool was available from sheep or, less frequently, from yaks. Yarn could be spun by women with distaff and spindle as a constant activity and woven on simple, portable looms. Carpets could be rolled up and were easily carried to provide cover for floors and walls in cold regions. They, and woven cloth, were often valuable items of trade and, indeed, some of the most enduring textile traditions in the world originated with the nomads of Central Asia. Small stone, bone or wooden implements and decorative objects could also be carved and easily carried.

The artefacts of the steppe tribes reflected their occupations as hunters and herders. They avidly adopted metal-working techniques for bronze tools and weapons, such as spears, swords, daggers and arrowheads vital for hunting and personal defence. Tools often had the handle and blade cast as one piece, such as adzes for working wood, knives for hunting and skinning animals, and awls for leather working. Most were small, light, and portable, easily made and capable of being carried and used as the need arose, often designed to hang from or be attached to a part of their clothing, through rings, loops, or similar devices.

Equipment for horses inevitably played a central role. To control draft animals and horses, harnesses, bridles, and cart or chariot fittings were produced in great numbers. Tribes continually on the move had little time, however, to make luxury goods. Although their way of life was self-sufficient in basic necessities, and small objects could be produced while on the move, numerous larger products and decorative objects were generated in oasis settlements or towns bordering the steppes.

Leather was a readily available material that must have played a prominent role in nomadic life. Little has survived, but a hint of the levels of quality attained are evident in a horn-shaped box from c.1000 BC. The component pieces are fastened by leather bindings and the surfaces are beautifully tooled in whorled patterns.

An early example of the potential of bronze working on a small scale in a nomadic society can be illustrated by the legacy of a group that emerged in the area known as Luristan in western Iran. Easily accessible mineral deposits, particularly copper, were mined there and by 2500 BC, bronze was widely worked, with a particularly rich spectrum of small artefacts dating from around 1300–500 BC found in graves. Not much is known about the people and their society, other than that they were nomads who migrated from Central Asia and became pastoralists, with some settlements possibly predating their arrival.

The pieces are generally small, capable of manufacture by itinerant metal smiths, with decorated horse-fittings predominating. Stylized animal forms, often compressed into twisting patterns to fit small spaces, are highly typical. Personal items include pins to clip cloaks or wraps, and whetstones to keep edges sharp, which nomadic horsemen habitually hung from their belts

Weapons, such as daggers, swords and axes are another major category. Some of these are highly utilitarian, while others are more decorated in ways that could hamper their use in battle and so probably had a more ceremonial nature. An example is a sword handle with eagles, tigers and human figures interwoven into its surface in a manner that would make it difficult to grip firmly in a hand-to-hand fight.

Some necessary artefacts for nomadic groups were larger, requiring more substantial resources, in terms of materials and tools, which were not easily transported. Regular interaction between tribes in their extensive wanderings and settlements scattered around the steppes provided more stable conditions for the development of larger scale work. There is also the possibility that itinerant craftsmen might have been a source of supply as indicated by an early Chinese source:

> Although the role of itinerant metal smiths, both Chinese and northern, has never been addressed, there is some evidence that they did exist, as passages in the *Han Shu* (History of the Former Han Dynasty) include references to itinerant Chinese armourers during the Han period.[6]

Similarities in patterns of life and regular interaction across large distances resulted from the livestock-raising common to all nomadic tribes, requiring them to habitually move great distances. Combined with the fact that the nomadic pattern of life was cyclic rather than evolutionary, this accounts to a large extent for recurrent common themes in imagery over large areas of Central Asian. The forms of steppe wildlife, in particular, were constantly used in dense, intricate patterns featuring animistic themes on small objects, such as belt-buckles, sword hilts and icons for the tips of standards. Larger forms have been found, but adapted in interesting ways to nomadic life. A bronze cooking vessel dating from c.200 BC, used for cooking meat over a fire, was 72 cm (over 28″) high, with walls cast of very thin bronze, compared to vessels used in settled regions, giving faster conduction of heat.

There were two ways, basically, in which the nomads could supplement their need for goods: firstly, by trading animals and other products at market centres in the frontier regions; secondly, by armed force—raiding expeditions with the intent of simply taking what they needed. The former was an activity dependent upon a market existing for what nomads could supply. When that market sagged for any reason, raiding would occur. What therefore emerged as a continual thread in frontier history was a symbiotic relationship between the nomads and the civilized states.

The balance of economic advantage lay with the latter when trading was based on goods crucial to the nomads. The civilized states possessed productive resources on a scale that nomadic societies could never match and there was often little they required from nomads. Governments of settled civilizations relied for income on appropriating the surplus production of lands under their control, primarily through taxes on agriculture and craft products that could be turned into long-term assets. The nomads' role in enabling and protecting trade routes, such as the Silk Road, was substantial, bringing income from tolls, but these were often difficult to gather and in many cases were evaded. If the continuing power and vitality of nomadic culture dominated events in Eurasia for so long, the plain fact was it basically relied upon an extractive approach, whether in terms of pasture, extorting tribute or trading tolls, or looting. It had little capacity to accumulate knowledge or wealth of the kind that generated continually increasing productive capacity. In this respect, the long-term advantage undoubtedly lay with the civilized states.

(ii) Trade

Agriculture, technology and political structures were vital elements in the evolution of human societies, but another factor of great significance was the emergence of commercial activity on a broad scale, epitomized by the early example of the Phoenician trading empire. The growth of trade meant that henceforward design functioned on two interacting levels: firstly, it continue to satisfy the specific needs and cultural values of particular localities; secondly, as long-distance trade in products grew it could extend to a global scale, which required coming to terms with cultural differences.

Such long-distance patterns of trade have their own cycles of rise and fall. New knowledge and discoveries, new technologies, changes in relationships or balance of power, and many other factors could stimulate new opportunities. These often involved substantial risk, which, if overcome, could translate into enduring commercial prosperity. As they grew and evolved, trading systems embodied accumulated knowledge and experience but were also vulnerable to disruption or fracture by same factors that created them. Trade routes could be attacked or blocked, conquest could destroy facilities or capabilities, tastes could change, new processes could make old skills outmoded, new discoveries could supersede old ones, changes in weather patterns could be disastrous, and so on.

A frequent accompaniment of trade was a widespread diffusion of religious beliefs. Conversion could be a matter of personal conviction, as it seems to have been with the enormous spread of Buddhism across East Asia and Hinduism in South-east Asia, or be imposed at sword point, as was the case in much of the rapid spread of Islam or the efforts of European Crusaders to regain possession of the lost Holy Land for Christendom. Religious belief, ritual and iconography also strongly determined what kind of forms and decorative motifs were suitable or tolerated in any society.

This chapter will therefore examine aspects of the growth of trading systems, patterns of conversion and cultural exchange and the influences they embodied and diffused in what can be called the Asian Triangle. Its geographical context can be envisaged in terms of an inverted triangle. Its horizontal axis was the Silk Road, one of the most fabled trading routes in the world. The other two sides were sea routes from China southwest to the apex of the triangle in Sri Lanka at the southern tip of the Indian sub-continent, and thence northwest to the Persian Gulf and the Red Sea. It encompassed lands with enormously rich and diverse cultures, including China, India and Arabia and from around 500AD, these regions were the most dynamic force for innovation in the world, generating enormous changes across Asia and in crucial aspects reaching far beyond.

As trading became more structured, markets were held in particular places at specified times, providing regular opportunities to buy and sell. When the scale and range of trade expanded beyond immediate localities, however, in addition to means of transportation, merchants increasingly required enabling systems to facilitate exchange, such as coinage, contracts and credit. If knowledge of distant places and people was tenuous, trusted institutions were needed to act as banks or agents, a function often provided by temples in trading centres. Facilities for travellers were also required, with chains of stations offering rest and succour for journeys. By such means trade came to be structured in patterns summarizing the knowledge and abilities of an age. Such routes established relationships based not only on exchange of desirable products, but the diffusion of ideas, of religious and social beliefs, technological and aesthetic concepts. Their existence was also intertwined with scientific and technical developments, such as cartography as an accurate representation of the known world and navigational instruments to more accurately locate oneself within it.

Early trading routes were simply tracks impressed by the repetitive movement of feet and hooves upon landscapes. Although roads were built comparatively early these were rare, primarily intended for administrative or military purposes. The first known road system of substantial size was the Royal Road in Persia, built c.3000BC and used until c.300BC. It extended from the Persian Gulf to the Aegean Sea in the north, a distance of almost 1800 miles. Other major systems were the Chinese Imperial Roads that extended for some 2,000 miles and Roman roads linking the empire. Most urban centres, however, had few paved roads and barely any worth the name connecting with their immediate hinterland, let alone with distant regions. Overland trade was often a necessity since not all regions had access to the sea or navigable rivers but it was slow, limited in capacity to packs carried by donkeys, (later camels and horses), and damaging to fragile articles, placing a premium on small, light and valuable goods. For bulky products, waterways, if accessible, were the best option.

The origins of long-range trading in Asia are difficult to pinpoint, although there are some indicators. Contact between Mesopotamia, Central Asia and India developed at least by the time the earliest urban settlements appeared and grew to substantial scale. "The network of overseas trade was impressively widespread: from the second half of the third millennium, ships made their way down the Arabian Gulf to Saudi Arabia and along the coasts of Iran and Pakistan as far as the north-west coast of India."[7]

In the second century AD a huge demand for Chinese silk in the Roman Empire led to as many as 120 ships sailing annually from the Red Sea ports of Egypt to carry cargoes from India, where the silk was carried overland caravan from China. On arrival in Egypt, cargoes were trans- shipped overland to the Nile and the Mediterranean. By this time, navigators understood the regular patterns of monsoons that could carry them speedily across open seas, instead of slowly hugging the coast. An early sailing manual, the Periplus Maris Erythraei, a Greek text dating from the 1st century AD described routes from the Red Sea to ports at the mouth of the Ganges in the Bay of Bengal. It referred "to several navigational techniques adopted in the western Indian Ocean, such as identifying the approaching coast by means of changes in the colour of the water; and the presence of sea snakes."[8] In the following century, the Greek geographer, Ptolemy, described an extension of this route to the Straits of Malacca and the Malayan peninsular. The relatively large capacity of cargo ships made it an enormously profitable trade, although the outflow of coin and bullion from Rome to pay for it substantially weakened the economy.[9]

Trading was not simply a matter of providing exotic materials for Europe, however, although much history has been written in such terms—patterns within Asia also became richly textured. Ships were sailing from Guangzhou in southern China from the second century BC, possibly as far as India. By 100BC, a shipyard near Guangzhou was building vessels capable of carrying 25–30 tons of cargo.[10]

Thereafter, growth in vessel size increased substantially: "One third-century Chinese text speaks already of large ships, over 200 feet in length, capable of carrying 600 or 700 persons and 5,000 bushels of cargo."[11] By the Tang dynasty, (618–906 AD) ceramics were the main cargo, being regularly dispatched westwards in large, well-built Chinese vessels as far as the Persian Gulf and Red Sea. From the second century AD these were constructed with transverse bulkheads, possibly based upon the structure of bamboo, creating a series of watertight compartments and substantially improving safety and seaworthiness.

Chinese shipping also created a dense regional network of trading relationships in South-east Asia and the island archipelagos of present-day Indonesia and the Philippines. Underwater archeology has been a vitally important source of invaluable information in this regard. One of the most dramatic discoveries is a wreck found off the Indonesian island of Belitung in 1998, the only example discovered of an ancient Arab or Indian vessel, with a hull that was stitched together, dating to the 8th century AD. Its cargo was over 50,000 pieces of ceramic wares from Changsha in China, thus providing solid evidence of direct trade between distant parts of Asia. Many of the ceramics were decorated with patterns echoing Islamic motifs and are evidently efforts by Chinese producers to adapt to the tastes of distant clients.

Another important discovery yielding detailed information on the evolution of junks and their cargoes was the discovery in 1973 near the port of Quanzhou, in Fukien province, of the remains of a merchant ship, dating to the Song dynasty (960–1279). The vessel is calculated to be about 110 feet in length, 34 feet across and weighing some 390 tons. It had a curved hull, to ride waves more easily, with a high stern and sails that were not totally raised and lowered, but had bamboo slats functioning more in the manner of louvres or Venetian blinds. Its cargo was predominantly aromatic woods imported "from Timor, Java and Champa; followed by pepper from Sunda, incense from Samatra, betal nuts from Tongking; amber, cinnamon and mercury."[12] By the eighth century there were also many reports of Indian, Persian and Arab vessels in Chinese harbours—a scale of seaborne trade difficult to envisage being sustained solely by luxury goods.

(iii) Craftsmanship in slavery

... An even greater source of wealth, however, based on an even greater degree of exploitation, stemmed from the exploration of the New World, subsequent colonization in the Americas and West Indies and, above all, the slave trade with Africa.

Slaves were taken from West Africa to Portugal in the early exchanges between the two regions, drawing on a long-existing slave trade in the Saharan regions. This was to satisfy a demand for domestic labour that had existed since mediaeval times in the Mediterranean region and it is sometimes overlooked how widespread slavery in Europe continued to be. There were substantial numbers of Asiatic slaves in Italy and, indeed, Venice gained considerable profits from selling Christian slaves to Egypt and other Islamic countries.[13] The difference in the Atlantic slave trade, however, was its enormous scale, the degrading conditions to which slaves were subjected, and the profound consequences for all involved. The origins of trade in human beings across the Atlantic can be traced to harsh conditions in Central and South America following the Spanish conquest, with populations decimated by epidemic diseases. New sources of labour had to be found and Africa was the answer. In 1518, slaves were first directly transported from Africa to Spanish colonies and as more countries acquired American lands the demand, going far beyond earlier requirements for household work. The primary use was now for fieldwork and with the establishment of sugar plantations by several European nations in the West Indies in the early seventeenth century, the trade expanded exponentially. The lowest estimates are that over the next three centuries some eleven million people were transported as slaves to the Americas.

Slavery was based on denying human identity and reducing people to basic labour functions. Rather than recognizing acquired or innate talents, slaves were defined solely by owners' economic requirements. In the British West Indies and the North American colonies that later became the United States, muscle power in fieldwork was the initial requirement. As plantations expanded, however, products required processing, requiring slaves to acquire new skills in virtually every craft needed for life on a large holding. The expansion of West Indian sugar plantations into distilling rum and bringing it to market, for example, required coopers to construct the barrels in which to mature and transport the final product. It was slave carpenters and blacksmiths who were responsible for constructing the veneer of elegance that was a characteristic of plantation life and the source of much subsequent nostalgia.

Neither was it only on plantations that slave artisans became essential. Towns housed the most specialized skills among both free people and slaves: goldsmiths and watchmakers, printers and skilled carpenters. This sometimes required slaves to be educated. William Collins of Antigua, planning to establish a printing office, declared in 1819 that "I have for that purpose long since caused three young negro men named Tom, Charles and Cato belonging to me to be properly taught to read, write and spell". Slaves living in ports acquired many skills in the shipping industry and were employed in repairing ships and making equipment as shipwrights, ships' carpenters, sail-makers and caulkers.[14]

In Barbados, settled by the English in 1627, the transfer of the technology necessary for establishing and running plantations as viable economic units initially drew on artisans recruited from England as indentured servants. Dissatisfaction with this system rapidly became apparent. A contemporary account of the island economy published in 1657 stated: "The shortage of free artisans at Barbados, especially those who could draw a plan, and pursue the design they framed with great diligence" was severe.[15] The expectation that artisans should be capable of drawing plans is an interesting comment on changes in craft practice. The white artisans available, however, were often unreliable and constantly demanding higher wages. Using slaves as craftsmen therefore had many advantages once skills were learned. So assiduous was the learning process that by the 1680s, slaves on plantations were "employed in handicraft trades, as Coopers, Joiners, Carpenters, Smiths, Masons, and the like."[16] In Barbados, the matter was raised in the representative council advising the Governor of the island.

Peter Colleton, planter and assemblyman, in 1675 noted that although he had no direct arguments against negro slavery, moral or otherwise, he was angered by its ruinous effects upon free artisans and craftsmen. Slavery, he said, had rendered disreputable the honorable occupations of artisans and created a sense of despair among them.[17]

By the mid-eighteenth century, it was estimated that slaves constituted ninety percent of the skilled craftsmen throughout the West Indies. From turning people into commodities, it was but a short step to regarding slave skills as marketable. They could be hired out by owners to provide additional income, further enhancing their economic value. This was reflected in slave market prices: "A good slave mechanic in the 1690s was valued at £150, compared to £20 to £40 for an unskilled slave."[18] They rapidly formed what has been termed a "slave elite." As a valued asset, the evidence is they received better treatment and a greater degree of unsupervised mobility.

We are so accustomed to thinking of black slavery in terms of its crude laboring form that we tend to overlook the ranks of skilled men and women whose crafts, experience and abilities enhanced the economic and social life of the slave colonies. But simply to look at the surviving artefacts of the former slave societies—the fields, the houses, the furnishings, the equipment—is to be confronted by the fruits of slave labours and skills. For among the ranks of those millions of Africans imported to labour in the fields of the slave colonies, there lurked some obviously remarkable people. ... But for all that ... they remained slaves; bought, sold, inherited, bequeathed and sought as other pieces of material property. Whatever his or her skill or talent, a slave was but a slave.[19]

A study of slave work in the American South estimated: "Skilled slaves like carpenters and blacksmiths represented ... about one in 50 slaves in Mississippi to about one in 20 in South Carolina."[20] The difference between fieldwork and skilled artisanship was a significant one:

> Unlike skilled slaves, field hands had few other opportunities in their work to express their autonomy. Carpenters, blacksmiths, and wheelwrights employed planning, judgement and initiative as they worked, which allowed them to take pride in their accomplishment, to attribute it to their own labor and skill.[21]

In his book *Art and Technics,* Lewis Mumford positioned aesthetic purpose as a central concern and a redeeming factor in otherwise harsh conditions:

> ... even the meanest slave, with a tool in his hand, would feel the impulse to give the object on which he was working something more that was required to make it work; he would linger over it, at the least, to heighten

its finish, or he would modify the form in some degree to make it delight the eye as well as perform its function.[22]

For slave craftspeople, there is strong support for the argument that skilled work could be an assertion of identity, but it could hardly have been compensation for their condition. Aesthetic consolation, if it was indeed involved, was a means, not an end. Pride in achievement must instead have been a fierce affirmation of personal worth, of human value, in a system that at every point denied this recognition.

The role of crafts in historical memories orally handed down through generations are illustrated in an example of skills used on the coastal rice plantations in South Carolina, where slaves wove both large baskets for transporting rice to market and finer, smaller pieces for domestic use from coiled sweetgrass. The techniques originated in age-old forms from Senegal and the Ivory Coast, (and the influence of slave trading throughout history should never be underestimated as a major means of diffusing forms and techniques[23]). The work was sufficiently valued to relieve basket makers from fieldwork, which was a small consolation, however, conditions on the rice plantations being brutal. Slaves were in a permanent condition of simmering resentment, which at intervals exploded into open rebellion. The craft therefore became a subversive means of keeping alive a communal sense of identity separate from that assigned by slave owners. As a descendent of the slaves commented:

> It reminded us of where we came from and that we came from someplace. The techniques were jealously guarded, and it was a cardinal sin to teach it to those outside the family structure, especially to whites.[24]

The sweetgrass basket makers also serve as an example of how crafts can adapt to new circumstances when their original function is superseded, with some three hundred families in and around the city of Charleston still making a living from weaving baskets for the tourist trade. Their livelihood is threatened from another direction, however, as the sea islands on which the sweetgrass was traditionally harvested are bought for holiday homes.

As occurred in antiquity, owners on the North American mainland, in the cotton-growing colonies of the Southeast—Virginia, the Carolinas and Georgia—set up profitable businesses using slave artisans. These widely displaced white practitioners, which hampered a more general development of crafts in the region. Neither slave artisans, without any rights in the businesses in which they worked nor white artisans, unable to compete against low-cost slave work, could derive any benefit from such a system.

Efforts were made to protect white artisans, but to little avail. At Charles Town (present day Charleston), slave craftsmen were so dominant that in 1751, the Town Assembly prohibited any inhabitant from having more than two slaves to hire out as craftsmen. In 1755, a further edict forbade any master to allow his slaves "to carry on any handicraft trade in a shop by himself, in town, on pain of forfeiting five pounds every day. Nor to put any Negro or slave apprentice to any mechanic trade or other in town in forfeit of one hundred pounds."[25]

The problems of white craftsmen in the Old South in earning a living were therefore compounded and few managed to obtain even a modest income. Their social standing was poor. In the aristocratic social structure with its values derived from a Classical education "... the English country gentleman's tendency to look down a well-bred nose at tradesmen was more pronounced in the southern planting provinces."[26]

When slaves were emancipated after the American Civil War, they constituted the overwhelming majority of artisans in the South. It has been estimated that in 1865, there were "100,000 black mechanics and artisans in the South as compared to 20,000 white artisans."[27] A sample listing of occupations held by black artisans at that time includes ninety different skills. In a sad postscript to this history of exploitation, when black people were legally free after emancipation but effectively deprived of political rights, several southern states passed legislation to break the craft dominance of black artisans. Certain skills were specifically reserved for whites and former slave artisans were widely forced into unskilled occupations.

With the onset of industrialization, substantially financed by profits from slavery, other priorities emerged in Europe and by the early nineteenth century, the slave trade was in decline. Its legacy, however, has been bitter. In sub-Saharan Africa, war became endemic to supply the incessant demand for slaves in return for gold and firearms, destroying the social fabric in many areas, with widespread depopulation in coastal regions. To add insult to injury, in the late nineteenth century the justification for carving up Africa into European colonial possessions was the need to impose order and bring civilization to the "Dark Continent".

The brutalities of the Atlantic passage and plantation work for the millions forced to endure it denied the humanity of slave and owner alike. By turning people into a cash commodity, Europe and the Americas derived economic benefit but became morally crippled by concepts of racial superiority, which, combined with religious exclusiveness and technological might, was and remains a heady, arrogant brew.

Notes

1   Kessler, Adam T. *Empires Beyond the Great Wall: The Heritage of Genghis Khan*, Los Angeles, CA, Natural History Museum of Los Angeles County, 1993, p. 44.

2   Lebedynsky, Jaroslav. *Les Nomades: Les Peuples nomades de la steppe des origines aux invasions mongoles IXe siècle av. J.C. – XIIIe siècle apr. J.C.* Paris: Editions Errance, 2003, p. 4.

3   Lebedynsky, *Les Nomads*. A good introduction to the spectrum of Asian nomadic groups.

4   Loewe, Michael and Shaughnessy, Edward L. (editors). *The Cambridge History of Ancient China: From the Origins of Civilization to 221 BC*, Cambridge, UK, Cambridge University Press, 1999, p. 937.

5   Barfield, Thomas. *The Perilous Frontier: Nomadic Empires and China.* Cambridge, MA: Basil Blackwell, 1989, p. 28.

6   So, Jenny F. and Emma C. Bunker. *Traders and Raiders on China's Northern Frontier,* Seattle and London, Arthur M. Sackler Gallery, Smithsonian Institution, in association with the University of Washington Press, 1995, p. 25.

7   Casson, *Travel in the Ancient World*, pp. 30–1.

8   Ray, Himanshu Prabha. *The Archeology of Seafaring in Ancient South Asia.* Cambridge: Cambridge University Press, 2003, p. 25.

9   Vollmer, John E., E. J. Keall and E. Nagai-Berthrong. *Silk Roads, China Ships.* Toronto: Royal Ontario Museum, 1983, pp. 28–9.

10 Ting, Joseph S.P. *The Maritime Silk Route: 2000 Years of Trade on the South China Sea.* Hong Kong: The Urban Council of Hong Kong, 1996, p. 33.

11 Holcombe, Charles. *The Genesis of East Asia, 221B.C.-A.D.907.* Honolulu: Association for Asian Studies and University of Hawai'i Press, 2001, p. 86.

12 Exhibit notes, Museu Maritimo, Macao.

13 Davidson, p. 214.

14 Walvin, James. *Black Ivory: A History of British Slavery.* Washington, D.C.: Howard University Press, 1994, pp. 112–13.

15 Ligon, Richard. A. *A True and Exact History of the Island of Barbados ...* London, 1657, p. 42, quoted in Beccles, Hilary McD. *White Servitude and Black Slavery in Barbados, 1627-1715.* Knoxville, University of Tennessee Press, 1989, p. 129.

16 Oldmixon, John. *The British Empire in North America. 2 vols.* London, 1689, 2:129; quoted in Beccles, p. 138.

17 Beccles, p. 147.

18 Beccles, p. 139.

19 Walvin, p. 118.

20 Johnson, Michael P. "Work, Culture, the Slave Community: Slave Occupations in the Cotton Belt in 1860." *Labor History*, vol. 27, Summer 1986, #3, p. 331.

21 Johnson, p. 348.

22 Mumford, Art and Technics, p. 60.

23 See White, Llyn, Jr. *Medieval Religion and Technology.* Berkeley, University of California Press, 1978, p. 50. Just as grass weaving techniques in South Carolina can be traced to West Africa, Llyn White Jr., in noting the influence of ideas from Tibet on the development of Italian technology in the medieval period, points to a population of thousands of so- called Tartar slaves in every Italian city in the mid-fifteenth century. They came predominantly from the areas of central Asia bordering Tibet and China. "Thus," he comments,

"we need not be astonished to find simple, but fundamental Tibetan devices appearing in fifteenth century Italy."

24 Mary Jackson, president of the Mount Pleasant Sweetgrass Basketmakers Association in 1993, emphasized how significant that influence had been.

25 Bridenbaugh, p. 141.

26 Bridenbaugh, p. 161.

27 Newton, James E. "Slave Artisans and Craftsmen: The Roots of Afro-American Art," *The Black Scholar*, November, 1977, p. 40.

(B)
Designing in the
Industrial World

8

The 'American System' and Mass-Production

As we have seen, the European response to industrialization was conditioned by a continuity of social and economic structures and attitudes. Craft techniques and processes were widely adapted and developed to produce large quantities of goods that, in form and design, reflected a conscious, if sometimes confused, recognition of past traditions. The significant and fundamental changes were mainly in the scale of commercial organization and production, rather than in the manufacturing methods by which goods were produced.

By the middle of the nineteenth century, however, largely as a result of the Great Exhibition of 1851, the rest of the world became aware of new methods of manufacture in the United States that established the fundamental patterns and processes of modern industrial mass-production. These were characterized by large-scale manufacture of standardized products, with interchangeable parts, using powered machine-tools in a sequence of simplified mechanical operations. The implications of this approach, which became widely known as the 'American system' of manufacture, were not confined to production methods, but also affected the whole organization and co-ordination of production, the nature of the work-process, the methods by which goods were marketed, and, not least, the type and form of the goods produced.

As with many developments in the United States, there were European precursors and influences. Around 1729, in Sweden, Christopher Pohlem had applied water-power to simple machine processes and precision measurement to produce interchangeable gears for clocks, at a factory in Stjarnsund. Later in the eighteenth century, a French armourer, known only as Le Blanc, applied similar methods to the production of muskets. After

---

First published as "The 'American System' and mass production" Chapter 3 of *Industrial Design,* Thames and Hudson, London, 1980, pp. 50–67. By permission of Thames and Hudson.

visiting Le Blanc's workshops in 1782, Thomas Jefferson, then American Minister to France, noted in a letter: 'An improvement is here made in construction of muskets. ... It consists in making every part of them so exactly alike, that what belongs to any one, may be used for every other musket in the magazine. . . . The advantages of this when arms need repair are evident.' Le Blanc's work met with considerable obstruction, however, from the official bureaucracy that administered government arsenals, and from craftsmen who saw their livelihood threatened.

French ideas were linked to English developments by one Marc Brunel, a Royalist refugee from the French Revolution, who designed machinery for the mass-production of pulley blocks for the Royal Navy, for Sir Samuel Bentham, then Inspector General of Naval Works and himself a pioneer inventor of many types of woodworking machinery. Once the exigencies of the Napoleonic Wars were past, however, the system was abandoned. The basic approach was taken up in the United States around 1800, and was developed on a scale that thoroughly justifies its being called the 'American system'. Eli Whitney is often cited as its founder, largely on the basis of a proposal he made to the American government in 1798 for the manufacture of ten thousand muskets in two years (though in fact the contract was not completed until eleven years later). Research on surviving Whitney muskets indicates that the number of interchangeable parts was limited, and their precision, and thus the extent to which they were interchangeable, was variable. Other armourers in the United States, such as Simeon North and John Hancock Hall, were at least as advanced in their thinking, and probably more advanced in production methods. The truth would seem to be that, rather than any one person possessing a unique claim to having invented the system, it was an idea that had general currency at the time, emerging in a continuous series of improvements, each being eagerly seized on by competitors.

Hall, in particular, emphasized and developed the decisive elements permitting interchangeability, namely, precision measurement and accuracy in production. This work culminated in a simplified breech-loading flintlock introduced in 1824 and produced for twenty years. His stated intention was to 'make every similar part of every gun so much alike that it will suit every gun, so that if a thousand guns were taken apart and the links thrown together promiscuously on a heap, they may be taken promiscuously from the heap and will come right'. In order to do this, Hall had to simplify each part as far as possible, and his products are a marked utilitarian contrast to the elegant, decorated products of master gunsmiths. His methods were later refined by firms that were to have international reputations in arms production, such as Sharp, Henry, Winchester and Remington.

The American system reached a high point of development by the mid-nineteenth century in another area of arms production—revolvers—with the establishment of Samuel Colt's armoury at Hartford, Connecticut. Colt was typical of this generation of American innovators, taking principles and inventions that were widely available, and combining them with a form that was distinctive and totally effective. Other contemporary armourers produced excellent weapons, but it was Colt's thoroughgoing application of mass-production methods, and an exceptional flair for salesmanship and promotion, that made him so successful. His factory contained over fourteen hundred machine-tools, and under the leadership of Elisha K. Root, a technical genius, was a magnet for anyone interested in the most advanced methods of manufacture. The United States Secretary for War referred to it as having 'the status of a national work.' Colt's Navy .36 Revolver of 1851 is typical of his products. Like Hall's flintlock, it was reduced to an essential simplicity, and the precision of its interchangeable parts defined standards for the form of hand-weapons for many years.

The fact that the American system developed in relation to the production of firearms is, in retrospect, hardly surprising. The supply of large quantities of reliable and inexpensive weapons was a corollary of the general expansion of the size of military forces, and the constant series of wars against neighbouring states and native inhabitants of the West in which the United States was involved. The only significant application of the American system abroad was also in armaments, the British government establishing the Enfield manufactory with American machine-tools in 1853, and American equipment also being supplied to Prussia and France. Government contracts were necessary in order to pay for the plant and equipment initially required to set up the new system.

What was unique to the United States, however, was the adaptation of the system to other areas of manufacture unsupported by government funds. In part, this was due to a lack of skilled labour and the absence of an entrenched craft tradition. Samuel Colt, in discussions with British engineers, stated that uneducated workers were best suited to the new mass-production methods since they had so little to unlearn. Innovation was not a challenge to established institutions and habits in the young Republic, and in an open, expanding society the commercial opportunities for wealth and advancement were a strong inducement. A British commission investigating the American system in 1853 noted 'the dissatisfaction frequently expressed in America with regard to present attainment in the manufacture and application of labour-saving machinery, and the avidity with which any new idea is laid hold of, and improved upon . . .'

By 1850 the American system had spread to other industries in New England, the centre of arms production, and later appeared in other districts. It was introduced to the manufacture of clocks in the 1830s by Eli Terry, who produced a clock movement from wooden parts, and in the following decade Chauncey Jerome took the process a step further by introducing metal gears stamped from thin, rolled-brass sheet, instead of brass castings. This resulted in a less bulky movement, and the clocks produced were very slim, suitable for wall-hanging without undue protuberance. The cases of plain wood were also mass-produced.

By 1838 the first attempt had been made to mass-produce watches, though with little success, the finer movements presenting greater difficulties. It was not until 1850 that sustained production began, started by the American Horologe Company of Roxbury, Massachusetts. Aaron L. Dennison, one of its founders, had visited the Springfield Armoury and decided that watches, as well as guns, could be made by mass-production methods. His pocket-watches with movement plates die-punched from rolled brass by steam-powered machinery had circular metal frames that could be hand-engraved for more expensive models, and printed metal dials with numerals in various typographic styles. By the end of the century the manufacture of watches was a major industry, the Waterbury company producing half a million a year, and the Ingersoll company marketing a watch that cost only one dollar. They were accessible to the whole population.

Some of the most dramatic effects resulted from the mass-production of agricultural machinery, an area that the Americans constantly improved and refined. In 1819 Jethro Wood of Scipio, New York, patented a cast-iron plough built from separated standardized and interchangeable parts. The most spectacular developments, however, radically influenced grain production. In 1833–4 both Obed Hussey and Cyrus McCormick produced practical reaping machines. By the 1850s these machines were mass-produced and being sold as fast as they could be manufactured. McCormick's was the most successful, selling about four thousand a year, a high figure for a relatively complicated mechanism.

American products were often criticized by European observers for their lack of finish and solidarity, their use of substitute materials, and their cheapness. The Great Exhibition of 1851 in London, however, marked a turning-point in attitudes. The exhibits for the American stand were assembled hastily and late, and were inadequate to fill the large space booked, causing considerable derision in the London press. The opportunity to study the products on show over a long period of time, however, enabled them to be taken more seriously, and by the end of the exhibition some had earned considerable respect, in particular Goodyear's rubber products, Colt's revolvers and the McCormick reaper. The rest of the world began to sit up and take notice, and the British Commission that subsequently visited the United States was to warn: 'the Americans display an amount of ingenuity, combined with undaunted energy, which as a nation we would do well to imitate, if we mean to hold our present position in the great market of the world.'

The difference between Europe and America was not limited, however, to production systems, but applied in a much wider sense to general cultural and social values. This was remarked on in the Official Catalogue of the Great Exhibition: 'The expenditure of months or years of labour upon a single article, not to increase its intrinsic value, but solely to augment its cost or its estimation as an object of *virtue,* is not common in the United States. On the contrary, both manual and mechanical labour are applied with direct reference to increasing the number or the quantity of articles suited to the wants of a whole people, and adapted to promote the enjoyment of that moderate competency which prevails upon them.' The comparison was between European attitudes, based on craft traditions, in which the value of a product, both economically and aesthetically, resided in the extent of skilled work it embodied, and the American approach, based on industrial methods, which emphasized quantity and utility for wider sections of the population. But was it true to say, as the catalogue asserted, that this difference gave 'the productions of American industry a character distinct from that of other countries'? In the opinion of George Wallis, a member of the British Commission of 1853, and head of the Birmingham School of Art and Design, a clear distinction had to be drawn between the means of production, in which he recognized the unique American achievement, and the goods produced, which he regarded as a reflection of prevailing European taste. The types of manufacture upon which he concentrated, however, were all traditional areas of European decorative art—furniture, metalware, ceramics, glassware and jewellery—in which American producers had to compete with European imports. In such areas of production, technical and commercial innovation did not inevitably lead to new forms. Wallis' judgment of the industries he considered was accurate and perceptive. At the time he made his report, however, the results of American ingenuity were beginning to be manifested in completely new products that did not fit comfortably into the European concept of decorative art," and these products were to proliferate to an extent that demanded attention. A crucial example was the sewing machine.

The process of sewing by hand requires a constant and subtle interplay of material, hand and eye. Many attempts had been made to replicate this manual dexterity by mechanical means, but it was not until 1844 when Elias Howe, a skilled mechanic from Boston, developed a needle with the eye placed at the point, using two to make an interlocking stitch below the surface of the material, that a mechanical sewing machine became feasible. After many vicissitudes, Howe finally managed to put his machine into production with considerable success. The idea was also taken up by Isaac Merrit Singer, who refined Howe's design, and by placing the sewing action on a vertical axis gave the machine its definitive form. Like Samuel Colt, Singer combined mechanical ingenuity with commercial flair. Realizing the potential of sewing machines, he marketed them with unflagging vigour, introducing what now seems an inevitable feature of modern life: hire purchase. The mass-production and sales generated by Singer also brought formal changes in his products. His first machine of 1851 was a very plain, functional mechanism, but an appreciation of the importance of appearance led to the mechanism being shrouded in a pressed, japanned-metal casing, decorated with stencilled floral patterns. The stand and foot-treadle drive, produced as optional extras, also had patterns of scrolls and latticework, designed to make them more acceptable in a domestic setting. The basic form of Singer's machines was dictated by mechanical function, but presentation conformed to conceptions of what was aesthetically appropriate to the social context in which the machines were used.

An interesting contrast is presented by another contemporary machine that radically altered working patterns: the typewriter. Like the sewing machine, it was the result of a long process of invention and refinement. In 1873 a machine built by Sholes and Glidden, which resolved many outstanding problems, was demonstrated to Philo Remington, whose family firm was well established as manufacturers of weapons, sewing machines and agricultural machinery. With the post-Civil-War slump in arms production, Remington was seeking new products, and signed a contract to produce the typewriter. Two of his best mechanics, William K. Jenne and Jefferson M. Clough, were assigned to the task of redesigning the machine for mass-production. They had been working on sewing machines, and the influence of that work is evident in the form and decoration of the casing, stand, and the treadle that operated the carriage change. The success of the typewriter was less immediate than that of the sewing machine, but eventually it came to be used extensively in the different visual context of business premises. As a result it evolved into a starker, non-decorated form, such as the Remington No. 10 of 1907, which reverted to a more emphatically functional appearance.

By 1870 the American system was well established in over twenty industries, including, in addition to the examples already cited, precision instruments and tools; machine-tools, especially woodworking machinery; railroad cars of the type discussed in the previous chapter; cutlery, using rollers to press out the form in a continuous process instead of stamping; musical instruments such as pianos and melodium, and domestic hardware. It was to spread even further as the pace of industrial growth in the United States increased at an explosive rate. The expansion of business stimulated the mass-production of simple, efficient office-furniture: desks, bureaux, filing cupboards, swivel chairs and adjustable typists' chairs. New inventions were avidly adopted. Some, such as bicycles, were produced by firms with existing and appropriate experience and equipment; others, such as telephones and phonographs, were to form the basis of new industries.

Photography, for example, was first popularized by George Eastman with his lightweight Kodak camera of 1888 incorporating a ready-loaded film. This feature had the disadvantage, however, of requiring the camera to be returned to the manufacturer for processing. A new method of loading, using roll-film, enabled a mass-produced camera, the Folding Pocket Kodak, to be produced in 1895. It was followed in 1900 by the Brownie, intended by its designer, Frank Brownell, to be suitable for children. The plain black box was an appropriate expression of the total simplicity and inexpensiveness of the apparatus, which de-mystified photography and made it accessible to the amateur.

Not all mass-produced goods were so utilitarian, however; many of them catered equally for the fashionable taste for ornamentation and decoration. This decorative tendency has often been criticized as a degeneration in taste, though dismissive judgments do little to provide an understanding of why it occurred in America.

In part it was due to the growth of the United States into a complex and diverse society, conscious of its standing in the world, and seeking a sense of cultural identity. An aesthetic eclecticism was capable of reflecting these diversities and aspirations, and if European examples were followed, it was hardly surprising. Disparaging comments by European visitors on the cultural deficiencies and alleged materialism of Americans did much to create a sense of inferiority, a feeling that 'culture' was something extraneous, and a desirable acquisition. Participation in international exhibitions with the inevitable comparisons these provoked, importation of goods, publications and pattern books, and the large numbers of European immigrants, were all influential factors. The European suspicion of machine products was also implanted in Americans through the writings of John Ruskin and William Morris. Simple and utilitarian products were regarded as evidence of the 'mere materialism' of which Americans were often accused. As in Europe, however, aesthetic symbols and allusion did not necessarily restrict efficiency. Frank Leslie in his *Historical Register of the Centennial Exposition of 1876* in Philadelphia, commended the 'application of art ideas' to gas implements and processes in the Mitchell Vance Company's exhibit. Much decoration remained just that, impairing neither the function of products nor the American enthusiasm for, and pursuit of, innovation.

The ability to combine efficiency and embellishment was clearly demonstrated in the furniture designs of firms clustered around the city of Grand Rapids, Michigan, which became the major centre of American furniture production in the late nineteenth century. The industry was based on a high degree of mechanization, with considerable technical and organizational ingenuity evident in the production process. In a study of its development Kenneth L. Ames has pointed out two special requirements in the design of Grand Rapids furniture, that were also characteristic of many other products: it had to appear familiar yet embody some unique feature, and have an appearance of quality without being expensive to make. Mechanization, he argued, was the key to satisfying these requirements. 'If an elaborate piece of furniture could be made primarily by machine, with a minimum of hand labor, it could be offered to, the public at a modest price.' In the competitive mass-market for furniture created by Grand Rapids firms close attention to public taste was necessary and design was correspondingly given great emphasis. Ames quotes a writer of 1887 on this subject: 'Each establishment maintains its own staff of designers and they are busy the whole year round planning articles of furniture as comfortable, unique and beautiful as the art of man can compass.' Typical of the eclectic use of Renaissance forms that dominated fashion in the 1870s was a chamber suite by the Phoenix Furniture Company, made in walnut. The pieces were sturdy and solid, and the height of the headboard and mirror-stand created an impression of stateliness. Decorative effect was achieved by jig-saw cut outlines, with turned roundels and cut panels glued to the basic structure. Innumerable designs for furniture of all kinds were produced in variations of the style, and became exceedingly popular.

A unified aesthetic in relation to mass-production did not, therefore, exist; in fact, the American system of manufacture catered for and encouraged diversity and eclecticism by the new modes of commercial organization and sales technique that it stimulated. Mass-production required mass-consumption, and there followed the establishment of department stores in cities, and later, mail order firms such as Montgomery Ward, founded in 1872, and Sears, Roebuck, founded in 1886. Both were established in Chicago at the hub of the railway system, and sold a vast range of products that catered for all a family's needs, across a wide geographical area.

With such highly competitive methods of selling, aesthetic appearance became a vital means of attracting interest. All tastes had to be catered for, and ever more complex and detailed effects became technically possible. The Montgomery Ward catalogue of 1895 offered fifty-six different kinds of clocks, many by leading manufacturers such as Seth Thomas and the Waterbury company, ranging from simple alarm clocks to extravagantly decorated wall and mantel models, the casing finishes including oak, walnut, enamelled iron and gilt. Different exterior forms often housed the same movement, as with the 'Dakota' and 'Cato' models. Sears, Roebuck followed a similar policy. The 1906 catalogue section on sewing machines contained a paragraph under the heading 'Design' for each machine and cabinet, commenting on the 'Minnesota B' model that it was 'extremely handsome and pleasing in appearance, the general design being worked out in easy curves and rounded corners so as to avoid any suggestions of harshness or angularity'. The cabinet was described as a 'model of beauty and artistic design.'

Towards the end of the century, the full consciousness of the extent to which mechanization and the American system were effecting a transformation of the environment led to attempts to arrive at a machine-aesthetic. An important figure in formulating and disseminating this aesthetic was the architect Frank Lloyd Wright. He had worked under Louis Sullivan, whose famous dictum 'form follows function' was to become one of the great polemical slogans of modern architecture and design. Often misinterpreted as expressing a somewhat crude structural and aesthetic determinism, Sullivan's phrase, in the context of his argument, was an attempt to formulate a concept of organic unity in architecture in which function, structure and appropriate decoration could be fused to give an artistic expression appropriate to the modern age. Wright adopted and developed this organic concept, and his early independent work included designs for furniture and fittings intended to be an integral part of the houses he designed. These, like his buildings, were based on the massing of simple elements. The chair built for his studio around 1895 by a Milwaukee cabinet maker was an expression of Wright's interest at that time in the Arts and Crafts movement and in handicraft. He came to realize, however, that the clean, straight lines of his furniture could be better achieved by the precision of machines than by hand. In a famous lecture given in Chicago in 1901, 'The Art and Craft of the Machine', Wright expressed his positive attitude to mechanization and its potential for aesthetic expression, mounting a scathing attack on the misuse of machines to produce 'butchered forms' from past cultures. The machine, argued Wright, was 'the creature, not the Creator of this iniquity'. It was a tool whose potential effect was to emancipate the modern mind. Through its tendency to simplify, the machine could reveal the true nature and beauty of materials. Taking wood as an instance, 'machines have undoubtedly placed within reach of the designer a technique enabling him to realize the true nature of wood in his designs harmoniously with man's sense of beauty, satisfying his material needs with such economy as to put this beauty of wood in use within the reach of everyone.'

For Wright, there was no contradiction between individual values and mass-production. He argued that the provision of a better life for everyone and a diminution of human drudgery were essential for the flowering of a democratic culture. 'What limits do we dare imagine to an Art that is organic fruit of an adequate life for the individual?' But for this potential to be realized, it was necessary that artists grasp and utilize creatively the power of the machine. Wright's romantic view of the artist's role took little account, however, of the realities of the industrial context in which mechanization was applied; and his success in building up a practice dependent largely on private commissions meant that an opportunity never arose for him to attempt to realize his ideals in terms of industrial production.

Nevertheless his ideas, particularly those relating to mechanization, had wide currency in the United States and Europe, and anticipated many of the central tenets of the Modern Movement of the 1920s. There were, however, several contradictions in Wright's arguments, as in those of the Modern Movement. The assertion that simple, geometric forms were alone appropriate to machine production took little account of the wide potential of modern mechanical technology. Wright's inflexible application of his aesthetic principles to some of his later designs resulted in some exceedingly uncomfortable geometric furniture. More fundamentally, although he appreciated the potential benefits of the products of modern industry in contributing to better conditions of life, he failed to perceive the human cost that the new methods of production entailed. In 1812 Eli Whitney had clearly stated the objective of the American System of manufacture as, to 'substitute correct and effective operations of machinery for that skill of the artist which is acquired only by long practice and experience'. At the same time as Wright was formulating his arguments, the American system was reaching a culminating point in the fulfilment of that objective.

Throughout most of the nineteenth century the progress of the American system had emphasized the analysis of objects and mechanisms, breaking them down into interchangeable constituent parts and designing them for mechanized mass-production. Between 1880 and 1900 an engineer, Frederick W. Taylor, began a series of studies of work-processes in which he sought to find 'the one best way' of performing tasks; in other words, to achieve a standardization of working methods in order to maximize production. By timing the most efficient workers by stop-watch and seeking to eliminate superfluous movements, he was in fact seeking to integrate human capacities into the sequence of machine operations. This marked a complete rejection of the craft concept of work, which depends upon the skill, judgment and responsibility of individuals. Taylor's methods became widely known in the early years of the twentieth century under the title 'scientific management', and were widely adopted. The adverse reaction they frequently aroused among workers, however, was to lead to an important modification, discussed in the following chapter, to take account of the harm to efficiency caused by fatigue depending not only on physical but also on psychological factors.

Co-ordination of all work-processes in pursuit of improved efficiency and production was first fully developed in the production of motor cars. The United States came late in the field of automobile manufacture, most of the initial development taking place in Europe, but it was in America that the low-priced mass-produced car emerged with astonishing rapidity. Early vehicles were individually craft-built in limited quantities. In 1901, however, Ransome E. Olds began to produce a small, lightweight car on a mass-production basis in Detroit. The machine was very basic and designed for non-mechanically minded customers, with a curved dashboard and folding hood clearly derived from horse-drawn carriage forms, and tiller steering. Six hundred were sold in 1901, rising to 6,500 in 1905. It was a staggering achievement at the time, and opened up motoring to a broad public.

Olds' achievement was, however, to be dwarfed by Henry Ford's. The 'Oldsmobile' was only suitable for urban conditions and good roads; Ford set out to design a car to cater specifically for a mass-market and the most rugged conditions. The outcome, in 1908, was the 'Model T'. From the first it was tremendously popular, and Ford and his team set out to produce it as cheaply as possible. As a result, in 1914 they brought together the constituent parts of the modern mass-production system: quantity production of a standard design with interchangeable parts, on a moving assembly line, to the pace and nature of which the workers were compelled to adapt.

The formula was decisive in increasing the volume of production and decreasing unit cost: in 1910 almost twenty thousand Model Ts were produced at a cost of $850 each; in 1916, nearly six hundred thousand at $360 each; before production ceased in 1927, nearly fifteen million had rolled off the production lines.

In design terms the Model T belonged to an interim stage: the influence of carriage design was still strong, for instance, in the spoked wheels and tonneau body with its folding hood; the body sat high on the chassis, in order to provide adequate clearance on poor rural roads; the bonnet was small, and the connecting panel to the body appeared ill-co-ordinated. But if the Model T was not the most beautiful car of its age, it was the most powerful symbol; the harbinger of a transformation in industrial work and industrial products that was to exceed anything previously experienced.

9

Writing the History of Design in the Industrial World: An Overview and Two Review Essays

Notes. Questions of substance concerning a field—say the history of design in the industrial world—are more dependent on questions of method, or, less abstractly, on questions of how a field, and a practice, should be understood than we think. The three pieces reproduced below consist of an extract from the chapter on "Industrial Design" from a student handbook on design, and two complementary and contrasting book reviews. The pieces both illustrate and discuss "questions of method" relevant to writing the history of design. It is important here to remember how important pedagogy was to Heskett. Heskett's own reflections in teaching (see reading #29) make clear that the pedagogical element was fundamental to his work—as indeed it was fundamental (at least in Britain) to the formation of design history between the 1970s and the 1990s. But the question of what is offered pedagogically as an understanding of design through history begs the question of asking what is to be understood and on what basis. These readings address this double issue; the first through the vehicle of a student guide to understanding industrial design and its history; the second and third by engaging with two contrasting instances of contemporary (1990s) scholarship on the history of design.

(i) "Industrial Design: A Student Guide"

Industrial design is concerned with the vast array of goods manufactured by serial- or mass-production methods. The profession of industrial designer

Previously published as "Industrial Design" in *Design History: A Student's Handbook*, ed. Hazel Conway (London, Allen and Unwin, 1987), pp. 110–17.

emerged in the twentieth century and can be seen as a feature of the division of labour and specialization characteristic of large-scale modern industry. Before this specialism developed the function of design in industry was less well-defined and was performed by a variety of people, from major artists to anonymous workers. These more obscure and distant circumstances present particular problems and challenges.

Modern practice for industrial designers generally falls into two broad categories, when s/he is either a direct employee of an organization and designing exclusively for it, or an independent consultant commissioned to design for a variety of clients. Examples of the first category are the design groups employed by all major motor-vehicle manufacturers, or by the giants of electrical goods manufacturers, such as the Dutch company Philips or Matsushita Electric of Japan. Such teams are responsible for translating the possibilities of scientific and technological invention into products that are appropriate and appealing to the buying public. Their success or failure can profoundly influence the performance of a company. Consultants perform a similar function but for a variety of clients and product types. Kenneth Grange of the consultancy Pentagram has been responsible for a range of work of as diverse a nature and scale as the front-end and cab of British Rail's High-Speed 125 train, kitchen appliances for Kenwood and disposable razors for Wilkinson's Sword.

Whatever the mode of employment, or type of product under consideration, the task of modern industrial designers is to produce a plan and specification of a form or mechanism for large-scale production. An essential feature of their work is the separation of concept from manufacture or realization.

The significance of industrial design in modern society

A key characteristic of industrial design is therefore the manufacturing context for which designs are created. Unlike design for ceramics, glass or textiles, it is not confined to one material, nor, as in furniture or interior design, to a particular category of artefact or environment. It can frequently overlap with other areas of design, indeed, practitioners have claimed its range of concerns extends from 'a lipstick to a steamship' or from 'a match to a city'. Such breadth can be problematic. The sheer extent and diversity of the innumerable products of industry is itself confusing. To illustrate this, consider some details of your own daily life. To simplify the illustration, concentrate on one area: the kitchen as working space and the preparation of food as a main activity. Basic fittings will include storage spaces and containers for food and equipment, with a table or cupboard-top surface at which to work. To prepare food, there will be hand-implements such as knives, spoons, ladles, vegetable-peelers and spatulas, for use with basins, jugs and cutting boards, and mechanical appliances such as a hand-whisk or powered mixer/beater. Vessels for cooking will include saucepans, frying-pans, baking-tins and casserole dishes, of varying shapes, materials and sizes. For cooking there will be a stove, using gas, electricity or solid fuel, possibly supplemented by appliances such as a toaster or electric kettle.

An examination of any other area of domestic life will reveal a similar diversity. Neither is such a consideration limited to the home environment. To go anywhere beyond immediate walking distance of where you live will require access to a form of transport, of a personal kind, perhaps; bicycle, moped, motor-cycle or car; or maybe public forms: bus, tram, underground or train. Whilst out you may wait at a bus-shelter, stop at a traffic light, or make a call from a telephone box. Whatever your destination, school, work, public buildings or sites for sport and recreation, there will again be a remarkable variety of objects to facilitate particular activities. All will have been conceived to serve a certain purpose and embody a particular set of values.

It would be possible to continue in similar vein and compile a lengthy catalogue. The examples given above are just the tip of a very large iceberg, but they do illustrate the degree to which our environment, in all its details, is composed of industrial products. They are so numerous and ubiquitous as to be frequently taken for granted. Yet they form the material framework of our existence, enabling it to function, not only in practical or utilitarian terms, but also in ways that give pleasure, meaning and significance to our lives. The public outcry in Britain in 1984, when British Telecom announced the replacement of the traditional red telephone booth by a bland modern design, ignored the undoubted efficiency of the latter and was essentially a lament for the loss of a familiar image, that communicated a strong sense of identity. Industrial products are therefore elements of our material culture, tangible expressions of individual and social values. This means objects cannot be studied simply in terms of visual characteristics and qualities, or as ends in themselves. Instead, visual analysis needs to be supplemented by questions exploring wider reaches of meaning.

What does the study of industrial design involve?

Basically, questions on the nature and role of industrial design point in two directions. The first concerns how artefacts come into existence: who designed what, when, how, where and why? This is obviously vital in establishing a basis of fact and understanding about the activity of design, though it is susceptible to differing interpretations and emphases, stemming from the variable meaning of the word 'design' itself. This can be illustrated by a seemingly nonsensical sentence: 'Design means designers design designs by means of designs.' The noun 'designers' refers to individuals or groups engaged in the activity, whose background, talent and achievement needs to be described and understood. The verb 'to design' describes an action or process, implying a development or sequence of thought and practice through which industrial designers create and evolve a concept for later production. The sentence also contains three usages of 'design' as a noun. The first word describes the total activity in an all-embracing and undifferentiated sense, as in: 'Design is an essential ingredient in successful industrial performance.' The final word refers to a concept or plan, the end result of the design process, e.g. 'The completed design was ready for production.' As used following the verb, however, 'design' describes the realized object after the process of production, e.g. 'Like all great designs, the Mini became the symbol of an entire generation.'

The second major direction of questioning explores the application of an object: who is it intended to be used for, who uses it, for what purposes, with what effect and what meaning. Widely differing conclusions can be drawn from these two channels of inquiry, since the meaning intended for an object by its designer may not be the same as the meaning of an object in use. The context may alter, and with it the manner in which an object is utilized or perceived.

An example indicating how these different approaches can combine in the history of industrial design is the German car, the Volkswagen, popularly known as the 'Beetle', which became the best-selling vehicle of all time, with over 20 million being produced. The character and career of its designer, the Austrian engineer Ferdinand Porsche, are obviously important and, in particular, the ideas and influences leading him to the conception of a small car with a rear-mounted air-cooled engine which he developed by the early 1930s. Attempts to have such a car manufactured commercially failed, but in 1936 he was commissioned by Adolf Hitler to produce an inexpensive 'People's Car' by mass-production methods similar to those earlier used by Henry Ford in the USA. This shift from the possibility of commercial to state-supported production in itself altered the significance of the concept. The intention was to manufacture a vehicle available to broad sections of the population previously unable to afford a car, as a means of securing support for the regime and diverting attention from its less savoury aspects. The detailed design process of how Porsche fulfilled a very tight brief on cost and performance to create the most enduring example of 1930s streamlined style is itself fascinating, and after models and plans had been approved by Hitler the first prototypes were demonstrated in 1938. The various stages of design as process, concept and object can all be identified in its development to this date.

The significance of the Volkswagen, however, does not end there. The car was promoted as an achievement of the Nazi regime but remained an unfulfilled promise. Few were produced before the outbreak of war, when the concept was adapted for a military vehicle. As such it was given an incredibly rigorous testing, from the snows of Russia to the sands of North Africa. After Germany's defeat, a new company was formed to commence commercial production of the original 'Beetle'. It became an astonishing success, a sound, reliable and inexpensive vehicle, capable of coping with rugged conditions. Even more remarkable was the way it became a cult object, particularly in the USA, where it became the star feature of the 'Herbie' series of films produced by the Walt Disney organization.

It was, in so many ways, an astonishing process: from being the symbol of the Third Reich, known pompously as the 'Strength-through-Joy' car, to the fun object of the 1950s. Its form and construction, though modified and improved in detail, remained unaltered, and its functional qualities, though refined, were also unchanged. Yet its meaning and significance had totally changed.

Of course, not all objects have such extensive a public impact or as dramatic a history as the Volkswagen. Many have more private and intimate significance, the importance of which was apparent to the American novelist Henry James. In his novels he used a technique of precisely detailed descriptions of the objects and interiors surrounding his main characters, which expressed their nature, as a means of increasing readers' awareness of their personalities. The importance of this ambience was summed up by him in the evocative phrase, 'the empire of "things"',[2] a term entirely appropriate to the role of industrial products in modern life.

The scope of industrial design history

The scope of the history of industrial design, is obviously closely linked to the development of industrialization, and much depends on how that term is interpreted. It is most commonly associated with the introduction of mechanization, mainly steam-power, and large-scale manu-facturing and commercial organization, which gathered momentum from the late eighteenth century, the period of the Industrial Revolution. Indeed, research on industrial design has overwhelmingly concentrated on Western Europe and North America since that revolution.

Industrialization has transformed virtually every aspect of material existence. Machines have been devised not only to produce age-old categories of artefacts, such as ceramics and furniture, but also to create new objects and other machines for use in daily life, from aircraft and cars, to refrigerators and vacuum cleaners. With mechanization values changed from an emphasis on tradition, the conservation of any history of industrial design.

There is, however, a strong case for extending the range of research further back in time and over a greater geographical area than is generally the case at present. This requires a distinction to be drawn between industrialization and steam- or electrically-powered mechanization. The two are often regarded as synonymous, but are not necessarily so.

If industrialization is defined in terms of organizational structure instead of sources of power, a different perspective becomes possible. Productive capacity on a scale beyond individual capacities, and based on specialization of tasks and division of labour, need not involve large-scale mechanization, but can be based on hand techniques. There is evidence, for example, of forty-five distinct pottery forms in Egypt in the Archaic Period, *c.* 3000 BC, being found in such profusion in excavations that an archeologist, W. B. Emery, writes of their 'mass-production'.[3] Archaeological research provides a wealth of information on the classification of forms and their identification in relation to place and time. There is a potential role for design historians not only to draw on such research, but also to contribute to it with studies of forms related to materials and processes, and analyses of the functions they performed.

The pottery and stoneware vessels of civilizations such as those of Archaic Egypt were precise solutions to particular functional and cultural requirements which emerged from centuries of craft adaptation. In this shadowy process of evolution it is generally impossible to identify individual figures or groups to whom specific forms can be attributed. This has given rise to a concept that has come to play an important role in histories of industrial design. Anonymous forms of this type are generally considered to be part of a vernacular or folk tradition. By this is meant those implements and artefacts which, over an extended period of time, have established basic forms appropriate to their function and cannot be fundamentally improved: for example, the shapes of tools such as spades, hoes, axes and saws, and domestic items such as jugs and ladles. Some may be specific to particular cultures, others may be more widespread: an example universally used as a cutting instrument, is scissors. Exactly when, where or how this solution to the problem of cleanly cutting material evolved is unknown, though it is believed to have been in the Bronze Age. Certainly, they were widespread over 2000 years ago as far afield as Ancient Rome and China. But whatever detailed variations have subsequently appeared, and they are innumerable, the fundamental configuration remains unaltered. The vernacular tradition is thus an important source of design concepts and forms, often known as type-forms, which have become firmly established due to their appropriateness and widely adapted to industrial mass-production. In principle, there is little difference of form in relation to function of modern scissors to those evolved long ago, despite the very different production techniques used.

The concept of the vernacular tradition can be romanticized in mystical terms as an expression of the soul of an age or people. Such treatments gloss over the fact that we simply do not know, and often have no conceivable way of knowing, what particular individuals, events or processes contributed to the evolution of a form. Neither is this kind of approach restricted to studies of the distant past; for example, writing of American design in the early nineteenth century, Arthur Pulos asserts: 'In the young and virile democracy it was thought that everyone was, or may have been, a contributor to the evolution ol a product... It would seem that anonymity was then, and continues to be, part of the burden that designers must bear for their role in democratic utilitarian design.'[4]

Anonymity is equated with democracy, but what this really means is that not enough research has been done or inadequate material is available for us to know what really took place.

Whatever the limitations and misuse of the concept of the vernacular tradition, it does have a positive side. It provides a useful corrective, in its acknowledgment of collective effort, to a one-sided emphasis on individualism and an important means of demonstrating the essential continuity of many design forms through time. The idea of continuity, however, needs complementing by an awareness of the forces producing change within a culture, of the contrasts existing between different cultural traditions and the extent of exchange between them.

Considered in terms of cultural awareness, the history of industrial design is afflicted with the academic equivalent of tunnel vision, an inability to focus other than in a very restricted range. The prevailing emphasis on recent events in an exceedingly limited number of countries has neglected trends that, even in the twentieth century, have had a profound impact in global terms. An example is the rise to economic power and the influence of designs from the countries of the Western Pacific arc, Japan in particular. Equally neglected are those countries under communist systems of government, or Third World countries, where differing economic and social structures have led to differences in design theory and practice. If this limited outlook is true of the present, it is even more marked in studies of the past.

Once again, however, a corpus of work from various disciplines exists which can give important leads to a wider understanding, such as Romila Thapar's history of her native India. She describes how, in the period c. AD 200-300, political and economic events combined to produce an expansion of trade:

> With the increasing demand for particular commodities and the consequent necessity to raise their output, some guilds began to employ hired labour and slaves ... Leading guilds were those of the potters, metalworkers, and carpenters. Their size can be gauged from the fact that even at an earlier period one wealthy potter named Saddalaputta had owned five hundred potter's workshops. In addition, he had organized his own distribution and owned a large number of boats which took the pottery from the workshops to the various ports on the Ganges.[5]

That raises many intriguing questions. Some relate to the effect increased trade and larger scale organization had on methods of production and the forms manufactured for expanded markets. Such research could be a valuable contribution to knowledge of the role of design for handicraft industry in one of the world's most diverse cultures, where continuities from the past provide distinctive challenges and problems for modern Indian industrial designers. It could also enable valuable comparisons with developments in other countries to be made. Perhaps even more significant, however, is the point Romila Thapar makes about the role of Indian traders as middlemen between East and West, based on a long association with Graeco-Roman civilization and their trading ventures into South-East Asia, which she succinctly sums up in the statement: 'Exchange of merchandise led inevitably to an exchange of ideas.'[6] It is a statement valid for all periods of history and has considerable, if yet inadequately explored, relevance to the development of industry and the design of its products.

(ii) Review: The American Design Adventure 1940–1975

by Arthur Pulos

Arthur Pulos has had a many-faceted career in the design profession, as chairman of the design department of Syracuse University, president of his own consultancy, and past president of the Industrial Designers Society of America and the International Congress of Societies of Industrial Design. This book is a sequel to his *American Design Ethic* (MIT Press 1983), on the evolution of industrial design in the United States to 1940. Both are informed by a belief that industrial design is a creative expression of the American democratic spirit in a free market system. If valid, it is an important argument in understanding the relationship of technology and culture in our time.

The book's organization, however, gives little help in introducing the potential complexities of this theme. Beginning with a chapter on the Second World War, others follow on modern living, "good design," education and professional organization, and design and national diplomacy. On page 268, the theme of the marketplace and design for various aspects of industry and commerce is discussed. The priorities in this structure are unexplained. The book is rich in detail and well illustrated, but the chapters sustain the impression of a lack of overall structure. The first, on the Second World War, describes the development of the Jeep, followed by examples of projects by various design consultancies, but the material is not integrated into an overall theme that reaches beyond the details. The specific demands of the war on American industry (the arsenal of democracy), the cumulative contribution of designers, the effects upon their work and organization, are not discussed. A later chapter on recreation and travel similarly discusses

First published as a review of Arthur Pulos, *The American Design Adventure 1940–1975*, in *Science, Technology and Human Values*, vol. 18, no. 2, Spring, 1993, pp. 263–4.

products of various kinds, without reference to why leisure opportunities became available to many Americans after the war, and how these changes affected the kind of projects on which designers worked.

The narrow focus would be sustainable if the book were simply a history of design ideas and practice. The introduction, however, makes broader claims for industrial designers as having "a commitment to human service beyond the cold touch of science and the predatory grasp of commerce. The role of the designer, as the humane and aesthetic conscience of industry, is that of a surrogate for the consumer" (p. vii). That requires a consideration of design in a broad context, including technology, business organization, and social change. Reference to this context, however, is often very generalized. For example, in a passage on kitchen appliance design, we read:

> Americans prefer individually powered products in the kitchen, although a single power source with attachments could perform as well Attempts to provide a single power source are applauded as rational but seldom universally accepted This is due both to the consumers impatience with the time it takes to change the attachments and to an affection for things that leads to the proliferation of appliances and tools. (p. 143)

It might all be true. But how do we know of Americans' preferences, impatience, and affections? How do designers make such judgments in their work? We are not directly told. A sneaking suspicion persists that the preference for proliferation is that of manufacturers, marketing, and advertising professionals and that suspicion is indeed fueled in a later chapter:

> The profession that had been established in the 1930s by talented artist-designers was now falling under the control of marketing men who saw design primarily as a means of ensuring profits in an increasingly competitive market. (p. 270)

What emerges is a gulf between the self-image of designers and the context in which they practice. The ideal of "talented artist-designers," simultaneously the key to business success and defenders of the people, motivates many design educators and practitioners. But designers also continually complain about the lack of understanding of design by business management. The reality is that far from being guardians of the public good, American designers have generally functioned as middle-level executants. "Cold" science and "grasping" commerce may be blamed, but designers have no sole franchise on creativity. Scientists and managers (and others) are equally capable of creative work.

The problem is that the scale of investment required for mass production is inimical to creativity and risk. The management techniques to run large businesses and the business schools that teach them emphasize financial analysis and market control—competency rather than creativity. Design, in the full sense, is remarkable by its absence. Its use in most mass-production industry is limited to short-term, superficial changes in the exterior form of products, that is, styling, as a means of stimulating short-term demand. On this, Arthur Pulos comments, "What was reprehensible was 'styling'— endowing a product with superficial and misleading forms and details that abused the consumer's faith" (p. 269). But the phenomenon goes beyond styling as a design choice and needs to be understood in the context of the whole system of mass production and its values.

If designers do represent the consumer whose faith has been abused, what have they done to redress the situation? What ideas have they generated to help them function at high levels in organizations and introduce change? Some, such as Richard Latham and Jay Doblin, have developed concepts of design planning as a strategic tool to ensure effective use of design. Pulos clearly disapproves of such developments, referring to the "unique character of the independent designer" being "replaced by organization men, operational diagrams, statistical analyses, and other substitutes for human instinct and concern" (p. 270). Another dichotomy in design, between methodology and creativity, raises its head.

It is not that Pulos's values are all wrong. He surely expresses a widespread anxiety in seeing in the industrial expansion of the postwar period "a shift from concern for human beings to a callous disregard for the public's well-being" (p. 417). But designers cannot sit in Olympian judgment; they are just as responsible for this as any other discipline. Ralph Caplan, former editor of *Industrial Design* magazine, writes of the 1960s; 'The designer ('the conscience of industry?') appeared to be at best collusive, at worst gratuitously aggressive. A prominent industrial designer with a brewery account once explained, when asked about his relationship to consumers, 'I'm the one who's gotta keep pumpin' that beer down their throats." (Caplan 1982, 48). Papanek (1971) indicted his fellow industrial design professionals as "a dangerous breed" involved in "concocting the tawdry idiocies hawked by advertisers." (p. xxi).

The reality is that designers in countries such as Germany, Italy, and Japan have made the running in creating products that people want to buy, resulting in the erosion of America's manufacturing base. Arthur Pulos tells us little about why in the last three decades, despite the title of his book, U.S. companies have been signally unadventurous in design policy (if indeed they have one) and have generally failed to compete on this vital level. Industrial designers can convert technological potential into commercial products that are accessible, useful, pleasurable, cost-effective, and environmentally friendly—and profitable, too. If they are ineffective, business values must be questioned, but particularist idealism in the design profession may be equally as culpable as cynical exploitation in hampering them. If that is so, *The American Design Adventure* must be seen as part of the problem.

(iii) Imagining Consumers: Design and Innovation from Wedgewood to Corning

by Regina Lee Blaszczyk

In established academic disciplines today researchers have become more and more focused on the minutiae of micro-topics, eschewing larger questions. Design, and specifically its history and theory, has never coalesced into a defined and recognized subject of scholarship, and on a public level, understanding of it is beset by an astonishing combination of ignorance and pretentiousness, as witness the current media absorption with "commodity chic." Attention to larger questions and treatments is therefore not just an option, but a vital necessity.

In this context, Regina Lee Blaszczyk's *Imagining Consumers: Design and Innovation from Wedgwood to Corning* is a significant contribution to a very large topic—understanding how design functions as the vital link between the interests of producers and consumers in a modem capitalist economy. In Great Britain, the history of design has become compartmented and reduced to not-so-splendid isolation, while in North America academic writing in this area has always drawn on a variety of disciplines, providing at best a richness of treatment and insight appropriate to a practice that reaches into all aspects of social and economic life, Blaszczyk describes herself as a historian of American business, technology, and culture, signaling the possibility that she will place design in an appropriately broad context. This is indeed the case.

The bulk of her book is essentially a series of case studies with commentary connecting them to her main theme. Blaszczyk begins with a brief account of the many levels of innovation by Josiah Wedgwood in Staffordshire, and then she presents a cross-section of American companies involved in manufacturing and retailing the products of the home furnishings industry, particularly ceramic and glass, through the nineteenth and into the mid-twentieth century. The thread she finds between the diverse range of companies was an approach to manufacturing that she terms flexible specialization, or flexible batch production, through which the managers of such companies constantly endeavored to keep close to consumers in order to understand them and better satisfy their needs. Her research is very detailed and heavily reliant on corporate archives which have yielded rich material—not just objects, samples, and catalogues, but documentation of decision-making processes, sales organization, design intentions, and market successes and failures. The diversity of these sources makes her detailed accounts of specific sequences of events in the evolution of companies

First published as a review of Regina Lee Blaszczyk, *Imagining consumers: Design and Innovation from Wedgewood to Corning*, 2002–3, pp. 147–9.

convincing, compelling, and occasionally surprising. Examples are accounts of detailed policy development in companies such as Woolworth and Kohler.

An especially valuable aspect of Blaszczyk's account is her avoidance of individualistic stereotypes of "the designer" and how he/she functions in "the design process." Instead, and this mirrors much design work in practice, she appraises the broad spectrum of people other than designers involved in design processes, broadly defined, and she is particularly interested in their role in ascertaining and defining consumer preferences. This was a feature of Josiah Wedgwood's business, with a number of people of different backgrounds acting as the firm's antennae in sensing what would sell in different markets. The bulk of *Imagining Consumers* is devoted to describing how a similar kaleidoscope of abilities also became an integral feature of the more successful American companies in the design field:

> Between 1865 and 1945, fashion intermediaries of various stripes—practical men, shopkeepers, salesmen, retail buyers, materials suppliers, art directors, showroom managers, color experts, home economists, advertising experts, and market researchers—assumed the major responsibility for the way things looked. Rather than impose their tastes, the most accomplished read the marketplace and cooperated with factory managers to design products for a spectrum of audiences (p.12).

Many people and competencies were involved, and high amounts of time and energy were dedicated to understanding potential customers. A specific example was the approach adopted in the late 1890s by Clinton Pierce Case, the first crockery buyer for the F. W. Woolworth retail chain. "On Frank Woolworth's orders," writes Blaszczyk, "people-watching became mandatory among buyers" (p.105). Case roamed the streets of New York, observing people, what they wore and purchased and what attracted them, joining in discussions when strollers commented on shop window displays. He would send samples of new lines to store managers and solicit their opinions, expecting them to have similarly precise knowledge of their localities and consumers' preferences. All this prepared him in huge detail for meetings with manufacturers about what Woolworth was prepared to order. "Consumers, in essence, spoke through the mouths of Woolworth's crockery buyers, the pottery industry's latest fashion intermediaries" (p. 107). Inevitably this leads Blaszczyk to a comparison with modern methods of defining consumer expectations, which can be simultaneously more numerically exact but more distanced from the realities of people's lives. Could the recent demise of the Woolworth chain have been averted if they had sustained this level of awareness of their customers as people and not just statistics?

The kind of companies that Blaszczyk examines were generally omitted from the most influential paradigm of American business development, that established by Alfred D. Chandler Jr., the Harvard Business School historian, who emphasized the dominance of large mass-production companies in American business. Mass production, as it emerged in the early twentieth century, was a highly inflexible system, requiring massive investment in production lines that could take up to six months to rebuild. The system could only function by manufacturing large quantities of identical items, to be sold at low cost. A further feature of mass production was that it required mass advertising, using mass media to create and sustain mass consumption. The immutable logic of the system was that it required control of markets and frequently used unsavory tactics in attempting to coerce consumers into buying what was good for producers, not necessarily for themselves. In that respect, design was used as a blandishment, with stylistic changes functioning as a manipulative tool of fashion to ensure the psychological obsolescence of products and keep the sales charts soaring.

Against that model, Blaszczyk sets an alternative, in which companies did not follow the logic of mass production, but instead established a system grounded in efforts to identify the needs and tastes of consumers accurately, with manufacturing systems that were innately different from the mass-production paradigm, maintaining in contrast a capability for rapidly and flexibly switching product forms and decorations. Design therefore had the role of an intermediary in interpreting the knowledge garnered about people. It was a vital tool in ensuring that what was produced met a specific, identifiable demand.

The recognition of this different business and market model is, I believe, absolutely right. Even today, in the United States and other leading industrial countries, the majority of businesses, around ninety to ninety-five percent belong in the category of small and medium enterprises many of which function in analogous ways. More important, the corrective validity of this model is that it emphasizes a process of dialogue between producers and consumers, rather than one of manipulative indifference. Producers are of necessity preoccupied with questions of profit levels, but in some cases this is not irreconcilable with a broader social concern about the role of their products in society and the lives of their customers. Similarly, consumers are depicted in a different light, not as a passive, malleable mass, but as people—in the household furnishing sector overwhelmingly women—who are credited with an intelligent sense of meaning about what is appropriate for their homes and their lives. Blaszczyk's argument for the validity of flexible manufacturing is finely nuanced. She does not seek to displace the mass-production business model—it was and remains extremely important—but she adds other dimensions to it in order to create a more richly textured account of both design and business. In this effort, she has succeeded exceedingly well.

There is so much in the book to admire that disputing any of its major points should not be seen as disparagement, but rather as an acceptance of its challenges to discussion. For example, another paradigm from which Blaszczyk specifically distances herself is that mainly identified with museums and the antiques trades, in which design is identified with what she variously terms "elite objects", "good taste" and "highbrow culture" (p. 273). Here, I have to admit being less convinced that this is a problem. There is no doubt in my mind that a significant responsibility in part for the distorted public image of design stems from exhibitions and publications focusing on what are indeed rarefied, elite, crafted objects. Setting such objects on pedestals in neutral surroundings inevitably strips away any possibility of understanding them as objects of use in context. Such an approach even encourages detachment among designers themselves, as was evident in a recent exhibition of so-called modern design at the Metropolitan Museum of Art in New York, consisting mostly of objects such as chairs and lamps in which forms were widely manipulated to the point of uselessness.

Considered from the standpoint of business, in which Blaszczyk locates design, this development causes her understandable dismay. What troubles me about the distancing of her text from elite and/or crafted objects, however, is that it thereby ignores an important relationship between them and their context. Even from her declared standpoint as a business historian, up-market products do constitute a market and companies do design and produce for it. Consider the French mercantilist tradition begun under Louis XIV of setting out to dominate such markets with the finest craftsmanship. The legacy of this is that France still has a forty percent share of the world's luxury trades: witness, for example, Hermes. Like it or not in these times of political correctness, there is a complex process recorded throughout history by which styles and fashions have been determined initially by wealthy elites in all societies and have thereafter trickled down to other segments of society. In other words, taste and preferences at the everyday level cannot be isolated from this wider pattern of influences, and may indeed be evidence of social emulation, an aspiration to a better standard of life based on images of how the wealthy live. It is probably only in the last two centuries that a reverse process has become discernible, with, for example, ghetto styles recently percolating upwards into high fashion—as with Louis Vuitton's best-selling "Graffiti Bags."

The mechanisms of emulation were evident in the production of glassware in the nineteenth century, which was characterized in the United States by two major processes. According to Blaszczyk, "Pressed glass represented the quintessential democratic consumer product; cut glass, its antithesis" (p. 26). Yet there surely was not such a simple division. Many pressed-glass forms, which did indeed open up a mass market for glass products, were derived from efforts to replicate the faceted effects of cut glass. The concept of a "democratic consumer product" is also problematic, confusing political and economic behavior. In the last two centuries, more products have clearly been made accessible to greater numbers of people, but this does not reflect a democratic process, since for the most part people have no voice in determining what is offered to them in a market. Even in the house furnishings business, the focus of this book, decisions determining products were taken by producers and intermediaries, not by users. Consumption has nothing to do with democracy. In a democratic ballot, a rich man's vote has no more value than a poor man's. In a market, if you have no money, you have no voice or choice.

Though Blaszczyk's case studies end with Corning glassware in the mid-twentieth century, approaches based on continuous and careful attention to the needs of users are of course still relevant. A process analogous to that adopted by Clinton Pierce Case of Woolworth's is used by ERCO, for example, a medium-sized German company that has become a world leader in architectural lighting systems, with an outstanding range of designs in their catalogue. When representatives of the company travel on business, they are similarly expected to observe developments in shops, museums, theaters, and factories and bring the intelligence back as a basis for future product development. The current pertinence of this modus operandi is, if anything, increasing, with the rapid expansion of flexible manufacturing techniques based on information technology. These are changing the emphasis from mass to niche markets, with a similar imperative for flexible, adaptable solutions oriented in great detail to users.

History has many purposes, but one of the most important is surely its promise of a more enlightened understanding of present and future possibilities. In a time of uncertainty, the one domain of apparent certitude may be the past. It may not repeat itself, but observing behavior in situations analogous to those of our own time can provide invaluable insights. This book is an outstanding example, a timely reminder of the latent power of thinking not in terms of consumption, but of use. Consumption is essentially a concept of exchange, defined in monetary terms. Emphasizing use means acknowledging the ongoing role of designs, on the levels of both practical utility and symbolic meaning, in the lives of people who purchase them. Blaszczyk's volume provides a counterweight to the banality of "commodity chic" with salutary cases and insights about the potential of design for embodying humanistic values in business procedures, a message of relevance far beyond the confines of academe.

References

Caplan, Ralph. *By Design*. New York: St. Martin, 1982.
Desmond, Adrian. *The Politics of Evolution: Morphology, Medicine, and Reform in Radical London* Chicago: University of Chicago Press, 1989.
Papanek, Victor. *Design for the Real World*. London: Thames & Hudson, 1971.

10

The Growth of Industrial Design in Japan

The arrival of Commodore Perry's Black Ships in 1854 marked the end of Japan's self-imposed isolation from the outside world and the point at which a process of modernization began to take place. Under government leadership, the most successful forms of government, administration, defense, and industry were carefully observed, absorbed and then implemented in a distinctly Japanese manner. Although modem Japanese industrial design is largely a phenomenon of the post-World War II period, it was still characterized by this pattern of assimilation.

Classifying Japanese industrial products in terms of their national characteristics is problematic given the pressures of globalization and the ubiquity of products. For these reasons, it is difficult to associate 'Japanese design' with a specific national aesthetic or particular trends in product forms. Nevertheless, design in Japan remains distinctive in terms of processes and values, both of which are heavily influenced by national cultural characteristics. For example, individuality is generally submerged in group identity. Consequently, industrial designers are rarely identified and the origins of products tend to be cloaked in the anonymity of group consensus. Linked to this is the belief that creativity is not only defined by originality, but can also manifest itself in sensitive renditions of past forms—a kind of creative recycling of past ideas. In other words, it is not necessarily what the Japanese design, but how they design it, that is distinctive.

Early industrialization, based on Western models, was primarily preoccupied with developing an industrial infrastructure and military capability. By the early twentieth century, Japan demonstrated technological know-how in such areas as shipbuilding, armaments, and locomotive

Published as "The Growth of Industrial Design in Japan," *Japan 2000: Architecture and Design for the Japanese Public,* John Zukowsky, ed., Art Institute of Chicago, 2001, pp. 83–93. By permission of Art Institute of Chicago.

building. As in other countries, the forms produced by early engineering designers often evinced a strong functional aesthetic. Honed by combat in Manchuria and China in the 1930s, Japanese ships and aircraft performed well against the United States in the early stage of the Pacific war.

The industrial design expertise that existed before World War II derived from European artistic or craft-based concepts, and was centered on the Industrial Arts Institute of Tokyo, a promotional body founded in 1928. The main emphasis was on adapting craft practices to serial production in traditional product categories, such as furniture, ceramics, and packaging. The consumer goods industry also emerged during this period, though the products were generally copied from Western models.

Defeat in World War II brought occupation by U. S. troops and enormous change, also in industrial design. For Atsuko Kamo-shida, later president of the Japan Industrial Designers' Association, the origins of Japanese industrial design lie in the powerful influence of the American life-style:

> Industrial design was to be seen in all the appliances and facilities at the service of US military personnel and their dependents. Although the concept was not part of the Japanese vocabulary yet, US life style was held in high esteem and was considered as being clean, efficient, and one that afforded comfort and was within the reach of anyone living within a democratic society.[1]

At the time, such a life-style was only an aspiration. Japan's industrial facilities lay largely in ruins but, again, the government took the initiative, by assigning the Ministry of International Trade and Industry (MITI) the task of devising plans for reconstruction and economic expansion based on exports. Its early policies had two main planks: introducing the latest foreign technology and protecting domestic industry while it was being rebuilt. The home market was viewed as a developmental springboard for exports.

Realizing that industrial design had emerged in America between the wars as a field concerned with the marketability of manufactured products, MITI began vigorously to promote it. An advisory group, invited from the Art Center College of Design in Pasadena in 1956, recommended improving design standards in Japanese products and packaging, encouraged the development of design education, and urged long-term goals in developing markets for new products.[2] It was deeply ironic, of course, that just as the example of American design was playing a seminal role in stimulating Japanese design, new methods of financial control and marketing emerging from business schools were already displacing design in domestic American business strategy.

The dilemma for MITI in its advocacy of design, however, was a dire shortage of practitioners. It therefore set out to create a cadre of qualified designers by sending talented young men overseas to be trained. In 1955–56, small groups were sent to the United States, to the Art Center College of Design, the Pratt Institute in New York, the Institute of Design at the Illinois Institute of Technology in Chicago, and to European schools as well. The need was urgent, so by special arrangement the customary four-year undergraduate courses were compressed into one year. The students faced acute pressures and enormous cultural differences.[3] Nevertheless, they learned rapidly and, on returning to Japan, were sent by MITI on tours around the country to speak about their experiences. Moreover, leading foreign designers were invited to Japan so that their experience and knowledge could be tapped.

Although it generally refrains from direct action, MITI has taken some decisive initiatives. In 1957, "to promote design activities to produce commodities of legitimate originality,"[4] i.e., original Japanese designs, and also to stimulate public awareness, "The Good Design Products Selection System," popularly known as the "G-Mark" competition, which is still held today, was established. Appointed judges select from between 1,000 and 1,200 products each year. Awards are given for the best product of a given category in each field and one Grand Prize is presented to the overall winner. The award criteria are much broader than those of most other competitions, and emphasize not only appearance, but also function, safety, value or cost, and after-sales service. Consequently, the award has become a respected guarantee of product quality in the Japanese market. Originally restricted to domestic goods, the competition was opened to foreign products in 1984.

To organize the competition, and provide for design promotion on a regular basis, the Japan Industrial Design Promotion Organization (JIDPO), a branch of MITI, was established and has subsequently organized a wide range of national and international design events. Further, to raise the profile of Japanese export products and discourage copying, the "Export Commodities Design Law" of 1959 gave MITI the power to control exports "from Japan in terms of the industrial property rights ... both domestic and international..."[5]

No laws or regulations required companies to employ designers, but the influence of innumerable, informal contacts between bureaucrats and businessmen through which ideas are channeled in Japan cannot be underestimated, and by the mid-1950s, many large Japanese companies had begun to establish design departments. While some new designers returning from overseas were so employed, others set up independent consultancies, such as Kenji Ekuan, who established GK Associates, and Takuo Hirano, who set up Hirano & Associates, which were leading organizations in creating awareness and acceptance of design in the business community. Soon, through new educational courses and on-the-job training, the number of qualified designers began to grow. MITI has continued over the years to view design as a strategic resource for Japan's economy, with ongoing policy reviews providing a framework of ideas and responses to new developments.

Not all initiatives were the result of government action, however, and already in the 1950s the first signs of typical Japanese approaches to product development were evident in the industrial sector, into which designers were hastily integrated. In areas of early industrial resurgence, such as motorcycles, consumer electrical goods, and photographic and optical equipment, a pattern emerged: variations on product themes were rapidly produced by means of sophisticated manufacturing techniques. Constant, incremental improvement, instead of radical solutions, were encouraged. This was not only a means of reducing risk; cumulatively, it represented a formidable competitive strategy.

It took time for the effects of these developments to become evident to the outside world, but the 1964 Olympic Games in Tokyo clearly signaled a change in perceptions of Japan, with advertising and television programs about the country featuring dramatic images of high-speed "bullet-trains" on the first Shin-kansen line between Tokyo and Osaka, opened in 1963 (Figs. 1, 2). These images must have astonished those who still thought that Japanese industry produced only cheap imitations.

Two main factors have marked the subsequent evolution of Japanese industrial design: firstly, the marketing strategies and policies used to implement design in business operations; secondly, designers' views about their trade and its relative merits.

The following are the salient characteristics of Japanese businesses use of design:

> —strong top-management support for the design department in major companies a survey published in the journal *Nikkei Design* in 1989 revealed that 80 percent of top executives affirmed the importance of design;

> —collaboration between designers, engineers, and marketers as flexible development teams involved in both long-term product planning and short-term product development;

> —use of off-the-shelf components rather than having everything designed anew this reduces costs and speeds up development, enabling designers to concentrate on the overall function of the products;

> —a continuous flow of information between manufacturers and suppliers, enabling the latter to become involved in the design process, and thereby further reducing costs and development time;

> —long-term investments in new technology and manufacturing and their continual development;

> —continual investment in design education the japan industrial designers' association was founded in 1952 with twenty-five members, by 1992, the number of industrial design practitioners had reached 21,000.

The strategies for using design to penetrate both domestic and foreign markets also follow typical patterns, whether the products are automobiles, pocket radios, or ball bearings. From an initial market position, expansion follows four basic strategies, singly or in combination, in an effort to increase market share. Each strategy requires different design attributes.

—*Product covering* is essentially a process of duplicating what is already on the market with minor variations, requiring little more than superficial changes to the product's form and the packaging.

—*Product churning*, especially in consumer electronic products, is a uniquely Japanese approach. In contrast to "rifle-shot" product development in other countries, where efforts focus at an early stage on one specific concept, product churning employs a "shotgun" approach, with designers in parallel teams developing numerous variations of product concepts. The results are then marketed and the public is left to decide which is more appropriate. The central Tokyo district of Akihabara—with its densely packed retail stores in an area of a few blocks accounting for some 10 percent of Japan's annual sales of consumer electronic devices—is where this outpouring of products is put to the test. A typical example is a range of some fifty vacuum cleaners offered by a single company at one time. Once a market preference becomes clear, unsuccessful variants are eliminated, and production is increased for national distribution and, later, for export. Product covering and product churning both require a substantial number of designers, although not necessarily highly skilled, and account for the large size of some corporate design departments.

There are occasions when product churning coupled with the flexibility to respond quickly can be a formidable competitive weapon. In a famous case, Yamaha decided to challenge Honda's lead in the domestic motorcycle market at a time when it was already flooded. To counter this move Honda, which like Yamaha normally produced about twenty-seven new models a year, promptly sent its car designers to the motorcycle division, and in 1982 produced forty-five new designs, almost one a week, most targeted at Yamaha's strongest market areas. Yamaha suffered losses that year estimated at some $150 million.[6]

The *"inch-up"* approach, in contrast, is more sharply focused, with design assuming a strategic role in breaking into higher levels of the market, where quality, distinctive forms, and exceptional service are fundamental requirements. Toyota, for example, entered international markets with small cars developed for Japanese conditions. Gradually, their models penetrated higher-value sectors, a process culminating in the "Lexus" range, which, following its introduction into the American market in 1989, immediately became a best-seller. A key to the success of Lexus was its systemic design approach, with a meticulous design not only of the automobile itself, but also of every visible aspect of the showrooms, sales offices, and service centers.

If Japanese designers have a particular forte, however, it is in *"scale-down"* strategies, with which they have continually redefined markets. An early example is the Honda "Supercub" of 1958—still in production today—which reduced motorcycles from the powerful machines that leather-clad males bestrode to a lightweight, small-engined, step-through model, offering inexpensive transportation to people of either sex in regular clothing. The tiny calculators of today derive from a Sharp "desk-top," solid-state calculator, weighing 55 pounds and introduced in 1965. Ten years later, Sony introduced the first VCR for consumer markets, after spending eighteen years developing them from broadcasting equipment, and the famous "Walkman," a miniaturized tapeplayer for portable use. In the early 1980s, Canon similarly scaled-down photocopiers from models affordable only to large businesses, to tabletop models appropriate to small businesses and home use.

It is not only the well-known giant corporations that employ this strategy. In the last four years, a medium-sized firm, Tanita Corporation, which earned its reputation manufacturing bathroom scales, has extended its product line by reducing the size and cost of body-fat analyzers from professional models costing $5,000 to consumer models priced at $200. The examples are innumerable, but the result of such ingenuity has been a profusion of products that has continually raised customers' expectations of design and quality.

At the same time, designers themselves have evolved new ideas about their role. Three major trends are discernible: the first concerns expanded ideas on design's role in society as exemplified in an MITI policy review of 1988, formulated by heads of design organizations and leading designers. Four key points were emphasized:

—going beyond material levels and contributing substantially to Japan's future quality of life;

—adapting to the latest information technology which introduces new opportunities in industry and in society and makes new demands on design;

—enhancing human and technical potential by combining hard-and software to meet new needs, as inherent, for example, in the changing demographic profile of Japan, with the proportion of elderly people growing rapidly;

—promoting the understanding of design at all levels if its potential contribution to society is to be realized.[7]

Both pragmatic and idealistic, the report combines economic with technological factors, and envisions design redefining Japan's cultural identity in the modern world.

A second trend is the emergence of multi-disciplinary consulting groups offering a wide range of design and planning services. They do not simply execute corporate briefs or design single products, but instead play a long-term strategic role in determining the future of a corporation, its products, services, and systems. An example is the relationship between Hirano & Associates and the CKD Corporation, a manufacturer of packaging machinery. Over a period of thirty years, the firm has emerged from being dependent on overseas licenses to being a world leader in the industry, based on a design policy that shapes every single aspect of corporate activities.

Thirdly, in sharp contrast, is the phenomenon of "star" designers, who project the image of innovative, lateral thinkers. They are independent trendsetters seeking to transcend the boundaries of product concepts and often cultivate a rebel image—and in the context of Japanese culture they are indeed rebels. One such designer, Naoki Sakai, explains: "My product is imagination, dreams, fantasies, desires... I make human desires."[8] Sakai does not always design products in detail, sometimes suggesting key images and features for others to execute, as in the Nissan "Pao" of 1988. Manufactured only for the Japanese market, this automobile was an example of so-called "retro-design," evoking the forms of the 1950s, and sparked an international trend in creating product forms derived from and recalling designs of the past.

The work of such designers is not strategic but open-ended, exploratory, and symbolic in nature, and the scale on which it has been manifested is yet another distinctive Japanese approach to design. Groups have also been established by major corporations to fulfill a similar function of generating new concepts, as with the "outside" group set up by Nissan in 1991 in Tokyo "to connect more closely user and maker,"[9] or Sony's design laboratory, which currently employs a staff of forty.[10]

Underlying all these developments, however, is the recurrent theme of how to humanize technology, as summed up by architect and designer Masayuki Kurokawa: "The next era is about the relation between humans and objects. Designers have to make things humans can love and that fit in with their life-style."[11]

Few people in the world remain unaffected by the shift in Japan from producing imitation goods to generating technically superior, well-designed products. In the process, Japan's economic standing in the world and its own standard of living have changed dramatically.

Yet, although the achievements of Japanese designers are substantial, a perceptible crisis of confidence among them has become evident in recent times. As in other areas of Japanese life, this stems from the collapse of the "bubble" economy in 1992, largely owing to speculative policies by major financial institutions, that sent shock waves through Japanese society. The annual growth rate of design services of nearly 9 percent prior to 1992 has fallen drastically, resulting in serious cutbacks and some design consultancies going bankrupt. Widespread soul-searching is evident on several levels. There are efforts to develop sophisticated design methodologies capable of handling the complexities of modern technology. In commercial contexts, there are problems with foreign competition in today's global market. Conversely, there is the desire to move beyond the uniformity of global products and to evolve forms truly expressive of Japanese culture and tradition. Another persistent note calls for more "emotional" approaches to design, free of commercial pressures.

The future evolution of Japanese industrial design seems likely to follow multiple paths, but it is precisely the vigor and diversity of debate and the new roles they envisage for themselves in Japanese society that is perhaps the best evidence of the distance Japanese designers have traveled since the 1950s. Design, however, is innately focused on the future and, if current aspirations to humanize technology are realized, Japanese designers could exceed their past achievements and make an even greater contribution to the lives of people across the globe.

Notes

1 Atsuko Kamoshida, "Foreword," in *Industrial Design Workshop: The Creative Process Behind Product Design.* Tokyo, 1993, p. 5.

2 E. A. Adams, George A. Jergenson, and John D. Coleman, *The Future of Japanese Industrial Design.* Los Angeles, 1957; repr. Pasadena, 1995.

3 For insight into the experience of a member belonging to these first groups, who later became one of Japan's most prominent designers, see Takuo Hirano, "The Development of Modern Japanese Design: A Personal Account," *Design Issues,* vol. 7, no. 2 (Spring 1991), p. 53.

4 *Good Design Products 1990.* Tokyo, 1990, p. 4.

5 Ibid.

6 Charles Smith, "Why Yamaha Was Forced to Re-Trench," *Financial Times,* Nov. 16, 1983, p. 5.

7 *Design Policy for the 1990s.* Tokyo, 1988.

8 S. Azbybrown, "The Shape of Things: Naoki Sakai Sees Himself as a Designer of Dreams, A Fulfiller of Fantasies," in *Winds,* July 1989, p. 54.

9 Leonard Koren, "Corporate Design Strategy: Nissan's New 'Outside' Group," in *Japan Design Close-Up,* no. 1 March/April 1991, p. 2.

10 Frank Gibney, Jr., and Sebastian Moffett, "Sony's Vision Factory," in *Time Digital* March/April 1997, p. 53.

11 Ibid., p. 54.

(C)
Design in Germany
1870–1945

11

The Role of Government Policy on German Design 1870–1918

It is entirely typical of John Heskett's approach to the history of designing that the longest chapter in his book on German design 1870–1918 should not be on individual designers but on the influence of government policies across the period. The chapter below discusses the attempts of the German Government to influence or encourage design in four main areas: demonstratively, through the support of, especially international, exhibitions of German design; pedagogically, through support for design education—and here Heskett shows just how advanced were some elements of education for design in Germany before the Bauhaus; ideologically and culturally, though support for the crafts and traditional values; and finally as infrastructure, with the development of government support for considerable involvement by professional designers in areas ranging from the interiors of naval as well as commercial shipping to the new Berlin urban and suburban railways.

The role of government

The tradition of government inherited by the Reich, indeed the social cohesiveness of Germany, hinged upon the subordination of individuality (which is not necessarily synonymous with its repression) to the community as represented by the state. The constitutional structure of the state was a hierarchical pyramid with power concentrated at the apex, ministers being ultimately responsible to the Emperor rather than the elected parliament,

First published as "The Role of Government Policy on German Design 1870-1918," in *German Design 1870–1918*, Trefoil Books, London, 1996, pp. 57–77.

the Reichstag. Policy thus devolved through a highly-trained and efficient bureaucracy rather than the elected representatives, with the state intervening widely in activities it wished to promote or saw in its interests. The result was not dictatorship, but rather a heavy-handed, autocratic paternalism, in which conformity was expected and generally conceded.

Under such a system, the patronage the Reich government and public bodies at all levels exercised was considerable, covering such forms as buildings, monuments, currency and postage stamps, uniforms and street furniture. Indirectly, the taste of the Emperor and court filtered down through the channels of government agencies, manifesting itself generally in a ponderous, highly-decorated symbolism drawing heavily on German mythology and a mélange of historical forms.

The aesthetic predilections of the theatrical Emperor Wilhelm II can be easily derided, but it would be a mistake to underestimate the influence of his authority, given the power structure of which he was head.

Senior appointments to the major art institutions of the capital were subject to his approval and the appointment of Wilhelm von Bode as General Director of Berlin's Museums in 1906 owed as much to his friendship with the Emperor as to his undoubted abilities. The main interest of the Emperor was in archaeology, where his patronage was generally enlightened and had a beneficent effect. He was completely intolerant of modern art, however, and the negative side of his authority became apparent in 1909, when Hugo Tschudi resigned his directorship of the National Gallery after the Emperor had vetoed the purchase of French Impressionist paintings.

The Emperor's attitudes were clearly expressed in a speech at the ceremonial opening in 1901 of the Siegesallee, a promenade in Berlin's Tiergarten lined with thirty huge statues of historical figures, a gift from the Emperor to the city. In his address, he equated art with the Ideal, a body of unchanging, eternal values, and castigated any concept of artistic freedom which did not conform to this as a sin against the nation. On the social role of art, he stated: '. . . art should help to educate a nation. . . The great ideals have become the heritage of us, the German nation, while other nations have lost them in greater or lesser degree. Only the German nation is left to follow the vocation of protecting, cherishing and propagating these great ideals, and one of these ideals is that we should give the working, the laborious classes, the opportunity to raise themselves up to what is beautiful and to work their way out of and above their other thoughts.'[1] For Wilhelm II, art was a social narcotic, his Ideal a sentimental confection of decorative embellishment glorifying his regime, bearing little relationship to the realities of the society he ruled. Indeed, perhaps the greatest task then facing the cultural reformers was to educate their monarch.

Fortunately for Germany, however, there were officials at various levels who were more enlightened than their Emperor. With the degree of power and patronage available to public bodies, and in a climate of opinion where visual form was of important representational significance, it could be possible for practitioners to be given considerable scope for innovative development. The Reich government, for example, provided a 'Standing Exhibition Commission for German Industry' under the Ministry of the Interior, which included representatives from the Foreign Ministry, the Prussian Ministries of Commerce and Education, and other interested parties. This was responsible for the presentation of official national exhibits at major international exhibitions, the normal method being to appoint a state official as commissioner responsible for the task, and provided direct funding. Subsidies were also available for exhibitions where a direct state involvement was inappropriate. With Germany's emergence as a major political and industrial power, such events were given high priority in the first decade of the century, as a means of impressing the world outside with the nation's strength and achievement, though in the consciousness of officials, this was not necessarily best expressed by new initiatives in architecture and applied art.

If idealism for renewal and change gained a new impulse in 1900, the major event of that year in architecture and design, the World Exposition in Paris, demonstrated that the legacy of the past was not easily jettisoned with a change of calendar. Paris was a special challenge, providing an opportunity to impress the arch-enemy in their own capital. Despite military defeat, the French cultural domination of Europe remained undisputed, a status generally acknowledged in German publications, though usually prefacing a hope of their country soon toppling the French from that supremacy. Some German reporting of the Paris Exposition displayed a distinctly *parvenu* quality in its mixture of arrogance and inferiority: stridently asserting their own power and pride, yet overawed by the assurance of French style and taste, and avidly reporting any compliments on their exhibits culled from the French press.

To design the German pavilion, two established architects were appointed, Karl Hoffacker of Berlin for the structure and Emanuel Seidl of Munich for the ceremonial room. Hoffacker's entrance court was large, flamboyant and intended to impress, essentially a piece of official bombast. Seidl had designed the pavilion for the 1888 *Kunstgewerbe* exhibition in Munich, and his ceremonial rooms showed little development from that earlier event. The decor was lush, with heavy, decorative furniture of obscure stylistic origins and grandiose proportions.

In its more positive aspects, the exhibition was the first major international venture for the *Vereinigte Werkstatten* of Munich. Bruno Paul designed a 'Hunting Room' with furniture in elm and wall-panelling in like materials, the latter surmounted by a marquetry frieze. It was a combination of rectangular and curvilinear forms, of richness and simplicity, the only jarring note being the vehement curves of the chairs which disturbed the general restraint. In contrast, Bernhard Pankok's interior was a more full-blooded and eccentric example of curvilinear *Jugendstil* in walnut and cherry. Its sweeping lines, rich materials and of carved ornament created a restless effect. This latter quality was also apparent in Richard Riemerschmid's 'Room of an Art Lover,' which had a frieze and ceiling on which the whiplash patterns widely characteristic of *Art Nouveau* were so combined and convoluted as to take on almost frenzied proportions. The furnishings and fittings were by several designers and whilst individual pieces were attractive, the overall effect was heavy, lacking in harmony.

The extent of progress in Germany was apparent from the international interest aroused by the German exhibits. A review by the French critic, Gabriel Mourey, opened by according 'Praise without reserve' for the honesty and excellent ideas 'which almost without exception reveal a truly Germanic sense of decorative art.' Mourey's somewhat stereotyped conception of the 'truly Germanic' had a sting in the tail, however, as subsequently became clear: 'Everything too -which is equally remarkable and commendable—is designedly modern in tendency, that is to say, as modern as it is possible to be, in regard to art, in Germany.' The reason given for this reservation, which contradicted his opening praise, was the power of the past over the German imagination. 'The Teuton has a thorough knowledge of his craft, his technical skill is unlimited, but he lacks freshness of inspiration; . . . Every production of art throughout the world, from the earliest times, is known to the Germans, and remembered too, for they assimilate easily, and have great receptive qualities. But how rare it is to find in their work a really novel aspect of things, anything showing that it has sprung spontaneously from the heart and the hand, from the very innermost being of the artist or the craftsman.'

Of the exhibits on which Mourey commented in detail, Bruno Paul's 'Hunting Room' was adjudged 'the best, because it is the most simple and the most harmonious, production . . .' and Max Lduger's ceramic work was also considered successful. Bernhard Pankok's room was 'somewhat sombre,' an impression reinforced by that of Richard Riemerschmid's room where a 'sense of depression' was generated: 'the style is gloomy and austere—almost sepulchral.' In contrast great enthusiasm was expressed for the work of the Darmstadt colony, where 'everything is bright and joyous, full of happy fancy and true elegance.'[2] Many of Mourey's detailed comments were apposite and justified, but in his general observations and conclusions he demonstrated that nationalist prejudice and bias were not the sole perquisites of German critics.

Although, as Paris clearly demonstrated, the old guard of academic practitioners was still to be reckoned with, a dramatic contrast was evident in the next important event outside Germany. The International Exhibition of Applied Art in Turin of 1902 was organized by several applied art organizations, though with government subsidy, through a committee chaired by Hans von Berlepsch, who was also responsible for the exhibition building. Peter Behrens' entrance hall, commissioned by the Hamburg Museum of Applied Art, aroused considerable comment. It was a total concept, spacious yet intimate in scale, a composition of restrained curvilinear forms. The detailed execution was by a group of Hamburg's leading craftsmen, utilizing some unusual materials, aluminium, leather and cane. Decorative effect was achieved by highlighting structures rather than applying extraneous effects, and a profusion of hanging plants provided a soft counterpoint to the man-made forms. With hindsight, it can be seen as one of the final expressions of *Jugendstil* by Behrens, who even then was exploring new directions. In its time and context, however, it appeared strikingly innovative, earning widespread approval, with one critic, Georg Fuchs, suggesting it was perhaps the first synthesis of Germany's lines of inner and outer power. In an article remarkable for its ecstatic chauvinism and breath-takingly florid prose, he designated it 'The House of Might and Beauty,' and proclaimed: "Enter stranger, here the German Reich holds sway; see with joyful heart of what it is capable!"—A sentence of this kind should be carved over the entrance-arch. For what the silent voices make known in this hall, is might, the might of the Reich of Wilhelm II, ready, prepared and determined, equally entitled, equally endowed amongst the world powers to assert its place in the new division of the globe, which the destiny of nations has declared as its immutable decree.'[3]

Behrens also designed a library-room commissioned by Alexander Koch, but generally the greatest praise was for three rooms by Olbricht, *The Studio* considering him 'almost a classic master.'[4] Apart from the Darmstadt influence, however, artists from other centres and firms associated with the applied art movement also exhibited, for example, Karl Gross, Wilhelm Kreis and the Kleinhempels from Dresden; almost inevitably, the *Vereinigte Werkstatten;* Kayser, and Villeroy & Boch, amongst many others. As a whole it was very well received and secured further international recognition for the scale and significance of developments in Germany.

The momentum was further maintained two years on, in 1904, at the St Louis Exposition in the USA, this time organized by state commissioners. Maude Oliver reported in *The Studio,* 'according to the verdict of their best critics, the German work seen at Turin, which had previously been unprecedented, was mediocre as compared with the St Louis showing, both in the matter of excellence and of effect.' She was obviously impressed herself, to judge by the number of superlatives in her article, commenting on the general impression: 'The beautiful and the useful are so united in sentiment and in substance, as to yield an equilibrium of repose.'[5]

Alexander Koch was so excited by the positive reaction that an article in *Deutsche Kunst und Dekoraten* was hurriedly advanced a month, and readers could hardly have been disappointed by it. The report, by Hermann Muthesius, said the German exhibits put those of other lands into the shade. 'Many of its achievements are so pure and stand on such an inassailable artistic height, that even the enemies of everything modern must lower their sails.' That mixture of metaphors was followed by the assertion: 'Germany has achieved a total indisputable applied art victory. Indeed, the German applied art presentation must necessarily arouse the idea in every visitor, that today the centre of applied art development lies in Germany, perhaps in the same measure, as it lay in France from the time of Louis XIV onward.'[6]

The array of talent represented in the German applied art section was most certainly impressive, a roll call of the best talent in the country, with all the familiar names and organizations represented, and what was particularly important, there was strength in depth, with many artists who were less familiar to an international audience making a considerable impact, such as Adalbert Niemayer and Karl Bertsch of the *Munchner Werkstatten fur Wohnungseinrichtungen,* which they had founded in 1902; Anton Huber of Berlin, whose dining room was thought by Maude Oliver to be 'particularly pleasing;' and a group from Magdeburg led by Albin Muller who presented a room, of which Theodor Volbehr commented: 'The content, moulded in such taut, clear, logical forms, is pronouncedly German. Not only because in it German materials have everywhere been utilized, but because everything' is created with an intimate sense for the still poetry of the home.'[7] Also, for the first time, the exhibition commission saw fit to allocate a room to the Verein *der Kunstlerinnen und Kunstfreundinnen* (Association of Women Artists and Art Lovers), which was of a high standard, though generally felt to be suffering from an attempt to include the diverse work of too many contributors. Across the whole range exhibited, there were fewer signs of the influence of *Jugendstil,* the prevailing note being of clearly articulated forms, emphasizing the quality of materials in a subtle and harmonious manner.

The St Louis Exposition was undoubtedly a crucial event for the reform movement, which had there gained representation under state auspices on such a large scale and had justified it with an outstanding success. Above all, from that time forward, a new note of confidence became apparent that encouraged further effort and achievement.

There were many other similar international events in subsequent years, but none had quite the impact of St Louis.

If government support for international exhibitions had paid off handsomely, there were also considerable advances under the aegis of the various state governments, particularly in education. In Prussia, for example, considerable influence was exercised by Hermann Muthesius.

An architect by training, Muthesius had visited Japan as a student, after which he joined the Prussian Civil Service. In 1896 he was posted to the German Embassy in London as architectural attache, to observe trends in British architecture and design relevant to German developments. The suggestion for such an appointment apparently stemmed from the Emperor, and was a clear indication of the importance attached to art and design in the national image. During his time in London, Muthesius became enthused by the Arts and Crafts movement, cultivating close relationships with many leading practitioners. In addition to official reports, a wider public was informed of his impressions through books and frequent articles. Returning to Germany in 1903 he was appointed to the Prussian Ministry of Trade and

Commerce with responsibility for art education and embarked on reform based on his observations of English practice.

Shortly after his appointment, Muthesius was the responsible official behind a ministerial decree which introduced workshop training in the crafts into Prussian schools of applied art. It was intended 'to emphatically give the student an awareness of the necessary relationship between raw materials and form and to educate him to develop his design more objectively, more economically and more functionally. Through engagement with materials the student will further eliminate misguided concepts, such as that the production of superficially pleasing drawings would be a worthwhile purpose, without concern for whether they paid adequate attention to the materials and its qualities. Also purely artistically, the workshops can only enable valuable stimulation, which instead of superficial accepted forms, is founded on the insight into constructional possibilities *(Gestaltungs-Moglichkeiten)* won through their own activity.'[8] The intention, therefore, was to end the emphasis on drawing detached from an understanding of materials, and the initiative was intended to be valid both for crafts and industry. It was seen by one commentator, at least, as a precondition for closer links between art and industry to the benefit of both: 'With the current application of new materials and taking into account the chemical and physical knowledge of our age, such a unification of theory and practice is essential to artistic and economic progress.'[9]

Muthesius used his patronage in appointments to directorships of schools to further this policy. In this and other activities he exemplified the considerable influence civil servants were capable of exercising in Germany. One of the first appointments in 1903, was of Peter Behrens as director of the Dusseldorf school, where he introduced sweeping reforms. His first programme stated: 'The Applied Arts School pursues the aim of training qualified workers for the requirements of applied arts and art industry and to have a generally stimulating and supportive influence on domestic applied art. This will be achieved through systematic education of the students to good taste and to a feeling for the organic in structure and arrangement, through instruction of the student in graphic and plastic representation, through close connection with the crafts and research into the means of construction and structure of materials, through education to artistic self-sufficiency and independence.'[10] The Vorschule (Preliminary School) of two years duration was the foundation of his teaching programme, in which general courses, nature studies and free-drawing were combined with technical construction exercises, technical drawing, letter-forms and workshop instruction. Five professional classes: architecture, sculpture, surface and graphic art, decorative painting and engraving, were subsequently available. These were all workshop based, to give a command of materials and technique.

Also in 1903, Hans Poelzig was appointed Director of the Royal School of Arts and Crafts at Breslau, though by the Prussian Ministry of Education under whose competence the school lay. There, he developed a curriculum emphasizing craft education as not simply a familiarization with technique but as an instrument for developing ethical values in students.

In 1907, at the instigation of Wilhelm von Bode, director of the Berlin Museum, Bruno Paul was invited to head the school attached to it. The need, according to Bode, was for someone to bring clear leadership to the institution. 'Our choice fell on Paul who had already mostly laid aside the bad habits of the *Jugendsfil* and appeared to us to most originally link-up with older models.'[11] Bode feared the Emperor would veto the appointment, for Paul had earlier contributed many drawings to *Simplicissimus,* often satirizing the monarch and his government, but it was, despite that, approved.

Paul, too, firmly believed in the workshop tradition of instruction and sought to reestablish its relevance. He introduced a dual system of instruction in basic courses, with *Werkmeister* (foremen) responsible for the craft side, alongside technically trained teachers responsible for artistic training. After passing a test, students were eligible for admission to a subject class, one of a large range of specialisms under a Professor. There, the work demands were increased but more was left to students' own initiative. Specially gifted students could later become assistants for up to six years, giving them an opportunity to develop their own work and earn a living, whilst the school had the stimulus of fresh, youthful ideas.

Another appointment of great significance, this time in Saxony, was of Henry van der Velde to Weimar. He was initially invited in 1902 by the Grand Duke of Saxe-Weimar to act as 'artistic counsellor charged with restoring the aesthetic level of all the craft and industrial production of the region.' That wording was deceptive; in fact his role was to help the crafts and small producers in the struggle to survive the competition of big industrial units. At Weimar, he initiated an 'Applied Arts Seminar' for young workers in employment. The concept was for students or apprentices to bring materials for a task of current relevance from their workplace, specifically commissioned by their master craftsman. Under the guidance of teachers at the seminar they would work towards a finished model to be taken back to the workplace and put into production. It was therefore intended to have an applied research function of immediate relevance and benefit to small producers. Van der Velde hoped the reliance on them for materials and tasks would eliminate the need for separate research workshops, and would help overcome any mistrust of the seminar as a threat. At the same time, work was underway on buildings for a Grand Ducal School of Applied Arts, to van der Velde's designs, which opened in 1906, with himself as principal. In the next few years he committed considerable energy to establishing contacts and good relationships with local small industry, for whom the courses at the school were intended, though with only limited success.

Thus in the first decade of the new century a significant challenge to the traditions of formal academic instruction emerged in Germany with widespread official support. Supporters of the old system could, however, also point to its successes. In 1909, an exhibition was held to celebrate the

45th anniversary of the Munich School of Applied Art. To comprehend this event, *The Studio* wrote, it must be borne in mind that it was organized 'by a single city with a population of little more than half a million.'[12] An article on French design in this period records a similar comment from *Le Figaro*, 'Here is a city of 500,000 inhabitants that, with its own resources, organizes a strictly local exhibition and manages to fill six large halls and four hundred rooms with the products of its own activity alone. I look in vain for another city where a work of such magnitude could have been produced.'[13] Another French visitor confessed his amazement at the progress evident in Munich. 'All these observations caused our surprise, but this was transformed into stupefaction when we saw the work exhibited by the Munich professional schools, from the elementary to the advanced level... As for the objects exhibited by the students of the College of Decorative Arts, they would be worthy of inclusion in our museums!'[14] Such praise from a Frenchman must have been music to the ears of any German who might have read it, but it was a serious indication of how fast Germany was progressing and of the contribution made by the education system at all levels.

The number of different agencies at all levels of government, and local and regional variations make it difficult to generalize about the influence of such bodies. They could just as easily champion conservative or restora-tionist values. In 1901, Karl Schmidt was involved with the *Verein fur sachsische Volkskunde* (Society for Saxon Folklore), which persuaded the Royal Saxon Ministry of the Interior to cooperate in a joint venture to encourage an awareness of traditional values and the protection of the environment. The Ministry directed all heads of architectural, applied art and technical schools to make pupils aware of local and traditional forms and to collect sketches of valuable examples to be shown in a public exhibition. Schmidt wrote of this exercise: 'We still stand under the influence of the speech given in Bonn by the Emperor, in which he—finding the most fortunate expression for the inner feelings of our nation—referred to the necessity of our development in a national German sense. And indeed architecture, as the most fundamental of all arts, requires such a development, such a requirement of the sense of German uniqueness, if the last remnant of German uniqueness and with it all that which is of value and irreplaceable in our inner and national life is not to be wholly lost. Should our Germany remain in the possession of the Germanic race, so it also needs in our architecture the resumption and more powerful emphasis of German nature. The understanding for this can, however, only be awakened, preserved and empowered if the works of our forebears find more appreciation, if everything foreign is held distant from the crystallization process and simply, or rather predominantly, the national element is emphasized.'[15] Such views explain why Schmidt later became a founder-member and leading activist in the Saxon *Heimatschutz*.

The Royal Saxon Ministry of the Interior also became involved in other, related, activities to help the crafts, for instance, commissioning an investigation and calling a conference in 1906 to inquire into whether traditional crafts were being seriously disadvantaged by new art tendencies. The result was recommendations to restrict the exhibition of novelties, and discussions between craft organizations and the Leipzig Museum of Applied Art and its *Kunstgewerbeverein* to effect positive initiatives.[16]

A further aspect of government influence was the possibility of exercising direct patronage through purchases and public commissions. The earliest government agency to bestow its patronage on the new applied art was, somewhat surprisingly, the Imperial German Navy. In an article published in 1907, Wilhelm Scholermann described a visit to the armoured cruiser *Furst Bismarck*, some eight years earlier, recalling the clash between exterior and interior design. In 1905 he wrote, invited on a short voyage in a torpedo-boat, this impression was revived. Of the outer lines and the mechanisms: 'Certainly there lay in them a new beauty.' In contrast, however, the officers' quarters, in late Renaissance and early Baroque style, stood 'in contradiction to the spirit and ideas of the present . . . Old and new complement each other quite well sometimes. But not bad stylistic imitation with the living spirit of modern technology.' Scholermann was of the opinion that artists needed to learn from engineers, many of whom had an instinct for form and style.[17]

These views were a reiteration of ideas widespread at this time, and it seems curious that Scholermann was unaware of recent events. In 1903, Karl Schmidt decided the *Dresdener Werkstatten* ought to become involved in producing ships-fittings and visited Hamburg and Kiel to explore the possibilities of business. Interestingly, his conservationist convictions did not in any respect conflict with his highly successful entrepreneurial career. According to his own account, he managed to get an interview in Kiel with a shipyard director, Dr Rossfeld, who on brusquely demanding Schmidt's purpose, was asked to listen to the latter for three minutes. The reply was an abrupt affirmative. Said Schmidt: 'If you build ships, you take the best engineers and constructors, and that is right. If you fit out ships, you take any kind of furnishings, and that is not right.' Rossfeld became interested and was persuaded to allow Richard Riemer-schmid to prepare some designs. On returning with plans and costings, Schmidt was met by the Admiral in charge of naval construction at Kiel and a team of directors and naval architects from the shipyard. Emphasis has rightly been placed on Schmidt's artistic and social idealism in many descriptions of him, but he must also have been a superb salesman. Not only did he secure acceptance for Riemerschmid's designs, which was not too difficult since they were enthusiastically received, but he convinced the shipyard team to alter the internal configuration of a vessel to allow the designs to be fully realized.[18]

As a further indication of his success, in the following decade, commissions to equip the captains' cabins and officers' messes of thirteen naval vessels, beginning with the armoured cruiser *Prinz Adalbert* and the light cruisers *Berlin* and Danzig in the period 1904-06, were received. The limited spatial dimensions called for great economy of means, with storage in box-forms tucked into niches and running along walls, enabling the maximum space allowable within available limits to be used to create a pleasant, relaxing atmosphere.

The patronage of land and city authorities could also be substantial. For example, in 1898 the first stages of construction began on a new electric overhead and underground railway system commissioned by the Berlin municipality. It provoked considerable debate on the need to take into account the effect of such major construction on the capital's street image. Deutsche Bauzeifung published a series of eight articles on the project by Albert Hoffmann, in which the purely functional approach adopted in similar projects in America and Britain were cited as an indication of the materialism prevalent in those countries. In contrast, German aspirations were to achieve pure beauty in construction which required a measure of 'aesthetic superfluity' and Hoffmann specifically rejected the proposition that 'functionality is beauty.'[19]

Four architects, Sepp Kaiser, Alfred Grenander, Bruno Mohring and Stadtbaurat Jautschuss were commissioned for work on the Berlin project under the consulting architect, Paul Wittig. Initially, they produced designs of a decorative nature for station street entrances and columnar supports for the overhead sections, but both city council and public were very concerned at the image of the railway, and work later broadened, with, for example, Alfred Grenander becoming responsible for designing stations, service buildings and rolling stock for the system up until 1914. Prior to 1897, Grenander had worked for seven years under the architect Wallot on the Reichstag building. In this work, however, he evolved clean, functional and well-detailed forms of a high standard. In moving away from applied decoration, he translated the concept of 'aesthetic superfluity' into something more subtle, a concern for form in relation to function, though not determined by it. Of his work as a whole, a critic commented: 'Practicality in the garment of taste is Grenander's ideal. He therefore cultivates straightness and parallelism. His ceilings and walls, his furniture and lighting apparatus, are treated with some of the soberness of the engineer. Yet the aesthetic is also active in him, and asserts itself in softening and embellishing; vertical lines are therefore sometimes gently inclined, and strong colours tempered. The logician cannot resist the temptation of the graces.'[20] If Grenander's designs for the Berlin transport network were in the context of a major public work, it is also worth noting that it would have been impossible without the support of the contractors for the project, Siemens Halske. Their role was recognized when the Rector and Senate of Berlin's Technical University unanimously approved the award of an honorary doctorate in 1906 to the retiring chief architect of Siemens, Heinrich Schwieger, for his contributions to the development of the city's transport system. Siemens had close links and worked in close co-operation with official bodies at all levels, like most large German companies. However, by the turn of the century these were developing an influence on design in their own right, offering a wide range of commissions that were often substantial in scope.

Citations

1   Quoted in Dube, W.-D., *The Expressionists,* London, 1972, pp. 157–8.

2   Mourey, G., 'Round the Exhibition — III. "German Decorative Art" in *The Studio,* 1901, pp. 44–50.

3   Fuchs, G., 'Die Vorhalle zum House der Macht und der Schonheit' in DKuD, 1902–3, p. 6.

4   'The International Exhibition of Modern Decorative Art at Turin. The German Section.' in The Studio, 1903, p. 194.

5   Oliver, M. 'German Arts and Crafts at the St Louis Exposition' in *The Studio,* 1905, p. 233.

6   Muthesius, H. 'Die Wohnungskunst auf der Welt-Austellung in St Louis' in DKuD, 1904–5, p. 209.

7   Volbehr, T. 'Die Magdeburger Gruppe in St Louis 1904' in DKuD, 1904, p. 492.

8   Quoted in Carstanjen, F. 'Kunstgewerbliche Erziehung' in DKuD, 1905, p. 478.

9   *Ibid,* p. 491.

10 Quoted in Moeller, G., 'Kunstgewerbeschule' in catalogue, *Der Westdeutsche Impuls 1900-1914: Kunst und Umweltgestaltung im Industriegebiet,* Dusseldorf, 1984, p. 40.

11 von Bode W., *Mein Leben,* Bd II, Berlin, 1930, p. 183.

12 Deubner, L. 'Decorative Art at the Munich Exhibition' in *The Studio,* 1909, p. 42.

13 The statement was by Jules Huret, quoted in: Troy, N., 'Towards a Redefinition of Tradition in French Design' in Design Issues, Fall 1984, p. 62.

14 Carabin, Rupert quoted in *Ibid,* p. 63.

15 Schmidt, K. 'Die Ausstellung von Darsfellung bauer-licher Kunst und Bauweise aus dem Konigreich Sachsen auf der Bruhl'schen Terrasse in Dresden' in DB, 1901, pp. 253–4.

16 'Handwerker und Neuere Kunst' in *ID,* 1907, p. 51.

17 Schloermann 'Gedanken u. Vorschlage zur Innen-Einrichtung moderner Kriegs- und Handels-Schiffe in ID, 1907, p. 255.

18 Quoted in Wichmann, H., *Aufbruch zum neuen Wohnen,* Basel and Stuttgart, 1978, p. 109.

19 Hoffman, A., 'Die elektrische Hoch- und Unter-grundbahn in Berlin von Siemens und Halske, in DB, 1902, pp. 265–9.

20 'Studio Talk' in *The Studio,* 1907, p. 232.

12

Germany: The Industrial Applications of Tubular Steel

It was in the years between the two world wars that tubular steel was of the greatest significance as an industrial material. Its application for avant-garde furniture designs in the 1920s is generally recognized, but what is not so clear is its wider use in industry, and the relationship between avant-garde developments and such industrial applications. A further question is why tubular steel came to be so important at that particular time in the inter-war years. Many of the factors involved require a consideration not only of aesthetic influences, but also of the technical and industrial developments, commercial factors, and in the 1930s, the influence of political decisions in the period of the Third Reich. Much more detailed research on these aspects is required and this attempt to describe some of the factors leading to the widespread use of tubular steel in German industry, with a number of examples that will illustrate the range and scope of its application, must necessarily be of a general and indicative nature, raising more questions than providing answers.

Early attempts to produce steel tubing involved rolling steel sheet around a former and brazing or welding the seam between the two edges. There were limitations to the strength and appearance of such tubes, however, and during the nineteenth century experiments were made in many countries to produce a seamless tube, that is, one in which the walls have not been separated at any point of the production process. The first generally successful process was patented in January, 1885 by two Germans, Max and Reinhard Mannesmann, which involved passing a heated billet through a piercing machine, which pierced a hole in the centre of the billet. The tube thus formed was rolled successively between rolls and over a mandrel to obtain

First published as "Germany: The Industrial Applications of Tubular Steel." in *Tubular Steel Furniture*, *ed.* Tim Benton, Architectural Association, London, 1980, pp. 22–5. By kind permission of the Architectural Association.

the required diameter of tube and thickness of wall. Large quantities of seamless tube were produced by the Mannesmann process for the production of bicycles; tubes of $^3/_8''$ – $1^1/_2''$ outside diameter being generally known as "bicycle tubing." Allied to the development and application of tubular steel in the bicycle industry were two other processes that were important for the exploitation of tube as a material: first, techniques of shaping tubes without distorting and thus weakening the strength of the tube wall, and secondly, welding techniques that enabled tubes to be extended end-on to form an unbroken run longer than that possible direct from the manufacturing process, and also enabled lengths of tube to be welded at an angle to each other to form a rigid frame. The precise details of the development and application of these processes is difficult to trace but it is clear that both were in general industrial use in the early years of the century. The question then arises: why was tubular steel not used for furniture at that time? Both material and techniques for working it were generally available, and there was a long history of metal being used for furniture production, especially cast iron. Any explanation must be speculative, but one possible reason is that the tubing produced for bicycle production had a thickness of wall that did not lend itself easily to the shaping of forms on the scale that was later to be used for furniture.

The expansion in the use of tubular steel was most evident in other areas of transport construction that developed rapidly after the turn of the century. The Dutch aircraft designer, Anthony Fokker, working in Germany, used welded steel tubing for his aircraft, the 'Spin' (Spider) Mark I of 1910. 'A factory in Frankfurt made the steel-tube frames for wings from rough drawings.'[1] Techniques at this point were evidently rule of thumb! His M1 monoplane of 1913 also had a welded steel tube frame and was to be produced in large numbers under the military designation 'E class' for widespread use in the early stages of the First World War. The factory established by Fokker at Schwerin must have gained considerable expertise because in 1916 they were ordered to build under license a rival company's design, the AEG CIV, the frame of the aircraft being to a large extent of varying gauges and diameters of steel tube. A British Ministry of Munitions report on a captured example spoke highly of the high quality of the welding.[2] Examples of Fokker's final wartime design, the D VII series, were handed over to the victorious powers after the armistice in 1918. Some were shipped to the U.S.A. where a study of the welded fuselage 'was to have a considerable effect on that country's pursuit aircraft design'.[3] As in many other respects the war acted as a catalyst, making commonplace what had been limited developments before 1914. In the 1920s welding equipment, for example, was produced and marketed on a large scale, some units being transportable, with petrol-driven generators mounted on a trailer, others being lightweight units that could be plugged into mains electricity supplies and used with extension leads over a wide area. The advances in technique are evident in a tram chassis of 1934 produced by the Schondorff company of Düsseldorf, in which steel tube of various lengths is shaped and welded into a strong, compact unit capable of sustaining the heavy strains of use on an urban tramway network.

There was also, in the immediate post-war period, a further development in the production methods of tubular steel. In 1921 a patent was granted to the Machinefabrik Sack G.m.b.H and Josef Gassen for 'improvements in skew rolling mechanism for the production of hollow bodies, especially thin wall finished tubes from solid stock or from hollow bodies.'[4] The Sack method resulted in tubing with thinner walls than that produced by the Mannesmann technique, which whilst retaining the essential strength of tubular steel, was lighter in weight, less rigid and thus more easily shaped into a potentially greater number of forms.

It is against this background of development in material and techniques, both being readily available and commercially viable, that the application of tubular steel begins to emerge on a large scale in the 1920s. Two main categories of use emerged: the first used the interior space of tubing as a flow channel for liquids or gases in industrial plant, and for domestic hot water and central heating systems. It was also used as an air channel in certain designs of domestic vacuum cleaners, such as the AEG 'Vam-pyr' range. A further use of this interior space was as a channel and protection for electrical cables. Lamps designed for industrial and commercial use by companies such as AEG, Siemens and Kanden were suspended from ceilings by a length of narrow steel tube that held the lamp in a fixed position, an essential requirement in large spaces such as factory workshops and open-plan offices where scientifically planned, constant light distribution was necessary for efficient working conditions. The second category of use, using tubular steel as a structural member, is more significant both in terms of architecture and industrial design. The qualities of tubing, strength and light weight, its smooth rounded surface, an absence of physical bulk in relation to its properties, gave it considerable potential. A diving platform in Germany, dating from the early 1930s, the location unidentified, shows these structural qualities to good advantage. This combination of strength and lightness had a wide application in architecture, where tubing could define space without the imposition of a solid physical barrier, as in balconies and fences, and it also offered distinct economic advantages. A report from 1928 on experiments in the use of welded tubular structures as against riveted angle-sections stated: 'The application of tubes in steel construction has long been the purpose of designers on the grounds that the most limited application of materials results in the most favourable relationship with stability.' The results of the experiments indicated that: 'The weight of tube construction amounted to a half of the riveted.'[5]

Such qualities were also recognized in the automobile industry in Germany which in the post-war period was absorbing the lessons of Henry Ford's mass-production methods and generating new markets. The exact details of when tubular steel began to be applied to the construction of automobile seats are not yet clear, but the reasons for it are obvious: strength and stability combined with minimum weight when compared with other materials. According to the account of Ferdinand Kramer it was the use of tubular steel for car seating that inspired Mart Stam to begin his work on tubular steel cantilever chairs. On a visit to the Weissenhof Siedlung in Stuttgart during its construction, Stam and Kramer drove in a small Hanomag car. When the front passenger seat was folded forward to let Stam out of the rear of the car, he noticed the tubular steel construction of the folded seat. According to Kramer he immediately began sketching ideas for a chair and on returning home constructed his first model.[6]

Its material qualities and aesthetic potential, together with the added attraction that it was a material unique to its time, do much to explain the attraction of tubular steel for the experiments of avant-garde artists and designers seeking to use materials and develop forms relevant to modern life and processes. If they were initially dependent upon developments in industry, their ideas were to feed back with tubular steel furniture being used in turn for a wide range of industrial applications. Photographs of the AEG exhibition stand at the 'Grosse Technische Messe und Baumesse' in Leipzig in 1935 shows the use of furniture designed by Mies van der Rohe. Its choice for this particular purpose is difficult to fault. The physical lightness of such furniture is perfect for transitory events where materials have to be rapidly installed and removed. Its sturdiness and comfort are necessary for the intensive use required, and above all, its insubstantial appearance did not detract in any way from the main focal point of the stand: the exhibits. For example, by 1936 tubular steel cantilever chairs were being used for the driver's seat in electric express locomotives of the Deutsche Reichsbahn. It is strong, comfortable, unobtrusive, well-secured and readily adjustable. Such qualities were widely utilized in seating for public transport vehicles such as passenger aircraft, railway carriages, trams and buses. The example of the tram interior constructed in 1934, shows an interesting adaptation of the cantilever frame enabling the chairs to be angled against the side of the coach, thus creating more space for standing passengers and access during entry and exit.

The best illustrations of its widespread application can be found, however, in aircraft design. An important factor in the design of aircraft is the power-to-weight ratio, and designers faced a problem in the First World War and the 1920s as the more extensive use of aircraft developed and more powerful engines with greater potential became available. In 1909 Victor Lougheed, a pioneer writer on aeronautics in the U.S.A., had written: 'Though weight for weight very few of the metals are stronger than the best woods, and these few are less superior than is commonly supposed, within a given volume of structure no materials approach metals.'[7] And on the subject of the most suitable metal form he wrote: 'Hollow rod or tubing, of the finest alloy steels, of circular cross section, of large diameter and with comparatively thin walls, is much the highest grade material—the strongest and lightest— that can be used for shafting . . . Always when it is possible unbroken shaft lengths should be used in any machine compelled to work under heavy duty, but when there are reasons preventing this, excellent joints can be made in shaft materials by brazing or by autogenous or electric welding.'[8] Tubular steel provided at that time the structural strength needed to house more powerful engines and to withstand the forces of higher performance, without an increase in weight or volume that would negate the increased engine power. As indicated above, German designers had considerable experience of tubular steel construction during the war. Many designs, however, in Germany, as in other countries, mixed both old and new technology. For example, the Focke-Wulf FW A17 'Mowe' (Seagull) of 1927 had a fuselage of welded steel tube with a plywood cover and wooden frame wings. It was the firm of Junkers, however, that developed the first all metal aircraft, the earliest experiments also being in the First World War. Their advanced technique is evident in the Junkers Ju A50 of 1929 which used both steel tube and strip for the fuselage frame, with steel tube as the main structural element in the wing construction, and a corrugated sheet metal skin that became a Junkers trademark. The cabin interior of the Junkers Ju 52/3 of 1932 shows a very ingenious exploitation of this basic structure. The supports of the roof rack are arcs of tubular steel welded within the circular frames used to form the fuselage. The arcs act as braces for the circular frames, and when linked longitudinally by the length of tubing along the fuselage, give additional structural reinforcement as well as continuous storage space. In addition the seats are made of a tubular steel frame covered with leather. Tubular steel furniture and fittings were also used in German airship construction, their lightness being an essential factor in their selection. The Fieseler Fi 156 'Storch' (Stork) of 1937, is another good example of the advantages of tubular steel. It used a welded steel frame for the fuselage not only for basic structural strength, but also with a configuration that allowed adequate vision downwards for pilot and observer in its primary role of reconnaissance and artillery spotting. Early German helicopter design also used tubing for airframes, such as the Focke-Wulf FW 61 of 1937, in which both fuselage and the twin outriggers carrying the rotors were welded tube frames.

In addition, the application tubular steel was evident not only in the aircraft structures alone, but also their production processes. Photographs of the Junkers factory at Oranienburg in 1937 reveal the extent of the use of tubular steel in ladders, platforms, guard rails, and supporting frames for aircraft under construction. It was taken a stage further in the production line of the Focke-Wulf factory at Bremen in the Second World War. There tubular steel provided the structure of the production-line itself, for the large scale manufacture of the FW 190A-4 fighter aircraft, giving good support, easy movement along the line, and clear access from all angles to workers at all stages.

In the 1930s, after Hitler's accession to power, political and military considerations began to play a more important role in the utilization of tubular steel. If in the preceding examples the majority of applications are related to transport or military use, this is no accident of personal selection, but rather a reflection of the realities of the Third Reich. Steel was a commodity in short supply under the provisions of the extensive rearmament programme embarked on by Hitler, and as a vital strategic material, was subject to a system of rationing and allocation that restricted its use to those processes given priority in the government's programme. As a result of these political pressures, economic and technical developments where emphasized that sought to replace steel tubing by alternative materials and techniques, such as stamped and pressed light-metal sections, which enabled more complex shapes to be formed that were equal in structural stability but even lighter than tubing. On the subject of light-metal fittings in aircraft construction it was stated in 1937: 'Cabin seating can be manufactured from pressed (light-metal) tubes having an extraordinary low structural weight. The tubes are welded together with the usual gas-welding methods. Comparative tests show that with the same strength, the relative structural weight of steel tube, duralumin tube and electron tube is in the order of 9 : 4 : 3.'[9]

Steel tubing was still used but: 'Only in mixed construction do we today meet with steel to any extent, and mainly in the form of welded fuselages and tail plane units of welded steel tube.'[10]

It is interesting that in this context of restrictions on the use of steel, tubular steel furniture continued to be manufactured by a number of firms including Thonet and Knoll, and not only that, was given official approval. Thonet furniture was exhibited at the exhibition 'A Working Nation' (Schaffendes Volk) held in Dusseldorf in 1937, the purpose of which was to publicize the aims of the Four Year Plan, an economic programme intended to prepare German industry for a state of 'war readiness.' Tubular steel furniture was also widely illustrated in the Deutsche Warenkunde,' a design index prepared under official auspices in 1938, which presented a wide selection of household goods considered to be of a high quality and value, that also conformed to the emphasis of the Four Year Plan. An explanation of the inclusion of tubular steel furniture in such projects can perhaps be found not in an appreciation of their aesthetic qualities by the authorities of the Third Reich, but in the fact thast they were among a range of products that had considerable export potential, and were therefore capable of earning foreign currency vital for the purchase of war materials.

The use of steel tubing thus underwent a process of relative decline and importance in the 1930s, its economic and technical advantages of strength in relation to weight being rendered marginal and even obsolete by further technical developments, and its aesthetic forms being exploited by a regime that denied the creators of those forms the right to work. Nevertheless a German commentator could write in 1935 that steel tubing 'has an outstanding share in the solution of the greatest problems of mankind in the last decades.'[11]

We may disagree with the overstatement of an obvious enthusiast, but have to recognize the significance of a development that aroused such enthusiasm. In any general evaluation of materials and innovative design in the early twentieth century, tubular steel undoubtedly has an important place.

Notes

1 Hegener, Henri: *Fokker—The Man and The Aircraft,* Letchworth, 1961, p. 14.

2 Gray, Peter and Thetford, Owen: *German Aircraft of the First World War,* London, 1962, p. 5.

3 Hegener: Fokker—*The Man and The Aircraft,* p. 15.

4 Evans, Gilbert: *Manufacture of Seamless Tubes: Ferrous and Non-Ferrous,* London, 1934, p. 26.

5 *Lichtbogenschweissung bei Eisenkonstruktionen* in RKW *Nacfirichten,* Vol. 2, No. 3, March 1928, pp. 35–8.

6 Taped interview of Ferdinand Kramer by the author—25 May 1977.

7 Lougheed, Victor: *Vehicles of ihe Air—A Popular Exposition of Modern Aeronautics,* Chicago, 1909, p. 381.

8 Lougheed: *Vehicles of the Air,* pp. 320–1.

9 Oberingcmcur De Ridder: *Leichtmetallkonstruktion im Flugzeugbau* in RTA *Nacfirichten,* 13 October 1937, p. 4.

10 *Dipl. Ing. Schlunk:* Werkstoffe im Flugzeugbau in RTA Nacfirichten 12 January 1938, p. 4.

11 *Krieger, Ulrich:* Stahlrohr in Gopfert, Arthur (ed.): Denkmal *Demscher Arbeit,* Vol. I, Leipzig, 1935, p. 231.

13

Modernism and Archaism in Design in the Third Reich

John Heskett Note. This article is based on a lecture given at a conference Fasehismus—Kunst und visuelle Medien, *organised by the Ulmer Vereins— Verband fur Kunstund Kulturwissenschaften, that took place at the Historisches Museum, Frankfurt/Main in October, 1977. It was subsequently published under the title 'Modernismus' und 'Archaismus' im* Design während des Nationalsozialismus *in Hinz, Mittig, Schache, Schonberger (eds.)* Die Dekoration der Gewalt: Kunst und Medien im Fasehismus, Giessen, 1979, *which contains a selection of papers from the conference. In preparing an English version, I have not simply translated from the original German text, but have taken the opportunity to expand and rewrite a number of passages.*

Design history encompasses the study of everyday objects of use in the past, such as interior furnishings and fittings, commercial and domestic appliances, and transport vehicles. As an academic discipline in its own right it is still undeveloped and there are naturally problems in defining the content and concerns of the subject, and in developing appropriate methodologies. In this article I will argue that design in the period of the Third Reich in Germany is of interest, not only as a neglected aspect of modern design history, but also because of its potential contribution to an understanding of the emerging role of designers in modem society and to an interpretation of the meaning and significance of their work.

In the majority of publications on design in the inter-war period there is a conspicuous gap. It would appear that modern design in Germany ended with the dissolution of the Bauhaus by the Nazi government shortly after its assumption of power in 1933. This interpretation is based essentially upon

First published in this version as "Modernism and Archaism in Design in the Third Reich," *Block 3*, 1980, pp. 13–24.

a limited definition of what constituted modern design in Germany before 1933, which concentrates heavily on the Bauhaus and the International Movement, and which has only been seriously questioned in the last decade. A major defect of this interpretation is its depiction of a particular range of aesthetic concepts and forms as 'modern design.' It thereby excludes a broad range of other work and ideas that in the 1920s was of great importance and widespread concern, much of which was considered to be 'modern'—a term of approbation or opprobrium in those years according to one's standpoint. A consequence of this failure to consider the full breadth of design in Weimar Germany has been the depiction of the Third Reich simply in terms of a negation of the avant-garde tendencies epitomized by the Bauhaus. This lack of consideration of what was one of the most crucial periods of German history by design historians is a marked contrast to the wide-ranging and often excellent work that has emanated from other historical disciplines.

One of the first published attempts to discuss design in the Third Reich was a three-part article by Hans Scheerer, that appeared in the German design magazine Form in 1975.[1] It sought to document 'the usefulness of aesthetics as an instrument of authoritarian state power,' and clearly demonstrated the importance of design in the policies of many party organizations. His depiction of the political and economic structure of the regime was somewhat too simplified, however, to clarify the complexities of the period. In particular, the political control of organizations such as the Reichskammer für bildenden Kunste (State Chamber of Visual Arts), and the influence of ideologues such as Alfred Rosenberg, were depicted as too deterministic on detailed design work. Despite such differences of opinion, however, Scheerer's article stimulated a serious discussion of design in the Third Reich in its social and political context, a marked contrast to its frequent dismissal by means of undefined phrases or labels such as 'Nazi kitsch.'

Another approach that was disturbing in its implications was revealed in a major exhibition that opened in Munich in 1977, under the title Schauplatz Deutschland: die Dreissiger Jahre (The German Scene in the Thirties), in which a limited view of material from the period was presented to justify a specific contemporary view of design. Objects of use were displayed in isolation as pure aesthetic forms under the caption of Sachlichkeit trotz Diktatur (Practicality despite Dictatorship). An irony was that the exhibition took place in the former Hans der deutschen Kunst, the exhibition complex designed by Paul Ludwig Troost on Hitler's orders as a cultural showplace for the regime. In the relevant chapter of the extensive catalogue, Erika Gysling-Billeter stated that the regime 'determined from now on what art in the Third Reich was to be and what taste the public had to follow.' Despite this, she argued, 'the heritage of the Bauhaus and the artists who sympathised with it revealed itself. Functionalism survived! The Neue Sachlichkeit outwitted the dictatorship.'[2] The Nazi party was thus depicted as having totalitarian control over the aesthetic taste of the nation with designers playing the role of cultural Schweiks undermining the regime by means of aesthetic form, and thereby constituting a cultural resistance movement. Frau Gysling-Billeter posed the question: 'Were there in fact works of meaning in the Germany of the regime that artistically survived this period?'[3] and came to the conclusion that, 'Thanks to the work of artists such as Wolfgang Tumpel, Wilhelm Wagenfeld, Marguerita Friedlander, Herman Gretsch etc., "Good Form" survived in the Third Reich, and after the war could be absorbed into the art of the present without a break.'[4] How it was possible, and why it was important for 'Good Form' to survive was not brought into question. The official positions of the artists named and the relationship between their work and their attitudes to the regime were not discussed. Neither was the attitude of the regime towards those artists and their work. 'Good Form' and its assumed beneficial value were regarded as independent of such relationships by virtue of their aesthetic quality.

Basically, this particular approach was an apologia for the concept of 'Good Form,' directed only towards a stylistic or formalistic understanding of the objects displayed, which included a prototype Volkswagen, Volksempfanger radios and Siemens telephones, as well as a wide range of ceramic and glass wares. Despite the fact that many of these objects were the products of government-sponsored projects, the approach adopted towards them could not offer any answers about the social role of design in this period, since such questions were simply not posed. This is not to suggest that form in design is irrelevant or should be omitted from consideration; the tangible form of designed objects should indeed be the focus of any study of design. Form, however, should be a starting-point, and not an end in itself.

In presenting an alternative view of the period to that described above, it is not possible in a brief account to fully discuss even a representative selection of design or designers in the Third Reich. There are few problems, however, in obtaining material on the designs of the period, since information was widely published and illustrated in journals, books and catalogues, that were often produced on a lavish scale, itself an indication of their importance. The many sources available indicate that there was in fact no single, stylistic tendency or direction, but instead a broad variety of manifestations, encompassing an extensive range of forms, techniques and manufacturing procedures.

Although no simple pattern can be perceived, and although more research is necessary before all the elements of this pattern can be identified, two apparently contradictory tendencies are discernible in the objects of the period: one, an emphasis on technical, industrial modernity, the other, an emphasis on traditional craft forms and techniques. A similar polarity has been noted in work on other aspects of the history of the Third Reich, and has been referred to as the 'Janus-headed' nature of the regime. In a discussion of the labour history of the period Tim Mason has identified these two tendencies as 'modernism' and 'archaism,' a designation that is highly appropriate to their manifestations in design.[5]

The origins and roots of these tendencies, as with many other aspects of the Third Reich, lie deep in German history. The First World War was an important turning point, however, acting as a catalyst and accelerator of social and economic trends that, together with the trauma of military defeat and the political collapse of the imperial monarchy, heavily conditioned developments and attitudes in the 1920s. In that decade a clear polarization between modern and archaic tendencies became clearly apparent. On one hand, there was an ever-increasing flow of mass-produced articles for an extending range of purposes, whose designers were often anonymous and which were usually identified with the name of the manufacturing company or its trade-mark. Such products were generally manufactured by means of standardized and rationalized mass-production processes after the American model, and exemplified the growth and consolidation of large industrial combines in Germany. On the other hand, there was a continuity of traditional craft organizations and methods, the products of which were made individually, or at most, in limited series, in small workshops. This dichotomy was noted by an American report on German industry published in 1931: 'From the point of view of production, the characteristic feature of German industry is the existence of numerous small establishments side by side with a small number of large enterprises employing a high proportion of industrial workers.'[6]

Another feature of this polarization in the 1920s was that, in addition to traditional industrial and professional bodies, a number of new groups and institutions were founded by both large industry and small craft organizations to promote and publicize their work, methods and interests. Two such institutions that represented new approaches in industry were the *Deutsche Normen Ausschuss* (German Standards Commission) and the *Reichskuratorium für Wirtschaftlichkeit* (State Efficiency Board).

The Deutsche Normen Ausschuss (DNA) was founded in 1916 as a result of military concern at the disparities and lack of technical compatibility between the products of different firms. Many large companies had established standard specifications for internal use, covering measurements, parts and procedures in the years before the war, but the DNA set out to prepare such specifications on a national basis. Its discussions involved both government and private industry through a network of committees covering all sectors of production. Standards were generally defined by agreement between all the parties concerned on the basis of the best of existing practice and the use of standards was voluntary. Although specific forms were rarely recommended as standards, the publication of a rapidly growing number of *Deutsche Industrie Normen* (DIN or German Industrial Standards) had considerable implications for designers. A major example was the DIN series of paper sizes based on the A-format, since adopted as the basis of an international standard. Published in 1927, it proposed a series of dimensions for sheet-paper that were multiplications or divisions of a basic unit of area, so that any size, from a postage-stamp to large sheets of drawing-paper were exactly proportional. It means that storage and filing units could also be designed to these basic dimensions, and the result was an extension of the concept of standardization into three-dimensions with the production of extendable modular storage units.

The *Reichkuratorium für Wirtschaftlichkeit* (RKW) concentrated on the problems of rationalization in industry, commerce, transport and the home. The concept of rationalization stemmed from the theories of F.W. Taylor on 'scientific management,' but the recommendations and publications of the RKW were not only concerned with the rational organization of production, but also promoted the adoption of technically efficient, functional forms. A good example of their approach was in the realm of light-fittings. It is possible to discuss the range produced by the AEG company in formal aesthetic terms as typical of the trend towards functional forms of geometric simplicity that was indeed characteristic of the period. (Attention has frequently been focussed in such terms on similar models by several Bauhaus designers for the 'Kandem' range of the Leipzig firm of Korting and Mathiesen). It is clear from the publications of the RKW, however, that there was another important level of meaning to the production of such forms.

In an article in the RKW-Nachrichten under the title of 'Functional Lighting and Rational Economy,' published in 1930, it was stated: 'Without a doubt the question of a functional form of light-fitting is also of the greatest significance in economic relationships, in view of the great influence, in psychical and physiological terms, which the light exercises on people.'[7] In other words, and this was strongly stressed, a modern form of light-fitting was an important instrument in attaining higher levels of efficiency in production. The article also reported that efforts were being made by the RKW to evolve general recommendations for the most favourable forms of natural and artificial lighting: 'Endeavours are generally in hand which extend from regulations on single questions of function to the whole economy of lighting, to bring in a more unified, rational approach.'[8] Functional form in lighting was thus part of a wider pattern of developments in industrial efficiency.

That the 'general directions' and 'more unified rational approach' meant a reduction of types in production and an increase in compatibility between types produced was evident in the work of the *Reichsausschuss für Lieferbedingungen* (RAL or State Commission for Specifications), a constituent body of the RKW. The RAL introduced amongst other things, a series of material specifications 'in which, for example, quality requirements, composition, properties, commercial quantities, packaging, sampling, quality control and simple test procedures were laid down.'[9] Quality marks were devised to be affixed to goods satisfying RAL recommendations and procedures, which emphasized a limited range of forms to satisfy specific needs.

The significance of such work, and that of the DNA, was that a considerable quantity of materials and parts produced by and for industry became standardized or subject to standards of performance specification, resulting in a convergence of form and concept between the products of different firms.

It was against this background that the role of designers in German industry evolved in the 1920s. Parallel to the process of standardization and convergence that accompanied the growth of mass-production and rationalization, and a direct consequence of it, the work of designers became predominantly oriented towards the creation of artificial and superficial differences between products. An example is a series of radio housings produced by AEG between 1927 and 1933. The set of 1927 comprised several units which still have a strong technical appearance without any attempt to refine or adorn the external form. The models of 1929—30 were still simple and undecorated, but the housings were more consciously formed with an eye to appearance. A major change is evident, however, in the housings for the 1933 models. Of pressed plastic, they were a stylistic exercise in the stepped Art Deco fashion of the period, completely eschewing any reference to technical function. The rationale of this trend was summed up in the house journal of one of AEG's major competitors, Siemens and Halske: 'The whole attitude of modem people, who see in a radio receiver not a technical apparatus but an object of use, demands... good-looking radio appliances, whose operation does not require practice or technical knowledge.'[10] Similar trends are apparent across the whole range of consumer goods design, particularly the expanding area of domestic appliances stimulated by the growth of electricity networks.

An unadorned, standardized functionality was therefore considered appropriate to the technical, productive side of industry in pursuit of higher levels of efficiency. With the design of consumer goods, however, there was, in contrast, an emphasis on artifice and fantasy as an instrument of marketing and sales strategies. The attitudes towards purchasers also shows considerable change. As in the example of radio design, the user was no longer considered as an active participant in a technical operation, but as a passive consumer of a packaged article. The role of designers in industry, as it evolved in the context of this transformation, with its emphasis on styling, on aestheticizing the benefits and significance of products for consumers, must therefore also be considered as an aspect of modernity in design.

In discussing contemporary developments in the crafts, it is first necessary to clarify an important difference between the German word *Handwerk* and its usual English translation of 'craft.' The earlier and more extensive process of industrialization of Britain resulted in many traditional crafts becoming obsolete or, if they survived, becoming adapted to or absorbed into industrial structures. The connotations of 'craft' have therefore come to be associated to a considerable extent with the ideas of craft revival associated with the Arts and Crafts Movement. The later industrialization of Germany, however, and its early concentration into a relatively few, highly capitalized units, meant that there was a greater unbroken continuity of traditional craft concepts and business organization. In both numbers employed and range of work encompassed, the concept of *Handwerk,* even though I will use the English translation, is much more extensive than its usage in British design history.

Despite its greater numerical size and economic significance when compared with Britain, the German craftsmen were under considerable pressure as a result of the growth of industry, a process all the more alarming for the speed with which it had taken place. To defend their interests new organizations were also formed in the 1920s. In 1922, for example, a major initiative was the foundation of an umbrella organization, the *Arbeitsgemeinschaft für Handwerkskulture* (The Council for Craft Culture), formed to co-ordinate the efforts of a diverse number of extant bodies. The driving force behind it and a leading figure in its activities was Dr. Edwin Redslob, who held the post of *Reichkunstwart* (State Art Officer) in the Ministry of the Interior, with responsibility for advising on all aspects of government activity that had artistic consequences, ranging from the design of postage stamps, emblems of state and currency, to buildings and public festivities. Redslob's purposes in founding the *Arbeitsgemeinschaft* was 'to systematically maintain the still existing heritage of German achievement in the German crafts, and simultaneously to prepare German work in time for new tasks.'[11] Later, in 1927, he expanded this theme: 'Our age needs a counterbalance to the tasks it has set itself: to dispute the spiritual penetration of machine work with a new appreciation of creative powers as they are evident in the eternally living sources of artistic creativity in the crafts and traditional art.'[12]

In pursuit of these ends, the *Arbeitsgemeinschaft* published books, pamphlets, a journal, organized exhibitions and publicized its views wherever possible. Despite these efforts, and Redslob's continuous attempts to evolve a state policy for the applied arts and design in which craftsmen would have an important role, their activities were insufficient to effect a fundamental change in public opinion or state policies.

The political links and influence of bodies such as the *Arbeitsgemeinschaft* and the RKW still require further research. It is clear, however, that in the Weimar Republic a considerable number of Reichstag members and government officials, of a broad spectrum of political convictions, consistently represented the different standpoints and policies of such organizations, and attempted to gain and use political influence for the promotion of their views.

The polarization of attitudes and organizations that influenced design at all levels, and political activity and involvement on their behalf, therefore provided a ready field of activity for the growing Nazi party when it began, in the late 1920s, to seek a broader basis of support. In particular, the grievances of the craft class made them very receptive to Nazi propaganda. During the decade, their economic position had continually deteriorated, and there was a similarity between the archaic elements of Nazi ideology, its anti-industrialism and reaction against modernity, and the attitudes of many craftsmen. The vituperative polemics of the debate on art and design that had raged throughout the Weimar Republic's existence were also put to use. From the early 1920's traditionalists had accused modern artists and designers of subverting the roots of German art and life with the rootless cosmopolitanism and 'cultural bolshevism' of their work and ideas. The Nazi front organization for the arts, the *Kampfbund für deutsche Kultur* (Fighting League for German Culture) and leading ideologues in the party, above all Gottfried Feder, the party's economic spokesman, continually and carefully exploited the fears and grievances of the craft class. Their support, together with that of similarly aggrieved groups who had become continually more disadvantaged in the Weimar period, became an important factor in the rise to political significance of the Nazi Party.

Indeed it seemed for a short time after Hitler was appointed Chancellor in January, 1933, that the plans and ambitions of the craft class to use the power of the new government as a means of reestablishing its former strength in the economic and social life of the country were going to be realized. Although Redslob himself was dismissed when the Nazis came to power for his open disavowal of the regime, the general outlook seemed promising. Craft guildsiwere reinstated, and at least in their constitutions and legal status, were accorded a new power and recognition. There were also a series of measures to protect craft interests, such as large department stores being forbidden to sell craft products.

Such measures, however, and in a wider sense, the danger of a 'conservative revolution,' a return to middle-class oriented production and economic concepts, alarmed the large industrial concerns, who saw their position in the German economy, and their hopes of using the Nazi party for their own ends, endangered by this threat.

The purposes of Hitler's government were clearly revealed by its intervention in this conflict during 1934. Their policies demonstrated that the regime did not intend to simply be a puppet of the disparate forces that had supported its rise to power, neither was its approach necessarily conditioned by its own proclaimed ideology. Even at that early stage, the dominant policy was rearmament and the rebuilding of Germany's military strength, as a precondition and preparation for the territorial expansion that Hitler believed would eventually be necessary. The great industrial concerns were an essential element of that policy, which the so-called 'second revolution' threatened to undermine. Instead of craft workshops, a highly developed technical-industrial base was an absolute necessity. The removal of Feder from power in the party and the elimination of the influence of the SA 'Brownshirt' private army were both steps in denying the 'second revolution' and reassuring the military hierarchy and large industry.

In terms of the effects of these events on design, it appeared that industrial modernity was victorious. The policy of military rearmament and national independence from the restrictions of the Treaty of Versailles meant the full application of the capacities of German industry. There was an increase in design and production in all areas that served the needs of the defence programme, which had considerable secondary influence in the civil sector. The policy of motorization, which primarily had a military rationale, led also to an acceleration of the autobahn construction programme and a stimulus to the design and construction of road transport vehicles of all kinds.

The economic consequences of these policies, however, created many problems. Resources were diverted from export industries to rearmament, imports were increasing to satisfy the burgeoning goods and materials, and the government's unwillingness to court political unpopularity by imposing restrictions on domestic consumption, led by 1935 to a serious foreign exchange problem.

The government's solution was the Four Year Plan of 1936, which specifically planned to place Germany on a war-footing by 1940. Economic planning was systematized and subordinated to military purposes, though at no time did it become all-embracing, but rather directed towards a limited number of strategic areas and objectives. Many measures were in themselves not new, such as the strengthening of the drive for standardization and rationalization begun in the 1920s, and indeed with the same institutions, the DNA and RKW, though now headed by party nominees. The development of new materials, such as plastics, and light metals, was encouraged and stimulated, as part of a co-ordinated attempt to reduce the level of imports and make Germany, as far as possible, self-sufficient. There were also some new measures, such as a programme of rationing and allocating essential materials. Collectively, these measures introduced a new dimension into German economic policies that had a strong influence on designers and their work in many sectors of industry. The use of steel-tubing for furniture production, for example, was not restricted on grounds of taste, or because of the avant-garde association of tubular steel furniture in Germany, but because steel was a vital constituent of defence requirements. Thonet steel tube furniture, including designs by Bauhaus members that were regarded as classics of modern design, were in fact included in the government-organized exhibition *Schaffendes Volk* (A Working Nation), that was intended to publicize the aim of the Four Year Plan, and which took place in Dusseldorf in 1937. Many aircraft fuselages, however, were also constructed from welded tubular steel frames, and their production, and other similar defence needs, had priority. Where furniture firms, such as Thonet, had an established export trade, though, they could obtain an allocation of materials in pursuit of the vital foreign exchange that was still desperately needed.

The effects of changes in economic policy were also evident, however, in goods produced for the domestic market. The electric-iron produced by AEG in 1937, for example, had an enamelled body instead of the nickel-plate finish used on earlier models. Many other domestic implements and fittings were produced from plastics or other substitute materials in the drive for self-sufficiency. Their use was in some cases disguised by conventional forms, as with the upholstered furniture shown at a State Chamber of Visual Arts exhibition in 1937. A cut-away cross-section of an armchair was shown revealing the extent to which synthetics and substitute materials had been used in its construction. The form of the chair, however, was unremarkable, a high-backed chair with enclosed arms of a type that was wholly characteristic of a broad range of contemporary designs. In other areas, however, new and innovatory forms were necessary to exploit the characteristics of new materials.

Articles and speeches in official journals and on numerous public occasions emphasized the need for the process of substituting new materials to be the occasion for a rethink of form and process, in order to at least maintain, and if possible to improve, levels of quality. As a result of this drive, German designers and technicians became very experienced and skilled in the use of many modern materials. By 1939, for example, Germany was producing and using more aluminium than the rest of the world put together.

The crafts were not left untouched by these developments either. In 1937, the number of people employed in craft occupations still totalled over $4^1/_2$ million.[13] Despite their loss of influence at the highest levels of government in 1934, they were simply too numerous to be ignored, and it became necessary to integrate their role and work into the economic plans of the regime. That role was explained in a major speech by Paul Walter, Leader of the German Crafts, at a crafts conference held in Frankfurt in 1937. He began by emphasizing the need for change: 'The way the crafts must go in order to solve the tasks [required of them by the nation] ... requires a complete change on the part of individual people belonging to particular trades. Many accustomed habits must be thrown overboard. Much that appears self-evident, must make way for these new attitudes.'[14] The major tasks referred to resulted, stated Walter, 'from cooperation on the Four Year Plan'[15], and can be briefly stated as: 1. The manufacture of new finished and semi-finished products from existing and new German raw materials; 2. Reduction of dependence of imported raw materials; 3. Adaptation of material requirements from foreign exchange-linked to existing and new German materials.

The trend of government policy was therefore clearly in the direction of subordinating the crafts to the principle of autarchy that was the foundation-stone of the Four Year Plan. There were further implications of this policy for the crafts, however, which were spelt out in a report of a speech in 1939 at the 'Greater German Crafts Rally' in Berlin: '*Reichshandwerksmeister Schramm* initially outlined the position of the crafts in the present-day economy, which is an instrument of power of the Fuhrer. In such an economy, rationalization has a totally different face to what existed earlier.'[16] He went on to state: Of greater further importance is the question of rationalization, that means the higher development of the economic structure in both large and small elements, on the basis of creating room for further improvement in performance.'[17]

Rationalization, as an instrument of large industry, had earlier been one of the main targets for bitter criticism by the craft organizations, and had been depicted as the soulless subordination of human values to mechanical processes. Now, in pursuit of higher efficiency, they were themselves being asked to conform to the very values they had earlier so vehemently rejected. The realization of the government's aim required, as a palliative, some acknowledgement of the identity and aims of craftsmen, but this rarely went beyond superficial features. For example, craft forms were often used by government and party organizations for furnishings and fittings in public and official buildings, as a kind of ideological housing or cosmetic. In a 'Furniture Book'[18] published by the *Schonheit der Arbeit* (Beauty of Labour) office of the *Deutsche Arbeitsfront* (German Labour Front), the body that replaced trade unions, designs were published for use in factories and offices. These were all of forms derived from traditional furniture, using German timber. Although in formal terms a clear example of archaism, the designs were nevertheless specified in the format of a RAL *Lieferbedingungen,* that is, as a technical specification that was strictly standardized and appropriate to mass-production. In other words, styling, the second aspect of industrial modernity in design, was here used to give an aesthetic, ideological veneer to the underlying aims of the regime.

The subordination of both technology and the crafts to the purposes of the party was consistently justified in Nazi propaganda by stressing the overriding importance of purpose rather than means. Industry had been the tool, it was argued, and the crafts the victim in the Weimar Republic of the self-seeking ends of capitalist exploitation, international cosmopolitanism and individual greed. The same means, it was stressed, could be beneficial if placed in the service of the regeneration of the German nation.

The policies of Hitler's government therefore established a framework that had a profound effect upon design in an indirect sense. It is necessary to ask, however, what specific influence these events and innovations had upon form in design and upon the role of designers in the Third Reich. Here, it is necessary to distinguish between propaganda and practice. Continuous efforts were made by party organizations and publicists to identify both technical modernity and traditional craft forms as integral cultural manifestations of the regime and the national resurgence it claimed to have stimulated. Yet an examination of the range of forms produced in this period shows that there was no particular set of design concepts and forms that can be regarded as specific to the regime, apart that is, from the range of signs and symbols that had the function of a corporate identity programme for the nation. Even when products were manufactured as a direct result of government-sponsored programmes, as with the Volkswagen car and Volksempfanger radios, the forms and design concepts employed in fact pre-dated the regime and were simply appropriated for or adapted to its purposes. Moreover, although the power of the government was extensive, it did not extend to total control over all areas of production in the pre-war period. Individual companies therefore retained a considerable degree of autonomy. Some did indeed attempt to identify themselves with the regime, as in the Adler advertisement of 1938, but again, neither the streamlined car, nor the Berlin exhibition hall in the stripped neo-classical style adopted for official buildings in the Nazi period, were specific to the regime. It could be argued that such attempts to identify with the regime, or what was believed to be the prevailing mood of the time, were as much concerned with commercial opportunism as anything else. Many firms in fact pursued a policy of self-interest, continuing to exploit sections of the market with goods that had commercial appeal but were frequently castigated as being detrimental to government aims, such as the furniture illustrated in a book entitled *Moderne Gebrauchsmöbel* (Modem Useful Furniture).[19] It contained 120 pages of furniture in an extensive variety of decorative styles for all parts of the house, even the simpler forms based on rural styles having a large, pretentious scale, with heavy proportions set on large ponderous feet being the only overall theme. There was, in fact, a continuity of the diversity found in the 1920s, and, moreover, a continuity of the debates and polemics on the elements of that diversity during the Third Reich. Although furniture such as that illustrated in *Moderne Gebrauchsmöbel* could not be forbidden, such products were the constant target for criticism by official bodies and critics sympathetic to the regime. The basis of the criticism was twofold: firstly, an advocacy of 'good design' and the beneficial role it could play in improving life; and secondly, the association of that concept with the ideology and policies of the regime. Typical of a large number of similar publications was the book *Unsere Wohnmöbel (Our Domestic Furniture)* by Fritz Spannagel, published in 1937. Spannagel associated the form of domestic furniture with one of the favourite themes of Nazi ideology, that of the family, the womb of the nation: '...the great task therefore falls to our domestic furniture to work for the reconstruction of the family and thereby of our state.'[20] In order to do this, furniture should embody the three characteristics of irreproachable quality, functionality, and also 'be so beautiful that through its formal language it delights and brings happiness.'[21]

This, he argued, could only be achieved by craftsmanship, though it was stressed that this did not mean hand production. '*No, craft work should know how to use machines and all* available technical achievements. But the progress of technology that enables a rational form of work, should above all be placed in the service of an honourable and craftsmanly achievement... Machines should not henceforward be used to produce qualitatively inferior mass-products that serve only commercially profit-minded sponsors.'[22] One can see a reflection in Spannagel's argument of the frequently recurring theme of the association and reconciliation of both technology and the crafts in the service of higher national ideals.

The role of design in the policies of the Nazi government, and the clearest and most extensive image of the specific forms it took, were to appear from 1939 onwards in a series of loose-leaved volumes under the collective title of the *Deutsche Warenkunde* (German Index of Goods).[23] Published at the instigation of Adolf Ziegier, head of the State Chamber of Visual Arts, it contained an impressive array of designs selected and approved by official bodies for a wide variety of domestic and commercial purposes. The standard, in a formalist sense, was generally very good and frequently outstanding, and it included a number of outstanding designs from the 1920s, many by avant-garde designers, that were still in production.

The official view of the function of the *Deutsche Warenkunde* was discussed in an article in the journal of the RKW, which praised the *Warenkunde* as 'visual and educative material for shaping artistic taste and education in the new German way of life. The Deutsche Warenkunde should be a guide to a racially pure material environment, free of foreign influences, of stupidities and deformations, that corresponds to our whole German renewal, and in addition stimulates designers and manufacturers of our objects of use to produce beautifully formed, well made and functional creations.' The place of the Warenkunde in the government's economic strategy was also stressed: 'The effect of the *Deutsche Warenkunde* in an economic sense relates to two main tasks: the carrying out of the Four Year Plan, and the external trade question. The Four Year Plan requires clarification and direction for producers and users, and it is therefore important to have a means of education by example, of current, characteristic craftsmanship and the increased application of domestic raw materials, which serve simultaneously the principles of efficiency and raw materials freedom. It can also serve foreign trade by providing a comprehensive catalogue of the best German quality manufactures.'[24] The concept of 'good design,' subordinated to such ends, can hardly be described as a subversion of the regime, but rather its precise opposite: it was seen as an appropriate expression of government policies and given extensive publicity and heavily-funded support.

Does this mean, however, that the work illustrated in the *Warenkunde* and other official publications was, as claimed, an expression of the regime? Here, one enters a discussion of the nature of the design process and the extent to which creative activity can be regarded as an instrument of social and political relationships. In this respect a quote from an article by Henryk Katz is highly appropriate: 'Every creator is a complicated, autonomous nature with individual relationships and a personal history that can be determined partly by social conditions, but also by biology, from the strength of intellect or by capacity for feeling.'[25] The emphasis in that passage on the need to consider a balance between uniquely individual characteristics and general social forces is important when considering design, since although designers depend upon their individual creative capacity, their work also requires an ability to reconcile the frequently competing demands placed upon them from a variety of external sources and resolve them into a formal unity.

The need to cope with these external demands makes a discussion of design untenable without a consideration of these factors, which severely restrict a designer's autonomy. The work of designers became even more restricted in the 1920s as their work evolved as one element in a complex division of labour in large industrial combines. In the Third Reich, their freedom of action was further contained by the government policies described above. Yet although the preconditions for designers' work became more strongly defined, the individual creative power that worked on the basis of those preconditions remained unaltered, enabling many formal solutions of high quality to be created. In this sense, it is possible to construct an argument that designers' work is independent of political and social influences.

To sustain such an argument, however, consideration would have to be limited to the relationship between designer and object, ignoring the social preconditions mentioned above, and equally importantly, ignoring the fact that the end product of the creative process of design is an object of use. Use is not an abstraction, but a tangible act that may be identified and responsibility for it established. In this sense, the whole context of design had indeed changed in the Third Reich.

The changes were twofold: firstly, the economic policies of the Third Reich were intended to encourage and tolerate only what was useful for its ends, and it is clear that modernity, on several levels of meaning, was regarded as vitally important for the realization of those ends; secondly, although the creative work of designers cannot be considered solely as an expression of political conditions, the application of a great many of the products of that creative act were used for the realization of the aims of the regime, and must therefore be considered as an instrument of those political purposes.

The general conclusions which emerge from a study of this period are that the emphasis on the strand of work and thought represented by the Bauhaus in the Weimar Republic and its subsequent closure by the Nazis has obscured the extent of the continuity that existed between Weimar and the Third Reich; further, the depiction of one avant-garde strand of 1920s design as being uniquely 'modern' has obscured the extent to which the Nazi regime not only used modernity, but depended upon it; finally, it places in question the widely asserted equation between concepts of 'good form' and desirable or beneficial political or ethical values. The history of German design between the wars shows clearly that identical design forms and concepts can be used for very dissimilar purposes, and it is therefore necessary in any study of design to include a consideration of the social conditions of production and use as an integral element.

In the 1920s and 1930s in Germany, there was an essential continuity in design in that it became progressively more closely linked to technological innovation and industrial organization and production. But, in the Third Reich, the paradox existed that modernity was placed in the service of an archaic political ideology and the military preparations for a war of aggression. The ironies and complexities of this situation have their origins not only in the policies of the National Socialist regime, but also in the nature of the modernization process itself and in the social and economic role played by large industry and craft organisations in Germany in these years, and it is necessary to range far beyond aesthetic factors alone in order to begin to probe this pattern and its meaning.

Notes

1 Scheerer, Hans. *Gestaltung im Dritten Reich*, in *Form*, Vol. 69, Nos. 1, 2 and 3, 1975.

2 Gysling-Billeter, Erika. *Die angewandte Kunst: Sachlichkeit trotz Diktatur*, in: *Die Dreissiger Jahre: Schauplatz Deutschland*, Munich, 1977, p. 171.

3 Ibid, p. 171.

4 Ibid, p. 171.

5 For further discussion of these terms, see Mason, Tim W. *Zur Entstehung des Gesetzes zur Ordnung der nationalen Arbeit vom 20. Januar 1934: Ein Versuch über das Verhältnis 'archaischer' und 'moderner' Momente in der neuesten deutschen Geschichte*, in: *Mommsen, Petzina and Weisbrod (eds.) Industrielles System und politische Entwicklung in der Weimarer Republik*, Düsseldorf, 1974.

6 National Industry Conference Board (eds.), *Rationalization of German Industry*, New York, 1931, p. vii.

7 *Zweckmässige Beleuchting und rationelle Wirtschaft*, in: *RKW-Nachrichten*, 4th Year, Nr. 6, 1933, p. 171.

8 Ibid, p. 171.

9 *RKW und RAL nehmen Stellung zur Frage der Gutesicherung*, in: *RKW-Nachrichten*, 7th Year, Nr. l, 1933, p. 3.

10 *Siemens & Halske auf der Funkausstellung 1932* in *Siemens Zeitschrift*, August 1932, p. 288.

11 Bundesarchiv Koblenz, Bestand R32/1. Quoted in a letter to Dr. E. Römer, 13.2.1933.

12 Bundesarchiv Koblens, Bestand R32/443. Letter from Dr. E, Redslob to Dr. P. Bruckmann, President of the German Werkbund, p. 5

13 Statistic from *Wirtschaftsbeobachter* in: *Der Vierjahresplan*, Vol. 3, 1939, p. 1028.

14 Paul Walter, *Handwerk auf neum Wegen*, Berlin, 1937, p. 12.

15 Ibid, p. 34.

16 *Grossdeutscher Handwerktag, Berlin 1939, Rede des Reiehshandwerkmeisters.* Typescript in Staatsbibliothek, Berlin, p. 15.

17 Ibid, p. 27.

18 Reichsamt Schönheit der Arbeit' (eds.), *Das Möbelbuch: Schönheit der Arbeit*, Berlin, 1937.

19 *Moderne Gebrauchsmöbel*, Berlin, 1937.

20 Fritz Spannagel, *Unsere Wohnmöbel*, Ravensburg, 1937, p. 6.

21 Ibid, pp. 59–60.

22 Ibid, p. 5.

23 Kunst-Dienst (eds.) *Deutsche Warenkunde*, Berlin, 1939–40.

24 *Eine deutsche Warenkunde* in: *RKW-Nachrichten*, 13th Year, Vol. 6, Sept. 1939, p. 12.

25 Katz, Henryk. *Arbeiter, Mittelklasse und die NSDAP: vRandbemerkungen zu zwei amerikanischen Studien, in Internationale wissentschaftliche Korrespondenz zur Geschichte der deutschen Arbeiterbewegung (IWK)*, Vol. 3, 1974, p. 307.

PART III

Design, Business, Economics

An Introduction to the Readings in Part III

As the reader works through the material below, it will become apparent that, more so than in the previous sections, the readings interact with one another and speak across the boundaries of the categories they have been placed under. For example, reading #20, 'Learning from Germany's integrated design policy', could be read with profit in between Heskett's critique of General Motor's (GM's) lack of corporate policy on the design of their cars (#14) and his wider critique of designer's attitude to business (#15) and his studies of the attempts in the late 1980s by the Phillips company in Holland and by RCA in the United States a few years later to create integral policies on corporate design and innovation (#16–17). Similarly, reading #22, which explores three suggestions for future design policy in the United Kingdom, does so by developing a number of propositions on the role of design in creating value and, in fact, acts as a kind of 'applied' version of reading #26, Heskett's major published attempt to articulate an economic theory of how value is created through, and as a result of, design.

This should not be surprising. Questions of corporate strategies, of national design policy and of the (economic) value created by design and value naturally flow into each other. Indeed, the interactions *between* (A) strategies and approaches in business, (B) wider questions of design policy and (C) how the creation of (economic) value through or by design should be understood is Heskett's particular field. It is how he understands what is at work in that triangle that gives his work its interest.

Allowing for that, however, the three major categories used to organize his writings in these areas – concerns with strategy at the company level, policy at national level and the value-creating possibilities of design – are those suggested by the material itself. These loose groupings, moreover, allow the reader to glimpse a body of work in each of these areas.

(a) Corporate design policies

A review of the dates of publication of these pieces would show that many, though not all, of the material presented springs from a very productive period in Heskett's life, his first few years in the United States between 1989 and the mid-1990s. During that time Heskett was adjusting to life in Chicago (and not least to a new marriage) and teaching on the graduate programmes in the Institute of Design. The focus of the latter on design strategy and design policy became, by necessity, Heskett's too. At the same time he was invited to become a contributing editor and to write a regular column on design and business for the (then) bimonthly magazine *I.D. International Design*. Meeting deadlines for these short columns – most are under three thousand words – was evidently not an easy task (as someone who was also writing columns for *I.D.* at the same time I can attest to the pressure), but it allowed, and perhaps even provoked, him into writing in a less guarded and less 'neutral' manner than in his more academic texts. The result was a series of sharp, pointed critiques and observations around corporate and national design policy and the relations of design and business (see readings #14, 15, 17, 20, 23). What was explored in these pieces, in turn, carried over into writings for bodies such as the American Center for Design (#3), the Industrial Designers Society of America (IDSA) (#24) and for other journals – for example, the important short article on the economic benefits of national design policies undertaken for the German magazine *MD* (#18). But as is pointed by Carlos Teixeira below, these chapters are by no means simply critiques in the negative sense, they also contain vigorous assertions for policies and for changes in attitude by both design and business. Taken together, these short pieces provide what I would call the 'observational matrix' which helps contextualize the more detailed case studies of design policy and design and business that he also undertook in these years – the case studies on Phillips and RCA, for example, referred to above (readings #16 and #17) and his extended studies of national design policy.

(b) National design policies

As Carlos Teixeira's introduction makes clear (see between readings #18 and #19), the issue of national design policies was important to Heskett in the early 1990s. Coming of age as a historian of industrial design in the 1970s and 1980s in the United Kingdom, Heskett not only had experienced first-hand government support for design in industry but also had watched both import penetration and, after 1979, the policies of the Thatcher government, work to set in chain the eventual destruction of much British manufacturing. Moving to the United States and specifically to Chicago, Heskett was immediately struck by the obvious parallels – the Midwest 'rust belt' being comparable in many ways to what was happening in the older industrial areas of Britain. The question of how then to develop adequate policy for design within companies and institutions and by nations became a central concern, not least pedagogically as he discussed the issue with students from a wide range of countries – and indeed later on he was invited by a number of governments or organizations to speak on developing design policy (for example, among others, Chile, Mexico, Finland, Taiwan, Hong Kong and South Africa). In 1993 he wrote a short piece (not reproduced here) on a possible US design policy ('Taking the Next Steps in Washington' *I.D.* March/April, 1993), and he had long been involved on and off with the UK Design Council (See for example 'Making Waves: Britain's new Design Council mandates a changing of the guards' in *I-D, International Design*, September/October, 1994, as well as reading #22). The first reading collected here (#19) provides a useful short survey of Heskett's views on the possibilities of national design policies. The second (#20) looks specifically at Germany as a model and lesson for the United States. Although written in the 1990s, its observations and prescriptions have lost nothing of their force. Finally, there are two 'applications' of Heskett's concern for policy, here taken from his contribution to the Cox report drafted for the UK government in 2005. Reading #21 is analytical, examining the mix of planning and non-planning in policies for design and industry in China. Reading #22 is prescriptive and suggestive, applying some of Heskett's ideas of 'creating economic value by design' to future design policy for the United Kingdom.

(c) Creating value by design

The short chapters on design and business and design policy prepare the way for – and importantly illustrate the necessity of – Heskett's major contribution to this whole field, his work on design and the creation of value. In the Reader, this work is represented by four chapters; two short pieces looking respectively at 'creative destruction' and the management of change (#23) and at product integrity (#24) and two extended studies – a talk on 'Cultural Human Factors', developed for the Institute of Design in Chicago in 1995 (#25), and which reflects some aspects of Heskett's teaching around cultural factors in successful product innovation – and the longest single reading in the whole book, the chapter 'Creating Economic Value by Design' (#26), which was published in the *International Journal of Design* (Taiwan) in 1998, and which is a partial digest of the seminar 'Design and the Creation of Value' referred to earlier. This paper links both to the policy proposals Heskett developed for the United Kingdom (reading #22 – which are developments of some points analysed here) and to the key reading on design and economics in Part I (#3). It ties together, therefore, in a single study, albeit in condensed form, some of Heskett's most important work on elucidating the economic value created by design.

Finally, and importantly, the chapters by Heskett in this section are complemented and introduced by chapters by three specialist authors who place Heskett's work on policy and value in its wider context. Carlos Teixeira, who was a PhD student of Heskett's at the Institute of Design in IIT in Chicago, and who is now a professor of design management in Parsons School of Design in New York, contributes a short chapter on Heskett's views on design policy in its national and corporate contexts. Tore Kristensen, a professor at the Copenhagen Business School, who has a very long-standing interest in the questions of design, business and innovation, offers an important contextualization of Heskett's work on design, value and economics. They are joined by Heskett's long-time colleague in Chicago and Hong Kong, Sharon Helmer Poggenpohl, who contributes a short but apposite introduction titled *Design between Economics and Practice*.

(A)
Corporate Design Strategies: Design between Economics and Practice

by Sharon Helmer Poggenpohl

In the nineteenth century, Victorian historian Thomas Carlyle coined the phrase 'the dismal science' with reference to economics. As twentieth- and twenty-first-century life is driven increasingly by seemingly imperative financial issues framed by quantitative metrics, it is foolhardy for design to downplay or ignore entirely its relationship to this unavoidable reality. But who among us has tried to understand this linkage?

Thoughtful and soft-spoken, John Heskett brought his background from the London School of Economics and his interest in history together, creating a new lens through which to examine design. He respected the quantitative, but was equally concerned with the more elusive qualitative aspects. His focus was to uncover and frame two essential ideas: how design delivered value to both business concerns and product users and how design might be better integrated in business and more fully incorporate its fundamental value – design thinking. He approached these two ideas through practical histories of design and business that went well beyond typical design histories that follow an art historical trajectory or celebrate short-term visual and material trends, and through scholarship based on his understanding of economic theory and business practice.

Design in its myriad realizations was hard to pin down in simple terms, but Heskett persevered, coming to the understanding that design was layered in multiple ways within business, culture and user experience. His investigations brought him to an international perspective regarding governmental policy as it influenced business and design. He was critical always, looking for the edge where improvement or newer ideas could flourish. No one's pawn, he worked from his own perspective and sought to help design better understand the integrity of product development and realization that made for business success through user satisfaction.

Heskett was critical of the state of design education. Design thinking could provide much more than superficial styling and technical expertise. He understood that difficult problems and emerging opportunities required collaborative effort from diverse people; that human-centred design approaches helped to eliminate some of the uncertainties that design necessarily faces; that business and design were partners in change; and that the pursuit of design history was more than objects, images and dates, but a search for effective patterns that pointed to an improved life environment.

His work provides a foundation that others may build upon. The lens he created for understanding and positioning design practice within business with quality-of-life improvement as the goal can sustain lively historical approaches to design in which we can learn from both successes and failures. Further, it suggests both a deeper look into economic theory and the practical integration of such theory with business and design. He was constantly interested in the question of what a case study in design might be. Compared with business or medical case histories, design is nowhere. Unfortunately, none of his students picked up this important investigation, but someone may yet establish a framework that could invite broad participation and provide for comparison among cases that could grow into a practical database. He leaves a legacy of critical thinking and research – opening design in a new and vital way.

14

GM's Current Woes Reveal the Price of Corporate Arrogance and Amnesia

Last December, while 1 was rereading the autobiography of Alfred P. Sloan Jr., *My Tears with General Motors,* news broke that the present chairman of GM, Robert Stempel, had announced more plant closings and the loss of 71,000 jobs. Sloan, who built GM into the greatest company the world has known, must have been spinning in his grave. Reaction in the media was widely unsympathetic. Mike Royko, the acerbic columnist of the Chicago Tribune, recounted his experience 30 years ago of buying a new Chevrolet that was a clunker, and getting no response from the company. "... GM did it to itself," he concluded. "If it had not been stiffing customers and had made quality products, there wouldn't have been much of a Japanese and European car invasion." But GM is not an isolated case. Rather it is symptomatic of a generation of companies once dominant but now struggling to adapt to competition and change. As the largest and most powerful of these firms, however, the problems of the automobile companies are more public and painful.

Sympathy for the automobile companies would flow more easily if they acknowledged their present woes as essentially of their own making, but such honesty is an exception. It is simpler in difficult times to blame problems on someone else. Scapegoats are easy targets, something Americans should well understand, having often been the butt of other countries' discontents over the years. Yet it often seems Americans are collectively intent on proving the old adage about those who fail to learn from history being condemned to repeat its errors.

First published as "GM's current woes reveal the price of corporate arrogance and amnesia," *I.D. International Design*, May/June, 1992, pp. 38–40. By permission of F & W Media (New York).

Detroit's amnesia

An example is the resentful implication that the Japanese have "stolen" or "copied" designs and processes developed in the U.S. and somehow, through underhanded dealing, made a commercial success of them. This conviction can be hilariously funny until one realizes that many people take it extremely seriously. They don't know, and maybe don't want to know, that the foundations of American industrial power were laid by very similar means.

Detroit's convenient amnesia, for example, omits mentioning that the automobile was not an American invention—it originated in Europe. And Americans did exactly what they accuse the Japanese of lately doing, namely, manufacturing a product invented somewhere else, in unprecedented quantities, to hitherto unknown standards of design and quality, at a price affordable by millions, and with great benefit to themselves. It is a perfectly legitimate thing to do, and good business if done well. We should get back to doing more of it.

Art, color and style

Mass manufacturing automobiles was, of course, the great achievement of Henry Ford. In 1907, he began to produce a single design, the Model T, and fundamentally changed American society. But Ford's dominance collapsed after two decades because Henry refused to acknowledge changing market conditions. Whether he actually made the apocryphal statement frequently attributed to him, "You can have any color you like, as long as it's black" is unclear, but it certainly epitomized his attitude. He knew what the public wanted, and what the public should want was what suited Ford. Success bred arrogance and inflexibility. Ford's rise and demise also set a pattern from which, seemingly, nothing has been learned.

Ford got his comeuppance in the mid-1920s from the aforesaid Alfred P. Sloan, who had overhauled GM, adding a new emphasis on mass marketing. Sloan's influence on the course of American design in the twentieth century has been little recognized—after all, he was a manager, not a designer— but in many ways he emerges as a decisive figure in shaping our concepts of what corporate design should be and how it should be organized. His strategy was to organize GM into vertical divisions corresponding to socio-economic market definitions based on income, in order to provide different models for the entire population at every stage of life. Basic engineering quality should be taken for granted, he argued, with standardized, mass-produced components used across model ranges. Variations in surface style were therefore to serve as the prime differentiator in the market.

To achieve this balance of visual change and technical continuity, Sloan appointed Harley Earl, from a coach building firm in California, to head a newly created Art and Color Section in 1927. Noting this was also the year that Ford finally withdrew the Model T, Sloan wrote, "Thus styling came into the picture as one era ended and another began." He was aware of the problems of inserting a new discipline into an existing managerial structure, and identified a perennial problem with the comment: "An automobile stylist is an advocate of change to a degree that was at first somewhat startling to production and engineering executives." To ensure acceptance of the new function, it was organized centrally, with Earl reporting directly to Sloan.

"In the 1930s I renamed the Art and Color Section the Styling Section," Sloan wrote. "In the terminology of the automobile business, model appearance is now generally called 'styling,' and the designers are 'stylists.'" He not only defined terminology, but established styling as central to his strategy and positioned it accordingly. "The growing importance of styling was symbolized by the appointment of Harley Earl as a vice president of the corporation on September 3, 1940. He was the first stylist to be given such a position, and indeed, I believe, the first designer in any major industry to become a vice president." By the 1950s, the Styling Section had grown to over 1400 employees.

When GM was impressive

The GM model of design was adopted by other automobile companies and by firms in other industries. Indeed, if one considers current arguments about promoting design in companies— support from the CEO, positioning design at a senior level, focusing on products, allocating adequate staff, facilities and so on—General Motors under Sloan was a pioneer and a model.

Apropos of introducing design into business school curricula, Sloan's autobiography is probably the only book with any reference to design read by several generations of business school students. As a result, his concept of design as styling still has enormous sway over American corporate consciousness.

As a formula it was incredibly effective. For many years, the cars that emerged from this system were truly impressive. (This was underlined for me recently when watching the film *Bugsy*. Set in the late 1940s, the period automobiles were compelling images, their appeal and character constantly provoking the question. Why can't they do the same today?) Moreover, GM not only dominated the U.S. economy, but successfully ventured out into the world.

By 1960, for example, it was taking over the Australian market. British automobile manufacturers responded similarly to Ford; dominant, believing they knew best, they complacently ignored the fact that driving vast distances on corrugated dirt roads imposed different demands on a car than taking local trips on well-paved English country lanes. GM bought a small company, Holden, for $15 million, applied its experience in designing bigger, more powerful cars to Australian conditions and manufactured a line of models there. Within a short time, the Australian subsidiary was shipping profits back to the U.S. that were annually many times the initial purchase price of Holden.

Design became parochial

So what went wrong? There are no simple answers. In part, Sloan's emphasis on external form as a marketing device eventually led to a gulf between form and function, between image and reality. The balance was lost. Harley Earl once said, "You can design a car so that every time you get in it, it's a relief—you have a little vacation for a while." This kind of escapism, achieved while the fundamentals of engineering were increasingly neglected in favor of financial manipulation, played a role in the company's subsequent decline.

GM's huge size and unwieldy bureaucracy also took a toll. Sloan had always sought a diversity of design ideas, insisting each division should have its own distinctive character. But his successors played it safe, massaged the numbers, and soon one product was indistinguishable from the next. Since all the automobile companies followed GM's lead, by the 1970s a depressing similarity and lack of quality had opened the door for overseas competitors.

And what of Sloan's concept of design as the cutting edge in recommending products to customers? It turns out that it wasn't design that was neglected, but the customers. Design became absorbed by a profound inertia stemming from success. It became parochial, refusing to acknowledge that other approaches might be valid. In 1989, the head of GM Design, Chuck Jordan, was quoted at the Tokyo Motor Show as saying, "The Japanese haven't gotten their act together, design-wise. There are some ugly, ugly cars here." Buyers across the world were deciding otherwise.

Meanwhile, back home in the U.S., GM ran a series of national advertisements trumpeting more design awards from the Industrial Designers Society of America over the last 10 years than any other corporation. Compare this with GM's loss of 10 percent of the total U.S. auto market in that same period, mainly to Japan's "ugly, ugly cars" and we have a negative correlation between design and commercial success!

The problem was not simply one of design, however. The question facing GM was what kind of company it was to be and, above all, how it would relate to its customers by what kind of design. It wasn't easy for the company's executives to accept that Sloan's legacy, his master formula, no longer applied. Neither did his concept of design. Times had changed.

Peter Drucker, a most thoughtful management analyst, points out that organizing production for a vertical market model based on socio-economic parameters ignores the way markets have evolved over the years, a process that was already evident some 15 years ago. Young people, argues Drucker, constitute a "lifestyle" market and it is for this group that the Japanese design.

The expression of values

The implications here are sweeping. Lifestyle cannot be conveniently categorized by the statistical groupings typical of the socio-economic model. It hinges instead on multiple decisions made by individual customers—how they define themselves, rather than how producers define them. Lifestyle is volatile, subtle and varied, sometimes dependent on intangibles and nuances, sometimes oriented toward consistency, dependability and safety.

Above all, lifestyle expresses values, and requires a corresponding expression of values in the products offered to meet that market's needs. Although the engineering quality of American automobiles has clearly improved recently, measures of success based on statistical conformance may not be enough. In a lifestyle market, performance quality is something everyone takes for granted. Adding value by design will need to mean what it implies: a content of real value, expressed through both aesthetic and economic dimensions.

Meanwhile, the continuing pleas for protection from Detroit ignore this trend, insisting instead that American designs be judged in terms different to what manufacturers in the rest of the world can provide. Protectionism of this kind is self-interested, seeking to deny the American public its right to purchase the best design from wherever it comes.

A clear vision of the future

Decline is not inevitable. Ford reversed a trend in the early 1980s by encouraging its designers to focus on what they believed to be the best. But staunching the hemorrhage at GM and other companies that dominated the age of mass production will require a fundamental cultural shift. From the illusion that everything can be altered but nothing has to change, there needs to be an acceptance that times are profoundly different. This means facing the future instead of trying to recreate the glories of the past, coming to terms with this different world, rather than expecting it to dance to your tune.

Understanding a user-oriented market requires another kind of business organization, with a radically different application of design, going far beyond the concept of styling. This shift represents an enormous challenge, requiring confidence and a clear vision of the future. In contrast, demands that Americans buy products they don't want and that Japanese buy products not even designed for their conditions, reinforce a sense of obsolete, producer-oriented arrogance.

I recall hearing that the CEOs of the big three auto companies would accompany President Bush to Japan from a news broadcast during a radio program of Christmas carols. I don't know if it was intentional, but the familiar sound of "We Three Kings of Orient Are" immediately followed the bulletin, reminding me of a childhood parody of the carol, but with just one word appropriately substituted for the 1990s:

We three kings of Detroit are,
One in a truck and one in a car.
One on a scooter, blowing his hooter,
Wondering just where we are.
Detroit's kings all seem to be wondering where they are.

15

Everything Alters, Nothing Changes: Why Don't American Companies Use Design More Intelligently?

Not too long ago, designers could complain, with justice, of a general lack of recognition from business and commerce. Over the last five years, however, all that has begun to change. Business newspapers and journals now show interest, with occasional articles and reviews of design. True, the level of understanding these reveal varies, often demonstrating the way news media operate as a self-justifying system, with, in particular, their penchant for scavenging whatever might be newsworthy from each other, resulting in them all saying much the same thing. Consequently, there tends to be a mind-numbing repetition of the people, points of view and quotations cited, without alternatives being brought into consideration. Another uniform feature is that such articles generally parrot the superficial belief that the purpose of design is, above all, to swell the profits of a corporation.

This has all been welcomed by the design community. They are grateful for some belated recognition, and are doing their best to demonstrate that they can indeed help convert some of the red or increase the black digits on corporate balance sheets. They excuse the trivialities with well-intentioned phrases about the need for a learning curve – "it's a start anyway, isn't it, and everything will in time improve?" Interestingly, their good-natured tolerance

First published as "Why don't American companies use design more intelligently?" *I.D. International Design*, January/February 1992, pp. 36–9. By permission of F & W Media (New York). "Everything Alters, Nothing Changes" was the original title of the ms. Heskett submitted to I.D.

overlooks the fact that if they made such excuses about their own work, they would have very little credibility as design professionals.

This would all be fine if it really did result in a greater awareness of design and what its contribution can be. But the rate at which companies are currently laying off design staff and cutting design budgets supports the belief that design is still one of the first functions in a business organization to be sliced up when times get tough. In addition, with design consultancies experiencing real difficulties and some going under, the plain fact is that all the recent recognition does not yet seem to be bringing home the bacon.

You will perhaps gather from the above that I have a somewhat jaundiced view of the new wave of design awareness and the expectations that it will transform the U.S. economy. But statements made in a business publication that design in the 'nineties is going to be for business what finance was to the seventies and marketing to the eighties, raise some nagging doubts. Just what were finance and marketing to business in those past decades, and just where have they led the U.S. economy?

Considered in an international context, at least, the answer has to be: into trade deficit and a lack of competitiveness. However, it isn't fair to criticize the business press when crass statements emanate from the design community, to the effect that the U.S. doesn't have a trade deficit, but a design deficit.

This reduces a highly complex problem to a ridiculous level of over-simplification. Promotional band-wagon jumping of that ilk suggests design is some kind of universal nostrum to solve all our problems. And that, frankly, worries me stiff. If such sweeping claims and expectations are established for design, it can easily be blamed for all setbacks and failures that occur in the future. And we will be back to design being discredited and ignored.

It isn't that recognition for design from the business community is unwelcome—on the contrary, it is desperately needed and long overdue. Neither should the contribution design can make to the success and profitability of a business venture be underestimated—it can be huge if managed intelligently.

The basic problem, however, remains: why are US companies in general so slow to introduce design as an integral part of determining what a product can be and do? Is it incompetence on the part of business management? Yet there are around 700 business schools in the USA, with figures being quoted of 25% of the annual output of graduates from higher education being in disciplines directly related to business management. This is a scale unparalleled in the world.

If the viability of industry and commerce was indeed dependent on educating management in a wide range of skills and competences in business schools, and on the seriousness with which business is regarded, indicated by the shelf length of books and publications, reinforced by widespread media coverage on business matters, the USA ought to be light years ahead of the rest of the world. The evidence, however, is too often to the contrary: that in many key areas it has fallen behind.

The realization of unpleasant facts such as this often leads to a search for scapegoats—the enemy without and the enemy within. Hence the trends of bashing the Japs and beating up on the MBAs. The Japanese, it is true, do have a stubborn tendency to market products that satisfy purchasers, and should be reprehended for this unfair practice. The MBAs, however, are as much victims as perpetrators. Their education is a reflection of current thinking on what is needed in industry and commerce. The fault lies not in their skills and abilities, but the context in which they are applied. And all too often, in that context, financial and marketing concepts have primacy over an understanding of design and manufacturing, over what it takes to make products.

Therefore, to simply suggest injecting competent designers into companies where there is no understanding of what design means and is capable of contributing, could be a recipe for disaster. In other words, taking design seriously is not just a matter of adding an embellishment, the icing on the cake, that will turn a quick profit but not disturb current concepts or organizations. It means changing the recipe, with a different mix and chemistry, and a different kind of outcome. It doesn't mean the primacy of design over other disciplines, but the integration of all necessary disciplines into a new configuration.

This process of change will also make great demands on designers and how they function in a business context. Essentially, the current campaign for their wider utilization says little about how they will have to adapt to rapidly changing conditions in organizations, technologies, products, markets and users, and with what consequences. Too often, it seems that designers expect a wider remit for their skills without this fundamentally affecting how they think or practice.

In addition, go to enough design conferences, listen a while to presentations and conversations afterwards in the bar, and it will become evident that many designers believe in Fairy Godfathers. What is needed to create the client of their dreams, is for some senior manager in a business to carry the banner for them, slay on demand the Dragons of Doubt about Design, and generally act as benevolent patron and protector. Across the present century, there have indeed been notable examples of such business leaders, for example, Camillo Olivetti, Frank Pick of London Transport, the Braun brothers, Thomas Watson Jr of IBM, and Klaus-Jiirgen Maack of ERCO, who made design a central feature of their company philosophy and practice and an example for their time.

While acknowledging deep respect for such people and their achievements, however, it also has to be remembered that in any age they are exceptions, a very small minority. If designers take them as a measure of what is desirable in a client, they will generally be disappointed. They will continue to be hostages to fortune, dependent upon whoever they happen to find themselves subordinate to, and never able to argue their own case in their own terms.

The point here is that designers too will need to fundamentally change if they are to break out of their present dominant function as middle-level executants, dancing to tunes others call, and make a genuinely effective contribution to business success. They will need to stop looking to other people to solve their problems and start developing the abilities necessary to function at the highest levels of corporate decision making.

Above all, the danger is of a situation in which everything alters and nothing changes. My skepticism is grounded in the belief that simply adding design to the way business in the United States is generally conceived and managed will not fundamentally alter much. It goes much deeper. To put it another way and more bluntly: American business attitudes are too often antithetical to design in any sense other than the most superficial.

That statement is sweeping and may cause offence to some of the businessmen and designers who are out there battling indifference and blinkered thinking in an effort to effect change. They do indeed need support and recognition. The combative tone stems, however, from a weariness with hearing the same old success stories too often, from too many sources, when the economic facts scream out that something is amiss. For example, Ford did a good job with the Taurus, but that was ten years ago and it didn't give Ford a decisive competitive edge because they didn't follow through fast enough with a consistent, comprehensive product development policy. Xerox effectively combined in-house and consultant designers to reverse a downward trend in market share against Japanese competition, also in the early eighties. Apple created a marvel with the Macintosh, but that too was way back. Even if more up-to-date examples are described, they fail to answer the question: why don't more U.S businesses use design intelligently? Maybe looking beyond the clichéd success stories to some of the problem cases can tell us more about what is amiss.

Consider, for example, some statements at a conference in Chicago by Douglas Stannard, former President of Beatrice Europe, on the role of design in that company. The role of design, he asserted, was to help him sell—a widely held and unexceptional point-of-view. Interestingly, however, he also identified a primary role of the company's design program as improving the image of Beatrice and raising its value. The program to increase awareness of the company and its brands had as direct result, according to Mr. Stannard, the raising of the stock price from $18–24 a share, to the price of $50 a share at which it was acquired, with consequent benefit to shareholders and investors. Moral disapproval of this action is water off a duck's back, and it must be clearly understood that Mr. Stannard and his company were totally within their rights to regard design as useful in this purpose. It is an example, however, of a tendency in U.S. business to regard the massaging of stock value (what the Japanese call "financial engineering") as more important than generating genuinely new products to keep a company viable. Another indicator is a statement of Coca-Cola CEO, Roberto Goizueta, in *Fortune* magazine, that the goal now is not to be a good marketer or good engineer (or presumably a good designer), but to invest to increase shareholder value.

The emphasis on share value, which stresses short-term thinking, and its effect on corporate philosophy and strategy is one problem. Another is the widespread belief in the power of imagery detached from reality. An example: in 1990, Oldsmobile found themselves in trouble with declining sales and market share. They had an advertising campaign which, according to surveys, achieved huge national recognition through the slogan, "This is not your father's automobile, this is a new generation of Olds." Not much wrong there, one might think, apart from the problem that the cars weren't selling. The solution was to shoot the messenger, i.e. fire the advertising agency, and hire a new one. The fresh minds applied to the task came up with the self-congratulatory slogan of "Your Gallant Men of Olds." Still the cars aren't selling in the desired quantities. While the latest ad-men slip on their bullet-proof vests, it might be pertinent to ask: could something be amiss with the design of the vehicles?

In contrast, in 1990 Nissan launched its "Infiniti" luxury car with an advertising campaign that didn't feature the product, but was filled with lovely scenes of nature and husky-voiced intonations of Zen-like sentiments. They made a restful change from the usual stuff pumped out on the small screen. Comment from the advertising trade, however, was on a scale from derisive to scathing and dealers were apprehensive. Yet, despite that, sales of the car are satisfactory, and improving.

The lesson? Clearly, it is much better if image and reality coincide. And it is encouraging to know that a good product can survive a lapse in image. It would also be nice to say that no amount of money spent on razzmatazz can compensate for a product that is less than satisfactory, but that would be spitting into the wind.

The persistence of the belief in image, and its capacity for survival, was graphically illustrated some eighteen months ago, when the *Wall Street Journal* reported that Mr. Coffee Inc. was spending $2 million of its $11 million annual marketing budget on two television advertisements. These would feature Joe DiMaggio, who was Mr. Coffee's spokesman in the 1970s, when the company dominated the automatic drip coffee maker market. In the 1980s, the company switched its advertising to more product-specific themes, which according to the company's president and CEO, Mr. Peter Howell, were not as successful as Mr. DiMaggio's. As evidence, a decline in the company's market share from 32% to about 29% was cited. Mr. Coffee has set a target of an increase to 35% by 1995. Mr. Howell was quoted as saying, "If you don't advertise, all you've got left is price."

The story is interesting on many levels, as much for what it leaves out as for what it includes. According to Mr. Howell's statement, the critical factors for his company's competiveness are cheapness and image. Design, which creates the tangible actuality of a product, is nowhere mentioned in the article and seems to have no role. If, as seems to be the case, the product is secondary to price and image, no wonder that product specific advertising was unsuccessful.

The question arises: if Mr. Coffee had money to splash on nostalgic advertising, turning back to images of past success, how much did the company spend annually on design and product development to ensure future success? Did it equal the annual marketing budget of $11 million, or even the $2 million spent on two commercials featuring Joltin' Joe? It is also worth noting that the overseas companies responsible for eroding Mr. Coffee's market share, such as Braun, Krups, and Philips, all place great emphasis on design and product quality, and all are established in the value-added segments of the market. To be fair to Mr. Coffee, a piece of anecdotal evidence is worth mentioning. The manager of a Chicago branch of a well-known chain of coffee-shops affirms that since the water temperature of Mr. Coffee's machines is higher than most competitors, they do in fact brew a superior beverage. If he is right, Mr. Coffee have a powerful competitive advantage, which could be enhanced by design.

Reliance on the power of imagery independent of the product has, however, probably done more to undermine a sense of the importance of product quality in American industry than any other factor. Belief that price and image are everything stems from the period when mass-production, mass-advertising and mass-consumption were the ruling ideas in the American economy. They were sustainable for a time under conditions when the domestic market was served by American companies playing to the same rules. As soon as competition opened up on a world scale, however, and was compounded by other changes, for example, new technology and changes in the nature of markets, the rules changed.

Under these more severe competitive conditions, playing to the old hackneyed rules which usually meant using designers as cosmetic stylists to drum up new images, can have little impact outside the short term. If an image fails in terms of advertising effectiveness, and is not substantiated by some reality behind the image, there is indeed nothing left but price competition at the lower end of the market. This, in fact, is the condition in which many American companies find themselves—a pattern repeated across a wide swathe of product categories—as a result of overseas competitors' belief that image can only be as good as the product, and that designers' abilities are best applied to the latter.

16

Philips: A Study of the Corporate Management of Design. Design Policy for a Global Market

Renewal at the top

(...) By the late 1970s, Philips Board of Management was concerned by the company's perform-ance in key areas compared to many leading competitors, particularly from Japan and other Asian countries. The reasons were complex, but Dr. Wisse Dekker, then Vice-Chairman of the Board, believed there was a danger that Philips with its long traditions, could become institutionalized and inflexible in responding to changes in technology, production methods and markets. A process of restructuring the company began, which sought to shake-up the structure and free it from inhibiting rigidities. In particular, there was a need to shift the balance of power from the national organizations, which could operate almost as independent bodies, back to the product divisions with a new concept of global policy. In addition emphasis was placed on devolving responsibility and accountability downwards, giving potential for and confidence in decision making to those best able to exercise it.

In 1980 Knut Yran reached retirement age and it became necessary to appoint a new Managing Director of CIDC. In considering the profile for the post, the Board of Management again decided the appointee should have a broad international orientation to match the range of Philips products and markets, with relevant experience in design and management. This could be in a totally different branch of industry, since design was regarded as a professional activity capable of flexible application. The net was cast world-wide for a suitable candidate.

Extract from *Philips: A Study of the Corporate Management of Design*, Trefoil Books, London, 1989.

In late 1980, Robert Blaich was appointed to the post. Educated in his native USA as an architect and industrial designer, he had worked for many years for Herman Miller Inc., a leading manufacturer of furnishing systems, which had employed some of the giants of modem design, such as Charles Eames and George Nelson. Blaich had risen to the post of Vice-President for Corporate Design and Communications, in charge of product development and all visual manifestations of the company. At one point he combined that post with Managing Director of Herman Miller/ Europe for two years, based in Basle, Switzerland. He had thus gained considerable managerial experience before he left in 1979, to establish his own design/communications consulting company.

This was beginning to be successful and when first approached about the possibility of working for Philips, Blaich was dubious. However, a conversation with Dr. Dekker in New York changed his mind, convincing him the post presented interesting possibilities. Subsequent visits to Eindhoven for in-depth discussions with a range of Philips top management confirmed his feeling that 'here was a company ready to make a move,' which presented a challenge and the opportunity to respond to it. From the side of the company, it was felt he was capable of providing leadership in line with the new policy direction.

The company he entered in 1980 was a giant of the electrical industry, but in Blaich's opinion the focus on national organizations and local requirements had led to design resources being spread without real control, duplication of products and confusion in decision-making. 'Moreover,' he later wrote in the STA Design Journal of 1986, 'the corporation's image in design and communications was very grey.'

Setting out the stall

Soon after his arrival at Eindhoven, Blaich was invited to give a presentation to the Board of Management of his thoughts on how design at Philips should develop. He began by stating his belief that the design of any product or communication must above all satisfy the customer, citing criteria for evaluating user satisfaction. To make design a consistent factor in Philips future competitiveness, he proposed a strategy with four major elements, namely design policy, design management, improved professional standards, and an equal partnership for design.

These four points were the foundation stones of Blaich's approach to the re-organization of CIDC and were subsequently elaborated and detailed.

Design, Blaich has continually stated, is crucial to industrial and commercial competitiveness in any undertaking: 'The product,' he emphasizes, 'is the most important statement a company can make about its image. It is the image.' However, if design was to play a significant role in Philips as a whole, a clear, coherent industrial design policy had to be established at corporate level, with the activities defined and consistently maintained throughout the company.

For design to be accepted as an effective competitive instrument it needed greater influence in management processes. To achieve this, however, the establishment and maintenance of industrial design itself had to be a managed process, with a coherent organizational structure and clearly defined responsibilities, relating to and compatible with the overall management structure of Philips.

Blaich also pointed out that demands on designers were rapidly changing. The design process could no longer be described simply in terms of a beginning and an end, it had become complex, evolutionary and on-going, no longer preoccupied with single objects and their aesthetics, but with an awareness that the environment must be designed holistically for it to be genuinely humane. If attitudes were to change and standards of design activity be improved and sustained at a high creative and professional level, a diverse and on-going programme of training and development was necessary.

Above all, for design to play a decisive role, it had to be integrated as an equal partner in the processes of development, production and marketing. To achieve this would not be easy, since in addition to designers taking new initiatives, it also required a similar response from other sectors of the company. Blaich also stressed that to effectively assess designs and communicate ideas about them, an emphasis on individual, subjective values was insufficient. Instead there must exist a set of criteria against which design at Philips could be judged and he set out a check list of six, which were later incorporated into the formal design policy of CIDC. The checklist asked: is the product ergonomically designed to satisfy human factors, and is it intelligible; does the product not only meet minimum safety standards, but extend to anticipating potentially dangerous situations; does the product successfully solve a consumer need; is it compatible with its environment; is the product designed to utilize materials, production processes and energy in the most efficient way; and finally are aesthetic elements such as form, colours and textures as well as graphic information integrated in an appropriate manner.

These criteria signalled an important change of emphasis, from the inwardly-focussed prof-essionalism of the Design Track to outwardly-focussed values stressing the constant testing of designs against the needs of commissioners and customers.

During the presentation, Blaich was asked by a Board member if the provision for design on the scale envisaged would not be expensive. 'What is the cost of no design?,' he replied. In elaborating on that answer, he emphasized the product creation process as a strategic issue for the company. Although Philips cannot be characterized as design-led, design is a part of its strategic policy. As part of a team generating future products on which the company depends, design should not be considered a cost centre, Blaich argues, but rather as a profit centre. There is, in fact, a paradox in the nature of the factors constituting the 'added value' of a product, which make it attractive and competitive, for they are frequently non-price qualities stemming from the design function. Later in 1981, in a keynote speech to a symposium held at Philips domestic appliance headquarters at Groningen in the north of The Netherlands, Blaich summed up his beliefs: 'I believe that design is an integral part of the company's strategy and policy, that design decisions are as important as those of the commercial and production departments and that designers must be part of a team with commercial/technical and other relevant disciplines.'

Selling the potential of design at Board level to an audience convinced of its importance was relatively easy, however, compared to the problems of delivering on the promises. In retrospect Blaich recalls, 'My fear was that I might be over selling. I was convincing top management we had all the marbles and then I looked here and saw we had some weaknesses.'

That was an understatement: the task facing him was huge. The scale of design activity at Philips was constantly increasing and design had become a truly multi-national activity. In early 1983, Philips had 194 designers and support staff of nineteen different nationalities, working in 30 locations in 20 countries. These broke down to 132 people in Europe, 36 in North and South America, and 26 in Asia. In 1982, a total of 632 projects of various scale and complexity were completed, increasing to 750 in 1983, 1,150 in 1984, and 1,360 in 1985. By 1987, the figure was over 2000. In addition, in an average year the CIDC Graphics and Packaging service completes over 200 jobs in packaging, advertising and point-of-sale design, direct mail and promotional literature. All these commissions originated from product divisions' requests for design work on new and existing products, and requests from National Organizations for assistance on locally developed products. Designers from CIDC were sometimes seconded to satellite centres for special projects. In one year, for example, personnel from CIDC worked on designs for refrigerators and domestic appliances in Mexico, radio recorders, HiFi and portables in India, and shavers and small domestic appliances in Japan.

Organization and delegation

Robert Blaich is emphatic that the design function in a company such as Philips must have a structure and policy objectives consonant with the structure and policy of the company as whole. The latter were undergoing substantial change, however, in the period of Blaich's appointment. Under the direction of Dr. Wisse Dekker, Chairman of the Board of Management from 1982 to 1986, and his successor Cor van der Klugt, the structure of the company has shifted away from the matrix system established in 1946 and the dual leadership of technical and commercial management derived from the founding brothers. Dr. Dekker changed the emphasis from technology and national organizations to a market driven, user-oriented policy of globalization. This opened possibilities for considerable change in the organization and role of designers. Cor van der Klugt, whilst continuing the process of change, has also been highly supportive of the role of design in the company. When he was Vice-Chairman of the Board of Management CID had reported to him, and he often visited the Design Center for personal reviews during which he made a strong impression with his detailed comments and many suggestions for improvements. 'Van der Klugt is a real product man,' says Robert Blaich. This level of understanding and support from the highest levels of Philips has undoubtedly been a very significant factor in establishing an appropriate climate in which design policy could develop.

There were some fundamental problems to be addressed. 'One of the myths,' says Blaich, 'was that the company had to design products for every different country. We attacked it here in-ternally, it was a design initiative and we were able to point out that this was a lot of nonsense. First of all if that was true, how were the Japanese getting such a stranglehold on Europe? Secondly, as a result, designers were sitting in factories and taking orders from the technology or commercial people. The product divisions did not control their destiny because of the national organizations' power.'

A further problem was the lack of adequate communication and interaction between product divisions. This resulted in considerable opportunities being missed. For example, a division developing the video recorder kept it as a technical product, so it was never fully developed for the consumer area. Even within product divisions, vertical separation resulted in product areas becoming virtually autonomous, each with its own design ideas.

To solve such problems, however, a clear priority on appointment for Robert Blaich was to establish a managerial structure for the design function, enabling decisions to be effectively made and executed. On arrival at Philips, Blaich found some twenty-five people reported directly to him, a situation emphasizing control rather than implementation. The scale of change required could not be devised overnight, however, it needed careful planning and consultation. His first step was to talk to people, evaluate the organization and establish the balance of strengths and weaknesses. His experience convinced him that a company with Philips scale of operations required both effective organization and delegation.

Immediately after taking up his post, Blaich organized a series of meetings for key staff, focussing on the role of design within the total Philips structure and then turning to the internal organization of the design function itself. The emphasis was on opportunities for clarifying this function both in its vertical relation ships with top management and its lateral relationships with those in other sectors of the company who commissioned work. As a result, by the end of 1981, the first outlines began to emerge for a new organizational structure. At the same time Philips commissioned an

Overhead Value Analysis, in the central corporation, to analyze the role, cost-effectiveness and aims of each area and the work of each member of staff, which was then checked against overall needs. The results of this independent survey, for CIDC, confirmed the in-house analysis. Discussions with commissioning agencies in the company provided a clearer view of their requirements.

The publication of the new structure in March 1982, emphasized the need for 'change to more effectively deal with change.' The declared goals of the reorganization were to create clearer lines of responsibility and authority, to increase involvement in decision making by line and staff personnel and to improve and focus project management. The plan also allowed for clearer career planning and personal growth for employees, for managing design research, and within that reducing indirect costs.

The operational scheme of 1969, which the new organization replaced, had three levels: at the top was the director, with his personal assistants and secretaries; the second was a substantial staff level including such functions as finance, administration and information; the final level consisted of a series of design groups with group leaders in charge. The new organizational concept grouped and simplified the staff functions of support services and administration, placing them under the control of a Manager for Design Affairs who also acted as deputy to the Director. Frans van der Put was appointed to this post and his long experience of Philips has been invaluable in implementing new policies. Blaich is warm in his tributes to the contribution made by van der Put: 'I couldn't have succeeded without him,' he says, 'Frans is the glue around here, he makes things stick.' The two men come from different backgrounds, with very different personalities, but in a real sense they complement each other and form a highly effective partnership.

The most radical organizational innovation was the creation of new posts of Design Manager for each major product sector: professional equipment, consumer electronics, major domestic appliances, small domestic appliances, personal care, light, with in addition, packaging and graphics, which crossed all product sectors. Each Design Manager had a brief to achieve the closest possible co-operation with their Product Division and had direct line responsibility to the Managing Director, Design. 'I want to manage the design process,' says Blaich, 'not manage the designers. Each one of them has to run their own area, and I will direct and support them, but I'm not going to be involved in every day to day activity.' The Design Managers were therefore given full responsibility for their own area. The introduction of the title 'Design Manager' was a deliberate choice, a key criterion being that each holder of the position should be selected for their capacity to assume managerial responsibility, in addition to other factors such as creativity, technical expertise and experience. Whilst in retrospect that might seem obvious, it had not pre-viously been the case. It therefore became necessary to identify people with the requisite man-agerial ability or potential. 'So throughout the organization I looked for the people who I felt were the most qualitative and could grow,' says Blaich. A major criterion was that design managers should be capable of bridging gulfs between product groups by using design as a link. In some cases the search for the right person meant giving accelerated promotion to young people who then had authority over those to whom they had previously been assistant. It was the start of a campaign to involve the Design Managers fully in creating a new consciousness of design—top down, bottom up, and sideways.

The devolution of control downwards was also important in allowing design managers to adapt to the varying and changing circumstances of their area of responsibility. Hugo Sterkenberg, in charge of Medical Systems I and E, and of special projects, comments: Its a continuous process of learning from decisions taken in the past, adjusting the rules, and meeting new market requirements. 'His work varies from the emphasis on commonality in the Harmonisation Programme to highly specific projects such as a Motorway Traffic Control and Signalling System for the Dutch Government. In Consumer Products, Peter Nagelkerke had to deal with highly personalized articles, such as shavers and now products for more general use such as television, each having their own emphasis. He sees his role as establishing a smooth running organization so he has time for 'inspiring people and supporting them in their work.' This extends to some highly structured and thought provoking theoretical work with which to back up design arguments. Stefano Marzano, of Major Domestic Appliances, based at Cassinetta in Italy, similarly believes design must be put on a more professional level: 'at the beginning of every PROCO [Product Committee] meeting, I always start the presentation with background information about the trends that influenced the product design. Along with these ideas I present the methodology involved in the design process.' Not only the range of ideas but the quality of initiatives originating from the design managers has immeasurably strengthened the lateral links with other disciplines in the product divisions.

The shake-up, and shake-out, resulting from the reorganization was absolutely necessary, Blaich believes, not only from the point of view of organizational efficiency, but to revive morale amongst the designers. 'Many designers here,' he observes, 'accepted their secondary role but in reality deeply resented it, and as a result we had lost many good people in the past.'

As a co-ordinating and policy-making body, the Design Policy Committee was established under the chairmanship of the Managing Director, CIDC, on which the Manager for Design Affairs and all Design Managers sat. This body was established to deal with on-going matters of design policy and to provide a review function for the work of the design teams. Rather than the weekly review of all projects previously used by DESTA, however, each major product area has a major review of its total performance every six months, with the form of the review left to Design Managers to determine.

As a further measure to ensure closer contact with the product divisions, fifteen contract des-igners, with line responsibility to the Design Managers, were appointed for specific product areas, such as video display systems, home entertainment systems, home information systems, or personal and car audio. They have charge of the day-to-day activities of a team including product designers, graphic designers and support assistants. In 1985, the title of CIDC, which referred specifically to the design centre located in Eindhoven, was altered to Corporate Industrial Design (CID), a change encompassing all Philips design activities and intended to reflect the globalist of the industrial design function worldwide.

Design policy

By 1984 the Design Policy Committee had prepared a definitive statement of design policy for publication. It began with a statement on CID's 'responsibility for the industrial design function and quality for Philips worldwide, from a corporate as well as a line function point of view.' This was to be achieved in four ways. Firstly, CID was to develop the corporate visual image, functioning as a 'connector' between the products, product systems and packaging of the Product Divisions, to create a strong visual image for all Philips products. A second responsibility was meeting users' expectations, as CID had specific skills in giving visual expression to products, which should 'satisfy the expectations and sensibilities of the ultimate users of Philips products.'

Thirdly there was meeting production and marketing requirements, by which designers were responsible for integrating these requirements into design work. Finally, CID was to be continually defining product design quality, emphasizing qualitative factors in design, as well as developing criteria and a continuing dialogue to increase understanding of these factors throughout the organization.

Another feature of the designers' remit is the need for 'continuous, optimal communication with all Product Divisions on product planning, policy, development and marketing.' However, if CID has responsibilities, the policy statement also proposes a formal status for design in the process of product development which broke new ground in the company. Whilst industrial design functioned as part of an inter-disciplinary team, it is emphasized that its expertise was contributed on a basis of equality with other participating disciplines. This was summarized in a diagram devised by Frans van der Put, in which successful product development was depicted as a three-way relationship of equality between design, development production and marketing, each capable of its unique contribution. To ensure industrial design quality is maintained 'as an integral part of the total quality of a product, product system, or packaging,' evaluation has to be included in the development process. The statement is a clear indication that in terms of policy, the days when design could be regarded as a last resort for styling exercises are over.

The policy document was deliberately concise, for elaborate statements can lead to confu-sion, and in any case are no substitute for action. Nevertheless, it gave clear commitment to a series of changes, some already achieved, others underway, which represented a wholly new function and image for design within the Philips organization.

The responsibility of the Design Policy Committee did not, of course, end with the publication of the policy document, since it has an on-going strategic responsibility for design. Its activities are intended to provide professional guidance for design quality, which it does by means of design reviews, and to interpret long term corporate requirements for product design quality and planning in terms of specific policy and its implementation.

The DPC thus has to be flexible in its response to development both within the company and outside. In 1984 it published a revision of the organizational structure, which reflected the mounting pace of change both in CID and the company as a whole. Change in the organization of product divisions was an important factor, resulting from the awareness of technical and functional overlap in many areas, with the need to integrate new concepts of design, development and marketing also playing a part. An obvious corollary was to realign the organization of CID design groups to match those developments.

The problems of decentralized design groups over which there was little control has been referred to earlier and a remedy was obviously necessary if control and coordination over all Philips design activities was to be effective. Therefore in a second major change of policy decentralized design groups within the company were brought into closer relationships with CID and the national organization design groups were linked in closer consultation. This was yet another step in establishing a unified approach across the whole Philips organization.

17

Teaching an Old Dog New Tricks: How RCA Is Using Design as a Strategic Tool

Like the afterglow of a brilliant sunset, images remain potent long after the substance behind them has disappeared. In innumerable antique shops in the 1980s, large sums of money were being asked for plaster images of Nipper the Dog, a Jack Russell terrier that once listened with cocked head to a phonograph loudspeaker in electrical goods stores across the nation. The mascot of the Radio Corporation of America, Nipper was the best known terrier in history, according to an illustrated history of American business from 1972. A decade later, RCA had become the dog of the consumer electronics industry. Acid comments were made about it being easier to buy the company than it was to acquire one of the pricey plaster canines from the nostalgia emporia.

How did this happen? The history of RCA in the last twenty years is a depressing chronicle typical of numerous American businesses that have crumbled under the competitive pressures of companies from around the world. Yet there are signs that RCA could be making a comeback, using design as the spearhead of recovery in every aspect of its business. In this, too, could Nipper be a symbol for a broader movement in U.S. industry in the 1990s?

Nipper was originally a dog inherited by painter Francis Barraud when his brother died. The dog's interest in listening to his phonograph inspired a painting that Barraud sold to The Gramophone Company. Following mergers, it later passed to the Victor Talking Machine Company and, in

First published as "Teaching an old dog new tricks: How RCA is using design as a strategic tool in its fight back," *I.D.*, March/April, 1992, By kind permission of F & W Media (New York).

1929, to the Radio Corporation of America. Together with the trademark of Nipper, the painting's original title, "His Master's Voice," helped to create an inimitable brand identity. It represented a company that, in the age of mass production, was a leader in radio, phonograph and, later, television technologies.

RCA's success continued after 1945, satisfying the demands pent up by the war and tapping into the expansion of television broadcasting. In the 1960s, key indicators, including figures for market leadership, product innovation, quality and cost, revealed that RCA still led the field. Japanese products were beginning to appear but did not yet have a high reputation. Here, as in many other sectors, however, the Japanese were learning fast.

Like many American companies that prospered on the basis of the large domestic market, RCA became complacent at precisely the time when Japanese and European competitors were starting to compete on a global basis. These overseas competitors had restructured in the post war period, introducing refined technology and new standards of manufacturing quality. Led by the Sony Trinitron, a revolution in consumer expectations took place in the 1970s, as import penetration increased to respond, RCA was forced into the lower end of the market to compete on cost alone.

By 1986, the company was in deep trouble, leading to what was officially termed a merger with General Electric. The reality, however, was an ignominious take-over and the dismemberment of the old RCA business.

No prospects of revival emerged from these wrenching changes. Investment was desperately needed, but GE was unwilling to make it. In fact, GE management considered RCA to be "outside the circle," lacking the profit potential that would warrant investment. By 1987, RCA had lost market share for eight years in a row. The company was sold that year for cash to Thomson, a French state-owned electronics company, and another round of reorganization and cuts ensued.

For long-time employees of RCA like Joseph R Clayton, these events were deeply painful. Reflecting on the merger, he shakes his head and says, "GE was too financially oriented. They simply wrote us off." Clayton was appointed senior vice-president for RCA's American television division in 1989; in other words, he was made responsible for the substance of RCAs TV business, based in Indianapolis with manufacturing plants in Canada and Mexico as well as the U.S. He came to his new position with the conviction that an entrepreneurial approach could revive the company, now officially known as Thomson Consumer Electronics, or TCE (although the RCA brand name was maintained). In terms of personnel, location and attitude, Clayton asserts, this is still an American company. "We created the market for consumer electronics in the U.S.," he says proudly. "No one owes us a living but we have a right to a place in that market. My aim is make sure we stay in it."

An entrepreneurial approach to design

Joe Clayton began his RCA career in sales, and something of that background is evident in the actions he took early on to revive staff morale. People still talk about the big meeting that he organized soon after his appointment as senior vice-president. Clayton drove into the packed gath-ering atop a vintage WWII tank on loan from a local collector. Dressed as General Patton, complete with a brace of pearl-handled revolvers, he blasted blank rounds at a large portrait of Akio Morita, then chairman of market leader Sony, to wild cheers from his staff.

Behind the razzmatazz, however, lay a serious purpose: Clayton was committed to conducting a sweeping reappraisal of RCA's business practices. Realizing that the old procedures were moribund, he became instrumental in bridging the gap between entrenched habits and new approaches. Above all, Clayton understood the importance of design, and the need to offer young talent the scope to create vital new products.

Clayton was assisted in his task by the fresh attitude Thomson brought to ownership of RCA. The French government wanted to enter the consumer electronics industry, viewing it as one engine driving the world economy. Buying RCA made sense in this strategic plan, providing the French with a substantial presence in the American market and a well established indigenous brand-name. Their willingness to make long-term investments was demonstrated in Thomson's decision to equip RCA with state-of-the-art facilities. Over $80 million was spent, for example, to upgrade a picture tube facility in Indiana for production of 31" and 35" television tubes, giving RCA control over its sources and quality. This type of investment was important, but Joe Clayton was convinced that techno logical competence alone was not enough. "Design," he says, "was the one area in which we could establish our own standards in a distinctive way."

Prior to his arrival, design at RCA had fulfilled what was essentially a cosmetic function, operating as a sub section of product planning. Clayton recognized that if its function was to be redefined, new leadership was an obvious priority, and so, after a lengthy search, Louis (Lou) E. Lenzi, Jr. was appointed manager of industrial design. Lenzi came to RCA in the late eighties with eight years of experience at IBM. As a condition of appointment, he had insisted on what he called "a place at the table" in order to function effectively. "I wanted to be able to talk directly to colleagues in planning, engineering and other areas, he explains. Too often, the problem with industrial design in companies is that more time is spent in negotiation than in meeting the competition." Clayton understood the logic of Lenzi's argument and positioned him on a level of functional parity with other senior management.

A group of like-minded executives quickly coalesced around Lenzi. Bruce Hutchinson, who had joined RCA in late 1986 at the time of the GE merger, was vice-president for national advertising, with previous experience working for D'Arcy, MacManus and Masius in Detroit. In early 1987, Sunil Mehrotra had come to RCA as a strategist after working for Chase Manhattan Bank; in 1990, he became brand manager for RCA. These two established a close working relationship with Lenzi and began to make decisions that brought immediate benefits. For example, RCA had traditionally offered over 200 color TV models, most of them only differentiated by such superficial details as oak, walnut or knotty pine finishes. An immediate cost reduction and a better definition of the range was made possible by streamlining the number of models to around one hundred.

The cooperation of Mehrotra, Hutchison and Lenzi was leading, however, to a more ambitious plan. With RCA having put its financial house in order thanks to Thomson's investments, the team saw the challenge of the nineties as cutting into the Japanese domination of the consumer electronics industry. There had to be some substance behind Joe Clayton's capers with the pearl-handled revolvers.

At the time of his appointment to brand manager, Mehrotra had already completed a wide-ranging analysis of the consumer electronics business which showed that the television and video markets in the U.S. were still huge. Annually, around 20 million color TVs, 10 million VCRs, and 3 million camcorders were sold, totaling some 33 million units. RCA's share was in the region of 3 million TVs, 1 million VCRs and half a million camcorders. Mehrotra also examined RCA's competitive position on the basis of consumer image, retailer support, product leadership, features and cost, market share, and whether the company could control its own destiny by manufacturing, sourcing and selling its own products.

The conclusion that emerged from his analysis was a surprise after all the traumas of recent years. Surveys revealed the consumer brand awareness of RCA ranked equal to that of Sony. There still existed a healthy customer base for the company, with nearly 25 percent of households in America owning an RCA color TV and 12 percent owning an RCA VCR. But RCA had a low-end market segment—it did not have much strength at the highend or in consumer opinion as a trendsetter. Nevertheless, the results revealed a platform on which to build.

In anticipating market development in the 1990s, four key changes were pinpointed. Industry output has tripled in the past decade but maintaining that rate of growth, even with the introduction of new technologies such as High Definition TV (HDTV), will be difficult. Secondly, the cost of a color TV has declined in real terms over the last decade hy almost 100 percent. Yet because major cost take-outs and price-slashing are no longer feasible, the cost gap between TVs and other products and services is unlikely to continue. A third factor for change lies in the growth of global alliances. With the Thomson/RCA and Philips/Magnavox link-ups, a new pattern of American-European alliances is emerging as a competitive response to Asian manufacturers. Finally, census data show the U.S. population profile changing in the next decade, as "boomers" move into the 35 to 45 year-old age range, the group with the greatest discretionary purchasing power.

The industry thus seems poised on the threshold of major changes. For Sunil Mehrotra, the implications were clear. "A door has closed on the past," he says. "The future will be completely different, and the rules that applied five to ten years ago are no longer valid. What emerged from his analysis was that to remain competitive, a new approach had to be adopted. It was a choice between radical change or nothing. The shared vision of Mehrotra, Hutchinson and Lenzi that change was necessary built into a compelling argument. But they faced not only the problems of the external market; the challenge was an internal one as well. The long-standing perception of design at RCA as something essentially trivial had to be overcome.

Before 1988, the company's products had revealed a limited exploration of form; traditional cabinets had dominated. This appearance standard had emerged from the styling exercises of engineers, who encased the chassis with front and back covers that were treated as separate entities. Designs had to take into account manufacturing capabilities, but the prime constituency to be satisfied was the network of distributors and dealers, whose viewpoint could be summarized as "If it's wood, it's good." Development cycles tended to be long, with endless presentations of renderings and realistic models, during which hours were spent picking over details.

There are, of course, problems inherent to the design of televisions: their screens are so dominant and their working parts must be shielded for safety reasons. The margin for variations on a box with a screen has been further diminished by the virtually uniform finish imposed in recent years by the larger retail purchasers, who demand vinyl imitation veneers. Commenting on this, Lenzi says simply, "We had to get rid of the wood grain."

The problem is a familiar one for designers: how to introduce change to signal a new approach without frightening customers away. The method adopted at RCA was an integrated approach to design, with all aspects of a product treated holistically. This meant changing the very notion, both within the company and among the dealerships, of what a television should look like. The risks of design statements that had no constituency had to be faced if a fresh product identity was to emerge. And since even the smallest details could contribute to the whole, Lenzi stressed human factors in improving hardware ergonomics and software interfaces.

The cold war with engineers

An example of this approach can be seen in the company's remote control units for VCRs, the operation of which has become a consumer nightmare. On one hand, the devices have become more complex. Therefore, one solution that Lenzi introduced is a remote control known as "Master Touch," compatible with all major brands of VCRs and cable boxes, and capable of controlling two VCRs, a cable box and TV set functions. Soft-touch, color-coded buttons, a simple grouping of functions, the use of shapes in controls as a guide to function, and clear graphics, both for controls and on-screen information, are some of the design details used to make its complexity more comprehensible. On the other hand, there also exists a need for greater simplicity. This is provided by another control, a hand-held wand known as "Simple Touch" with six buttons for the most frequently used functions. Further developments include an interesting example of how software can open up new possibilities in product design: using a technology exclusive to RCA called VCR-plus, three-digit codes that are published in TV program guides identify broadcasts, enabling users to pre-set VCRs by simply keying in the numerical codes.

Lenzi's group also identified a trend towards "media rooms" and integrated systems. To meet this interest, the concept of a "home theater" was developed, based on improvements in RCA's integrated audio/visual systems. The company's designers had to create consistency for customers from the splintered product and marketing approach that had prevailed. The implications here for design were profound: no longer a superficial afterthought, it was now crucial to realizing the company's brand strategy.

Lenzi's total approach had the further advantage of positioning industrial design to contribute to both technological innovation and cost reduction. Significantly new forms could be created and manufacturing costs could be cut by reducing the number of parts and assembly operations. For example, a new chassis design oriented front-to-back, instead of side-to-side, reduces overall mass, and combines an elegantly compact form with a reduction of materials and parts. The industrial design team now also tracks costs from the point of initial concept, providing convincing support for the effectiveness of design.

Perhaps most importantly, the integration of design in RCA's product strategy and its contribution to reducing costs have led to attitudinal changes in other departments. This comes from involving people in a common achievement, rather than from publicizing design as such. Lenzi says, "Design is in here, but the word is not used."

Whether articulated or not, the design process at RCA is a model of cross-disciplinary cooperation. As director of industrial design, Lenzi heads a staff of 28, fully half of whom work in RCA's extensive model shop; the rest are broken out into groups of principal designers and com-puter specialists with design backgrounds. The unusual emphasis on model makers is indicative of the physical approach to design taken by Lenzi's staff, but it also directly relates to his primary strategic design goal: to create a distinctive visual identity for RCA.

Prior to his arrival, the relationship between the design and engineering departments at RCA was marked by what Lenzi terms a "cold war" mentality. "Previously, there really wasn't any interaction between designers and engineers," he says, "and each department had its own objectives." When the inevitable conflicts arose, it fell to senior management to resolve the problem. Now, however, principal designers head up product development teams composed of representatives from design, marketing, engineering and purchasing—these groups even include the designers of the integrated circuit chips. "Design has an obligation to solve problems; we're not simply involved with cosmetic issues," Lenzi explains.

That designers can have so much impact stems in part from the unusual control RCA has over the basic components that go into its sets. The company is vertically integrated to an extraordinary degree, producing everything from the sand used to make the glass for picture tubes on up. But with the high profile of design within Thomson America's television division comes added responsibilities. The 10,000-employee television division accounts for a full 25 percent of Thomson's global revenue, so there is a lot riding on the success of its design strategy.

In order to remain responsive to current consumer needs and desires, the company's designers now conduct their own research into the changing role of television in the home; this information helps them to anticipate new opportunities in the marketplace. But to explore future technology and design innovations, Lenzi also initiated the practice of contracting outside consultants—among them, Design Logic, Fitch Richardson Smith and Metaphase—to create conceptual designs. "Sitting here in Indianapolis, we simply don't know everything there is to know about the future of the television business," he says. "I try to use people who are going to challenge our way of thinking and hopefully enable us to create a superior product down the road."

From concept to production

A case in point is the design of a conceptual projection television commissioned from Chicago-based Design Logic. The brief was simple and wide open: here's what this product looks like now; what are the possibilities for this type of product in ten years' time? Lenzi is quick to stress that these conceptual designs are not vanity exercises, since many of the concepts do find their way into production. In the case of Design Logic's project, the firm proposed innovative approaches to the format of the chassis kits and the way in which the lenses and mirrors fit inside the unit that were later incorporated into some of RCA's own production designs. "Developing these concepts is a useful tool for us," Lenzi says. "It's invaluable in terms of opening up new ways of looking at our own products."

The fact that the design group is able to move quickly from concept proposals into production stems, in part, from the model makers that constitute half of the design staff. In fact, a quick look around the design studio might lead a visitor to wonder if RCA remains in the dark ages of design technology: extensive work is still done in clay. The design process always begins with a quick sketch and then moves directly into clay or foam models. The models are scanned with a laser digitizer and the data is down loaded to computer-aided design systems for technical refinements. This approach makes the most efficient use of time, because the laborious process of inputing data to form the CAD database is handled by the digitizer. The CAD information, when complete, is then sent directly to engineering.

This emphasis on tactile design is also revealed in some of RCA's recent products, which challenge traditional thinking about televisions. A few, in fact, are radical departures. For example, the first in a line of what can be described as "biomorphic televisions" is due out later this year, with the rest on the market in 1993. "Tastes are changing in this country," Lenzi asserts, "and when these new televisions hit the market, RCA will be making a very strong statement about what a TV can and should be. It will take some people a while to adjust to, but others, I think, will just say, 'Well, it's about time.'"

Whether or not biomorphic televisions mean that the future is now, the future of the industry is a subject that RCA's designers take very seriously. With the onset of cable providers that can bring over 150 different channels into a consumer's home, televisions, remotes and on-screen menus will need to be entirely rethought. "And it's not going to be simply ISO channels offering MTV," says Lenzi. "You have to think in terms of 150 different channels of information. The information revolution is really coming home to the consumer, and we have to be ready to address these issues now."

One step taken to this end has been to hire a full-time human factors consultant to help define the usability issues that will arise in designing the complex, multifunction televisions of the future. Another measure has been to concentrate on reducing the cycle time of RCA's products from concept to production, a capability that is absolutely necessary if RCA is to be a fierce competitor. For most products, the cycle time is currently at around 18 months, but the hope is to bring it down to 12 or 14 months in time.

Mark Fleischmann, a freelance writer on consumer electronics for magazines such as Rolling Stone, Premier and Audio/video Interiors, has already noticed the differences. "Lou Lenzi is hardly a greybeard," he says, "and it's nice to see a big corporation give a young design staff creative freedom." He points out that the first of a new generation of what are now really video monitors with much improved technology first appeared with the Proton 600M in 1983, followed by the Sony XBR Pro. "It seems that all these companies had to have 'Pro' somewhere in their product names," he notes, "so I was sceptical when I heard RCA was launching the 'ProScan.' But in fact, RCA's design is very original—this is no 'me-too' product. The company took its time to respond but did so extremely well with a handsome and distinctive line."

Fleischmann is particularly impressed by the attention to detail obvious in RCA's product. "The user interface goes one step beyond the on-screen menus that everyone is developing. It is more readable, with well-chosen fonts and shadowing." He also points out that the features added to make products more attractive generally result in simply more buttons, creating a barrier between product and consumer. "The remote control is the item closest to people," he observes, "and RCA's Master Touch is well thought out in its detailing of shapes, colors and graphics. Above all, it has a really nice feel."

A new corporate culture

Market implementation of these new designs also required a significant in-house realignment for RCA. As Sunil Mehrotra says, "We're no longer involved in technology for its own sake, we are in the business of technology for human entertainment. We've redefined our own business." To effect this change, a three-pronged strategy was needed: sales people had to understand the strategy and sell it to retailers; retailers had to support it and sell it to customers; customers had to hear it and believe it.

Here, too, design had a vital contribution to make. For example, the concept of the "home theater" is predicated upon making technology easier to understand. Selling the concept begins with a basic step-by-step training of sales people. A pocket-size sales and training guide, created by the graphic design firm Pentagram, then outlines for retailers the building blocks that constitute the home theater concept. To address the final link, RCA's potential customers, interactive laser-disc sequences at the point of sale are used to communicate directly between producer and user. A home theater kit gives more detail, with a toll-free number to answer queries and brochures serving as follow-up material. These take customers through a series of stages in which they can determine which elements are suitable for them, using a simple matrix based on suggested screen sizes and viewing distances.

The benefits of this approach are noticeable, according to Dave Lauchenbruch, editorial director of Television Digest, a weekly publication for the industry. He says, "Many retailers were losing interest in RCA because of all the turmoil at the company. Now it seems to have got its act together and looks like it's here to stay. Market share is improving and goodwill among the dealers has been regained, in part because of this educational process."

A coordinated message was also launched in national advertising, promotional programs, catalogues, spread sheets, point-of-sale materials, sales training and interactive display materials—in short, in everything the company designs. Previously, these functions had all been parcelled out to various departments. "Bringing the planning and design of these materials together not only works externally, but it can be used to motivate our own people in creating a new culture," notes Mehrotra. "Everything must be synergistic, everything must say exactly the same thing inside and outside the company."

For Bruce Hutchison, the key feature in giving focus to RCAs brand identity, both externally and internally, was an advertising campaign revolving around the image of Nipper the Dog. Research studies had revealed an enormous brand equity accumulated by RCA from this image over the years. It is still RCA's most recognizable contribution to the American collective memory, with broad appeal running across different generations. The return of the venerable Nipper, accompanied now by a little puppy as a symbol of renewal, was to signal a major change "We wanted to shake up the consumer, but we really also wanted to shake ourselves up internally," explains Hutchison. He had first thought of bringing back the image four years ago, recognizing its positive connotations He had worried, however, that Nipper might be perceived as old-fashioned—the kiss of death in a volatile industry. The solution: the puppy, named Chipper as a result of a promotional competition, to personify the new generation of RCAs products. But the critical focus of the campaign, emphasizes Hutchison, still had to be on product quality. The new advertisements that appeared last year were thus deliberately humorous but featured, along with the dogs, the product as hero.

Any assessment of RCA's course over the last three years has to be suspended because of the long-term nature of all these decisions. In November of 1991, Sunil Mehrotra left RCA to become executive vice-president of JBL Consumer Electronics. The ultimate test of his ideas will be the extent to which they survive his departure. Yet the new strategy has already begun to make an impact. Dave Lauchenbruch comments, "RCA has decided to take the high road of design rather than simply compete on price. The products have steadily improved and the company is assuming the mantle of leadership in the industry. This means taking on companies like Sony and Mitsubishi at the high end of the market, where RCA never had a presence, with some beautiful designs that show a lot of imagination."

Similarly, it will take time to form a comprehensive judgement of the French government's industrial policy and the decisions taken by Thomson. Stuart Malin, a partner at The Doblin Group, a Chicago-based strategic planning organization, agrees that Thomson's acquisition of RCA makes good long-term sense, but questions the wisdom of large investments in current technology. "Looking at television technology," he says, "we could be right on the fulcrum of significant changes. Maybe picture tubes are at the end of their life-cycle; maybe the future belongs to flat-screen technology. Infact, televisions and computers may be about to fuse into some new kind of product."

Despite such caution, Mehrotra, Hutchison and Lenzi have undoubtedly achieved a great deal in three years. "Shifting a juggernaut is never easy," says Mehrotra, while Lenzi uses the metaphor of teaching an elephant to dance. Yet the team set their sights high, intent on matching RCA's performance with their leading competitor, Sony, as an indicator of achievement. There was pressure to achieve results, with many structural problems that could not be solved easily. Nevertheless, Thomson's corporate strategy allowed them to take a "medium-term" perspective, without the constant pressure for immediate results that often chokes off initiative in America.

Ultimately, of course, the design team's efforts will be judged by results in the harsh spotlight of the marketplace, but preliminary figures give encouraging signs of a positive turnaround. In the latest annual market share survey of U.S. color television sales by Television Digest, RCA remained the top brand. Although the industry showed little overall change, there was real encouragement for RCA's strategy in that its share of the high-price segment increased in the last year. The average selling price of units increased by 10 percent in 1990 to 1991, and so RCA is increasing its proportion of the 15 percent of sales at the top of the market, where 50 percent of the industry's profits are made.

Some other numbers are worth pondering. When appointed to their positions in Thomson's new structure, Joe Clayton was 39 years old, Mehrotra and Hutchison were also in their late 30s, and Lou Lenzi was 31. At a time of widespread and well-merited criticism of American business for its aversion to risk, it is heartening to discover a team of young managers who, even if under French patronage, are developing new approaches, using design intelligently, and taking on the world's best.

18

Current and Future Demands on Hong Kong Designers

There is always a problem with change when it affects habits and procedures that have given good service in the past. This is particularly so with the viability and value of Hong Kong designers' skills and competencies. These have been commercially viable and valuable to clients for a long time, and in some respects may continue to do so. They are unlikely to suffice, however, in future situations characterized by change on multiple levels. This raises questions about the relationship of existing capabilities to the likely needs of the Hong Kong economy in the near and medium future and the implications of any conclusions for design education.

It needs to be stressed that while at some levels of practice design might sometimes involve an individual designer working alone on a project, it can also frequently involve several designers, possibly from several different specialties, working in cooperation with colleagues from other disciplines, such as marketing or engineering. In other words the scale and complexity of design projects varies considerably.

Another variation can be identified in terms of the product type on which design input is required. To give an extreme example, jewellery, clocks and watches require a very different kind of design approach to that necessary for machine tools or medical equipment.

Further variations of design input are conditioned by the stage of a product life-cycle, in that significantly new products require an experimental approach different to what is desirable for mature, standardized products; the state of technology in different product sectors; and the special design needs of the small and medium enterprises (SMEs).

Since the size and outputs of Hong Kong companies are highly diverse, they correspondingly differ in the design approaches necessary to enhance

Extracted from the *Interim Report of the Hong Kong Polytechnic University Design Task Force on the Future of Design Education in Hong Kong*, 2003.

their competitiveness. A simple theoretical model can illustrate some of these differences in design approach:

Existing products

Figure 18.1 shows two axes, the vertical one distinguishing between a company's existing range of products and new product concepts. The horizontal axis distinguishes between the activities in any company that relate to single products or a product-line, and those that have implications across the whole company. The bottom-left quadrant that results is therefore concerned with the activities of designers working on existing concepts on a product-line basis. This involves them generally in work that gives form to pre-existing ideas handed to them without involvement in decisions about their nature. This is a situation typical of OEM work, in which client companies provide specifications for work, often in great detail. The top-left quadrant is concerned with new concepts for product lines and here designers are required to develop innovative forms and treatments for products, corresponding to ODM. The bottom-right quadrant shifts attention to how existing products and other aspects of design, such as those related to packaging, collateral information, web-sites, environments, etc., can be combined in ways that defines a brand for a product line or

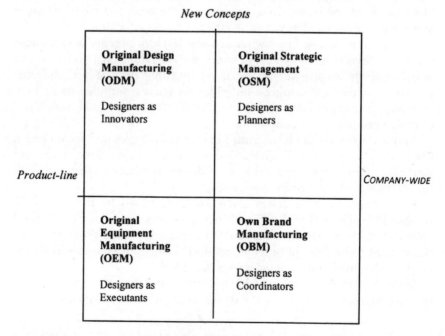

FIGURE 18.1 *From OEM to OSM.*

through a corporate identity programme (OBM). The top-right quadrant indicates the zone of decision-making where new concepts have widespread implications for strategy across the whole company, which can involve the use of designers as planners and strategists (OSM).

Original equipment manufacturing

Basically, in the manufacturing sector, Hong Kong has built its prosperity upon OEM. A recent report of the TDC provides an excellent description of the nature of OEM processes: "Over the years, Hong Kong companies have been engaged mainly in original equipment manufacturing (OEM) arrangements, under which overseas buyers provide the design and draw up the product specifications for a new product. They then look around the world for suppliers to produce and deliver the goods in the most satisfactory way. Overseas buyers usually own the brand name and the design of the product, and they are also responsible for the distribution and promotion of the product in the end market."[1]

OEM requires a good command of production technology and an organization capable of speedily delivering products to tight quality and cost specifications. Some advantages pointed out by the TDC were:

- OEM relationships, if successful, can represent steady business.
- OEM arrangements provide opportunities for Hong Kong Manufacturers to learn about new technologies or techniques.
- No need to be involved in marketing and distribution in overseas markets.
- No need to provide after sales service.[2]

OEM undoubtedly represents an important platform of manufacturing capability that has many virtues. It depends substantially, however, upon sustaining good relationships with purchasers, who take most of the risk and most of the profits, and does not give manufacturers control of the products they make.

A disadvantage increasingly obvious to many Hong Kong manufacturers at the present time, however, is that competition in OEM too easily becomes predominantly focussed upon cost, and with numerous other lower-cost alternatives available, future profits and viability appear vulnerable for Hong Kong OEM companies, whether located in the SAR or the mainland. Companies capitalized in China are overwhelmingly seen as major competitors, and Malaysia, Thailand, Vietnam, Indonesia are also emerging on the basis of cost advantage. Taiwan and Korea are now competitive on two levels: they have introduced more sophisticated approaches to move up-market in their home production; and have been through a rapid learning curve in the context of manufacturing in China.

It may be that Hong Kong will continue to be competitive in some aspects of OEM, but it is unlikely that design will be a significant element at that level.

Original design manufacturing

Many companies have moved on from OEM to the stage known as ODM or Original Design Manufacturing. The TDC uses a diagram, which has been adapted here, to illustrate this process of upgrading the value added in manufacturing (Figure 18.2). "One option that has been chosen by Hong Kong companies is to upgrade the OEM production by moving up the value-added U-curve of the product development cycle. At the front end of this cycle, pre-production activities, such as product research, product design and prototype creation, usually entail higher value-added."[3]

The move to ODM may be required as a condition of operating in a particular product sector, where there are long-established practices of companies designing the products they manufacture, from which buyers select those they consider appropriate for their needs. This is widespread in some sectors of toy manufacture and fashionable products such as jewellery. ODM effectively means that a company takes over specific design functions at the pre-production stage, among them being a set identified by a TDC survey:

Moving to ODM by developing their own design capabilities may also reflect an effort by firms to enhance competitiveness. An electrical appliance

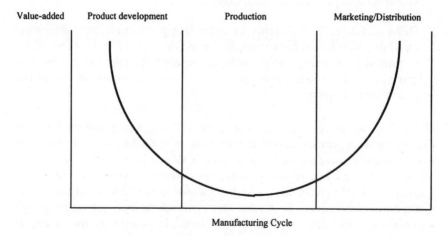

FIGURE 18.2 *The value-added "U-curve".*

Table 18.1 *Processes of Product Design Involved in ODM*

	% Share of respondents having ODM production
Detailed product design	78.2
Prototype production	69.9
Product concept development	63.4
Market testing	32.8

manufacturer gave as a reason: "To help our customers solve problems related to product design and the making of prototypes."[4] However, while manufacturers can expect a premium for adding enhanced design to their other capabilities, buyers still generally have command of brand, marketing and distributing—the more risk-laden end of the production spectrum—and expect to reap greater profits as a consequence. The significantly lower response for market testing in the above table indicates the bias of ODM activities to pre-production stages.

It should also be noted that at the ODM level, design approaches need to be differentiated to meet the needs of firms and their products in the conditions of specific, established markets. Some options are indicated in the diagram below (Figure 18.3):

Product covering is an approach that takes an existing product range as the norm and seeks to cover these approaches with minor variations or differentiation. This often linked to the concept of "fast follower" and is an

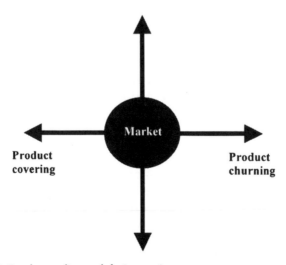

FIGURE 18.3 *Product policy and design options.*

approach typical of many manufacturers of small electrical and electronic products intent upon obtaining a share of a large existing market. Product churning is a process of seeking to turn out as wide a range of products as possible to give buyers the maximum possible incentive to purchase, and is typical of such sectors as toy manufacture. Scale-down can mean miniaturization in a physical sense, but also encompasses other approaches to make existing products accessible to larger markets: the development of cell-phone products in recent years is a notable example. Inch-up is an attempt to design products that can push up into higher-end markets where levels of profitability are more rewarding. Samsung is an example of a company that has been consistently raising the standards of its product lines in this way. Any combination of these approaches might be appropriate across the product range of a company. It is important to stress, however, that the implications for design in each approach point to very different concepts and outcomes being necessary.

The TDC has found that while design capability was viewed as a major attribute of successful ODM business, respondents in their surveys also pointed to a relatively low availability of product designers.[5] The same TDC survey predicts: "In order to differentiate themselves from indigenous Chinese suppliers, Hong Kong companies will need to offer better quality and better designed products. The further development of the mainland market will thus foster continued expansion of ODM or brand name production."[6] If this is indeed so, the fact that demand is currently high and is likely to substantially increase, should be a signal for action by the School of Design to meet what appears to be an expanding need.

Own brand manufacturing

OBM, or own brand manufacture, is a major step for any company because it entails taking command of all stages of manufacturing through to the post-production phase of bringing products to market, including "a number of post manufacturing activities such as quality control, brand name development, transportation and marketing, which also have great commercial value."[7] They also entail a greater element of risk. Among important factors to be considered are that building a brand takes time and needs to be based on a long-term business strategy, and the launch of a brand needs to be based on a unique product or a distinctive approach to design, in order to give customers a reason for purchasing the new brand.

Developing a brand is therefore more than just applying a unique logo to a product. A crucial shift in any move towards OBM is that it requires a new mind-set by manufacturers who now have to take direct responsibility for how their product is viewed by users, involving them in a much broader view of the processes in which they are involved. An important element in this shift is the role of design in creating and sustaining trust in a brand.

The Golin/Harris Trust in Asian Business Survey conducted in the summer of 2002 in Tokyo, Taipei, Hong Kong and Singapore, reported that a mix of ethical factors and experience are crucial factors in building trust in a brand.[8] Some of the key factors that topped the list of trust builders were:

1. Good customer service and relationships   88%
2. Quality products and services   87%
3. Value for money   84%
4. Well-managed and stable business   84%
5. Clear and frequent communications   82%
6. Healthy, safe, ecological products   81%
7. Responsible, ethical corporate behaviour   81%

Of these factors, design can be argued to be a critical element in numbers 1, 2, 3, 5 and 6, and a contributory factor to the other two, numbers 4 and 7.

Yet there seems to be gaps in the awareness of what is required to make this transition. The TDC reports: "Neither product design capability nor the development of new designs featured significantly in the reasons for attempting to develop brand name business."[9] Simply labeling existing products with a logo is hardly a recipe for the qualities necessary to sustain a brand. There are numerous companies in Hong Kong, however, that have very successfully established strong brand reputations over a long period, such as Cathay Pacific Airways and the Hong Kong and Shanghai Bank. Neither is size a necessary criterion for achieving this level of competitive recognition.

Some small and medium Hong Kong companies have also made the transition, and indicate some important lessons. When Kin Yip Metal & Plastic Pty. Ltd. set out to manufacture its own brand of kitchenware, its executive director in 1991, Cliff Sun, pointed out that good design, style, safety and quality were crucial factors in selling household products.[10] He also emphasized that once a brand name is established it is necessary to be constantly on the alert for improvements and product innovation in order to sustain the viability of a brand.[11] Twelve years later, the continuing success of the company, now Kinox Enterprises Limited, based in Kwun Tong, is a testimony to the soundness of this approach. It has two brand names, Connoisserve and Kinox, and specializes in Barbecue Articles, Plastic Housewares and Stainless Steel Cookware with worldwide markets, including USA, UK, Canada, Europe and the Middle East. In a typical pattern, manufacturing has been shifted to Shenzen where 95% of the company's 1,000 employees are located, with 5% located at the Hong Kong headquarters. The company uses two to three freelance designers on a regular basis, commissioning them to generate aesthetic concepts of products in accordance with briefs setting out rough concepts and guidelines provided by the marketing department. When approved these design concepts are translated into production specifications by engineers in the mainland factories. Marketing Director N.D. Sun, the executive director's brother, observes that many companies are reluctant to invest in design, but emphasizes the benefits of relationships with consultant designers who provide strengths not normally available inside a firm.

To establish the integrity of a brand, high levels of design input are required at multiple levels of a firm's activities. Above all, a managerial capacity is necessary that thoroughly understands how the coordination of all these design activities can reinforce the projection not just of an image, but also a reality, in terms of reliability in product and service, which underpins any durable brand.

Original strategy management

It has to be said that this concept has not featured in discussions about the economic future of Hong Kong and it must be concluded that this indicates a general lack of awareness of its potential. OSM is an approach where a company sets out not just to cater for existing market needs in currently identifiable ways, but endeavours to create new markets by means of innovative products, communications, environments, and services combined into systems intended to demonstrate that the whole exceeds the sum of its parts. It entails building internal capabilities in a company, with substantial emphasis on generating new ideas and bringing them to market. An example is the continuous record of innovation by 3M, or the way in which Sony has sustained leadership in the field of small electrical and electronic devices. Sony, for example, has a design-planning department reporting to the President with a remit of shaping the future of the company. Putting design at the centre of corporate concerns in this manner requires a long-term commitment to excellence in every visual dimension of corporate activity. Neither does it have to be restricted to giant corporations - it should be remembered that Sony was a start-up in the 1950s and that big companies were once small companies with ambition. An example is a privately owned German company, ERCO, which has established a world leadership position in the field of architectural lighting, emphasizing not just lighting fittings, but the quality of light they afford. At the time it designed the lighting of the Hong Kong and Shanghai Bank building in Central, completed in 1986, it employed some 400 people, which has since grown to over 1000.

None of the business approaches discussed here are mutually exclusive, neither is it necessary to sequentially progress from one to another. The processes of development can take innumerable paths in many combinations. This points to an important need in design education to enable students to understand and adapt to a range of situations and demands. Investigating, assessing and making known the different levels and ways in which design could potentially be applied in Hong Kong and China needs to be a central activity in the School of Design and a vital element of its courses and outreach activities.

Notes

1 *Competitiveness and Prospects of Hong Kong's OEM, ODM and Brand Name Business*, Hong Kong: Research Department, Hong Kong Trade Development Council, July, 2000, p. 2.

2 *Competitiveness and Prospects*, p. 11.

3 *Competitiveness and Prospects*, p. 2.

4 *Competitiveness and Prospects*, p. 18.

5 *Competitiveness and Prospects*, p. 21.

6 *Competitiveness and Prospects*, p. 38.

7 *Competitiveness and Prospects*, p. 2.

8 Forrest, Anne. "Asia survey shows that trust in a brand is built, not born." *South China Morning Post*, Sunday Money section, December 22, 2002, p. 6.

9 *Competitiveness and Prospects*, p. 35.

10 *Establishing a Brand Name: The Experience of some Hong Kong Companies.* Hong Kong: Research Department of Hong Kong Trade Development Council, 1991, pp. 8–9.

11 *Establishing a Brand Name*, pp. 10–11.

(B)
National Design Policies: John Heskett and Design Policy

by Carlos Teixeira

The question that John Heskett asked himself in regard to design policy, both corporate and national, was ostensibly a simple one: How should design be thought as a resource, within companies, territories and nations? The chapters in this section – and those in the section on design, business and the creation of value – bring to the foreground the cornerstones of Heskett's understanding of effective design policies. Beginning largely from when Heskett moved to the United States in 1989, these pieces range in date across the 1990s and through into the early years of this century. They focus on multiple contexts, from the United States, Germany and the United Kingdom through to China, South Korea, Hong Kong and Taiwan.

Heskett's interest and work on design policy is probably best explained by his admiration for well-designed products. But the process of designing products with integrity (see reading #25, 'Product Integrity') can only be achieved through the orchestration of fragmented and dispersed design capabilities. However, such orchestration confronts two major challenges: having the building blocks available and awareness and understanding of the (economic, but also more than economic) results it can produce.

In this context, design policy is an instrument used by companies, territories and nations to build and manage design capacity very effectively.

Probably, the most noticeable characteristic of Heskett's views on design policy is the conviction that product (in whatever sense this terms means, including services, systems, environments and communications) should always be the axis that defines priorities and decision-making regarding investments in design. Products in this wide sense are the nexus of multiple competing social, cultural and economic imperatives; therefore, they should be the point of reference that regulates what type of design is needed. Consequently, design policy should function as the support system for embedding design practice as the bridge between companies and users for the development of products. According to Heskett, effective design policy requires widespread application of design in multi-levels and multi-sectors, long-term commitment to design, continuous capacity building of new design practices based on research and education, and a shared sense of awareness, seriousness and integrity regarding the role that design plays in promoting economic prosperity and determining the quality of everyday life.

Heskett's argument is simple, nevertheless ambitious: design policy is effective when design is seamlessly embedded into production, consumption, innovation and education systems, creating the consciousness and infrastructure for the development of products that are of social, cultural and economic relevance.

The widespread application of design in this sense is considered by Heskett as one of the key success factors in design policy. That's because the challenge of rigorously engaging with multiple competing imperatives when designing products requires a pluralistic approach to design practice. In the chapter 'Lessons Abroad: What America can learn from Germany's integrated design policy' (#20), Heskett illustrates the integration of design and engineering for the development of products in German companies. But the highlight of this strategy is the fact that it can be found both at the large corporations, such as BMW, Siemens and Braun, and at medium-sized companies. Clearly, design is present in multi-levels at German companies; it plays multiple roles and can be found in multiple incarnations such as engineering design, product design, communication design and strategic design. Applying design at multi-levels across multi-sectors creates a robust and sophisticated design capacity to successfully bridge and mediate companies' and users' expectations. Heskett reinforces his argument by calling the attention to the fact that, at that time, Germany didn't perform well in emerging sectors such as information technology where design was not yet widespread.

As a historian, Heskett considered time sequences, periods and transitions as a fundamental dimension for understanding the role of design. According to Heskett, design policy can be effective only if it is based on a long-term commitment to design. Longitudinal alliance with design ensures navigating multiple product life cycles with the ability to keep or upgrade the quality of the products through long periods of time. In moments of transition, design functions as the facilitator for product innovation, when significant and disruptive shifts occur in industries and markets demanding new solutions.

Conversely, it is the absence of these factors within the product development understanding of a company that leads to economic disaster – as Heskett unsparingly noted in one of the sharpest pieces of design journalism he wrote in the early 1990s when he excoriated the then incompetence of GM in almost all these aspects. In 'GM's current woes reveal the price of corporate arrogance and amnesia' (#14), he takes powerfully to task GM's almost complete failure to have effective and well-designed product development programmes in-house. GM's problems in the 1990s are a clear example of the importance of a long-term commitment to design. Despite the shifts occurring in production and consumption, the absence of design in GM was a contributing factor in its continuous offering of products that lack updates and innovation. But as Heskett pointed out, 'GM is not an isolated case. Rather it is symptomatic of a generation of companies once dominant but now struggling to adapt to competition and change. As the largest and most powerful of these firms, however, the problems of the automobile companies are more public and painful' (#14). Heskett claims that when design doesn't adapt to changes that happen through time, products lose their integrity and appropriateness, thereby disrupting customers' long-term loyalty to a product and its identity.

His article on GM was not the only time Heskett took US industry to task in the early 1990s (see also reading #15). But he was never only a critic. His short paper 'National Design Policy and Economic Change' (#19) presents instances of national design policies from France, Japan, South Korea and Taiwan to illustrate the commitment of national governments to design for economic advantage. While they were momentarily successful during a period in time, they were limited when confronting the new imperatives brought by globalization. In this new context, Heskett argued, design policies should mirror successful cases of product development, such as the vacuum cleaner with double cyclone by the industrial designer James Dyson in the UK. Heskett explains: 'Design creativity linked to technological competence and entrepreneurial capability can be a powerful means not only of resisting the penetration of global companies in existing product markets, but enhancing a nation's competitiveness. Establishing clear concepts of entrepreneurial approaches to design in small companies should be at the heart of any national design policy.' Heskett's conclusion is clear: if commitment to design is momentary, the ability to mediate the constant shift of imperatives influencing product upgrades and product innovation is impaired, consequently disrupting the ability of the industry to develop products with social, cultural and economic relevance. Therefore, long-term commitment to product development and design should be a cornerstone for any design policy that is intended to be effective.

Based on historical patterns, Heskett was equally clear about the need for design practice to change and adapt to new challenges, demands and opportunities. If design doesn't evolve as contexts change, it would be 'just another problem confronting our societies, rather than a contributor to solutions'. In one of his last works on design policy, his contribution to the Cox Report, written for the UK government and which looked at national design policies in China, South Korea and Taiwan (see readings #21 and #22) and then tried to take lessons from these for the UK, Heskett highlights another very important cornerstone of any design policy, namely that it should invest on continuous capacity building of new design practices on the basis of research and education.

As product has always been Heskett's reference point, interpreting the future demanded a holistic understanding of the shifts in social, cultural and economic imperatives that determine the fitness of products in people's everyday life. New imperatives would demand new types of products, consequently opening up the opportunity for new sorts of designers and design practice. Therefore, research and education in design should function as the innovator, incubator and disseminator of design practice capable of confronting the imperatives of a new time and helping the transition to a new order. Such commitment to new design practice, according to Heskett, should be a priority for any design policy that is sensitive to historical patterns of change. He would say that 'who fail to learn from history being condemned to repeat its errors' (#14).

In the Cox Report, Heskett recommends a design policy for the UK that would significantly invest on the unique combination of academic research and higher education, especially graduate-level programmes. 'The greatest possibility of rapidly introducing new concepts of design practice would be the establishment of suitable courses at Master's level.' Such spaces would serve as incubators of entrepreneurial design practice concerning the development of new types of products. 'Such new organizational applications of design in all its diversity and multiplicity can be vital means of harnessing talent in ways that can also engage users, whoever they are and wherever they may be; they do not need large investments of capital or resources, but do require new, more intelligent thinking on the part of management and designers.' Such a strategy would provide the UK with a competitive advantage over the design policies from China, South Korea and Taiwan because being small, agile and user-centred is the foundation for being innovative. A design policy focusing on entrepreneurship and innovation allows the UK to compete by differentiating itself from the design policies of the leading Asian countries, which still focus on spreading design capabilities widely in multi-levels and multi-sectors of their industry which is centred on the development of mass-produced products at low cost. This approach improves the competitiveness of their products, but is a limiting condition for entrepreneurship and the creation of innovative high value-added products.

While most of Heskett's design policy recommendations focused on tactical solutions, such as embedding design practice in business and changes in design practice through research and education, one recommendation, however, is predominantly about morality regarding the identity of design and its role in society. Heskett advocates for seriousness in any discourse and practice related to design. In the chapter already referred to, 'Lessons Abroad: What America can learn from Germany's integrated design policy' (#20), Heskett points out the seriousness with which design is regarded and discussed by senior executives and the press in Germany. As a counterpoint, in the chapter, 'Everything alters, Nothing changes: Why don't American Companies use design more intelligently?' (#15), Heskett highlights the limited awareness and superficial hope that design would transform the US economy. Through these chapters he advocates against a simplistic interpretation of the role of products and the utilitarian application of design. Given that design's influence in society can be so deep through the products it creates – if effective it can promote prosperity, if as malpractice it can create disorder, if absent it can paralyse behaviour, beliefs and discourse – then design, by necessity, should be of very high moral standard.

For Heskett, seriousness and integrity regarding the role that design plays in promoting economic prosperity and determining the quality of everyday life should be the moral foundation of any design policy. Such seriousness promotes the values, beliefs and discourses that can drive conscious and systematic investments in design at multi-levels across multi-sectors, over long periods of time, and simultaneously lead to incubation and dissemination of new practices. Design policy is resilient only when it is based on a strong moral foundation, which provides the ethos for design practice necessary to play a significant role in society. According to Heskett, 'Adding value by design will need to mean what it implies: a content of real value, expressed through both aesthetic and economic dimensions' (#14).

19

National Design Policy and Economic Change

Design has been the subject of policy decisions by governments at many levels in the twentieth century, but has received comparatively little attention. No theoretical framework exists to identify different modes of policy and assess what they can achieve, which, in an age of globalization, is an urgent need.

Objectives of national design policy

Historically, two broad categories of government design policy are evident, with the aim:

1 of creating imagery symbolizing the government and its power.
2 to gain economic advantage in international trade.

The first, a symbol of power, has deep historical roots, with modern examples ranging from the first Napoleonic empire, to the Fascist regimes of the early twentieth century, and the search for representative imagery in states created by the collapse of socialism in the late 1980s. The assertion of national identity through visual imagery may indeed increasingly be a compensation for diminished national self-determination, particularly in the economic sphere. The growth of global corporations, the seamless flow of world financial markets, and the growth of regional organizations such as the European Union, all result in a major reduction of national government's abilities to control affairs within their own borders.

First published as "National Design Policy and Economic Change," (in German and English) *MD-Magazine* (Germany) August 1999, pp. 59–60. By permission of MD Magazine.

Policies of economic advantage also have a long history, but have become more systematic in recent centuries, with the growth of modern government organizations. The results, however, have been mixed.

A common approach is the protection of domestic markets by controlling imports, while using design to promote exports. In France, Jean-Baptiste Colbert, Louis XIV's Chief Minister from 1661 to 1683, implemented what became known as the mercantilist system based on a static view of the world economy. The total volume of production and commerce possible at any time was fixed, and French commercial policy aimed to obtain the maximum share at the expense of other nations. Believing visual style could create competitive advantage, policies to stimulate high levels of design and craft skill, and the promotion of design education, made France the centre of taste in luxury goods, a position it has never entirely lost. The negative aspects were close control of markets, with the result that France eventually lost its economic lead to Britain where a more open system enabled rapid industrialization from the late eighteenth century onwards. More recent Japanese policy shows similar characteristics. Realizing industrial design had emerged in the inter-war years in America as a means of making products more desirable and marketable, the Ministry of International Trade and Industry began to vigorously promote it in the 1950s. MITl sent young people to train as designers in Europe and America; invited leading designers to Japan; worked closely with businesses for the long-term development of markets for new products; and encouraged the development of design education. By 1992, the number of industrial designers reached 1,000. Although many were employed in relatively low-level work, the growth in design competence at higher levels has been important in the success of the Japanese export economy. Just as in France, however, success in one phase of history has left Japan struggling in the 1990s to adapt to a wave of change that requires other approaches.

Other countries in East Asia, such as Taiwan and South Korea successfully followed the Japanese model. Similarly, important factors in their success were the direct linkage of design policy to economic aims, and close cooperation with business in developing design practice.

In contrast, the history of government involvement in design in Britain has been less successful, despite investment in design education beginning in the 1830s, and a succession of organizations to promote design, particularly for export markets. Yet, after a century and half of design policy, in 1983, Britain for the first time in modern history had a trade deficit in manufactured goods, in contrast to its Asian competitors, British design policy was neither closely linked to economic policy, nor actively developed in cooperation with businesses and design organizations promoted design in a power vacuum. The latest reorganization of the Design Council in 1994 was belatedly intended to remedy these problems.

Mixed evidence

The evidence that design policy can promote economic competitiveness is therefore mixed. Success seems to depend on two factors: the existence of authoritarian characteristics in government, such as absolutist France, or the guided economy of Japan; and relative industrial stability, as in ceramics and tapestries in the eighteenth century, or automobiles and domestic electrical products in the late twentieth century, in which innovation tends to be incremental and gradual. How then can national governments handle the dramatic changes on multiple levels and technologies, of global markets, and business organization and that are currently causing major economic disruption and unemployment? The answer, I believe, is they cannot: government policy exercised through bureaucratic organizations is ill-equipped to understand and dynamically respond to change on any level. The world economy is at present so diverse and dynamic that attempts to control it through mercantilist-style policies will be not only be futile but extremely damaging.

Are national governments then doomed to be marginalized, becoming an obstacle to progress, as some commentators suggest? This does not have to be so, but it requires that national policies become oriented less to targeting a specific range of aims, defined by government, and devoted more to building design capability as a flexible means of coping with change. On this level, there is still great potential for effective government policies.

Globalization is a process that in essence rests upon the activities of a limited number of large companies. It is often overlooked that these had small origins. In most countries, 90–95% of companies are small or medium-sized. Many giants have long histories, Kodak and Siemens are over a century old. Others have more recent origins: Sony and Honda in Japan were founded after the Second World War. This power of small companies to rapidly grow is illustrated by James Dyson, an industrial designer, whose radically new vacuum cleaner based on "dual-cyclone" technology was introduced in 1993. It became market leader in Britain within two years against established global players such as Hoover, Electrolux, Matsushita and Hitachi, and is now penetrating overseas markets. Moreover, the growth of his company has not only earned a large personal fortune for Dyson, but has ended unemployment in the area in which it is located.

Design enhances national competitiveness

In other words, the success of Dyson, and similar small companies in other countries, demonstrates that design creativity linked to technological competence and entrepreneurial capability can be a powerful means not only of resisting the penetration of global companies in existing product markets, but enhancing a nation's competitiveness. Establishing clear concepts of entrepreneurial approaches to design in small companies should be at the heart of any national design policy. Equally significant is the way companies in the United States, such as Apple and Microsoft, have used design to introduce new technologies and create totally new markets. Similar developments are currently apparent with companies being established on the Internet on the basis of new approaches to interactive design.

If governments wish to encourage such developments, they will need to understand what they can and cannot do well. They can continue on the basis of the status quo, attempting to control or influence overall trends, or they can encourage a diversity of new design initiatives. They can do this by building infrastructure and exploring possibilities of how to use design in their own activities, demonstrating in environments, communications and products not just an aesthetic veneer for bureaucratic inertia, but leadership through an encouragement of possibility.

Chances of influence exertion

Above all, policies for promoting design and for design education are the most powerful tools available to governments, but these need to emphasize the new demands being made on business and design practice. Businesses that do not adapt to change disappear. In contrast, design education continues to exist in old forms, and its failure is evident in the low numbers of design graduates obtaining employment in design, less than 3% in Britain, with similar trends in the U.S. and Japan.

Yet where are there national policies to explore new concepts of what design education and practice are likely to be in the twenty-first century? They are conspicuous by their absence.

Nations will continue to exist as focal points, not just of cultural identity, but of a substantial proportion of economic activity. Policies based on understanding design as a dynamic element in innovation and adaptation to change, will mean that design itself must change—becoming a creator of economic value by enabling people to understand and adapt new technological potential in their lives. National design policies, if they do not help producers and users navigate the difficult processes of economic change, in ways enabling cultures to evolve rather than repeat old patterns, will be just another problem confronting our societies, rather than a contributor to solutions.

20

Lessons Abroad: Learning from Germany's Integrated Design Policy

When Ford's Taurus supplanted the Honda Accord as the best-selling passenger car of 1992, an air of exultation was detectable in reports that the automobile industry might be regaining market share lost to the Japanese. It's almost as though American national prowess is defined in terms of some elemental shoot-out between the products of the two countries, particularly automobiles.

The Land of the Rising Sun isn't our only major competitor, however. Balance of trade statistics make it clear that German imports into the U.S., although not on the scale of Japanese products, are still very substantial. Yet where are the bookstore shelves full of journal articles dissecting German manufacturing procedures, management organization and social relationships?

The reasons may have something to do with what Robert Reich in his book, *Tales of a New America,* identifies as American society's need for an "enemy without," a myth of threat in the face of which it can unite and define itself. With the Cold War over and the Russians in such deep mire they can't even feed their soldiers, our armory of available mythological stereotypes has been sadly depleted. Putting the spotlight on Japan and reducing problems of competitiveness to the level of *Gunfight at the O.K. Corral* provides a convenient scapegoat on which to blame economic ills. German companies, in contrast, have deflected the possibility of serving this role by not focusing on the American market to quite the extent their Japanese counterparts do.

First published as "Lessons abroad: Learning from Germany's integrated design policy," *I.D. International Design*, May/June, 1993, pp. 34, 36. By permission of F & W Media (New York).

Nevertheless, we should remember that Germany exports a greater proportion of its gross national product than Japan—the difference is a more even distribution across the world. Integral to this success has been a passion for engineering quality, combined with the application of design to many aspects of business, commerce and government. Prominent examples come easily to mind: the automobiles of Daimler-Benz, BMW, Audi and VW; major electrical products by Siemens and Bosch; consumer electrical products by Braun, Rowenta and Krups; the corporate identity of Lufthansa; lighting by ERCO; and a host of fine porcelain and cutlery firms. Some are very large in size, but many belong to what is called the Mittelstand—small and medium companies that are the real backbone of the German economy.

The seriousness with which design is regarded is also reflected in the German press. A recent example was a major supplement on design published by a leading newspaper, the Frankfurter AUaemeine Zeitirag (FAZ), in November of last year. Fourteen pages were packed with over 30 articles, providing a comprehensive survey of what is happening in German design and its role at home and abroad.

The FAZ supplement is interesting on two levels. Firstly, it demonstrates the possibility of nurturing a consciousness of design to the point where it becomes embedded in business and society as a normal ingredient of understanding how our world is shaped and what it means. It also provides pointers to current efforts to promote the role of design in the U.S.

The importance of long-term thinking is an obvious element of why German design has such a high profile. The firms mentioned earlier have pursued consistent policies over many years, which implies not only a fundamentally different attitude to design, but also a different concept of business practice.

An example is an article by a Siemens executive for a catalogue introducing a major exhibition of his company's products in 1987. Design was important, he said, not only in terms of "the role a company played in its markets, but also in the role it played and was seen to play in society and how it defined and proved its cultural responsibility." The writer was Dr. Dankwart Rost, an advertising specialist and head of the Advertising and Design Department of Siemens. Corporate cultural responsibility in society, as he depicted it, had nothing to do with financial support for operas and art exhibitions, or other obeisances in the direction of "high" culture useful for PR purposes. It focused, instead, on the concept of quality, expressed through the function and design of products, and their role in shaping contemporary culture in everyday work and life.

Now my opinion of advertising executives is normally so jaundiced that suggesting the culture of our society ranks high in their concerns has all the credibility of the wolf pretending to be Red Riding Hood's grandma. They do create large chunks of our culture, but with responsibility? There is a pattern of behaviour observable in some German companies, however, that gives Dr. Rost's statements credibility. The Braun brothers' vision was based on the belief that design had a definite role in constructing a new postwar German society. Klaus-Jurgen Maack, managing director of ERCO, insists that every new lighting product his firm develops must be a genuine improvement over what is currently available in the belief it cannot otherwise be socially justified. He once sent visiting representatives of the local city council of Lüdenscheid packing, telling them to return when they were empowered to discuss culture, in terms of how to improve life in the community. BMW has taken the concept of design for disposability into new levels of achievement and consciousness in its latest cars. On a macro-level, German legislation on environmental and ecological protection is the most far-reaching in the world, with the active participation of many German companies and designers.

There is nothing inevitable about this, no secret ingredient specific to this society. In fact, a hundred years ago, deep concern existed at the "cheap and nasty" reputation of German goods in world markets. As a result, a broad coalition of government officials, industrialists, educators, designers and journalists emerged early in this century, advocating that in an industrial age, machines should be used to create a new national culture typical of its time. To achieve this also required higher standards of understanding in the public at large. One of the veterans of this movement, Theodor Heuss, a writer and former business manager of the German Werkbund, an organization formed in 1907 to promote design, became the first President of the Federal German Republic in 1948. He did much to encourage renewed interest in design in economic recovery after World War II.

The idea of a Design President in that sense is somewhat incomprehensible for anyone in the U.S. But the success of German design cannot be attributed to political patronage, no matter how enlightened. It worked because many designers fervently believed in the social relevance of what they were doing, and sufficient owners and executives in companies of all kinds, over many years, committed themselves to this idea. The emphasis is important, because at no time were the majority of German companies even remotely involved. Indeed, a recent report for the German Ministry of Economics contained a rough estimate that in the old Federal Republic just before unification, no more than 1,500 to 2,000 firms of all sizes were more or less design active. The figures and the wording are interesting, and are seen in Germany as proof of how much they have yet to do to strengthen design consciousness in industry and the public.

Although German design has generally been very successful, we must keep it in perspective. The German economy, like Japan, is currently in recession, not only as a result of having to digest the consequences of Communist misrule in East Germany, but also from fundamental problems of high labor costs, the shift to electronic/information technology, the demands of global marketing and the growing transnational nature of corporations and manufacturers. In such a situation, the fact that design has become so established may indeed be an obstacle to change and adaptation, a possibility that preoccupies many younger designers.

Despite such problems, however, the German model is important. It demonstrates that over time, a core of committed companies supported by governmental and professional bodies, with publications that discuss design as a substantive issue rather than ephemeral trivia, can establish a critical mass to change how design is applied and perceived, and that the process is more powerful if the general public is regarded as indispensable participants in the process. Above all, it also shows that an essential element of this transformation is the role designers can themselves play. Of the 33 articles published in the FAZ design supplement, not one was done by a professional journalist. One-third of the articles were written by businessmen or representatives of major design organizations; two-thirds were by designers intelligently articulating, ideas about their work and the role it plays in society at large. The ideas expressed in these articles are not particularly unique or more advanced than the best current thinking in the U.S. But in their capacity to be their own best advocates to a broad public, German designers definitely show the way.

21

Design and Industry in China

Readings #21 and #22 are extracts from **Design In Asia: Review of national design policies and business use of design in China, South Korea and Taiwan**, *a research report commissioned by the Design Council, UK as a contribution to the Cox Committee's report to the Government on the future of design in the United Kingdom. As part of the work of the committee Heskett was survey the national design policies in China, South Korea and Taiwan and then to take lessons from these for the UK. The extra below is from the chapter on design and industry in China. Reading #22 gives Heskett's propositions for developing an adequate policy of design and development for the UK. Both are previously unpublished.*

Context

(...) Amidst the richness and variety of Chinese culture, four broad factors can be cited as pertinent to understanding the current situation in industry and design.

It is easy to forget that for a thousand years, until around the mid-eighteenth century, China was the leading technological and economic power in the world. Many Chinese people are natural entrepreneurs and wherever they have migrated they have enjoyed remarkable economic success. It therefore should not be surprising they are similarly succeeding in their homeland now that opportunities for them to do so have again opened up.

Secondly, unlike most other major cultures, China is not dominated by the influence of monotheistic religion. Instead, the tenets of Confucius and Lao-tse-tu have been woven into a powerful secular morality based on social hierarchy in which mutual responsibility and respect, right-thinking and right-doing, are the basis of social cohesion. These values are strikingly apparent in the management practices and pronouncements of Chinese companies of all kinds.

Thirdly, China is not homogenous, but is huge and diverse on every level, landscape, climate, ethnicity, culture and society. The gulf between conurbations, smaller cities and rural districts, and between rich and poor is large and growing. In addition, while the power of central government is paramount, there are many ways that regional and local government find to adapt to the needs of their local environment.

Finally, superimposed upon characteristics long ingrained in the culture has been the more recent influence of Communist rule since 1948. Again, with the remarkable industrial expansion since the open-door policy was introduced in the early 1980s by Deng Shao-ping (resulting in him being known as "the Great Designer"), it is easy to overlook or dismiss the fact that the Communist party still rules China; that in some respects, there is still a command economy; and that as a result, no part of government or the economy is entirely free from central directives or the need to appoint to responsible positions people who are acceptable to the party rather than qualified for the job. At least 30% of the labour force still work for government-owned companies propped up by an inefficient banking system. For international companies to do business in China, a good relationship to the government is a must, but this incurs costs. The juxtaposition of commercial wealth and a powerful but ill-paid bureaucracy is a recipe for corruption, graft and bribery (colloquially known as "fragrant grease"). A major feature of the command economy is that it literally has no concept of markets. Neither is there any consciousness of consumer rights or needs. There are still huge problems for Chinese industry and its managers in coming to terms with approaches that focus upon customers, their needs and desires.

The current situation is therefore complex and volatile, with rapid change on many levels juxtaposed with traditional cultural values that are still a binding influence and a state and provincial government structure still capable of intervention and control on many levels.

Central government initiatives and organizations

As yet, China has no design policy although the State Development and Reform Commission of the State Council is currently reported to be considering one. Design has been mentioned in a recent report on Modernization by the commission, which also discussed the development of Korea and Japan. An important influence in this new emphasis is widely cited to be China's accession to the WTO and the need to think not only in terms of its own internal market, but of meeting competitive challenges around the world. There are a number of signs and comments confirming this, but given the secrecy with which government is still transacted, it is not easy to grasp what the direction of such discussions is. A draft of proposals on policy from a professional design organisation is appended and, on a personal note, a straw in the wind is an invitation to discuss preparing a syllabus on design policy for and giving a lecture to what can be considered the staff college of the Chinese Communist Party that educates cadres of future party administrators.

It is relevant to ask, why has China lagged so far behind in discussing the role of design in industry? A partial answer is that the Communist Party has always viewed science and technology as the necessary building blocks of the economic base—with Marxist economic theory still a crucial frame for policy. Insofar as design has been considered, it is not in the mainstream of economic thought or policy, but as a visual tool for propaganda purposes. That may be about to change in policy terms but to the extent to which policy statements signal a real change in attitudes and practices is uncertain.

Beijing industrial design centre

The only practical government initiative of any note in design by a government body in recent years has been the establishment of the Beijing Industrial Design Centre (BIDC), founded in 1995 as a branch of the Beijing Productivity Promotion Centre, which reports to the Beijing Municipal Science and Technology Commission.

The government five-year plan of 1995–1999 had the aim "to enhance competitiveness by technology". It was under this plan that the design centre was established in 1995. According to its Director, Chen Dongliang, it represents the voice of the government in promoting industrial design and communicating between the government and industry. This positioning as an intermediary between government and industry seems to be a prerequisite for the functioning of any design promotion body in China, with no private organisations allowed.

BIDC is funded by the government and industry and has two major functions:

- To promote industrial design;
- To provide design services appropriate to the needs of industries, "as there were only few designers available at that time."

What the latter comment meant, it emerged in subsequent discussion, was that the educational system does not produce industrial design graduates capable of a wide range of work in industry, particularly in technically-oriented fields such as medical equipment and machine tools. The centre therefore plays a compensatory role in a situation of fierce competition for appropriate design services from industries seeking to development their own intellectual property through innovatory designs, whose needs are inadequately met by the education system. There have been some projects where the BIDC design input has contributed to market success, such as ultrasound equipment for cancer treatment that has been outstandingly successful in the US market with reportedly US$20 million in profit. At present, however, their human resources are stretched due to work for the Beijing Olympics, which is confidential but said to be demanding.

BIDC has 43 staff in total: 20 in the design team, comprising industrial designers and engineers, and the remaining 23 focusing on promotion. The head of the design group is British, a devout Christian whose declared mission is to promote industrial design in China and is thus prepared to accept the low salary paid. Design projects comprise 20% of work, with 80% spent on promotion. They organize training sessions, awards and events, exhibitions, conferences and overseas visits and cooperate closely with university design departments. There are branch offices of BIDC in, Gongzhe, Shantong, Mongolia and Wu Bei.

BIDC's services cover both big corporations and SMEs, with different needs emerging in terms of large companies' ability to plan in the long term, compared with SMEs demand for design service for immediate production.

A glimpse of some of the problems of change in China emerged in descriptions of projects for the government undertaken by BIDC, such as a campaign to ease the unemployment problem of peasants whose land has been appropriated by the government by designing simple products for them to make. Similarly, a handicraft design competition was held for women who had to leave the fields, as an opportunity to develop new ways of earning a living. The scale of rural displacement is so huge, however, that it is inconceivable for such measures to have any substantial effect.

A new venture of BIDC is Design Resource Cooperation (DRC), an initiative for information sharing, which should be in full operation by the end of the year when the Centre moves into a new building. It will offer:

- Technology resources (Applied Technology Centre, material and handicraft research and exhibition centre, testing centre, Rapid Prototype Centre and CAD centre)
- Creativity resource (Universities, design organization, design community and "dream workshop of design"—a forum for blue-sky thinking);
- Service resource (information, law and finance consultant, information of reference books and images, business centre, knowledge and technological exchange and training, also a media centre)

Regional government design organizations

Consciousness of the need for design promotion has been evident far earlier at the provincial level, which is capable of moving faster and more flexibly to stay ahead of the central government.

The most prominent design organizations established by regional governments are:

- Beijing Industrial Design Promotion Organization (BIDPO)
- Shanghai Industrial Design Promotion Organization (SIDPO)
- Guangdong Industrial Design Association (GIDA)
- Guangzhou Industrial Design Promotion Organization (GIDPO)
- Shenzen Design Forum (SDF)

BIDPO has adopted a high-profile approach to publicising a wide range of design events, using its position in the capital to bring in exhibitions and organise functions featuring overseas design.

Shanghai is vigorously promoting itself as a creative city and is particularly strong in graphic design and interior design, which are strongly featured by SIDPO.

The Pearl River Delta (PRD) has the greatest concentration of manufacturing in China with Guangdong province recording annual export products of US$18 billion,[1] representing a very large proportion of China's 2005 first quarter exports of US$60.87 billion. It should be remembered that a substantial proportion of investment in the PRD is based on Hong Kong capital but the figures are nevertheless staggering.

The region has several overlapping promotional bodies. GIDA is a provincial body for Guangdong province; GIDPO is a municipal association in the city of Guangzhou, as is SDF, which was established by the Shenzen municipality.

The Guangdong industrial design association

GIDA was established in 1991 by the Economic and Trade Commission of Guangdong Province. To organize the association, Xian Chao Zhang, an engineer by training who was at that time in charge of the technologies division at the Light Industries Office of Guangdong Province was appointed as Secretary-General, a post he still holds. The provincial government offers funding for special events, however, daily operations are self financed.

The aims of GIDA include:

- The popularisation and promotion of industrial design, through media and education;
- Organizing exchange visits to the USA for major industries: in 1992, 28 delegates had visited major companies and design firms in Washington and the Art Centre College of Design in Pasadena;
- Inviting foreign experts, for example, from the US, Germany and Japan to give lectures;

- Presenting design awards to industries for innovative manufactured products;
- In 1999–2000 it cooperated with the British Council, which invited design students from universities in South China to visit Britain;
- Organizing special provincial events with both overseas and local expertise;
- Guiding industries to move from cosmetic designs to in-depth analysis and development of their own products.

The expectation is that big firms have developed their own industrial design teams and therefore need little assistance. The main work of GIDA, therefore, is with SMEs. In this regard, they act as matchmakers, helping to find appropriate professional designers for the needs of companies and the nature of their products, such as consumer electronics, or furniture; they also seek to extend the concept of industrial design service, "from mock up to injection moulding." According to Mr. Xian, two levels of training are necessary for SMEs, both involving changing "mindsets:" for owners of companies, there is a need to change their concept of design, which is too superficial, to include such elements as a products utility, structure and human factors; designers also need to change their approach to understand better what kinds of tools and methods can facilitate a successful and profitable design at reasonable production cost. SMEs, he says, should be able to afford to pay for design services providing better design, pointing out that Guangdong has designers from all over the world and some local ones who were educated in other countries. This enables Guangdong companies to pay greater attention to the needs of the European and US markets.

Guangdong has 10 higher education institutions offering Industrial Design programmes, divided into those focusing on human factor engineering, materials and structures, the other one is fine art, focusing on form. Feedback from industries indicates graduates do not have sufficient hands-on skill to work out designs independently. It usually takes half to a year to train them up.

Guangzhou industrial design promotion organization

In the early 1990s, the municipal government of Guangzhou became aware of the importance of industrial design and began to organize events like design awards to motivate students and strengthen understanding of design. GIDPO was established in 1995 by the municipality on an initiative of the mayor to provide for the needs of local industries. All organisations in China must be established in a relationship with a central government unit, in GIDPO's case, the Ministry of Science and Technology, in order to function as a bridge between the industry and the government. It has a budget of RMB 200–300,000, funded annually by the city government to organize for special events and it has premises provided that include rental-free offices for designers.

The aims of GIDPO are to:

- help industry reflect ideas to the government;
- help economic and industrial development;
- organise technical exchanges with foreign countries;
- organize seminars to enhance design standards;
- organize award activities;
- enable a facilitative environment for design;
- develop relationships and collaborations with the rest of the world.

Shenzhen design union

SDU had its origins in the Shenzhen Industrial Design Association, established in 1987 by the Shenzhen Science and Technology Association of the local municipality to enhance the competitiveness of local industry. The government influence is evident in the fact that it is chaired by a local party official in charge of propaganda—under which design is subsumed—but it is basically a self-financing operation, with occasional funding on a small scale for special events. Its current emphasis in on the need to develop original designs in place of copies and its main target audiences are SMEs and designers.

SMEs are viewed as problematic, with little idea of how to use designers, of what the role and value of design can be or of how much designers should be paid. They do, however, have a clearer concept of advertising and media and feel it worth paying a higher rate for a corporate identity, in the pragmatic belief that once designed it can be used over several years. Time is seen as what matters in SMEs' development cycle, above all, getting products to market speedily with instant feed-back on their performance as a preliminary to the next development cycle.

Professional organizations—China industrial designers association (CIDA)

CIDA is a privately-founded professional body dominated by academics. As with other design organizations, various government agencies provide funds only for special events. In general, CIDA makes great claims for its role, (e.g. that it is similar to the UK Design Council) but even its members admit that it is not very effective—good ideas can be generated by its members but it lacks the manpower and finance to be effective.

CIDA is preparing a document on design policy for the central government, (see Appendix 3) covering the following areas:

- Policy on Technologies
- Management of Design Industry
- Design Organization
- Intellectual Property
- Human Resource, Education and Training
- Promotion to Society
- International collaboration and exchange
- Fund raising and taxation

The role of design in business

In general, in large Chinese manufacturing companies, design functions at best at a middle level, buried in large marketing or engineering departments. Its role is to give an aesthetic veneer and not to be involved in conceptual work. Even in companies considered leaders in China, such as Lenovo or TCL, there has in practice been very limited success in using design as more integral element of development processes. Although the core of corporate strategy is professedly innovation and design this has not been implemented consistently and products are not of a particularly high standard. In 2002, for example, TCL's new line of cell-phone designs featured patterns of diamonds (industrial standard) on the lid that were a flop in the market and had to be speedily withdrawn.

Huawei Technologies Co.

Huawei Technologies, founded in 1988, is one of the largest telecommunications equipment manufacturers in China with headquarters in Shenzhen. Revenue for 2004 was 46.2 billion yuan ($5.6 billion), up 113% from 2003, in which overseas sales comprising $2.3 billion soared 120% and profit was 5 billion yuan ($600 million). The company employs 22,000 people and about 13,000 are engaged in R&D. In 1993, the first designers were employed by the company, with 4 on the staff in 1997, rising to a present total of 54, working in several divisions:
2005

- 16 designers for server terminal, modem equipment
- 25 designers for mobile terminals, cordless phone and Fixed Wireless Terminals
- 13 designers working for user interface (graphics & interactions)

The designers work in separate areas with no real contact between them. Design is moving slowly away from concept of cosmetic design with some brand work after 2000 when the company moved into domestic products, but design still has no role in proposing product concepts.

Decisions on what to produce are taken by an Investment Product Management Team (IPMT), comprising R&D leaders, vice-presidents and the company president, to which the product development team reports. Ideas are fed to the IPMT by the marketing department.

Product development teams include, in addition to industrial designers, mechanical engineering designers, hardware and software developments specialists and marketing and sales personnel. They work on approximately thirty projects a year. Designers can call meetings to present new ideas but is not a normal practice. There is also a problem of time to develop new ideas since design managers and senior designers are engaged for half their working hours in meetings.

Shenzhen Konka Telecommunications Technology Co Ltd

Konka, based in Shenzhen, has two major product lines, televisions, in which it is China's largest manufacturer, and mobile phones, in which it ranks third.

The company first set up an industrial design department in the mid-1990s and it is currently positioned as one of four divisions in the R&D Centre:

- Industrial Design team (25 ID designers, reduced from 40 last January), plus 6 designers working on graphical user interface projects;
- Software
- Hardware
- Mechanical engineering

Two-thirds of projects are developed in-house, the rest are outsourced. They work with Korean consultancies and have an office in Japan, to which four designers are sent to work.

Product concepts and strategies are determined by a consumer research department and a product team working in the Marketing department. Designers are sometimes invited into the product team. Designers have developed products but their ideas are usually different from marketing colleagues. Decisions on product proposals and designs are made by a panel comprised of the President and team leaders. They used to hire research companies to conduct research in order to confirm and evaluate product concepts. The manager of the design division, Frank Yao, believes

Chinese designers will be promoted into top management positions in ten years time.

Founder technology

Founder Technology is a manufacturer of computers, in which sector it is ranked second in the Chinese market after Lenovo. Based in Beijing with 800 employees, it is part of the larger Founder Group that has 6,000 employees.

Design is positioned in the company's Product Centre that also comprises mechanical engineering and strategic planning. The latter has responsibility for market research and analysis, but according to Wu Wei, a designer and Director of the Product Centre, it is not a high level operation.

Wu has been working in the company for 7 years, but is frustrated by frequent changes of Vice Presidents to whom he reports due to constant restructuring of the company's management—five in the time he has been in the company. The problem is to educate these people about design, which becomes impossible with such rapid turnover.

Founder's early focus was on R&D with design responsible for form. Gradually, more research was undertaken but it is still restricted to the local market only. Product ideas are generated top down, with the top management giving a rough idea in terms of price range as the direction for new products. Wu can propose ideas as well but this is infrequent. There are 20-30 projects per year.

Few companies have any design vision, says Wu, they are only cost oriented and want to get to market as fast as they can.

Lotusland Furniture Co.

Lotusland was founded by Weiyang Ye, its Managing Director. Weiyang is forty years old. After studying literature at university, in 1988 he entered a Buddhist monastery and edited publications for National Buddhist Association. In 1989 he was heavily involved in the Tien An Mun demonstrations and subsequently left China for Australia, where he eventually became involved in furniture production and design. "Designers," he says, "should be thinkers. One's state of being establishes the rules for what is good and bad design. Get the philosophy right and the design will be right."

Returning to China he set up his own furniture factory in Shenzhen in 1996, with early products based on OEM contracts, supplying colonial-style four-poster beds for American clients. Later he developed a friendship with a leading American designer Chuck Pelly, founder of a company, Design

Works, in Los Angeles that developed into BMW's advanced concept studio. Pelly is now designing several lines for Lotusland, which is the only Chinese furniture company trying to compete on original designs and now has 400 employees, with an office in Australia and a unit of three designers in Milan. Weiyang points out that in the furniture industry, designers are mostly expected to produce what is cheap—some don't even have to provide sketches, but just cut out images from magazines and catalogues which are then copied in factories. Copying is seen as the most economic and efficient way of learning and the quickest and cheapest form of business practice. During Milan Furniture Week, he asserts, not one senior manager can be found in PRD furniture factories.

The lack of any real sense of design at all levels angers Weiyang. The bitter legacy of China's recent past, he says, has left people just grabbing for as much money and possessions as they can lay their hands on. He talks of setting up a centre so that young designers can meet together and develop their ideas and consciousness of what design can achieve in society.

Weiyang Ye is one of a generation who represent a new wave in Chinese business management. They have travelled or studied abroad, understand the world outside China, speak foreign languages and feel the need to contribute something back to Chinese society to rebuild it after the terrible events it has endured in the last fifty years.

Design consultancies

Consultancies have also evolved in China but are spread unevenly, with a concentration of industrial design practitioners located in the Pearl River Delta, close to the manufacturing companies they serve. The scale of establishment ranges from 5–6 staff, with very few having over 10 people.

Estimated number of industrial design consultancies:

Beijing	19
Guangzhou	80
Dong Guang	30
Foshan	40

UTOP Design (Guangzhou) Co Ltd

UTOP is located in Guangzhou with a staff of 14 people, and projects ranging from information technology to transport. It is linked to partner companies in Sydney and Montreal run by former classmates and colleagues of Billie Xiao Ning, the founder and general manager of UTOP. The company has worked to maintain long term relationships with clients, with some 80% of projects being repeat orders.

Anyone founding a design consultancy faces the initial problem of how to get started and obtain the first client. Billie Xiao Ning spent the first year seeking clients by visiting company offices and promoting himself and the services he aspired to provide. His portfolio of previous work was the means of persuasion and he obtained his first project within two months. Other means of obtaining clients are exhibitions, the website, publicity brochures and referrals.

UTOP aims to build its reputation on continuous innovation skill to cope with the rapidly changing China market, such as electronic products, IT, digital cameras and MP3. Much depends on the client's experience in design. Their approach is to be professional but without adhering to a fixed process, which is slow and costly for clients. Profitability is maintained by continually improving the standard of design. This has been helped by an improvement in the design understanding of clients, which has significantly improved since the accession to WTO in 2003, widely regarded as a benchmark for change after clients felt the pressure of competition.

Design education in China

With the command economy, manufacturing facilities and quantities of commodities were all controlled by the State. Consequently, design of products at that time was basically ignored and visual education focused on arts and crafts. With the opening up of China in the early 1989s it became rapidly clear that this emphasis needed to be changed. An important shift in the nature of industrial design education was the re-definition of the subject as science-and-technology-based, although the baggage of the earlier arts and crafts emphasis is still hampering development. Nevertheless, the growth of design courses in general has mushroomed.

The overall figures for design courses vary wildly, ranging from 500 to over a thousand, but the most authoritative source available on the number of industrial design courses at present gives a figure of 126. Within that total there are probably ten universities, including some of the most prestigious universities in China, that have courses in industrial design with good standards of professional training in basic skills. Outside that inner circle in the wider generality of courses, however, there are many problems.

The reasons for the huge growth of design education programmes have been above all the pace of economic development, or as one academic aptly put it: "we need industrial design—being the world's factory". Design has also been a popular choice with students who, influenced by growing publicity that it would offer the next wave of development, replacing science and technology, believed it offered a good, lucrative career compared to computing or engineering, allowing them to do freelance work for additional income. Over half of the students recently surveyed before applying for university expressed an interest in design. If demand has been strong, this has been bolstered by other factors on the supply side. Since the Open Door policy was introduced the social welfare structure of China has been largely dismantled and funds for education have been drastically cut. Design courses in China yield the highest tuition fees of any discipline, a legacy of when art courses charged for materials, such as brushes, paints, inks, paper, etc. In a situation of increasing constraints, therefore, universities and colleges are naturally attracted by the potential of higher tuition income by offering ID programmes.

A chronic shortage of good teachers is exacerbated by better incomes being available to any competent person by working in industry. Teachers are drawn from diverse backgrounds, frequently with no experience or knowledge of design practice. Of eight teachers in the industrial design department of Shenzhen University, only one is a practitioner. Teachers are often incompetent and are badly paid. They have little awareness or involvement in international events other than a superficial knowledge of fashion. A group of professors interviewed at Tsinghua University in Beijing explained that recent changes in China's higher education system had resulted in job cuts, leading many teachers to seize opportunities to keep their jobs by switching to industrial design from other disciplines, such as engineering. For many, teaching is often a cover for personal consultancy activities using students as cheap labour. A professor at Shenzhen University explained that five-month-long semesters required only two months teaching, leaving the remainder free for independent consultancy.

A confusion of aims about design also results from the influx of people from art or engineering, with the former believing it comprises packaging and posters and the latter focusing on technical skills without any understanding of ideas or processes on how these might be applied. Few industrial design courses in China have workshops where students can gain practical experience of materials and processes through hands-on activities and those with workshops generally don't know how to use them. Instead, students learn to use computers and become competent at visualization, which is not the same as designing. There is a heavy emphasis on fashionable forms for IT products and following the market, but little experience in how to design for more fundamental problems across a wide spectrum of products.

Another problem is a tendency to blindly adopt what is known or observed in overseas schools without considering their relevance or how they might be adapted to Chinese circumstances. Even at Tsinghua University, one professor spoke of his involvement in the Business School's MBA course on design and user research and complained that they adopted everything from Harvard and the US market, with case studies belonging to the past.

Advantages

- Design is becoming a recognized tool in Chinese manufacturing, albeit within certain limits.

- There are some designers who now have several years experience and are capable of more complex work but they need more effective management.

- Some consultants also have a wider outlook, either from being educated overseas or from an intelligent appraisal of their working environment and have built relationship of trust with owners of companies over long periods. This is a key element in changing managers' understanding and attitudes.

- There has been a fast learning curve, with copying widely seen as quick way to learn but more recently with a growing emphasis by promotional bodies and some companies on creating higher-added-value through original designs.

- Consumers are becoming very sophisticated. Many people interviewed commented that consumers were in many respects far more sophisticated than companies, due to the influence of retail expansion, advertising, films and publications. The increase in wealth, particularly in the big conurbations, is evident in the avid consumption of imports of the world's outstanding brands.

- There are early signs of a new generation of more sophisticated managers and entrepreneurs in industry who are showing greater innovative spirit.

Disadvantages

- The basic skills of visualization using computer systems that are compatible with those used by most companies and meet their demands are well taught in design schools. Visualisation, however, is not designing, which is not widely understood. Design students are therefore widely prepared for a limited repertoire of skills in a narrow range of consumer industries. There are widespread complaints about the need for a period of 6–12 months to "train them up".

- There are severe problems in designing more complex products or systems, where skills of superficial design are inadequate to understand the nature of intricate problems. There is a lack of sophisticated methodologies or means of generating solutions applicable to a broad spectrum of product and systems.

- The influence of rote learning is evident in a lack of initiative, with a pattern of looking to the rule book for guidance.
- The pattern of appointing bureaucrats from other state bodies to run design promotion organisations can be seen as a necessity throughout China in the absence of any designers qualified to do so, although there is also a tendency for organizational appointments to be preserved by bureaucrats. There are widespread complaints, however, that the bureaucrats do not understand design.
- Management attitudes and a widespread lack of any understanding of design are a continuing barrier to progress and it will take time for this to change.

Conclusions

China has undoubtedly established world-dominance in the production of goods on a quantitative basis where cost is the primary criterion. As yet, however, it still widely lacks the ability to successfully design products for the mass markets of the world, with overseas companies still controlling the design and distribution of products in these sectors. For the time being, most Chinese companies have their hands full attempting to successfully compete in the Chinese market, which is large, growing and very diverse. If and when they successfully solve those problems, it should be expected that they will then use the home market as a springboard for entry to global markets. Neither at present does China have the sophistication to compete in those sectors where quality of design concept is a prerequisite. Even with the Chinese capacity for hard work and rapid learning, it will take time for the necessary cultural shifts required to work at the highest level will work their way through.

22

A Design Policy for the UK: Three Suggestions

How can design contribute to a more competitive economy in the UK, in ways that would not be easily copied or emulated in Asian countries? The key factor I would emphasise above all others is the need to develop a new, more effective and more sophisticated relationship between business and design and to embed this in design and corporate culture. To achieve that level of change, industrial design has to be understood as a complex business tool capable of providing concepts and operational processes that enhance performance and profitability.

Suggestion #1

Stop talking of industrial design in the context of creative industry.

Design is multi-faceted as shown in the following list of specialisations and applications:

engineering design, product design, industrial design, ceramic design, decorative design, graphic design, illustration design, information design, typographic design, advertising design, packaging design, brand design, interior design, fashion design, textile design, pattern design, software design, systems design, interactive design, hair design, floral design, funeral design ...

Extracted from *Design In Asia: Review of national design policies and business use of design in China, South Korea and Taiwan,* a research report commissioned by the Design Council, UK as a contribution to the *The Cox Review of Creativity in Business: Building on the UK's Strengths* commissioned by the UK Government in 2005. Previously unpublished.

Some of the above may indeed be appropriately grouped under the rubric of creative industries, but there are real problems in the perception of industrial design in these terms.

An illustration is a project in the *New York Times* magazine in December, 2002, when serveral designers were asked to redefine common objects of everyday life. One, Jonathan Adler, chose the toilet. (Fig. 22.1)

What the relevance of a fashion trend from France in the aftermath of World War II is, or how to convince a business client that the major characteristcis of a toilet are that it should be "cheerful," "cute," "fun" and playful," are not addressed.

My primary objection to this approach being depicted as appropriate for industrial products, however, is that it reduces design to a limited level incapable of delivering anything else but whimsical and superficial

Toilet | **Jonathan Adler**

"I chose to redesign a toilet because even though everybody has one, they're always so dreary. I wanted to create a cheerful toilet. I was inspired by Dior's New Look, with its wasp-waisted silhouettes, from the 40's and 50's. The shape makes it a little cuter; the graphic element makes it fun. There are a number of functional issues that would need to be addressed for this to actually work, but the toilet really is the perfect arena for playfulness."

FIGURE 22.1

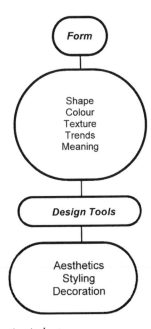

FIGURE 22.2 *Design as creative industry.*

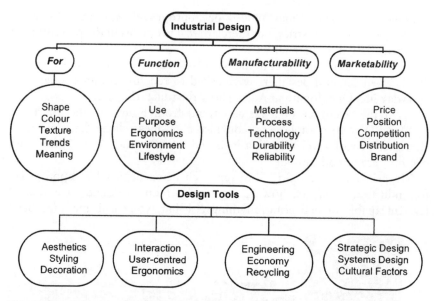

FIGURE 22.3 *Design as a Complex Business Activity.*

decorative or formal solutions. The contrast is apparent in a comparison of these two diagrams. (Fig. 22.2, Fig. 22.3).

The factors set out in the diagram Design as a Complex Business Activity are not intended to be comprehensive but indicative. The simple point is that industrial design is a practice involving a wide range of aims, methods and procedures that are relevant to the activities of manufacturing companies on multiple levels. A more complex point is that design is morphing into new methods and applications that offer a diverse range of strategic options appropriate to many different circumstances. Unless this is understood, bringing business and design together on the basis of concepts that no longer have general validity could be an exercise in futility.

Suggestion #2

Theory, whether explicit or implicit, frames practice; business and design need rethinking on both levels.

For example, a concept of a Generic Value Chain developed by McKinsey & Co., one of the foremost management consultancies in the world, shows product design in terms that again are very limited (Fig. 22.4). Indeed, this specification does not go much beyond what managers in China expect of design and certainly does not encourage thinking about it as a strategic factor. Another problem with this linear concept is the positioning of

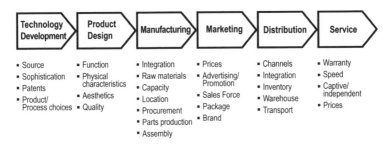

FIGURE 22.4 *Generic Value Chain.*

technology as the primary driver of development—ignoring other sources of ideas. Above all, this is a producer-centred concept typical of business education and practice, essentially devoid of any consideration of users.

Michael Porter's model of the Value Chain, published in his book *Competitive Advantage* (1985) acknowledged the McKinsey model as a source but went no further in discussing design, which was positioned as one of several "support factors". His approach similarly epitomises American economic thinking in halting at the point of sale with no consideration of the context of use. In doing so he privileges management decisions in the context of production as the primary source of value.

Another distinguished American theorist, Jay Barney, takes a different approach in a concept that focuses on the distinctive characteristics enabling a company to distinguish itself from competitors. The questions raised are highly relevant to any company, but again there is a total lack of any extension of them to include the actual or latent needs of users.

The VRIO Framework – Four Questions

- *The question of value*

  Do a firm's resources and capabilities enable it to respond to environmental threats or opportunities?

- *The question of rareness*

  How many competing firms already possess valuable resources and capabilities?

- *The question of imitability*

  Do firms without a resource or capability face a cost disadvantage in obtaining it compared to firms that already possess it?

- *The question of organization*

  Is a firm organized to exploit the full competitive potential of its resources and capabilities.

From: Jay B. Barney. *Gaining and Sustaining Competitive Advantage.* Reading, MA: Addison Wesley, 1996, p.145.

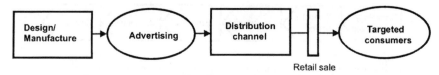

FIGURE 22.5 *Designer as formgiver.*

It would be possible to continue citing examples. What conventional business school approaches widely ignore is the matter of translating the functions and data represented in their theories into products and services that represent solutions to the needs of people— users.

This producer-centric approach also encourages an interpretation of design that essentially limits it to the role of designer as "formgiver", a terms translated from the German word *formgeber,* which literally implies the creation of form (Fig. 22.5). This is the design corollary of producer-centred business theory, a process in which forms are designed, manufactured and distributed, with various blandishments to purchase. Form on this level is created and validated in terms of producer concerns and there is simply a choice for consumers to accept it or not.

There are, however, other paradigms of how design functions that alters the relationship with users and also changes how product development processes can function. User-centred design (fig. 22.6) focuses on efforts to identify and understand people's actual and latent needs. Knowledge of users based on observation can form part of a virtuous cycle in which concepts are developed, implemented and their validity constantly monitored and evaluated in the context of use. Such knowledge can be the source of scenarios of user behaviour that are springboards for further design concepts embodying deep insights of actual and latent need. Early prototyping methods of a simple, inexpensive kind can be used to test concepts with users, aiming at getting ideas right in terms acceptable to them at the earliest stage of product development and, in addition, establishing a broad

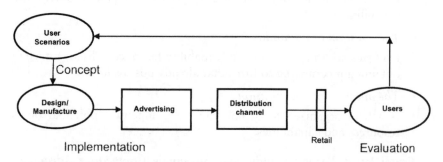

FIGURE 22.6 *User-centred design.*

consensus of agreement by all parties involved in development processes before moving to the vital and costly stage of production prototypes and ramp-up for manufacture.

The power of user-centred approaches is illustrated by the Freedom Chair (1998), an office chair that Niels Diffrient, one of the leading designers in the USA, designed to give complete lumbar support, capable of flexing and adapting to movements in body position. The manufacturer previously only had experience of smaller products such as keyboard supports and the project required substantial investment in new production facilities. The risk has paid off, however, with the Freedom Chair being the first of a series of products by Diffrient that have positioned the Humanscale Corporation as one of the world's leading companies in ergonomic seating. On his relationship with the company, Diffrient commented: "Since the company that is producing this product is very advanced in their thinking (just as I would think), it has been a very satisfying development without too much compromise." That level of unity between company and designer about what design can and should achieve, is, however, rare.

A further extension of the spectrum of design approaches emerging at present is the role of designer as enabler (Fig. 22.7). This stems from the development of information technology and flexible manufacturing that shifts the focus away from mass-production to more niche-oriented.

The pattern of nodal firms acting as leaders in a coalition of manufacturers, with information technology yielding immense efficiencies in business-to-business applications, has become widespread. Nike is an example, with a large design and marketing staff at its headquarters in Seattle and its manufacturing in the hands of Asian OEM producers. Nevertheless, Nike is typical of many companies in that it still thinks of getting its products to market via conventional value-chain ideas targeting consumers. The implications of information technology, however, are that consumers can be more effectively drawn into the processes of defining products and determining their value in a complex pattern of communication through multiple channels. The resultant diversity of viewpoint among large groups of people creates problems requiring a shift to a concept of designer as enabler.

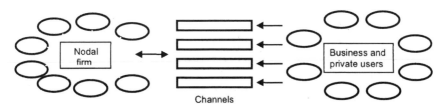

FIGURE 22.7 *Designer as enabler.*

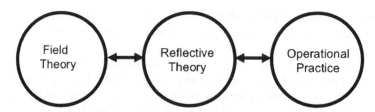

FIGURE 22.8 *Design as research.*

Diversity implies flexibility—they are two sides of the same coin. For diverse patterns of need, a single product designed by a formgiver will meet but a small percentage of actual requirements. The role of designer as enabler in contrast seeks solutions enabling users to flexibly adapt products or systems to their needs, in this sense becoming co-producers of value. An indicator of this trend is that 70% of automobile sales in the USA now result from users researching options on the Internet and specifying their needs in advance, rather than buying "as is."

Another feature of the evolution of industrial design into more complex patterns is the need for bodies of coded knowledge and information to supplement older methods of trial and error and reliance on tacit knowledge derived from experience. A key to this is the role of designer as researcher (Fig. 22.8). For reasons too tangled to discuss in detail here, there existed a long-standing antipathy in the design community to theory, regarded as something that hampered creativity. With the growth of greater complexity and larger scale in design projects such attitudes have become outmoded while research and theory have made considerable advances. The danger is that academic research, in particular, can take off on its own trajectory without any relevance to practice, which obviously needs to be avoided.

Research can function on several levels in design. It has become obvious in its more complex operations there is a need for research at an operational level during projects. Earlier mention of user observation is a case in point. There has been a tendency to adapt methods of observation from disciplines such as anthropology, which, however, functions in a manner that eschews involvement in what is being observed and takes a long time to formulate its conclusions. Design projects, on the other hand, cannot be objective since their purpose is to implement change—which implies involvement in the effects of change - and projects are often relatively short in duration. More formalised methods of researching are therefore a necessity in design but need to be appropriate to its context.

Reflective theory, or as Aristotle termed it, "practical wisdom", in contrast, examines a body of practice and seeks to identify commonalities or problems that are capable of new approaches that can be tested and if proven valid introduced into practice. The difference between this and operational practice is neatly illustrated by an example used by Aristotle: a carpenter, he said, will attempt to make a table with legs that are stable;

in contrast the geometrician will seek to understand the nature of angles, knowledge that can be embodied in tools such as the carpenter's square, enabling standards of work to be consistently enhanced. An area suitable for research in this sense is to evolve new approaches for the trend in manufacturing whereby products integrating substantial bodies of information cannot be designed solely in terms of form.

The third category of field theory in design research refers to efforts to understand broader patterns of cause and effect and wider contextual questions and, in general, will not be immediately applicable to the context of practice.

The growth of scale in design projects often requires a spectrum of disciplines, and not only design, which have to be organized through coordinated systems. This can require sophisticated computer programmes to specify and organize often bewildering arrays of data and ensure all necessary tasks are acknowledge and programmed. The need here is to break down complex systems into their component elements to determine which ideas or subsystems can be improved in combination and which might be in conflict with one another. In other words, the more complex a project, the greater will be the degree of coded knowledge and methodology required as a necessary prerequisite for what can be termed high-level creativity in design at a strategic level (Fig. 22.9).

There is currently much talk of design as strategy but scant clarity about what it really means or can mean. Considered in the most elemental terms, any business has three functions: it needs a strategy that explicitly or implicitly sets out what it intends to do and be; it requires a managerial structure to organize implementation; and implementation in tangible or intangible form.

Design also needs to be defined in terms of these three functions (Fig. 22.10) but is mostly found at the level of implementation; design

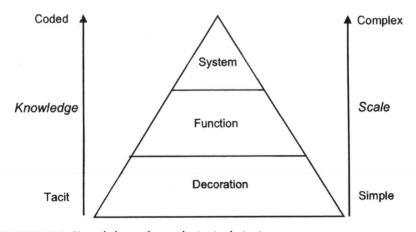

FIGURE 22.9 *Knowledge and complexity in designing.*

FIGURE 22.10 *Design as strategy.*

management has emerged as a trend in the last two decades, but a separate form of management for design emphasises its difference—do we really need separate management for engineering or marketing? Then why design management, which represents particularly for small companies a significant extra cost? The emphasis of the introduction to the Design Council's submission to the Cox Review seems to me to give exactly the right emphasis: "... our primary goal must be to make UK managers the best users of design in the world" - in other words, the management of design as an aspect of its integration into all aspects of corporate activity. Although this emphasis is rare in practice and ill-defined in theory, however, where it does function successfully, as at Samsung, the results of strategically positioning design can be spectacular.

If design is to be effectively implemented other aspects requiring consideration are the different ways in which it can be used. In the diagram (fig. 22.11), Different levels of design practice, The vertical axis represents a strategic emphasis ranging between innovative and existing products; the horizontal axis positions the organisational emphasis between the poles of product line and corporate-wide strategies. The four quadrants each illustrates a very different positioning of how design functions in an organisation.

The lower left quadrant has designers functioning as interpreters of existing products late in the process, a product-line emphasis that is superficial with little differentiation. This is essentially an executant role carrying out ideas generated by other functions in the company or clients—a situation typical of Original Equipment Manufacturing (OEM).

The upper left still focuses on product-lines but here designers function as differentiators in the search for a distinct market position. It is here that the "design as star" can also be found whose products win prizes in

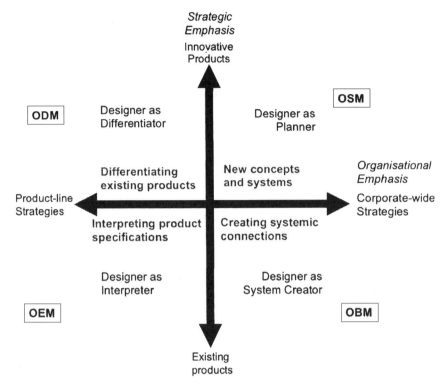

FIGURE 22.11 *Different levels of design practice.*

competitions. It is a segment typical of Original Design Manufacturing (ODM) manufacturing.

The lower right quadrant stresses the role of designers as system builders, which involves not just design competency but a managerial role. Here the emphasis might be on constructing systemic approaches to the overall output of a company, which could lead to the evolution of Original Brand Management (OBM) approaches, brand concepts founded on a total impression of what a company is and how it functions.

The upper right quadrant is where designers can become involved in innovative plans for the company as a whole at the Original Strategic Management (OSM) level. Design Planning aims to identify strategies for systemic innovations, including new products, services and systems that are harder for competitors to replicate because of their complexity and incorporation of user needs into their development, which can lead to long-term competitive advantage. This involves continuous innovation rather than single projects. To function at this level depends on being able to communicate and defend ideas with clarity and conviction, with supporting evidence that justifies investment decisions, in conditions that may vary from known or uncertain to unknown. Knowledge is a prerequisite at this level, which in design terms, involves the interaction of both tacit and coded forms.

Design planning in this sense enables a company to formulate a strategy that:

- can enable a company to bridge the creative and analytical aspects of its business at the highest level and thus throughout the organisation. Creative planning of design's role in a company should be an imperative, not an oxymoron;
- can effectively be realized in any circumstances that a company selects;
- allows for ambiguity and uncertainty by being flexible and able to adapt to new circumstances;
- can offer tangible insights into future possibilities through a range of scenarios exploring future potential technologies, markets, users and products, which can provide the basis for assessing their desirability, suitability, feasibility and practicability. Scenarios will not anticipate every eventuality, but can prepare companies to respond to rapidly changing competitive challenges;
- can promote different types and scales of innovation appropriate to a specific company's needs by using a spectrum of design methods in product development processes;
- can accumulate knowledge from the cumulative experience of a company in product development processes;
- can not only create profit but when embedded in processes and the experience of people represent an accumulation of human capital that is also difficult to copy by competitors.

Suggestion #3

The role of design needs to be understood as providing a bridge between a company and the users of its products that acknowledges very different imperatives in each.

In the context of production, at least three major points of emphasis in the role of designers needs to be taken into account:

- They must be capable through innovation of contributing to creating and adding new economic value.
- They need an ability to understand technological opportunity and act upon it as required.

- They have to function within institutional structures of various kinds (organizations, laws and customs) that enable and constrain their endeavours.

In contrast, of fundamental importance in the context of use is the factor of utility, which in design terms relates to the capability provided for users by a design, or in other words, what it enables them to do. In addition, designs assume meaning and significance in people's lives, which may stem from alignment with the beliefs and symbols current in the outside world, or may be of private significance to particular individuals. A third factor is variations in the systemic nature of the context of use. This can be subdivided into the physical systems, such as the electrical system or TV broadcasting system, and cultural systems, such as patterns of belief and behaviour that are embedded in a pattern of life. These latter often have a profound effect upon how what aspects of utility or meaning people will consider significant and in a global world require close and detailed attention.

The essential role of designers is in providing the tangible linkage between the two contexts, of production and use (Fig. 22.12). Any product, communication, environment or system has the potential to be an interface, which is the essential concept in translating the internal imperatives of any company, its organisation, analysis and action into solutions appropriate to users. The concept of interface is set in a wider context, however, in which recognition of its role in contributing to long-term competitiveness and profitability has other ramifications capable of being profoundly influenced by design. Design on this level should be one of the most demanding and

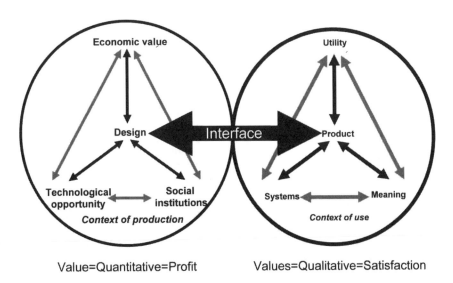

FIGURE 22.12 *The context of design practice.*

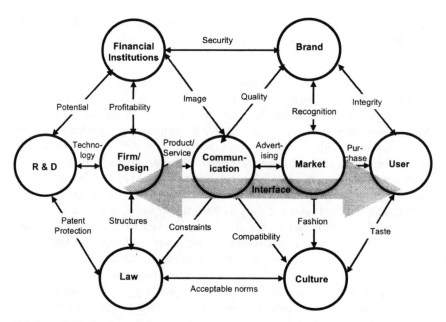

FIGURE 22.13 *The context of design.*

exciting of disciplines for the best talents of the nation, rather than a haven for refugees from discipline and rigour (Fig. 22.13).

Conclusion

In all the volatile changes affecting every part of the globe and every aspect of life, only one thing is certain: the future will require continuous adaptation to new priorities. The alternative for any country that fails to adapt will be a slow wasting away to a position of irrelevance in the world's affairs and economy, rather like Spain, India or China from their positions of pre-eminence during the eighteenth century. While many aspects of design in the UK are exemplary, there is a danger of complacency in any assumptions about what exists now being appropriate for the future. To suggest the need for radical change will undoubtedly arouse resistance from some people whose practices and attitudes are placed in question but an encouraging sign is the leadership apparent from bodies such as the DTI and Design Council, which is stronger and, I believe, more soundly based than at any time in my forty years of experience of working in the field of design.

It is widely accepted that the UK cannot compete across the broad swathes of mass-production industry and low-cost services now located in Asia. The problem is what to do about it, in particular, how to stem and even reverse the loss of manufacturing capability. James Dyson's example could be followed, with a focus on using the UK as its base for large-scale technological research and complementary design efforts, functioning in nodal terms with overseas manufacturing facilities that ensure cost competitiveness. There are also some possibilities of exploiting technological leadership although in this area the UK is hardly likely to remain unchallenged. Neither does producing "star" designers who can function around the world, developing products for our competitors, seem to offer any viable economic solution for the future. In addition, the failure of any western design consultancy to successfully function in China places in question illusions of a vast market waiting for the talented few.

On the other hand, generating a flow of a new kind of design professionals who can find challenging opportunities to excel in UK companies and organisations with coordinated support from government at national and regional level, from the Design Council, and from universities undertaking serious research into the future potential of design, does offer possibilities of a competitive edge. I can only reiterate the point, however, that this has no chance of success without a corresponding transformation, not just in manufacturing companies, but also in the financial and service companies that are vital to their needs.

Behind my comments and suggestions in this second part of the report is a belief that if the United Kingdom is indeed to "futureproof" itself, an interesting term currently being used by the Design Council in its activities, then fundamental change is required above all in how design is thought of and practiced in business contexts. The Design Immersion projects introduced by the Design Council seem to me to offer an excellent starting point for operational development capable of demonstrating not just the viability of new relationships but their necessity.

While the changes suggested in this section are capable of being couched in terms of making the application of design in business more efficient and effective, however, there are wider implications. Significant social efficiencies are also possible: applying systemic concepts of user-centred design in contexts such as hospitals, educational institutions and transport systems, for example, has vast untapped potential for the development of innovative processes, products and systems that could stimulate demand in export markets. As the Design Council has also argued, although there are practical problems to be overcome, government procurement could also play a similar role in providing a vital seed-bed for manufacturing initiatives.

Education is obviously crucial in preparing the ground for future needs. Engendering new business attitudes, creating a demand for designers with abilities to function at various levels, obviously needs to be met by a suitable supply. The conventional linking of terminology that so easily trips from the tongue—"art and design"—is perhaps the heaviest baggage from a past that bears scant resemblance to what is currently emerging in industry and design. My reasons for emphasising the distinction between art and design are simple: with art, only an artist can determine whether a work is valid; in design, a spectrum of other people, clients and users of all kinds, determine validity; moreover, it is possible for anyone to walk away from what they consider a bad painting or poem without any harm on either side; people cannot walk away from bad design, such as public seating or confusing information. The imperative for design to relate to users must therefore be reinforced at all levels.

While undergraduate education is the basic platform, the greatest possibility of rapidly introducing new concepts of design practice would be the establishment of suitable courses at Master's level. To prepare designers for more complex responsibilities implies a shift from older concepts of what is appropriate at this level, which basically meant a "playpen" approach, giving students space to do their own work with minimal teaching. To function at a high level in business, however, requires a rigorous teaching programme to bridge disciplines and acquire knowledge, methodologies and, above all, the ability to communicate with clarity and conviction what design can contribute to businesses through enhancing the lives of those using their products and services.

Another essential change to reposition design in the business context is in the growing field of design research. The research and monitoring activities of the Design Council are providing essential data to support its programmes in convincing manner but there needs to be a positioning of design research as a whole at a high level in its own right. Finland provides a good example, with design research being supervised and administered by the Finnish Academy, the highest research authority in the country, which has had a powerful influence in changing the nature of work undertaken in universities and research institutes and has stimulated much cooperation across business and design institutions.

The most important argument, however, is that these ideas of how design can function are different to widespread current practice around the world and if formulated in operational terms and embedded in business culture could be difficult to rapidly or easily replicate. Such new organisational applications of design in all its diversity and multiplicity can be vital means of harnessing talent in ways that can also engage users, whoever they are and wherever they may be; they do not need large investments of capital or resources, but do require new, more intelligent thinking on the part of management and designers. In terms of the possibilities of regenerating manufacturing in the UK, two concluding comments are pertinent. One is that there are many small companies around the world integrating design into all their activities that are leaders in their field—size is not crucial to success; secondly, and again there are many examples around the world, big companies were once small companies with vision and ambition.

After working in the US and Hong Kong for seventeen years, my viewpoint on the situation in the UK is somewhat ambiguous, simultaneously outsider and insider. The former makes me cautious about assertions of superiority, but the latter makes me aware of what I have missed in working overseas for so long. Compared with societies around the world where there are still many political and social barriers to open thinking—not only in underdeveloped countries but industrial competitors such as the United States—the free-play of a spate of ideas could be Britain's greatest resource. The country's reputation as a cradle of often brilliant inventions developed by others is, however, essentially a failure to acknowledge the role of innovation and application in businesses. Design is a vital element in reorienting thought and practice in this regard and government does not need to intervene with extensive resources to have profound influence in stimulating a re-evaluation of its role and meaning of design for all our futures.

(C)
Creating Value by Design: John Heskett's Contributions to the Business and Economics of Design

Tore Kristensen

Introduction

John Heskett was mainly known for his books and articles about design. Many of them had a historic dimension and some a contemporary one, notably the book on design management in Philips and *Logos and Toothpicks*, later published as '*Design: a very short introduction*'. However in the 1990s and later, he was committed to economic approaches and worked mainly as a conceptual researcher exploring how we may conceive of design in an economic context and framework. Among his unfortunately not realized plans was an edited book where economics of design was to play a major role. Being educated as an economist in LSE, Heskett was constantly aware of, and motivated by, the potential of economic and strategic analyses of design. The Philips book, for example (see the extract as reading #16 in this volume), was an analysis of how the Philips Corporation in the 1980s represented one of a few companies where design, linked with but not subservient to, engineering and marketing was one of the pillars of Philips' success.

In this introduction we will look into Heskett's interpretation of economic sources for researching design, his application of economics of innovation and growth theories. Then we focus on the issues of strategic character, how Heskett used his acquired findings to set the stage for better strategic decision-making. Finally, we will look into the programme explored and ask whether we are seeing the contours of a paradigm or research programme with a progressive future.

Economic background for design studies

Since the early 1990s, Heskett was very clear about which traditions in economics were useful and which were not. As the extracts or versions from the seminar manuscript 'Design and the Creation of Value' published in this volume begin to show (see readings #3, #22, #26), he never saw neoclassical theory as very useful. The theory mainly applied an aggregate market view on the basis of the assumptions of rational choice. Neoclassical economists may speak of 'the consumer', but it means an average of a prototypical persona rather than the individual in flesh and blood. To deal with design as Heskett does means to focus on design *as the human capacity to shape and make our environment in ways without precedent in nature, to serve our needs and give meaning to our lives* (Heskett 2005, p. 5). Although an assumption is that our environments may be rational, neoclassical theory seems unable to grasp the concept of design. Neoclassical theory assumes rational action because the number of consumers and firms is high and the typical consumer is assumed to behave rationally. Problem-solving and meaning must be highly individualistic although there may be a common need for nutrition, heat, sustainable surroundings, etc., but the way they are materialized is highly individual. People use individual expressions to create and express their identities. Neoclassical economics seem unable to support this. (An attempt would probably rely on the comparative statistics of Cobb Douglas' growth theory, modelling design as an investment that is assumed to reduce costs or increase consumer utilities (e.g. Kaldor 1961). To identify design in such a framework is impossible and so far no serious attempts have been made. Heskett would have found such attempts highly improbable).

Design as a Complex Business Activity

As Figure 1 shows, design in business is a very complex issue. While design in a creative context is restricted to shape, colour, context, texture, trends and meaning, with aesthetics, styling, etc. as its main tools, design in business means much more. Issues of form and function have been well documented before Heskett added *manufacturability* and *marketability* into the picture. The understanding of manufacturing and marketing is far beyond what is taught in many design schools even today (2016). While the tools of aesthetics, styling, etc. were established, user-centred interaction, drawing on cognitive psychology and ergonomics, engineering economy, cultural factors and economics and business factors are still considerable challenges to designers and their education. One the other hand, many of the design tools dealing with form and function as well as the finer details of manufacturing, marketing and branding are not explored in business schools.

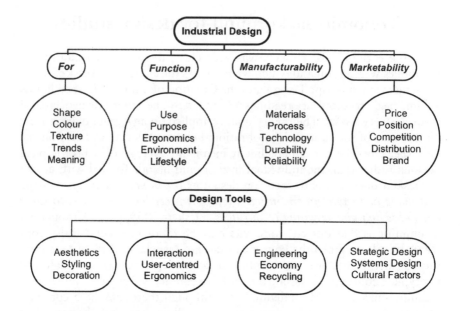

FIGURE 1 *Design as a Complex Business Activity.*
Source: Heskett, reading #18.

Maybe it was the tradition of the LSE, which hosted the Austrian economist Friedrich August von Hayek over several periods, that gave John Heskett an impetus to look elsewhere in economics. He found in the Austrian school the beginnings of a model of the economy that might be more capable of encompassing design as an economic factor. In contrast to the neoclassical approach, which assumed comparative analyses between various equilibrium states of the economy, the Austrian school was process oriented. The economic system and its role in dealing with resource allocation were seen as a fundamental knowledge base distributed in small bits among a large population. Integrated in this view was a fundamental aspect called *method individualism*. It meant that all kinds of behaviour should, in principle, be explainable as the action of a single person with his or her values, options and opportunities (Elster 2007). Having such an explanation, one could aggregate into social networks, as we would call it today, or more simply into markets and social structures. The knowledge needed includes consumer valuations, embedded as problem-solving and meanings in products, environments, artefacts and systems (Hayek 1945). As seen in von Hayek's articles on the emergence of markets from 1937 to 1945, this meant that the focus could be on the individual user or customer and that markets were the aggregate emergence of the efforts of many actors acting in a kind of uncoordinated, but still concerted, action–each pursuing his or her own targets. This would give a rationale for the importance of design as a necessity for each person to be involved with. Meaning implies that design also connects people.

Economics of innovation and growth

In a similar manner, an economics of design requires grasping the roles of innovation and growth. Building on the Austrian school, evolutionary economics, especially in the hands of its master Joseph Schumpeter (1934, 1950), became central to Heskett's work. Schumpeter's contributions are multiple, but his theory of *entrepreneurship* on individual level as well as the process of *creative destruction* introduces a complex, dynamic and multi-level concept of innovation. Creative destruction means making a way for new innovations, new designs and new structures. For instance, many mechanical devices and ways of undertaking, for example, counting and regulation, only exist as historical objects as they are replaced by digital systems. Owners of old watches must look for watchmakers to repair their old inherited watches as there are very few of them and they have no apprentices and do not invest in new workshops and the like. This brings design into the closeness of market creation. New digital technologies lead to new systems of distribution, shops and investments in system at all levels. This John Heskett saw very early and explains how designers and groups of business and design often were uncomfortable with rapid and disruptive change. This may be seen today in the discrepancies sometimes met when design relies on workmanship (Veblen 1999), while new technologies press the focus towards digitalization and 'big data'. A point is that there is still a place for crafts and workmanship, but the materials have changed rapidly and education and practice are challenged to follow apace.

Tacit knowledge is an integral aspect of design and crafts, and even Simon's (1996) definition of design may seem to cover this important issue: 'Changing from existing to preferred states' may sound very conscious and strategic, but the ability to make this transformation is similar to art and not well articulated. If we follow Damasios' (2003) view of the feeling of what happens, it is clearly a mix between conscious action, feelings and emotion. To design is to conduct a kind of quasi-experimentation, where sketching, modelling and testing lead to possible solutions. The process is often only partly conscious and may be regulated through the designer's bodily reactions to the process.

Economics of design

A concern expressed in Heskett (#27) is that design is not well accounted for in neoclassical economics. He came to this point of view in part through listening to U.S. Department of Commerce officials and their Council of Competitiveness who did not recognize the value of design in economic terms. The reason is the static–comparative nature of the neoclassical models and their failing ability to deal with problem-solving and in particular the non-existent, imaginable. Herbert Simon (1978) is an exception here, and is duly emphasized in Heskett's work.

One challenge to economic reasoning could be the vantage point and level of analysis. From the outset, this is usually attributed to the single designer working to solve particular challenges experienced by a single user. Clearly, economic reasoning may often refer to the user, the customer or the consumer, in ways that make one think of an individual. However, this is deceptive and Heskett was very much aware of this when he referred to the Austrian school, which takes the individual into account when that individual makes an effort to conduct transactions aiming at building a market. Heskett, on the other hand, also thinks in terms of the market as the outcome level of aggregate performances of many producers, consumers and traders. Yet, contrary to most economic reasoning, it is the individual level that prevails for most of Heskett's reasoning.

The value statement that flowed from this approach was expressed in profound clarity by the Austrian management guru and immigrant Peter Drucker:

Quality in a product or service is not what the supplier puts in. It is what the customer gets out and is willing to pay for. A product is not quality because it is hard to make and costs a lot of money, as manufacturers typically believe. This is incompetence. Customers pay only for what is of use to them and gives them value. Nothing else constitutes quality. (Drucker 1986)

This was a quotation that Heskett repeatedly presented in his speeches: it grasps the point, essential to any economics of design, that quality and value were very closely associated.

Heskett's first reference to the term 'economic value' comes from Adam Smith (1776) who distinguishes between value(s) in use versus value as exchange. In practice, economists tend to disregard this since it does not make much sense in economic reasoning. Also, the Marxian concept of work as a foundation of values is disregarded, but is covered by the Drucker quote above. In the 2008 article, however (#27), his aim is to assess the contributions of economic theories to explore the value of design. The exchange value is usually identical to the market price, the amount a customer (not user) is willing to sacrifice.

In this chapter, Heskett quotes the Austrian economist Carl Menger (1871) for stating that value is not a quality of the object per se, but is an element of consciousness of men (#27). This qualification is later affirmed by another Austrian economist, Von Wieser, and even adopted by a more neoclassical economist Kelvin Lancaster (1966) in his theory of consumer choice. This means that value itself is of a subjective nature and no unique scale can determine its quality according to a fixed scale. The Drucker quote indicates that it is the customer or user who decides what is quality.

The concept of value is treated in some detail in several of Heskett's chapters, especially #3 and #27. The value of a single object, artefact, service or experience may, therefore, change according to circumstances. To exemplify this point, Heskett quotes Thorstein Veblen (1899) whose *Theory of The Leisure Class*, the class of capital owners, especially the newly rich in Eastern United States around the turn of the nineteenth century, demonstrates the vulgarity of attitudes and the disrespect of the crafts qualities that emerge when consumers engage in superficial orgies of styling. The concept of value then is not a stable issue, as required by neoclassical theory, but something related to history and the qualities of trade, for instance, fashion. It is in excess of the value of craft or engineering engaged in design and production (Veblen 1921).

Heskett starts by attributing the theories of growth to Joseph Schumpeter (1950). This makes sense as Schumpeter is the founder of the much modern theory of growth in an evolutionary perspective. His direct followers were, among others, Romer and Nelson. Heskett's (1993) chapter (reading #24) quoted Schumpeter (1950) when explaining how the term creative destruction could denote a radical change in habits, patterns of consumption, satisfaction of needs, etc. While Schumpeter's ideas were left hanging for a number of years, Nelson and Winter (1982) took up the heritage of ideas and specified *routines* as genes and bearer of information and procedures, including design, to be carried over to new generations, with competition serving as selection mechanism.

The concepts of routines were helpful as a way of dealing with the concepts of tacit knowledge, known both from the crafts studies and the skill studies of Michael Polanyi (1958). Obviously, a routine in daily language is not very dynamic, but concepts of *meta-routines* easily match the dynamic skills of good design work. Tacit knowledge may sound like a contradiction in terms if one follows the definition inherited by Plato as 'justified, true, belief', but it makes a lot of sense that crafts were to a large extent the work of the hand and to a large extent a matter of emotions and feelings. This provides a place for the intuitive aspects of design, totally incomprehensible in neoclassical theory.

These studies impressed Heskett on a general level and gave him a framework for thinking of how design served the routine/incremental aspects of value creation and also helped to create value through radical innovation. Perhaps even stronger statements were made by Paul David and Brian Arthur. Both built on the evolutionary approaches and also built a framework, which supported the growth created by design. In particular, the works on diffusion of innovation and the establishing of industrial standards by David were able to show how the growth of problem-solving industrial systems was able to create value as a function of compatibility in systems and in the number of users. This has become even more important now with the connectedness of the World Wide Web; when the numbers of connected users increase, it means better usability for all. This, of course, depends on the systems working investigated by David (1992). Arthur's (1996) contribution here, also appreciated by Heskett (2008), was the nature of *increasing returns to scale* and *positive feedbacks*. Positive feedbacks could be said to be an upside downturn of Schumpeter's creative destruction concept (#3). Heskett did not explore the empirical ideas, but was very clear in the conceptual understanding of the importance of these issues.

Value is the qualitative appreciation, by the individual consumer, of the worth of things linked in social networks by a *meaning creation* or *sign* effect as well as reputation and accounts of (good) experiences. This way, Heskett connected the individual with systems or networks. Such systems are essential when analysing growth. The mechanisms are similar to the problem-solving mechanism, but since no technical standards or compliance were necessary, these systems could advance the growth even more. The full extent of this was seen in mega events like football matches, Olympic Games, etc. (Chwe 2001) where the number of spectators was extreme and the prices for advertising reached higher levels than ever before. In these systems, concepts known from game theory, another triumph of neoclassical economics like common knowledge, were realized in large masses of people. Millions could share the sports masters and music idols and using them as carriers for commercial messages means growth.

Strategic design

A basic concept for strategic thinking in design was Heskett's categorization of strategic decisions as regular (or incremental) versus innovative and product-focussed versus corporate-focussed. While the model was not published [though see #23], he often presented it and it is available in several presentations. This text, which aims at giving suggestions for various design policies in the UK, is also an excellent introduction to some of the models that Heskett deployed to explain the value created by design.

The distinction between innovation and regular business is concerned with resources in general. No company can be fully preoccupied by innovation all the time. March (1991) suggested a division between explorations and exploitation, hinting that a balance between the two had to be optimal in times when major environmental changes occur. Companies need to explore their opportunities and threats in order to commit resources to adapt to future challenges. In a stable environment this may happen less frequently and there is more available time and resources to build exploitation and accumulation. It has been seen, that in companies owned by a family fund, having less obligations to satisfy the stockowners on a frequent basis, more capital can build up over a long period because there is time to commit resources into long-term plans (Thomsen and Pedersen 2000). In times of rapid change, the opposite is essential and companies may have to adapt to changing conditions more often. Design competencies may play a very important role in both exploitation and explorations. Innovation is investment, which means holding back financial resources in the hope that they may yield better payback. To make the best investment, strategic explorations are essential, and investment may indeed include new designs. The regular business is harvesting earlier investments.

In exploration, design performs its traditional assignments of sketching, modelling and building products, artefacts, services and experiences. In times of exploration, design skills may provide the ability of 'seeing' threats and opportunities, weak and strong signals, using sketching techniques for scenario-building and exploring various sets of consequences. Design skills and methods may support managerial approaches by delivering clear models and instructions for product definition, taking care of some of the uncertainties and ambiguities that traditional managerial methods diminish in importance. This way, among others, Heskett's good friend Robert (Bob) Blaich (1993) was able to convince the CEO and the financial director at Phillips that design had to be a core competency due to its central position in navigating the strategic operations of the firm. Heskett did not make analyses of how the strategic operations were organized but was concerned with the contributions that design could offer to a variety of strategic considerations and decisions.

The horizontal distinction concerns perhaps an important historical reading: the 2000 borderline. This means a sort of change between the age of mass production and the age of digitalized production. The date is perhaps somewhat arbitrary, but there seems to be clear evidence that mass production is currently fading out in the Western world, while digitalized production will gradually be implemented. Managerial models of product decisions in mass production were essentially taking a narrow focus in the portfolio of existing and prospective products, for example, the *Ansoff matrix* (1957) and many similar models. In these models, the mixing and matching of products made the portfolio of future prosperities for firms. Porter (1980) extended this reasoning by building more neoclassical industrial economics into the so-called *five forces* model. But it was still essentially built on the idea of a portfolio of products.

But beginning with high-technology firms in Silicon Valley (e.g. IDEO Product development often associated with Stanford University) and with figures like Jay Doblin and the Doblin group who were associated with IIT's Institute of Design in Chicago, companies and design firms began to extend their focus to designing corporate strategy as a whole. In the 1990s, considerable analyses, examples and success stories were built around this new focus. The brief logic of the new approach is that in order to organize and manage the complexity of increasingly *organic* firms (as contrasted to the traditional hierarchic and mechanical firms), communication, motivation, problem-finding and solving have to build on *concerted action* involving the whole organization.

The synthesis of these ideas Heskett built into a simple matrix.

The full model is shown here (Figure 2).

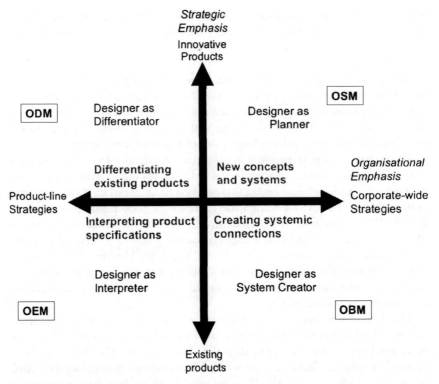

FIGURE 2 *Different levels of design practice.*
Source: Heskett, reading #18.

The four fields have been labelled OEM (originally thought of as *Original Equipment Manufacturer*), because the prototype was a company taking orders for sub-supply of parts for larger companies which would assemble the complete product on the basis of modular designs. The design challenge for these firms was to interpret product specifications and adapt them for the production system in order to secure effective production or at least to reduce the cost to make a profit. Many such companies, such as the ones Heskett often referred to operating in the Pearl River Delta, work in this way as sub-suppliers, producing for other companies. Their hope for the future was to get their own products, to move from the left lower corner to the upper corner, developing whole new concepts and systems, including customer education and services, and integrating the whole company. This means developing their own products and to employ design for products. It also means developing marketing research, distribution networks and marketing management. This would require investments and explorations and most likely the acquisition of new skills and managerial competences. Perhaps, the pursuit for these companies would stop here, or it could, if successful, lead to aspirations for a corporate focus where cross-disciplinary teams and branding would work for new concerted action.

Innovations were seen in the context of OSM (or *Original Systems manufacturing*). It was here the inspiration of the IDEO and Doblin Group was strong and often realized in prosperous companies such as Google, Apple and others. The big trick of this trade was to exploit the innovation into branding (OBM or *Own Brand Manufacturing*) where markets were *domesticated* to create loyal long-term customers with little wish to try the offers of the competitors. The solution was rarely to change the whole company from an innovative into a stable brand mode, but to keep a steady pace in innovative departments, while branding would work elsewhere to deal with customers. This was never an easy approach as seen when NOKIA was acquired by Microsoft. Also, the book on *Steve Jobs* by Isaacson (2011) gives deep insights into how difficult this balance is. Design must play a major role by reconciling research and development with branding and customers to create a visual culture that can channel new solutions in a steady, but not too fast stream, to the marketing and customers. Overall managerial challenge then is a complex one – finding a balance between exploration and exploitation.

The challenges, however, as Heskett saw them (#20, #22), were even bigger. While we can say that the economic theories aim at explaining certain economic phenomena, Heskett's aim seems to be more normative than most economic reasoning. He wanted to make recommendations and to suggest to students, business decision makers, designers and policy makers criteria for how they might act. Heskett rarely discusses this issue explicitly, but the texts clearly indicate such a purpose.

Product differentiation

One instance of this is how he adapted and used the term 'product differentiation', used by many, but mostly associated with Lancaster (1966). In the 'New theory of consumer demand' by Kelvin Lancaster (1966), it was not the goods themselves (e.g. cars or train journeys) but their *characteristics* that were central. What could the users or consumers get out of the objects, artefacts, systems or services? Food was not just calories to support combustion in the body. It was an attempt to manipulate the basic constituents of flavour and nutrition into a satisfying gastronomic experience. The qualities offered were labelled 'characteristics space'. The starting point is an existing product with its technology, reputation, costs and price seen from the vantage point of the producer (or in design terms, to differentiation in colours, in styles, in shapes, in flavours, in tastes, in competitive brands). For instance, Zara is on terms with H&M, but yet different. Products differing according to features that are not ranked on a monotonous value scale are horizontally differentiated. Another example of horizontal differentiation is represented by films: each film is different from the others, while the price of entry to cinema is always the same. This example shows that the internal organization of the differentiation space can be structured around 'genres' and several similarity measures can be taken (e.g. two films having in common the film-maker, an actor, etc.), without being linear and continuous (nor too precise!).

In speaking of such examples, Heskett operated with two basic forms, 'covering strategies' versus 'churning'. The assumptions were that in a competitive market companies would imitate each other. If the lead time was sufficient, like in the automobile industry, companies would not directly copy but design their own version of a car of a certain size, fuel economy and usability, like a car for the small family of parents with two children churning happens when time is very short such as in areas like fashion and toys where companies feel that they have to get products out very fast.

If horizontal differentiation operates in terms of product (and brand) characteristics, vertical differentiation occurs in a market where the several goods that are present can be ordered according to their objective quality from the highest to the lowest. It's possible to say in this case that one good is 'better' than another. Heskett makes his own interpretation of this to accommodate strategic design decisions. A vertical direction upwards signals a higher-quality or even luxury product. His example often used in lectures was how a Lexus automobile is an 'inch up' strategy for Toyota. The quality is improved at all levels and the car has its own luxury brand competing with Mercedes Bens, BMW and Audi, while the Toyota, being itself of a high quality, competes with Ford, Volkswagen, Peugeot, Citroen, Saab, etc. A scale-down strategy means taking a luxury or high-quality product and gradually thinning down its characteristics and functionality. A much-used example is the Canon EON camera. The first version aimed at high functionality and quality to the professional user. The next step was simplification of the optics and triggers to accommodate the skilled amateur, then the average amateur. The final step was a simple and cheap and disposable one-time camera for any untrained person who just wanted to push the button. This model is perhaps a way a company can use design to accommodate its techniques in an environment of creative destruction and hang on to its competitiveness. It may also be a consideration for the product life cycle consideration, where a general product concept may initially serve the needs of the advanced, pioneering users and grow into a larger market to finally reach the late adopters (Rogers 1972).

Obviously, creative destruction itself depends on technology, changing needs, new technology and cultural openings. Before they introduced the Lexus, the Toyota group was, in fact, flourishing, being among the leading producers of high-quality automobiles. Still they aimed higher. Rather than attempting to improve the Toyota to compete with Audi, BMW and Mercedes Benz, they decided to develop and design a completely new concept from scratch. The Lexus was a complete qualitative improvement on the previous models and in that way was able to compete with the German automotive industry. The similar downwards design strategy is not as such an indication of falling quality, although it can be a deliberate strategy of designing cheaper alternatives.

Conclusions: What remains today of Heskett's research programme for the economics of design?

Interpreting and assessing the value of, and future for, Heskett's economics of design as well as the issues in design strategy it opens is not as easy as it may seem. There are several concepts to consider in relation to this. According to Karl Popper's 'falsificationism', we may ask if he proposed falsifiable hypotheses and whether some important ones have indeed been falsified. If this is the case, then we may leave it here. We must admit that, although many of the writings are good approximations to an empirical reality, we find few real testable hypotheses; on the other hand, many of Heskett's descriptions, assessments and predictions seem well corroborated. Heskett himself did not test hypotheses as such and his style of research was explorative rather than corroborative. That is perhaps a very good idea, because Heskett's interest was more to stimulate the fire of contemporary designers and others interested in these issues rather than in digging up the ashes of the past. This said, he did indeed engage in the *archaeology of design*. He spent a lot of time visiting collections, museums and factories to explore how design was actually conceived and realized. He was also very active in teaching design both to designers and others and this way he was very up-to-date about current practices.

Perhaps, Paul Feyerabend (1979), who suggested an *epistemological anarchistic approach* covering the possible scientific progress, seems best suited to describe and assess Heskett's contributions. Feyerabend was in no way a real anarchist, who despised rules. Only when he assessed the history of progress in science could he see that no formalistic set of rules were constantly followed. With Heskett's work, it is more like he followed the Norwegian philosopher Arne Næss who claimed that if you gradually light up a square, you see more details of it, but you also see the contour of an increasing area where there is darkness. Heskett was indeed knowledgeable, but he was also humble as to how much we still did not know. We may also look into Heskett's style, which was a very elegant narrative combining conceptual and empirical issues. This is no criticism in the sense that it enhances readability and interest. But it also makes the text less testable than if it followed simple hypothesis formulations. Testing his theories may sometimes require reformulations.

His engagements in design policies in Hong Kong, South Korea and Britain indicate a strong interest in supporting design by helping policies. The analyses are thorough and aim at practical and implementable policies that, in turn, would be evaluated. Therefore, rather than aiming at pure academic corroboration, Heskett really had an intention of trying out his concepts and theories in the form of policies. This way, the theories can be interpreted as hypotheses just waiting to be tested in a practical setting.

In assessing the possible 'research agenda' that he opens, we may look at three main points. The first is to assess his contribution vis-à-vis using economics to understand design in its proper context. The second is how well design may add to the understanding of business. The third is whether we see a progress in the sense that is worthwhile to build on his contributions and reach new future insights.

1. On economics, Heskett's criticism of neoclassical economics was profound.* He saw very limited options for using equilibrium theory, which he saw did not build on the individual, but assumes a rational behaviour in an assumed market. This all seems contradictory if your aim is to show how (strategic) design may contribute to create the very same institutions and rules of conduct. The Austrian school and its followers on the other hand assumed an individual foundation where one should explain the individual behaviour (a bottom-up approach) before aggregating (top-down) to make sure that one did not accidentally create *inferential constructions*, to quote McCloskey and Ziliac (2008). Coming from a neoclassical tradition, they were also critical but rather working from inside the tradition and asking serious questions in particular about the creation of concepts that they did not see covered a real entity. It seems safe to say that they agree with Heskett's criticism.

2. How important, and how well does Heskett explain the value of design in business? We know that he often spoke to business people and on occasion that his messages got through. But we still see that many business people are not on a par with the understanding of design. The founder of SONY, Akira Morita, himself educated as an engineer, claimed that he thought a designer could easily become a marketing practitioner, but never the other way around. There could be several good reasons. The selection and education of the two is very different. A designer is supposed to command visual understanding and expression. Marketing students may be educated in research, but they may follow reason-based approaches like hedonic scales, where the prospective customer is asked to suggest a numeric valuation. The calculation of numeric values may not itself be a challenge, and Heskett was very much aware of the possibility of using statistics in so-called qualitative studies (personal communication). However, much of the use of statistics in business drops the essential focus on the individual. Many marketing people simply ask 'how many' (people will demand to own this new product), rather than 'how much' it means for the individual, and take the extra round of time to understand whether those with a strong favour are a minority or majority. It is again the warning from Ziliac and McCloskey (2008) that

---

*Editorial note: See the forthcoming *Design and the Creation of Value* (Bloomsbury, 2017).

should nudge us. It was very clear from the conversation with Heskett that he also approved of quantitative approaches if they were done well enough.

3. The last question is, of course, the most speculative of those three. Will there develop a research tradition that can build on Heskett's insights? It is important here to refer to the work of Heskett's PhD student and collaborator Suzan Boztepe (2007). Over the last few years she developed a set of concepts of value, where value was seen and a constant exchange between exchange, sign and experiential value. Such a concept opens for a constant negotiation between the three value concepts where a sign fits Heskett's element of design as creation of meaning, while experiential value is the value in use. In such a view, which I believe is intrinsic to Heskett's view, design becomes a very complex issue, where multiple levels of analysis as well as several systems coexist. The criticism of economic theory becomes strong, since economics basically can deal with only a single system, the price or competitive system. Yet, this is not isolated from the others. As seen in the design of very symbolic objects such as fashion and other expressions of conspicuous consumption, the willingness to pay is strongly dependent on ever-changing fashions and the symbolic values of certain objects or artefacts, experiences or services. Also, a consumer or user experience (which usually means the same) may strongly influence the economic value or price. Rumours of failing quality or safety of an air travel service, for example, can rapidly set the brakes to the demand when one or more planes crash or when people get sick in a restaurant. Heskett's work serves as an inspiration to young researchers in Hong Kong. Lucy Liu who was also a PhD student with Heskett as her supervisor works on strategies for Chinese companies using, among others, the framework OEM, ODM, OSM, OBM. There is a strong interest in understanding the strategic use of design among many researchers in Asia, Europe and the United States. For example, there are researchers like Kristensen and Gabrielsen (2012) who conduct a number of experiments to explore the value of design and even how design studies could be used to explore the effectiveness of markets. These studies aim at creating a sequence of experiments, documenting how well design is approved by customers and users, how well the markets are able to carry the messages from the designers and the companies and how well the intentions of good design can be shown to also be a good business, that is, create investment payoff. Heskett was very much interested in these quantitative studies and believed they would give new insights into the qualitative aspects of design.

Overall, it would appear that in the areas that Heskett tried to open, from the study of design in relation to economic theory to the role of design in adding value, the work of bringing together economists, those in design studies and in management, remains to be achieved. The different fields at the moment remain relatively isolated. What Heskett's work begins to show is how these disciplines could come together to their mutual profit and benefit.

References

Ansoff, Igor (1957), 'Strategies for Diversification', *Harvard Business Review*, 35 (5): September to October, 113–24.

Blaich, Robert (1993), *Product Design and Corporate Strategy*, New York: McGraw-Hill.

Boztepe (2007), 'User Value: Competing Theories and Models', *International Journal of Design*, 1 (2): 57–65.

Chwe, Michael Suk-Young (2001), *Rational Ritual Culture, Coordination, and Common Knowledge*, Princeton: Princeton University Press.

Drucker, Peter (1985), *Innovation and Entrepreneurship*, New York: Harper & Row.

Elster, Jon (2007), *Explaining Social Behavior More Nuts and Bolts for The Social Sciences*, Cambridge: Cambridge University Press.

Hayek, F. A. (1945), 'The Use of Knowledge in Society', *American Economic Review*, 35 (4): 519–30. Reprinted in *Individualism and Economic Order*.

Isaacson, Walter (2011), *Steve Jobs*, London: Little, Brown.

Kaldor, N. (1961), 'Capital Accumulation and Economic Growth', in F. A. Lutz, and D. C. Hague (eds), *The Theory of Capital*, New York: St. Martins Press.

Kristensen, Tore and Gorm Gabrielsen (2012), 'How Valuable is a Well-Crafted Design and Name Brand?: Recognition and Willingness to Pay', *Journal of Consumer Behaviour*, 11 (1): 44–55.

Lancaster, Kelvin (1971), *A New Approach to Consumer Demands*, New York: Columbia University Press.

March, James G. (February 1991), 'Exploration and Exploitation in Organizational Learning', *Organization Science*, 2 (1): 71–87.

Næss, Arne (1969), *Hvilken verden er den virkelige*, Oslo: Universitetsforlaget ('Which world is the real one?').

Porter, Michael (1980), *Competitive Strategy*, New York: Free Press.

Rogers, Everett (1972), *Diffusion of Innovation*, 3rd edn, Cambridge, MA: MIT Press.

Thomsen Steen and Torben Pedersen (2000), 'Ownership structure and economic performance in the largest European companies', *Strategic Management Journal*, 21 (6): 689–705.

Ziliak, S. T., and McCloskey, D. N. (2008), *The Cult of Statistical Significance: How the Standard Error Costs Us Jobs, Justice, and Lives*, Ann Arbor, MI: University of Michigan Press.

23

Creative Destruction:
The Nature and Consequences
of Change through Design

Above and beyond all the definitions that abound, design, of whatever kind, is concerned with possibilities of change. The capability of introducing change that will result in improvement in some way is one of the implicit assumptions of the activity. Yet to what extent do we really understand the nature and consequences of change through design?

The plain fact is, change is disruptive, and many people aren't comfortable with it. How many designs fail in the market because they don't adequately take into account prejudices about how things should be, or because they underestimate the change in behavior required? It isn't only a problem in the marketplace, but a serious problem for designers in businesses.

Since the Industrial Revolution, change has been justified by progress. In practice, it is widely resisted as companies, and sometimes governments, seek to establish market control or monopoly in their favor. Ideas and organizations tend to become rigid, fixed in convenient, self-justifying patterns. Just witness any government organization in Washington or innumerable large businesses, such as GM and IBM.

Consequently, many businesses are struggling to cope with the spate of new ideas, products and services that are transforming markets and social patterns and undermining attempts to sustain stable systems on both macro and micro-economic levels. In such a period of flux, innovation ought to be the defining criterion for achieving efficiency in the battle for commercial survival, and design should be a key discipline in making innovation appropriate, accessible and acceptable to the public. Why then isn't it widely recognized as such? Clinging to existing practices in the face of accelerating

---

First published as "Creative Destruction," *I.D. International Design*, September/October 1993, pp. 8–9. By kind permission of F & W Media (New York).

changes in technology, global patterns of trade and information ought to be increasingly difficult to sustain. All too often, however, resistance increases in proportion to the seriousness of the challenge.

An explanation of the profound scale of current change can be found in the work of Austrian economist Joseph Schumpeter, whose ideas have been widely publicized in economic and business publications. He has taken issue with conventional economists who describe the problem of management in terms of choices possible in an existing system. Schumpeter points out that the congenital instability of capitalist economies is due to what he calls "perennial gales of creative destruction," or the result of innovations that totally redefine product concepts. Progress, he argues in a classic example, depended not on one harness-maker seeking to make a better or cheaper product than any other harness-maker, but on the development of a viable automobile that destroyed harness-making as an economic activity.

Clearly, it isn't possible to explain this process solely in terms of available technology, for the existence of a technology alone doesn't guarantee acceptance. Economic opportunity, the awareness of market potential, can also drive a search for solutions that push the development of scientific or technological knowledge beyond existing boundaries. The current efforts by drug companies to develop new treatments for AIDS is a case in point. There is a need that has to be satisfied. On the other hand, who wanted or needed a microwave oven before one appeared on the market? An innovation may therefore be stimulated by either market-pull or producer-push. Whatever the cause, a distinction between invention and innovation is necessary. If invention is regarded as the original discovery of a principle or process, innovation is the point at which it becomes introduced, and accepted in widespread use—which is where design comes in and why it is so important. It is precisely this process of translating technological potential into market feasibility that is one of the most essential functions of design.

Why then are there not more examples of business organizations genuinely committed to innovation and to using design as a major strategic instrument? The answer seems to be that the consequences of innovation are not easy to accept: innovation involves constant disruption and, above all, risk. Making a radically new product that is both functional and viable in the market involves wide-ranging obsolescence within an organization; of people's knowledge, experience and self-justification, as well as more tangible aspects, such as equipment and systems. And in many businesses at present, there is little guarantee that what is new today will not be outmoded tomorrow.

An additional complication is that different products, technologies and markets may not all change at the same pace. Intervals of quietude have not been entirely eliminated by permanent disruption. For example, rapid change in industries based on computers and information currently coexists with relative stability in the production of many domestic electrical goods—just how much have blenders and hairdryers really changed over the last 50 years?

Innovation ought to be the defining criterion for achieving efficiency and supremacy in the battle for commercial survival, and design should be a key discipline in making innovation accessible.

If designers are to cope with the demands of varying cycles of change, the concept of innovation must be understood on many different levels—from radical and incremental innovation. Radical innovations are the basis of Schumpeter's "creative destruction" concept, which provides new industries and needs. An example of this would be the creation of the personal computer. Radical innovations alter or create patterns of use, change user behavior. Often expensive to implement, they have a high risk of not being accepted. More typically, innovation in a period of product or market stability is incremental in nature, using little new technology, with few new benefits and requiring little change in user behavior. With products such as vacuum cleaners or electric irons, little more than incremental improvement is feasible.

However, the simple division of radical and incremental innovation doesn't cover all the possibilities. A third type is application innovations, which can be highly successful since they create new market demand from existing technology. The Sony Walkman is a classic example: who wanted a miniature tape recorder that didn't record? Great emphasis is currently being given to synthetic innovation, such as the potential combination of different media in interactive format, or a combination of hardware and software.

Innovations in distribution and service can also be important. Way back in the '40s, Earl Tupper had the radical idea of circumventing conventional channels of distribution for his plastic container-ware and the Tupperware Party was born. Anyone wanting evidence of the impact of service innovation should look at J.D. Power's latest listing of customer satisfaction in automobiles, which is headed by Lexus, Infiniti and Saturn. These are companies in different segments of the market, but each integrates obsessive attention to customer service into their overall strategy.

Each type of innovation, its relevance and the possibility of combination, varies in importance over time. The introductory stage, for example, is by nature based on radical innovation, which, if successful, leads to a product concept emerging as a dominant design—an invaluable standard. Once established, the next phase will emphasize process innovation and product enhancement, opening it to a wider customer base. The personal computer, a dramatically radical innovation when it was first introduced in the early '80s, is currently entering this succeeding phase. Different approaches to design therefore become appropriate to each stage.

Such concepts also point up the need to understand variations in types of companies and their capacity to cope with and implement innovation.

Flexibly operating companies, defining strategies that aim to create markets, will innately be better equipped to think in terms of innovation than hierarchical companies that take the market as given and compete primarily on cost. 3M, for example, has a remarkable record of actively encouraging innovation at every level. More recently, Gillette's investment in the Sensor program redefined a market dominated by low-cost disposables, generating an impressive range of innovative extensions.

Setting design in the context of such ideas goes some way toward explaining why it is not easily accepted or understood in so many business organizations. In both design education and practice, there is a widespread assumption that design is a ubiquitous process that can be easily adapted to any circumstance, and that its primary role is radical change. Assigning itself this role might be acceptable in some organizations at some stage of a product or market cycle, but under other conditions, it could very easily be seen as a threat to existing practice. There is, therefore, a need in design to develop theories capable of articulating the challenges of the different phases of product and market cycles in different types of organizations. Such theories should not aim at being predictive, but help focus on defining opportunities, making innate assumptions explicit and taking us a little further along the road of explaining and justifying design to a wider audience.

24

Product Integrity

Reality vs. image

In the mid-1970s, the German electrical appliance company, Braun, wanted to enter the market for coffee machines. Its first model won numerous design prizes for quality, but was far more expensive than competitive models and so failed to reach viable sales levels. Consequently, Braun put a stop-gap model on the market to retain a presence and spent three years perfecting a new, distinctive design that offered high quality at a competitive price—the KM 40. This model was used with great success to open the US market in the 1980s as part of a campaign to transform the company from serving a well-established, but limited, European niche into a global player.

In the US, Braun competes with the American company, Mr. Coffee, whose strategy for meeting its competition contrasts markedly. It was recently announced that they are reviving the format of a successful series of advertisements from the early 1970s, featuring the retired baseball star, Joe Di Maggio, who was to be paid some $2 million for his endorsement. A company spokesperson quoted in the *Wall Street Journal* said they expected the campaign to raise Mr. Coffee's market share from 28 to 35 percent.

In a different product category, the *Wall Street Journal* provides another interesting comparison. Nissan, concerned about its automobiles being perceived as reliable but stodgy and uninteresting, wanted to improve its market position. It set out on a program to redesign its model range in every detail. The chief designer in its California office was reported to have spent one month working on the small knob at the end of an indicator stalk, searching for fingerprint compatibility.

In contrast, Oldsmobile was the subject of another *Journal* report when it fired its advertising agency. It wasn't that its advertising was unsuccessful.

First published as "Product Integrity," *Innovation*, Spring 1992, pp. 17–19. By kind permission of Industrial Designers Society of America.

Surveys indicated that the slogan, "This is not your father's automobile, this is a new generation of Olds," was known and recognized across the country. Nevertheless, the cars were not selling. The remedy: a new agency to provide a new campaign that would sell the vehicles. Apparently, that too is not having the desired result.

These anecdotal comparisons illustrate why product—be that a component, information, an environment or service—must be emphasized as the focus of business activity. They reveal the problems that arise when image is invested in rather than reality. The belief that the market can be indefinitely manipulated by means of superficial transformations of image, either in terms of styling or of advertising, is deeply ingrained in business attitudes and practices, but is becoming increasingly difficult to sustain in the long term. It is a problem that many US companies face, as customers become increasingly skeptical of claims that are not substantiated in reality by the artifact or service.

The product: Where corporate reality meets user needs

No business can remain viable for long under current competitive conditions if its product does not satisfy end users. The product is the point where the internal realities of companies meet the real needs of people. If sale is the point of attraction to a product, use provides a continuing point of judgment of it and of the company that made it. It is the product that ultimately communicates to users the values implicit in a company or a brand name.

If a product convinces users that a company is exploitative, indifferent or disdainful about their needs, no amount of advertising or image creation will convince them otherwise. Indeed, it will only increase cynicism, and the company will fail ignominiously. On the other hand, if a product is right for the user, if it is functional, appropriate, comprehensible, satisfying in use—even pleasurable—it establishes a firm platform for success.

Paradoxically, while a poor product will generally lead to failure, a good product does not necessarily lead to success. There are innumerable cases of well-designed and well-made products that have been market failures because critical factors in the competitive mix have been neglected. Clearly, among other factors, a good product has to be positioned in the market at the right place, at the right time and at the right cost.

It is in this respect that the concept of "product integrity" has value. The word "integrity" implies a sense of wholeness, of completeness, of values that can be relied upon. Product integrity is a concept that represents the totality of qualities needed to conceive, make and market a successful product. That is not to say it is an absolute, relevant for all circumstances; rather it is something that emerges from the practices and values of any organization and can work in many ways, on many levels. It is more easily recognized in hindsight than prescribed in advance. It is created neither quickly nor easily, and it is not something that can be conveniently applied as a quick fix. Therein lies a fundamental problem.

The problem resides in the distinction between what can be codified and laid out as a theoretical or methodological construct, and what can be recognized as accumulated value and experience—the difference between procedure and sensitivity. Both are necessary in any kind of organization, but because procedures are more easily described, understood and applied, values and sensitivities tend to be downplayed. If the effectiveness of a business sector could be judged in terms of the organizations, educational institutions and volume of publications studying procedures and methodology, then the United States would lead the world. The US may have a trade deficit, but it has a huge surplus of information about management. Yet, if learning by concept is not effectively combined with learning from experience, if theory is not combined with practice within a framework of accepted values, then all that information will ultimately be sterile.

The wholeness factor

Product integrity is innately difficult to define; it is not just a sum of qualities, it encapsulates a sense of wholeness that goes beyond arithmetical addition. Consider a rowing eight as an example. There are many theories on the design of craft and of rowing technique. Ultimately, however, success comes from going out on a river and rowing day after day until, suddenly, a common rhythm emerges. Everyone in the boat knows it and feels it as something beyond themselves, of which they are a part. A sense of wholeness, of course, goes beyond simply acting in unison. Consider sports that call for differentiated functions within a team framework, such as basketball or rugby.

What have these analogies of teamwork to do with product integrity? If 80 percent of musical performances were unsatisfactory, an ensemble would disband, no one would book it. Yet, in some product categories, research studies suggest that 80 percent of products fail! This means the waste of enormous amounts of time and resources on products that are unsuccessful in terms of both market and use.

Whether you are talking about music, sports or business, the development process requires people from a range of different disciplines, with different competencies, tools and methods, often using different concepts and language. For the most part, however, the participants in product development have been educated in isolation, without regard to others with whom they will have to cooperate. In contrast, musicians are not only trained to hone their individual skills, but are trained specifically to apply those skills in the context of ensemble work.

Without that overarching framework, there is all too often a cacophony of competing ideas instead of harmony. A power struggle emerges among competing points of view. With no real understanding and cooperation among disciplines, a dominant idea is introduced and passed sequentially from group to group, without regard for cooperation and without the potential for synergy. We need to acknowledge the problems of specialization and accept the virtuoso capabilities of each contributing element. Rather than submerge them, we must combine them so each can give their best, with a result that exceeds the sum of the individual capabilities.

Finding an effective product development structure

It is in project teams that conflicting values and competing egos must be addressed and resolved. Connections have to be made, and energies have to be focused in a clearly defined decision-making process. If they are to be venues for defining problems and creating and implementing solutions, product development projects must be effectively structured and managed— not just for any single project, but for every individual product undertaken by a company.

This need implies two things:

- That a company has a vision of the future expressed in terms of what its products should be and the functions they should perform. This requires a process of planning at the strategic level.
- That what a company is, as manifested through any single product, is reflected on every other product that comes out of the company. This effect mandates the establishment and general acceptance of procedures for product development to realize the strategic plan.

Product development procedures take a plethora of organizational forms; therefore, any theoretical model of the process must be a composite and abstract construct which will have to be modified when matched against what actually takes place in individual companies. With that said, there are six basic stages in the development process.

- Origination of product concept; decision as to theoretical feasibility.
- Definition of product concept and strategic analysis; positioning brief.
- Preliminary development, visualization and product development testing.
- Detailed development and refinement; final model approval.
- Specification to production preparation and prototype.
- Manufacture; follow-up review.

Although set out sequentially here, these stages can be run in parallel with great benefit in terms of interaction and faster development cycles. However, regardless of how they are specifically organized, the possibilities for genuinely innovative, creative thinking become more limited as the process progresses and the number of firm commitments increases. Within stages 1 to 4, decisions committing 80 percent of the total development cost will usually have been made. While the implications of this rule are profound, the actual costs of stages 1 to 4 are minuscule in proportion to total development costs. Therefore, if all the potential of the contributing disciplines, with their various concepts of quality, can be harnessed in the early stages of product development, better products can be brought more quickly to market.

That this approach powerfully assists competitiveness is confirmed in detail by many management theorists. But faster product development alone does not guarantee success. As an advantage, it, too, can be eroded rapidly and easily by competitors adopting similar procedures. So how can a decisive, competitive advantage be gained that is not easily emulated?

The answer lies in another question: how is it possible to move beyond current possibilities to develop products that do not simply cater to customers' current understanding in terms of giving them what they want, but take them a stage further to give them something they never knew they wanted—something that makes an essential difference in how they interact with the world around them? The key is an emphasis on product as differentiator at a level fundamental enough to create a sense of integrity—an emphasis that goes well beyond short-term opportunism.

Achieving integrity: The human factor

Who can achieve this integrity? R&D develops technical ideas that are new; engineers make those ideas technically feasible for production; marketing specialists tend to tell us what people will currently accept (although there are marketing practices that focus on future possibilities); financial controllers often try to gouge out the heart of a project in order to save money; managers on bonuses look to the next quarter's result. How about designers?

Designers have many specialist competencies, such as product, information or environmental design; however, whatever their specialization, their work is innately concerned with the future, with anticipating what the future reality of products will be. All are concerned with the tangible reality of a product in a way that no other discipline is. No one else can as comprehensively create and structure the reality of artifact, information or environment. Above all, they are concerned with making products accessible, comprehensible and acceptable to users.

In this respect, human factors plays a key role, helping determine how products fit people.

Human factors has four major aspects:

- **Physiological**—concerned with human body dimensions and the physical compatibility between people and products; e.g., chairs should fit the body, tools should fit the hand.
- **Cognitive**—concerned with how people perceive the world beyond themselves; e.g., the influence of color, form and layout on how controls on appliances or blocks of information on reports are understood.
- **Social**—concerned with what helps or inhibits the interaction of people within social groups; e.g., elements of behavior attributable to generational, class and economic differences.
- **Cultural**—concerned with differences among societies, and subdivisions or subcultures within societies, and how these affect the capacity to accept or use products.

Making products fit the needs of people on the basis of such concepts—in ways that they find functional and pleasurable, in forms that are distinguished by accessibility and ease of use, and in arrangements that pay close attention to continuing service—can provide a decisive competitive edge that, if constantly refined, will not be quickly or easily eroded. Designers cannot achieve all that on their own. They need to work in close cooperation with specialists from many other disciplines. But without designers' decisive emphasis on user needs and requirements, the critical dimension in adapting products to people will be lacking.

Product integrity is not based on concepts of absolute quality nor limited to concepts of "good" design in an elitist sense. It is equally applicable to the most basic of products as well as to the most complex. Consequently, it can extend possibilities for improvement through all price levels as long as at each level there is consonance of judgment between designer, producer, seller and user.

The undervalued value of company pride

Product integrity is a concept that, although derived primarily from the needs of users, has a wealth of important ramifications. Company wide belief and pride—in the product, in its purpose and meaning—is a potent and underestimated competitive weapon. Integrity of product can be a powerful symbol for integrity of relationships at all levels.

Achieved at all levels, from manufacturer to customer, such belief means the integration of image and reality. Advertising based in such belief becomes a confirmation of what is, rather than a manipulation of perception. In fact, the reality becomes the image. Which is, ultimately, what integrity is all about.

25

Cultural Human Factors

Abstract

Cultural human factors, recognition of a society's learned behavior regarding social organization, patterns of object use and values in relation to design and global business, are the focus of this paper. Problem areas regarding respect for cultural difference or the imposition of cultural change are explored with diverse specific examples from Euro Disney to British Telecom. Elements of communication and identity as well as organization and pattern of use are cited as the possible loci for conflict. The connection between human factors and business strategy is examined as a competitive tool in the global marketplace.

The concept underlying this discussion is that culture encompasses the fabric of everyday life and how it is lived in all its aspects. Yet of the four categories of human factors (physical, cognitive, social, cultural), cultural factors are the most vague and unspecific, the least known, the most difficult to codify, but perhaps, for precisely these reasons, the most To begin with, a definition of culture, as it will be used in this presentation is, at this stage, a important very simple one: Culture is the distinctive way of life of social groups, the learned behavior patterns expressed through language, values, organizations and artifacts.

How does this relate to design? Design is concerned with products, communications, environments, services and systems. All can be considered artifacts, they use language and manifest values, and most originate from organizations of one kind or another. The connections are therefore close.

First published as "Cultural Human Factors," *Design Innovation for Global Competition*, Sharon Poggenpohl ed., Institute of Design, IIT, Chicago, 1995, pp. 26–40. By permission of the Institute of Design, IIT, Chicago.

Respecting cultural difference

So how can cultural issues be defined as relevant to business? The answers are on two levels, the simple and the complex. On the simple level, sensitivity to cultural difference can avoid obvious mistakes made by companies. All it requires is a clear understanding that the cultural context in which products or services originate may be very different from the cultural context in which they are used or applied. It is surprising, however, how often this is overlooked. Some of the more obvious aspects are

- *Language and meaning*
- *Sensitivity to context*
- *Visual imagery*
- *Cultural mistakes in market forecasting*
- *Destruction of cultural identity.*

Language and meaning. Differences in language and meaning are obvious examples. A widespread approach is to ignore them, as did Rolls-Royce, the epitome of social status, which had a series of models with names such as the Silver Wraith, Silver Cloud and Silver Mist, which sold around the world. Trouble occurred when the company put a model on the German market under its English name of "Silver Mist." A perfunctory check in a German/ English dictionary would have saved the company considerable embarrassment. The Schoffler-Weiss dictionary gives the following translations (which are hardly suitable to describe the epitome of automobile elegance!): Mist: dung, manure; (Animals) droppings; (maritime) fog; dirt, trash, rubbish, junk.

Sensitivity to context. This is also problematic, as in an example of a huge Marlboro cigarette advertisement, a block long and five stories high, brightly illuminated at night, that used to sit high on a wall of the main public mortuary of Kowloon, Hong Kong.

Visual imagery. Visual imagery can also be a minefield. One of the stranger illustrations of the cultural perils of buying an overseas company was a leading brand of toothpaste in Hong Kong, marketed for decades under the brand name of Darkie, with an illustration of caricatured, stereotyped, black-face minstrel, teeth gleaming pearly white. No one in its market of origin found this troublesome. When Colgate-Palmolive bought the Hong Kong manufacturer of this product in 1989, however, the illustration rapidly rebounded on the company when placed in this new American context. A rumor spread in the United States that Colgate was selling a racist product in Asia. Banner-carrying pickets appeared outside its New York headquarters.

To appease its American critics without destroying a well-known brand in Asia, where people were generally oblivious to the racist implications,

Colgate-Palmolive sought to redefine the brand name as Darlie, with a visual redesign that changed in stages. By 1992, through adjusting the illustrative conventions, the image became that of an elegant man-about-town of indeterminate ethnic origin. Colgate-Palmolive could have saved itself considerable expense and bad publicity, however, had it foreseen the situation, rather than belatedly react to it.

Cultural miscalculation. A more serious illustration of cultural miscalculation in market forecasting is the performance of Electrolux in Europe in recent years. In 1983, the management of Electrolux made a comparison of large domestic appliance manufacturing and found that whereas the United States had only four major manufacturers, Europe had one hundred. They became convinced that Europe would become a single market like the American and embarked on a program of acquisitions to make it a major player in large domestic appliances, with the intention of providing a limited range of designs to supply all of Europe.

Ten years later, the policy proved costly, as the divergent cultures of Europe intransigently failed to inevitably follow the American pattern. In northern Europe, people shop weekly and need equal freezer and refrigerator space. Southern Europeans shop daily in small local markets and need smaller units. The British eat more frozen vegetables than anywhere in the world and need sixty percent freezer space. Some want the freezer on top, some on the bottom. Electrolux attempted to streamline operations, but seven years later, the company still operated six refrigerator factories in Europe (it closed two), sold products under forty brand names and produced one hundred-twenty basic designs with fifteen-thousand variants. In fact, it found it necessary to launch new specialty refrigerators to appeal to certain market niches. By 1989, profits were down forty percent from 1988, and in 1992 dividends were slashed.

Destruction of cultural identity. Problems exist not only between cultures. Even within a culture, enormous offense can be generated when a corporation acts without adequate regard for context. In Britain, under Mrs. Thatcher's government, the telephone services were separated from the Post Office and privatized as British Telecom (BT), which wanted to impress its independent status on the populace. It decided to replace the long-established and famous red telephone kiosks across the country with a new version, bought off-the-shelf from an American manufacturer. On the face of it, this hardly seems to have the makings of a cultural crisis. The old kiosks, however, had been around since 1936 and had assumed the role of an icon of British identity, widely used on travel posters and tourist postcards. The proposal generated public outrage and an appalling press, fueled by an arrogant response from BT, which insisted the new kiosk was cheaper and more functional, claims that were hotly disputed, even at the annual general meeting of BT.

The battle was renewed with BT's introduction in 1991 of a new corporate identity which drew heavy criticism. It's a strange situation: one of the more successful and profitable businesses of the United Kingdom, which has become a world player in the field of telecommunications, is viewed with derision in its home country because it removed a familiar, unique element of the landscape.

Problems of this nature can be handled adequately with sensitivity, some research and a willingness to adapt. Coca-Cola, for example, found when entering the Chinese market that the phonetics of the famous brand name translated into Chinese as "Bite the wax tadpole." The characters were modified to mean "Tasty, evoking happiness." Another example of fitting into an environment is provided by MacDonalds' advertising in Switzerland, which stresses the contribution of the Swiss agricultural economy in maintaining the food chain's standards of quality.

On the level of market projections, Whirlpool avoided the problems of Electrolux by introducing in 1992 a lightweight "world washer" for India, Brazil and Mexico, designed to accommodate the different manufacturing capabilities and conditions of use in each country, such as washing eighteen-foot-long saris without tangling in India and adding a soak cycle for Brazil to cater to a local belief that only pre-soaking yields a really clean wash.

Changing cultural patterns

So far, I've talked about the simple level of cultural factors. Two main levels of problem occur. The first arises from the need to conform to existing cultural patterns, to integrate or assimilate in ways that cause no disruption. The second level involves changes in that pattern, and this level is infinitely more complex and problematic. Whirlpool adapted to the market as it exists; Electrolux sought to move down a path of inevitable change; Colgate-Palmolive sought to adapt in two different contexts without serious change in either; but British Telecom walked into a storm by stimulating change. The argument would seem to tend towards the less problematic approach of assimilation, but change cannot always be avoided—the opportunities opened up by global manufacturing and marketing frequently require it on a considerable scale. It can be a condition of success in terms of competitiveness and opening up markets, but it also involves substantial risk and therefore needs to be planned consciously and sensitively.

It is important to emphasize the cultural dimension of globalization, which is not just about widening markets or the production base. There is a strong possibility that the trends in technology and communications currently linking the globe together will result in a radical reconfiguration of our notions of culture.

Globalization means moving from culture being dependent on a specific environment, to having a culture different from those around us; in other words, cultural multiplicity rather than homogeneity; and culture creation rather than cultural derivation. That sounds very abstract, but to put it on a personal level: in cultural terms, how does one categorize an Englishman who speaks fluent German, teaches in Chicago and consults for a Japanese design company?

Another example is the film industry. Not long ago we could rightly speak of a Hollywood film, in the sense of it being a product of that particular location in America. A current success, *Schindler's List,* is based on a novel by an Australian of Irish origin. The subject is a German living in Czechoslovakia who helps Jewish people in Poland. The director is American, most leading actors are British and it was made in various European locations. The technical staff and financing were similarly drawn from an international spectrum. On another level, examine a source list of the parts that go into any so-called American or Detroit automobile. They are also drawn from a similarly cosmopolitan and diverse range of sources around the globe.

If I am right concerning the direction of the pattern of cultural change, the consequences are huge. However, it will involve considerable friction, as is evident by the many current reactions to globalization and its consequences. French nationalism, Russian fascism or Islamic fundamentalism are very different in origin and rationale, but a characteristic of all of them is the attempt to resist new patterns of cosmopolitanism, and particularly the freer flow of trade and communications, in the name of protecting cultural identity.

We need a cultural answer to these reactions, to counter, in particular, the perception that trade is an aspect of so-called cultural imperialism, that trade follows the flag. One answer is provided by a line of people standing outside the Kentucky Fried Chicken restaurant in Shanghai. They are not, I believe, voting for democracy, the free market or the American Way. They are opting, rather, for new experience and enjoyment, for eating in clean surroundings, at reasonable prices and a standard of service that contrasts with the locally found "service with a snarl." Equally interesting is a local variant of KFC next door to the original, the Shanghai Rong Hua Chicken restaurant. It too has long lines outside, so something is being learned.

In other words, the answer of business to attempts to assert the local cultural status quo is powerful when focused on people's needs in ways that improve their lives; by making products and services accessible, appropriate, understandable and pleasurable, in ways they can absorb into their pattern of life.

An important point to emphasize here is that culture is not fixed and immutable, but is capable of adaptation in many ways and on many levels. Throughout human history people have interacted with innovations that have created not just new tools, but also new choices, new options, new thoughts, new values. We need to be careful, however, because products may take on a different meaning as they cross cultural boundaries, as the Darkie/Darlie episode illustrated in a negative sense. A classic example of a more positive change was the Volkswagen Beetle, which originated in 1930s

Germany as a gleam in the eye of Adolf Hitler, a motoring enthusiast, and when produced in prototype in 1937 was widely promoted as an icon of the achievements of the Nazi Party. After production recommenced on a large scale after the Second World War, the VW appeared in the United States in the 1950s and became a raging economic success. The design was virtually identical across this period of time, but the image of the product and its cultural value showed a remarkable transformation from an icon of fascism in the 1930s—the "Strength through Joy car"—to the lovable "Bug" and hero of Walt Disney's Herbie films in 1960s America.

Another example, but on a very complex and problematic level, is that of Disney's recent experience in attempting cultural transfer. How do we explain the different reception of the two Disneylands built overseas, those in Japan and France? The approach brought to each was basically similar. The Disney organization has a unique product, impressive technology, a formidable organization and an impressive record of success.

In Japan, the Tokyo Disneyland has been embraced and absorbed unreservedly by the Japanese population. Indeed, it is so successful that a marine-theme Disney park is being planned adjacent to the original. On the other hand, the disastrous start for Euro Disney, located outside Paris, not only cost a huge initial investment of four billion dollars, but had considerable losses in its first year of operation on a scale that places its continued existence in question.

The answer, let me emphasize, does not lie in ignorance of cultural factors by Disney staff. Disney's Imagineers went to great lengths to accommodate plans to what they perceived as European requirements and culture. For example, observing the French habit of taking dogs everywhere with them, Disney built a kennel that "is more like a hotel than a kennel." The reason might lie more in a strategic decision that was culturally askew, if a story in *Newsweek* is accurate. Apparently, when a question was raised at a strategic planning meeting about whether the French would line up in February to visit Euro Disney, the reply was, "Well, the Japanese do." Differences between the Japanese and French were ignored, despite financial projections of attendance and income based on this assumption being crucial to the viability of the project.

Other cultural factors were important. First, the success of Tokyo Disneyland is due in part to the consistency and efficiency of the operation— it fits the way Japanese people think such an operation should function. The high degree of organization of visitors also fits—watch the behavior of any Japanese tour group anywhere in the world. Another factor, a ubiquitous feature of Japanese life, is the widespread use of cartoon figures and comics, which makes them amenable to Disneyland.

Most important, however, is the Japanese capacity for role-playing in new settings as a way of escaping the pressures of a conformist society. But, paradoxically, escapist fantasies must also be clearly structured and signposted.

Above all, they are fascinated by America. So with the Tokyo Disneyland, the Japanese wanted pure Disney without concessions to Japanese culture. In other words, the product was accepted unconditionally and the processes involved happened to fit perfectly, so little substantial change was required for the Disney operation to culturally fit in Japan.

In comparison, France, in many of these key characteristics, is the diametrical opposite. French culture is not conformist, but highly individualistic and verges on the anarchic. There are reports of Euro Disney staff resenting being made to conform to dress and presentation codes; of public resentment that wine and beer were initially not available with food; with the press constantly sniping at how the project was run. Above all, rather than fantasy and role playing, French culture is more notable for rationality and logic. And it is not noted for being receptive to cultural imports.

In other words, two decisive differences emerge. Disney emphasizes behavioral characteristics that place value on conformity, the presence or absence of which will determine whether the tendency in a culture is to cluster in patterns of group behavior or its opposite, non-conformity, to break out in individual patterns of behavior. Secondly, in behavioral terms, the process of exporting this particular product requires a willingness on the part of the receiver to understand and accept it. Another basic characteristic of cultures that I call cultural permeability—the ability of a culture to accept ideas or products from a variety of sources, to absorb them and make them its own—is also critical.

Plotted on a scale of behavioral conformity, the Japanese would be positioned at one end in terms of strong group consciousness and conformity. The French would be at the other end, with an almost anarchic disdain for rules that inconvenience them. In terms of cultural permeability, the two countries are also at polar opposites. For example, over forty percent of Japanese vocabulary consists of imported words. In contrast, in the 1960s, the French head of state, President Charles de Gaulle, initiated a campaign to remove such Anglicisms as "le weekend" from everyday usage in the country (a demand that periodically recurs); while a book by leading politician, Jean-Jacques Servan-Schreiber, *La Defi Americaine,* published in 1972, warning against the cultural take-over of Europe by America, became a best-seller. In the recent GATT negotiations concluding the Uruguay Round, a major stumbling block was an attempt to restrict imports of American films and television programs in France and limit their showing to no more than fifteen percent of total broadcast time.

A senior vice-president of Walt Disney Imagineering said in 1992 that he wanted visitors to feel they were discovering dreams of what they imagined America and an American theme park to be. Yet, interestingly, an employee of Tokyo Disneyland visiting Euro Disney in 1993 found it "too European." Maybe Disney fell into a trap, therefore, when it diluted its product without modifying its own behavior, or what it expected of staff and visitors, and got the worst of both worlds. Its present response to staunch the flow of losses is to cut costs and advertise heavily. If this doesn't work, what then? Whether it is possible at this stage to reverse cultural priorities, that is, asserting the integrity of the product, while adapting behavior, and whether this would improve the situation, is open to debate. More importantly for Disney are the implications for future strategy: are these huge blockbuster theme parks a viable proposition any more?

Connections between cultural factors and business management. The case of Euro Disney demonstrates the importance of cultural factors, but also their difficulties and complexities in practice, and how they are intertwined with other aspects of business management. How then can design contribute in specific terms to identifying problems such as those Disney encountered, before they become critical? It can do so on several levels.

The trend in many product and service sectors towards parity in terms of technical quality and functional performance, makes effective differentiation among competitors' offerings increasingly difficult. In existing markets where cost is not the determining factor, four factors can be identified as critical to decisive competitive advantage:

1. Innovation
2. Value
3. User focus
4. Speed.

To be effective, all involve, at least, understanding existing cultural values. To the extent they involve change, it is important for us to understand the consequences of change. In both cases, whether that of cultural integration or change, design is a vital instrument. To talk of cultural human factors in design being a pro-active tool in this way requires defining markets in cultural terms—which is not easy. I began with a simple definition of culture, but in fact it is highly complex and capable of many interpretations. Without getting into detail, in addition to national culture, we can talk of tribal, ethnic or regional culture; of high and low culture; elite culture, popular culture, mass culture, street culture; urban culture, folk culture or sub-culture; last but not least, professional and corporate culture.

All are useful, but none provide an adequate working methodology. Some are capable of bridging the whole globe, such as youth culture with its icons of rock music, jeans and MacDonalds; or for hthat matter, the professional global culture of designers. Others, such as preferences for color of a particular ethnic group, or the particular class composition of the sub-culture of British or German skinheads, are highly localized in place or social structure. Frequently, global, regional and local all overlap. The tools available to handle this diversity are still limited, varying in sophistication and reliability and needing much greater development. They are summarized in the following list:

1. *Language analysis*
2. *Artifact analysis*
3. *Behavioral analysis*
4. *Cultural characteristic mapping*
5. *Extrapolation and projection*
6. *Scenario building.*

—*Language analysis* means a precise and detailed analysis of meaning in the use of language, not just translation.

—Another means is *analysis of artifacts*, not just for an understanding of form, but for an understanding of behavior and attitudes, which can also yield valuable information and insights. Even the smallest item can be important in this process. Artifact analysis can reveal attitudes to such factors as detail, scale or space. If we are talking of more people in the future working from home, these kinds of factors will obviously take on very different significance in America, Britain and Japan—but exactly how? Techniques for identifying and mapping existing cultural characteristics are possible on many scales. Although it has the limitation of being primarily descriptive, it can provide data useful for other, more analytical exercises.

—*Extrapolation and projection of existing characteristics*, trend spotting, is another possibility, but it is a fragile tool since all too often it is based more on biased enthusiasms of the present rather than the realities of the future. (Electrolux is a case in point.) How does one avoid such blunders? A key in all this, it seems to me, is core characteristic analysis, identifying and cross-referencing the characteristics of vital players in any process of change. This means not only understanding the cultural context of a market, but also a rigorous understanding of one's own organization and cultural values—the real problem is the dynamics of interaction between the two. The characteristics analyzed will obviously vary according to context, but a constant element should be a comparison of images of the future between whoever is initiating change and the people affected by change.

—Another tool used in the early stages of design definition as a means of projecting into the future is *scenario building*—initial visualizations that are complete cultural stories: narratives of the landscape in which products are intended to exist and be used. In the development of the Mazda Miata, for example, the design team wrote short stories featuring the car they envisaged as a means of establishing a common vision. Techniques of this kind were so successful that Mazda abandoned conventional market research on products intended for emerging rather than existing markets.

Challenging accepted assumptions, whether of a market, a cultural group or a corporate strategy, and using design as a culture creating instrument, can allow a company to move a culture, including its own, in new directions, or at least to understand directions in which it may inevitably be moving. To evolve and use scenarios to the extent suggested here requires that the strategy of a company's future be defined not only in terms of technology and economics, but also with respect to the cultural ramifications of new products and services. If done comprehensively and executed creatively, they can help customers visualize the future and negotiate change more assuredly, even to the extent of becoming a self-fulfilling prophecy.

This is what really should be meant by customer focus. Working to make technological change as fluid as possible (which also involves ensuring continuity by building on established cultural norms) requires that change be evolutionary where possible, rather than in conflict or dependent on the imposition of a new culture. The magnitude of the change may require the latter, but the former is undeniably less stressful.

To conclude: navigating cultural change smoothly is more than a concession to customers, for whom uncertain futures provoke anxiety. It should be a corporate goal formulated in strategy as a key competitive tool.

26

Creating Economic Value by Design

Abstract

This paper examines the influence of major economic theories in shaping views of what constitutes value as created by design. It begins by examining Neo-Classical theory, which is dominant in the English-speaking world and underpins the ideology of the so-called "free market" system. Its focus on markets and prices as set by market forces are believed to solve all problems if left free from government interference. The implosion of this system and its emphasis on unrestricted individualism is a crisis of theory as well as practice. There are, however, other economic systems that relate to design in a more positive manner, such as Austrian theory and its belief that users determine value; institutional theory, which examines the influence of contexts and organizations; or New Growth Theory, which asserts the power of ideas as an unlimited resource in economic activity. These offer a window to business activity that enables designers to communicate the value of their work. Moreover, if the practical implications of these theoretical positions are understood by designers, it becomes possible to construct an extension of them that specifically addresses what the economic contribution of design can be in terms that business managers can understand.

Introduction

This paper is an attempt to summarize work undertaken over several years on the relationship between economics and design. The origins of the

First published as "Creating Economic Value by Design," *International Journal of Design*, vol. 3, no. 1, 2008, pp. 71–84. By permission of the editors.

project go back to meetings with officials of the U.S. Federal Department of Commerce and the Council on Competitiveness in the mid-1990s. The officials were all economists and it rapidly became clear their concept of design was of something superficial, easily copied and not really capable of generating value. They were educated, intelligent and courteous people, but it was clear that design had no role of any significance in their view of the economic world.

Obviously for some reason, the discipline of economics does not acknowledge design. To be fair it must also be acknowledged that the discipline of design is deficient in communicating its economic role. Some designers might ask: why bother? My answer to that would be that basically, design is a professional business activity practiced overwhelmingly within business contexts and if designers cannot argue the economic relevance of their practice in convincing terms, the views of the officials I met in Washington will be justified and they will remain what the American designer, George Nelson, long ago termed "exotic menials." The work of Herbert Simon, Nobel Laureate in Economics in 1978, is a rare exception of design being considered as a factor in economic theory. His starting point was acknowledging that the world we inhabit is increasingly artificial, created by human beings. For Simon (1981), design was not restricted to making material artefacts, but was a fundamental professional competence extending to policy-making and practices of many kinds and on many levels:

> Everyone designs who devises courses of action aimed at changing existing situations into preferred ones. The intellectual activity that produces material artifacts is no different fundamentally from the one that prescribes remedies for a sick patient or the one that devises a new sales plan for a company or a social welfare policy for a state. Design, so construed, is the core of all professional training; it is the principal mark that distinguishes the professions from the sciences. (p. 129)

Implicit in Simon's reasoning is an emphasis on design as a thought-process underpinning all kinds of professional activities; yet the varied skills through which design is manifested are not discussed. He did indicate, however, why design is so rarely considered in economic theory. Economics, he stated, works on three levels, those of the individual; the market; and the entire economy (p. 31). The centre of interest in traditional economics, however, is markets and not individuals or businesses (p. 37). A serious problem is thereby raised at the outset: two important considerations relating to design—how goods and services are developed for the market place and how they are used—receive scant attention.

Markets and prices—Neo-Classical theory

The focus on markets as the major arena of economic activity is a characteristic of Neo-Classical theory, which emerged during the late-nineteenth century to become the mainstream of economic thought in the modern world. Its context was Great Britain's rise to global industrial dominance, later overtaken by the United States—so its origins are deeply rooted in the English-speaking world. At its heart is a concept of markets and how they operate as mechanisms to allocate resources. Out of the processes of competition, the theory claims that market mechanisms, if left to their own workings, will yield the most efficient allocation.

In fact, the arguments go much further than that. Their most influential advocate in modern times has been Milton Friedman (1962), who argued that markets are an indispensable component of political freedom, by ensuring diversity of choice and by limiting the scope and power of governments to a minimal role.

> What the market does is to reduce greatly the range of issues that must be decided through political means, and thereby to minimize the extent to which government need participate directly in the game. ... The great advantage of the market, on the other hand, is that it permits wide diversity. It is, in political terms, a system of proportional representation. (p. 15)

The argument that the market can be considered politically as a form of proportional representation is typical of Friedman's popularization of an idealized assessment of the efficacy of markets. In contrast, it is possible to argue that markets are a form of disproportionate representation. Possessors of great wealth and major business organizations have a power in modern society that is hardly justifiable in terms of political democracy, particularly since Friedman (1962) rejected any view of "social responsibility" for corporations "beyond serving the interest of their stockholders or their members" (p. 133).

Originally, markets were specific places in towns or villages where people gathered to exchange goods and services. Today, these are overlaid by markets that range across the globe and are complex, impersonal and intangible, but nevertheless still remain essential mechanisms for exchanging goods and services.

Basic concepts in Neo-Classical theory explain how supply and demand are reconciled in any market. A market only exists because of scarcity: it fills the need to allocate goods that are scarce in relation to the number of people desiring them. A further assumption about supply is that the price of each unit decreases as the quantity produced increases, which is made possible by economies of scale due to increased efficiency in manufacturing large quantities.

Complementing supply is demand: what people are prepared to pay for goods and services. Demand increases as larger quantities become available at lower prices.

Equilibrium is the point where supply and demand intersect and determine the price customers are prepared to pay. Equilibrium implies balance and is essentially a static condition.

These concepts are rudimentary—the kind any student of economics learns in their first lessons; obviously, Neo-Classical theory is immensely more sophisticated. Nevertheless, some important points arise even at this simple level. Firstly, price is the major determinant of value, which ignores other factors such as quality or differentiation; secondly, goods are assumed to appear on the market without any consideration of how they got there, i.e., consideration of product development processes and the role design plays in them are conspicuously absent; thirdly, firms have no role in this theoretical depiction, they are assumed to be price-takers, passively accepting the price determined by the market; and fourthly, markets are depicted as static, but in fact are constantly changing in innumerable ways.

Harold Demsetz (1977), a distinguished American economist, stated the situation very clearly:

> Neo-Classical theory's objective is to understand price-guided, not management-guided, resource allocation. The firm does not play a central role in the theory. (p. 426)

This clearly positions design outside the parameters of Neo-Classical theory. Yet in reality, many companies function as price-setters—targeting people who will willingly pay more for products embodying superior qualities. James Dyson's first vacuum cleanerr introduced in Britain in 1993 were double the price of his cheapest competitors. Yet against established multi-national companies, the superior performance of his start-up products attained market leadership in the UK inside two years, an achievement subsequently mirrored in other markets.

Design, as demonstrated by the Dyson example, is essentially about change, and concepts of equilibrium have limited relevance in explaining change. Neo-Classicism explains how goods and services are generated for markets in terms of two main production functions: the amounts of labour and capital employed in production. Again, these production functions can be quantified to explain the cost of what is produced, but do nothing to help understand what is produced, why or how. Neither do they explain beyond the dimension of cost, what quality and value might be in other terms than monetary value.

Consumers are assumed to act in terms of rational calculation in market decisions and have three characteristics (McCormick, 1997):

1. Their tastes are consistent.
2. Their cost calculations are correct.
3. They make those decisions that maximize utility.

Rationality is expressed in quantifiable terms. Mathematical methodology stresses what is consistent and calculable and whatever is unstable or indefinable is discarded, or as critics of Neo-Classicism assert, facts must fit the methodology.

Another static model is the condition termed perfect competition, in which the interplay of supply and demand in the market is assumed to be subject to no hindrances of any kind. Everyone has access to the same information about the same products. Choice is assumed to be a matter of rationally selecting what is available within an established range.

Curiously, these beliefs about how markets work to efficiently allocate resources rests upon what can only be described as an act of faith without rational proof. The founder of modern economics, Adam Smith (1776/1937), explained this in terms of a concept of "the invisible hand of the market" (p. 423). He wrote of any individual being led in their investment of capital "by an invisible hand to promote an end which was no part of his intention" (p. 423).

If not interfered with, (under conditions of perfect competition,) the pursuit of enlightened self-interest by each entrepreneur and consumer produces the most efficient result to the greatest benefit of all.

Markets are therefore the sum total of each individual's attempts to maximize their own advantage. However, if any buyer or seller can manipulate a good's price or distort the market mechanism, then a condition of imperfect competition occurs, a condition that encompasses most design work.

On the important question of value, Adam Smith defined two aspects, which he termed value in use and value in exchange. Beyond acknowledging its importance, he has little to say about value in use since it has no direct economic relevance.

> The things which have the greatest value in use have frequently little or no value in exchange; and on the contrary, those which have the greatest value in exchange have frequently little or no value in use. Nothing is more useful than water: but it will purchase scarce any thing; scarce any thing can be had in exchange for it. A diamond, on the contrary, has scarce any value in use; but a very great quantity of other goods may frequently be had in exchange for it. (Smith, 1776/1937, p. 28)

Just as there is little in Smith's Wealth of Nations to enlighten us as to why people find things useful or desirable, neither in Neo-Classical theory is there substantial concern with how products might be different. If market decisions are indeed based on goods which already exist, there is little left on which to focus beyond price and quantity.

How can these static assumptions be credible? The answer is that in reality, markets for many products do indeed fit these criteria.

Highly standardized products, for example, basic commodities such as oil or wheat, or consumer products such as beer, soft drinks and cigarettes, or shares on any stock exchange transaction, are not generally subject to change in their essential character or how they are produced. This being the case, they are open to rational, numerical inquiry, as Demsetz (1977) points out:

> When economists analyze the consumption behavior of households, the employment choices of workers, and the investments of capitalists, their conclusions are largely drawn from the wealth consequences that flow from alternative decisions. We do not have much to say about tastes and how these may differ across persons and situations, but, in principle, variations in tastes also explain variations in behavior. Our focus, not exclusively but most often, is on wages, prices, rates of return, and budget constraints. This works quite well in practice *if most tastes change only slowly* (my emphasis, JH). (p. 8)

Demsetz confirms the importance of innate "measurability" and avoids "taste" with all its uncertainties and volatile unpredictability.

If the assumptions of Neo-Classical theory explain commodity markets, they are more fragile in situations where criteria other than cost and quantity become significant in market choice. The processes of creating new products or product variations, based on an assumption that someone has a better idea than their competitors, by definition creates *imperfect competition* and, inevitably, a state of *disequilibrium* as a permanent condition.

Another frequent criticism of Neoclassicism revolves around its stress on an individualistic view of society, with social values considered as an arithmetical sum total of individual intentions.

> Neoclassical economics involves an individualistic view of efficiency. Efficiency is defined as the allocation of resources to "the highest," that is, monetarily most remunerative, uses. Social efficiency is additive, that is, the summation of private individual efficiencies. (Klein & Miller, 1996, p. 267)

The potential tension between individuals' desires to pursue their own benefit and their simultaneous need for protection from the actions of others requires people to behave in very different ways in varying situations.

> Culturally, ...a key requirement for a market system will be a set of values in society that offer vigorous encouragement to self-interest in the market and yet maintain powerful normative inhibitions on the expression of self-interest in many other less socially acceptable areas. (Nelson, 2001, p. 6)

As is apparent at present, self-interest easily translates into greed. Therefore, if self-interest is encouraged in economic affairs, how do we reconcile this with the need to prevent other people from stealing the contents of our home, mugging us on the street, or pirating a shipment of goods? Choices have to be made in reality between pizza and police forces, or cigarettes and social welfare programs. In Neo-Classical theory this leads to a distinction between private goods—bought at a price—and public goods—paid for by taxes. The former are included in the market model and therefore are depicted as beneficial. The latter are not subject to market forces and are widely viewed as a distortion of market models. Once in existence, public goods are available to additional people at no cost. An example is street lighting—there is no competition between suppliers that enables us to choose between alternative lighting systems when we move down a street.

An important criterion by which private goods are distinguished from public goods is excludability, or in other words, private goods are those where one person's consumption precludes consumption of the same item by another person. When a supplier can prevent some people from consuming the product—those who do not pay—then the product is excludable and can be supplied by means of a market.

For those preaching the virtues of "free markets," excludability is at the heart of the economic system and there is a constant struggle to extend and protect its boundaries. A good example of such an extension is parking. In the early days of automobiles, parking on the sides of roads in cities was open to anyone and was therefore non-excludable. As soon as spaces were demarcated and parking meters installed, with payment enforceable by law, parking became excludable. An even more remarkable extension is the tangled web of "intellectual property rights," based on the proposition that even ideas can be owned.

In terms of these concepts, it is easy to see how design can be regarded as non-excludable and therefore of little economic value. On some levels, its outcomes are easily copied. New fashion designs, for example, will be on the streets around the world via major clothing chains within two weeks of them appearing at exclusive fashion shows in Paris, Milan, London or New York.

Attempts to give designs protection by licensing systems analogous to patenting can be evaded by slight modifications of form, pattern or colour. Product or graphic designs are also widely imitated by competitors. Innumerable companies around the world specialize in being "fast-followers," adept at rapidly producing imitations of successful innovations at low cost. For this reason, design can be considered as something virtually impossible to exclude, something that can be easily acquired at no cost by competitors.

However, nowadays Neo-Classicism is increasingly questioned because it does not explain many crucial aspects of development. Technological innovations on every level of life, changing products, processes and organizations, have created economic growth and substantially improved living standards. Yet, strangely, in Neo-Classical theory, technological progress is not explained, but has the status of an exogenous variable, something known to be an influence, but outside the loop of what is clearly understood and can be quantified, in contrast to an endogenous factor— something integral to a process or model and clearly definable. In Neo-Classical thinking, technology functions in indefinable ways, as a black box, the workings of which cannot be known. This creates a strange situation:

> Technological progress was seen as something that simply rained down from heaven. Studies show that, in most economies, higher inputs of labour and capital account for barely half the total growth in output

this century. The huge unexplained residual was labeled "technological change", but in truth it was a measure of economists' ignorance. (Anonymous, 1996, p. 57)

If it is "a measure of economists' ignorance," as *The Economist* termed it, (and which journal is better qualified to judge this?), then it also has the more serious implication that Neo-Classical theory addresses only half of what it purports to explain. If increases in investment do not adequately account for an economy's long-term rate of growth, it requires greater understanding of the role of technology and design than has hitherto existed. Fortunately, other tendencies in economic theory with alternative models of how markets function offer greater hope for opportunities to explore the economic role of design.

Value and change: Austrian theory

Many aspects of Neo-Classical theory were questioned and modified by a group of scholars who initially came from Austria, although adherents are now found in many countries. This group of scholars and their theories are now referred to as the Austrian School. An important emphasis in their early work was on how value is attributed to products, which was also a major emphasis of the founder of the Austrian School, Carl Menger (1840–1921). In 1871, he wrote:

Value is thus nothing inherent in goods, no property of them, nor an independent thing existing by itself. It is a judgment economizing men make about the importance of the goods at their disposal for the maintenance of their lives and well-being. Hence value does not exist outside the consciousness of men. (Menger, 1871/1976, p. 121)

It is difficult to overestimate the importance of this insight. Understanding that value is subjective and determined by users is of crucial importance for design and business, and yet many designers and managers continue to believe that their decisions determine value. Menger (1871/1976) is emphatic on this point:

There is no necessary and direct connection between the value of a good and whether, or in what quantities, labor and other goods of higher order were applied to its production. (p. 147)

Menger's followers extended his ideas, among them Friedrich von Wieser (1891), who argued that although value in exchange is objective in terms of being defined by price, value in use is not only particular to individuals but is subjective, leading to the further question: "why do men prize commodities?" (p. 118). Neglecting subjective values, Wieser argued further, "would thereby leave unexplained all individual decisions in economic matters, e.g. it would not even explain why any one buys" (p. 119). Wieser therefore emphasizes that although the subjective dimension is indeed not easily specified, this is no reason to omit it from any explanation of buyers' behaviour. Thus the early work and ideas of the Austrian School explored a radical concept of value, which more closely approximates the behaviour of users in purchasing. This can be illustrated by an object with a basically simple function, such as a lemon squeezer, which yet reveals great diversity in the forms and materials used and equally great price differentials. Why this diversity? All the examples perform the required function effectively, but the actual range of forms and materials is exceedingly varied and confirms the arguments of Menger and Wieser on the role of value and taste in choice decisions, in contrast to the stress on price and rationality in Neo-Classical theory. The Austrian school therefore opens up more accurate depictions of how design innately functions and generates value in an economic context.

Austrian ideas were further elaborated in the twentieth century by Ludwig von Mises and Friedrich von Hayek. For Mises (1949), action is only comprehensible in terms of the ideas that generate it. "Human action," he wrote, "is purposeful behavior" (p. 11). Its aim is change to achieve improvement in some way.

> Acting man is eager to substitute a more satisfactory state of affairs for a less satisfactory. His mind imagines conditions which suit him better, and his action aims at bringing about this desired state. (Mises, 1949, p. 13)

Human meaning and action, therefore, do not derive from a static world, but one that is in ceaseless ferment.

Hayek (1948) similarly argued that if theory was to be validated in empirical reality, it had to be dynamic. "It is, perhaps, worth stressing," he wrote, "that economic problems arise always and only in consequence of change" (p. 82). Competition innately involves change, and he noted that Neo-Classical theory tended to avoid its consequences: "... competition is by its nature a dynamic process whose essential characteristics are assumed away by the assumptions underlying static analysis" (p. 94). The concept of "perfect competition" was another target in his critique of how Neo-Classical models eliminated some of the most important elements of how markets actually worked:

> ... how many of the devices adopted in ordinary life to that end would still be open to a seller in a market in which so-called "perfect competition" prevails? I believe that the answer is exactly none. Advertising, undercutting, and improving ("differentiating") the goods and services produced are all excluded by definition—"perfect" competition means indeed the absence of all competitive activities. (Hayek, 1948, p. 96)

Hayek did not explore the concept of "differentiating," or other references to branding and advertising in anything other than the most general terms, but he was clearly aware of their role as vital elements in competitive processes.

In fact, it need hardly be said, no products of two producers are ever exactly alike ... These differences are part of the facts which create our economic problem, and it is little help to answer it on the assumption that they are absent. (Hayek, 1948, p. 98)

Hayek's emphasis on economics being innately concerned with the consequences of change and its relevance to design can be illustrated by substituting the word "design" for "economic" in the quotation below.

> The solution of the economic problem of society is in this respect always a voyage of exploration into the unknown, an attempt to discover new ways of doing things better than they have been done before. ...all economic problems are created by unforeseen changes which require adaptation. (Hayek, 1948, p. 101)

Acknowledging the huge range of human skills, knowledge, tastes and needs meant for Hayek that attempts by the state to impose centralized solutions on problems would not only reduce economic efficiency, but restrict individual freedom. In this regard, Hayek is most famous for his book, *The Road to Serfdom,* published at the end of the Second World War, which is a compelling defence of individualism against the centralized planning he saw emerging in even ostensibly democratic societies.

The influence of the Austrian School reached far beyond the geographical boundaries of Austria. In the United States it also had a profound impact on management theory through the work of Peter Drucker, who was born and educated in Austria and whose views are a classic manifestation of Austrian economic ideas. One hundred and fifteen years after Menger (1871/1976) articulated the basic principles of the school, Drucker (1986) trenchantly restated them in terms that have been a constant theme in his writings:

> "Quality" in a product or service is not what the supplier puts in. It is what the customer gets out and is willing to pay for. A product is not "quality" because it is hard to make and costs a lot of money, as manufacturers typically believe. That is incompetence. Customers pay only for what is of use to them and gives them value. Nothing else constitutes "quality." (p. 228)

If quality is a factor in competitive success, it is highly relevant in discussing the economic value of design.

Conspicuous consumption and workmanship: Institutional theory

Austrian theory locates economics in the context of a broader human concept of nature, and a further broadening is evident in Institutional theory, which seeks to explain differing levels of economic performance in firms and nations by examining the influence of history, culture and institutions.

The generally acknowledged founder of Institutional theory is Thorsten Veblen, who from the 1890s onward framed arguments that throughout history two human tendencies were in conflict over responses to new developments, distinguished by an emphasis on production and acquisition. The first, production, strove for creative adjustment to the new, expressed primarily in efforts to shape new materials and processes into useful artefacts; in contrast, acquisition was characterized by possession, preserving privilege and averting or restricting the new. The latter was the target of his first major book, *The Theory of the Leisure Class* (Veblen, 1899/1994), in which he coined the phrase "conspicuous consumption" (p. 75). He depicted the emergence of a leisure class as synonymous with ownership, which has nothing to do with the necessary subsistence minimum, being instead concerned with the demonstration of superfluity, either in terms of time or of goods.

The relation of the leisure (that is, propertied non-industrial) class to the economic process is a pecuniary relation—a relation of acquisition, not of production; of exploitation, not of serviceability. (Veblen, 1899/1994, p. 209)

Veblen's concept of conspicuous consumption extended far beyond what was functionally necessary and focused on the display of products as an index of wealth and status:

> ... most objects alleged to be beautiful, and doing duty as such, show considerable ingenuity of design and are calculated to puzzle the beholder— to bewilder him with irrelevant suggestions and hints of the improbable—at the same time that they give evidence of an expenditure of labour in excess of what would give them their fullest efficiency for the ostensible economic end. (Veblen, 1899/1994, p. 152)

The other pole of Veblen's thought was the subject of another seminal work *The Instinct of Workmanship* (Veblen, 1918/1990), which focused on the role of production and examined the linkage between technology and institutional organization across human history through "practical expedients, ways and means, devices and contrivances of efficiency and economy, proficiency, creative work and technological mastery of facts" (p. 33). However, this concept of workmanship does not exist in isolation, but instead is drawn into value systems other than those unique to it, creating a problem that Veblen calls "contamination":

> So also, to the current common sense in a community trained to pecuniary rather than to workmanlike discrimination between articles of use, those articles which serve their material use in a conspicuously wasteful manner commend themselves as more serviceable, nobler and more beautiful than such goods as do not embody such a margin of waste. (p. 217)

Veblen's (1899/1994) identification of "economic beauty" in terms of simplicity of form anticipated the emergence of the body of aesthetic theory collectively known as Modernism:

> So far as the economic interest enters into the constitution of beauty, it enters as a suggestion or expression of adequacy to a purpose, a manifest and readily inferable subservience to the life process. This expression of economic facility or economic serviceability in any object—what may be called the economic beauty of the object—is best served by neat and unambiguous suggestion of its office and its efficiency for the material ends of life. (p. 209)

Veblen's criticism targeted the often vulgar manifestations of wealth by elites in the so-called Gilded Age of new commercial wealth in late nineteenth-century America that moved in top-down manner to influence a broader spectrum of society. In the contemporary world, however, conspicuous consumption has moved down-market. In China, for example, where Western brands have become an index of status, the Louis Vuitton logo is prized as an indicator of social aspiration to a degree that young women working in relatively low paid jobs will spend a month's salary on a Vuitton wallet.

Another development that did not feature in Veblen's day, was a bottom-up tendency that can affect broad swathes of society. In the USA, what began as a movement among deprived inner-city African-American youth known as Hip-Hop, has spread to middle-class white suburban youth and morphed into a huge commercial phenomenon with an elaborately decorative visual expression known as "bling-bling" based on exotic and often bizarre forms. In this case, conspicuous consumption has become a powerful assertion of cultural identity.

This distinction between "the productive" and "the acquisitive," or "the industrial" and "the pecuniary" in modern society remained a central and generally pessimistic feature of Veblen's theories and they are still of great importance in understanding not just contemporary design, but the financial crash that is sweeping the world at the time of writing.

Another important contribution of Institutional theory has been on the subject of the firm. "The Nature of the Firm," a landmark paper in this direction written by Ronald Coase in 1937, questioned Neo-Classical arguments that the price mechanism determines how markets allocate resources. If this was so, he asked, what was the reason for the existence of firms?

In examining the actual workings of firms, he identified functions beyond those associated with production termed "transaction costs," which included everything essential to how a firm undertook its business, such as purchases of materials and supplies, banking, legal and insurance costs, information and promotion, design and delivery. Minimizing transaction costs was therefore suggested as the primary function for firms. Otherwise, Coase (1998) asserted in a trenchant critique of Neo-Classicism, the situation will remain that "economists study how supply and demand determine prices but not the factors that determine what goods and services are traded on markets and therefore are priced" (p. 72).

In recent years, C. Douglass North has emerged as a powerful influence in institutional thinking. The first economic historian to be awarded the Nobel Prize in Economics in 1993, he believes history is important not for its own sake, but as a crucial means of understanding the present and facing the problems of the future. He emphasises the role of institutions in giving structure to life in a society. Basically, they establish the rules of the game, which leads to a distinction between institutions and organizations or between the rules and the players. In comparable social terms, institutions such as laws, customs and habits set the essential framework of activity, within which organizations are the players.

If institutions can be described as self-imposed constraints that bring order and structure to a society, what then is their economic importance? According to North (1990), this lies in how they affect the costs of exchange and production. In addition, institutions are crucial in explaining historical patterns of how societies have changed in such divergent ways with very different performance characteristics, and can give insights into how change might take place in the future. The manner, for example, in which a firm organizes, structures and manages design will very largely determine the quality of work generated.

An example is the Italian electrical manufacturer Olivetti, which insisted that its designers, no matter how prestigious, should only work no more than half-time for them. The designers were expected to do work of other kinds with other companies to keep themselves fresh and stimulated. The outcome was a very high standard on many levels - products, graphics, exhibitions and packaging—that was sustained over forty years. Olivetti became a design icon among the world's manufacturing companies, which was also reflected in sustained and competitive sales of its products. By the 1990s, however, that institutional advantage proved inadequate to cope with changes resulting from the spread of digital technology—illustrating that institutional forms are indeed powerful, but not immutable over time.

Understanding how institutions function is in large measure dependent upon the concept of human nature that informs any social theory. In rejecting the rational theory assumptions of perfect competition, North (1990) asserts, similarly to adherents of Austrian theory, that when purchasing anything individuals make subjective choices on the basis of incomplete information. He points out:

> We get utility from the diverse attributes of a good or service or, in the case of the performance of an agent, from the multitude of separate activities that constitute performance. ... when I buy an automobile, I get a particular color, acceleration, style, interior design, leg room, gasoline mileage - all valued attributes, even though it is only an automobile I buy.

... The value of an exchange to the parties, then, is the value of the different attributes lumped into the good or service. ...

From the particulars in the foregoing illustrations we can generalize as follows: commodities, services, and the performance of agents have numerous attributes and their levels vary from one specimen or agent to another. The measurement of these levels is too costly to be comprehensive or fully accurate. (pp. 28–9)

North identifies here a prime difficulty in providing quantifiable demonstrations of design's value—when integrated into product development processes it is virtually impossible to disentangle the precise contribution of design, or any other discipline, to the final outcome.

The task of management, according to North, is to acquire the appropriate knowledge of products, production and markets in situations of uncertainty and risk. What knowledge is acquired and how it is applied will be decisive for the future not only of firms but also of societies. He therefore identifies institutions and technology as the building blocks of change, although technology is more open to the effects of individual decision-making since institutions are more embedded in a complex range of political, economic, social and cultural influences.

While North acknowledges the need for formal rules, he also stresses informal behaviour: rationality is balanced by subjectivity, stability by change, the macro-economic dimension related to the micro-economic. His reference point in history gives an awareness of how change has actually taken place and enables theoretical positions to be tested against a spectrum of historical occurrences.

Knowledge and technology: New Growth Theory

New Growth Theory emerged in the U.S. in the 1980s. A forerunner was Joseph Schumpeter, who was born in Austria, but in 1932 left for the USA on appointment to Harvard University.

By the 1930s, Schumpeter was depicting growth as innate to capitalism, driven by the interaction of technological development and competition between firms. This also directly opposed the static views of Neo-Classicism:

Capitalism, then, is by nature a form or method of economic change and not only never is but never can be stationary. ... The fundamental impulse that sets and keeps the capitalist engine in motion comes from new consumers' goods, the new methods of production or transportation, the new markets, the new forms of industrial organization that capitalist enterprise creates. (Schumpeter, 1942, p. 83)

Schumpeter did not detail the new goods and markets generated by this dynamism, but strongly emphasized the role of innovation as the main stimulant of growth. Historically, he discerned waves of technological revolution sweeping old industries away and replacing them by new ones in a process of "creative destruction," (perhaps Schumpeter's most famous phrase). Each new wave would fire-up investment and provide jobs to replace those lost. Schumpeter (1942) also criticized the incapacity of Neo-Classical theory to deal with dynamic changes:

> ... the problem that is usually being visualized is how capitalism administers existing structures, whereas the relevant problem is how it creates and destroys them. (p. 84)

Price, Schumpeter concluded, was therefore not the dominant criterion in competition. To expand upon Schumpeter's basic insights has been the role of the leading proponents of New Growth Theory, among them, Paul Romer, Paul David, Nathan Rosenberg and W. Brian Arthur.

Romer's (1992) emphasis is the missing element of technology, incorporating it directly into models of economic growth by explaining how knowledge is created and spread. Unlike the two conventional factors of production, labour and capital, he argues, ideas are not scarce. Therefore a sustained flow of ideas for more efficient processes and new products potentially makes continuous growth possible. Knowledge of technology and experience in its applications can appreciate into human capital, a powerful concept in explaining why many firms are more proficient than others in innovation. To labour and capital, Romer added knowledge as a production function, making it more plausible.

Nathan Rosenberg (1982) similarly emphasizes knowledge in making technology into an effective instrument beyond price competition:

> ... technical progress is not one thing; it is many things. Perhaps the most useful common denominator underlying its multitude of forms is that it constitutes certain kinds of knowledge that make it possible to produce (1) a greater volume of output or (2) a qualitatively superior output from a given amount of resources. (p. 3)

For Romer (1992), emphasising knowledge requires a basic shift in approach: "... the difference between the economics of ideas and the economics of objects is important for our understanding of growth and development" (p. 63). This point is vital in comprehending many developments in contemporary economies:

> ... take oranges as an example of a product that's an ordinary object. There's a cost of producing each additional orange, and the cost of the next orange is pretty much the same as the cost of the last one. You've

got to give up the use of some land, plant new orange trees, harvest the oranges and so on. So each orange has a constant cost of production. (Robinson, 1995, p. 66)

Increases in the production of objects achieved by a replication of existing, known methods of production will therefore yield an increase on the basis of constant or diminishing returns to scale. Romer then compares the economics of objects with the economics of ideas, using the example of the polymerase chain reaction (PCR), which is a simple technology for taking a tiny amount of DNA and multiplying it.

An incredible amount of research expense went into the discovery of PCR. But once it was discovered, it was just basically a recipe. The recipe could just be published on the Internet, and then anybody in the world would be able to use this amazing technology at zero additional cost. So the key difference between objects and ideas—between oranges and a high- tech process like PCR—is this: Objects tend to have a constant cost per unit. But ideas have a huge cost for the first unit, then essentially zero costs for each additional unit. (Robinson, 1995, p. 66)

"Ideas," says Romer, "are routinely ignored" (Robinson, 1995, p. 67). He points out, however, that they are crucial generators of value, making a decisive difference not only in big discoveries, but also in constant incremental improvements, as illustrated by Japanese manufacturers in their extraordinary rise to global leadership in many product sectors.

On Japanese assembly lines, the workers were supposed to experiment with slightly different ways of doing their jobs. Japanese workers were given the freedom, for example, to try putting the rearview mirror on the door before putting the door on the car, and then to try it the other way around, finding out which was more efficient. Over time, the Japanese gained a big competitive advantage. ... This move toward institutionalizing the whole process of discovery is a really profound change in the nature of economic activity. (Robinson, 1995, p. 67)

Companies clearly need to understand that knowledge workers involved in various levels of discovery are significantly growing in numbers, becoming vital elements in the existence and success of firms, with a corresponding reduction in numbers of those who actually carry out the manufacturing function.

... if you think about it in terms of production at a company like Microsoft or a big drug company, you'll see that by far the most important activity at those companies is getting the instructions right. ...The fraction of workers at Microsoft who actually manufacture the physical product is very small. (Robinson, 1995, p. 67)

The concept of increasing returns, which is another substantial challenge to traditional economic theory, perhaps provides the best understanding of the potential for growth unlocked by these new theories. W. Brian Arthur (1996) argues that diminishing returns was a valid concept in the days of nineteenth century smokestack industry, and still is valid in resource-based industries such as agriculture and mining, but not in the new knowledge-based industries.

> ... steadily and continuously in this century, Western economies have undergone a transformation from bulk-material manufacturing to design and use of technology—from processing of resources to processing of information, from application of raw energy to application of ideas. As this shift has occurred, the underlying mechanisms that determine economic behavior have shifted from ones of diminishing to ones of increasing returns. (p. 100)

In high technology industries, when one firm gets an initial toehold in the market, it can establish a position of dominance, ensuring increasing returns rather than the slow wastage of diminishing returns.

The establishment of such dominance is characterized by the concept of lock-in, with one product or system establishing total control of a market. Arthur illustrates this with examples such as the DOS system, which became locked-in as the operating system of preference over Apple's Macintosh system, and the victory of VHS over Betamax in the video-recorder market. In both cases, victory did not go necessarily to the best system either in terms of technical quality or operating simplicity, but to the system that established early dominance and reinforced it in every available direction.

A classic contemporary example is the way Apple created a new market with the introduction of its iPod and the iTunes system in late 2001, which revolutionized the retail music business. Despite intense competition from imitators around the globe, it has maintained its superiority due to consistent development of the product range, the continuing quality of its technology, and the strong design identity that characterizes it. By March 2008, over 150 million iPods had been sold worldwide, making it the best-selling digital audio player series ever. It is neither the cheapest, nor even the most technologically advanced product of its kind, yet it has a dedicated following locked into to what they believe is its innate superiority. It is surely one of the most compelling contemporary examples of the power of design when embedded in the culture of a business in all its aspects (iPod, n.d.).

The emphasis on technology and ideas also opens up a greater emphasis on what is termed human capital, the kinds of knowledge important in sustaining growth. Paul David (1993) uses a distinction between tacit knowledge and coded knowledge, which draws on earlier work by Michael Polanyi (1983). Tacit knowledge refers to a vast range of procedures, a build- up of innate knowledge and inherent skills, derived from practical experience. The result, as Polanyi (1983) points out is that "... we know more than we can tell. ... So most of this knowledge cannot be put into words" (p. 4).

A commonplace example of tacit knowledge is learning to ride a bicycle. No set of instructions can give a recipe for this—one person's knowledge cannot be directly transferred to another. The only way is through the slow and often painful process of trial and error. This type of knowledge is a crucial element in innumerable skills vital to firms and particularly important in design practice. The skills of drawing, for example, enable potential solutions to be probed in a variety of forms, without there always being an exact rationale for each. Choices of materials and colours can also rely more on this experiential sense of the "rightness" of a solution that is not always capable of logical explanation since it is rooted in a sensitivity based on substantial experience.

In contrast, however, other vital kinds of knowledge may need to be coded and explicitly communicated. This can take many forms–documentation in the form of patents, licensing agreements, proprietary information, contracts, formulae, data and manuals, or other formats. As projects increase in scale and complexity, so this other kind of knowledge also begins to assume greater importance in design practice.

In economic terms, this kind of coded knowledge is potentially a public good–in published forms it is potentially available to anyone with the ability to understand it. Once ideas are coded, they can be possessed by numerous people at the same time, and be made available to any number of people with little or no additional cost.

Romer's ideas, although influential, have nevertheless been challenged from several directions. Once asked in an interview (CIO Insight, 2003): "If a greater and greater portion of the value of new ideas is going to the consumer and not to companies, will that reduce the incentives to create new ideas?" He replied:

> The evidence seems to point in that direction. The very same highly competitive conditions that benefit consumers mean that a new entrant who has a valuable new idea doesn't actually capture all of the value they create with that new idea. Lots of the value created by the new idea flows through to the consumer. The person who comes up with the new idea cannot patent and control all its benefits. What that means for the economy as a whole is there isn't as much new idea creation as would be ideal. The incentives for creating new ideas aren't as big as they should be. (p. 28)

This is a curious question and an even more curious response. It seems to imply that any value delivered to customers is in some way a deprivation of producers, who in addition, are liable to lose control of the idea. The emphasis is on producer-centred control and benefit, detached from any relationship to the customer and enhancement of the value delivered to them. Romer (CIO Insight, 2003) continues his answer to the problem in more detail:

> So other economists and I have been arguing for a long time that the government has an important role in encouraging the creation of new ideas, and letting them get fed out into a market system where people can capture profits from innovating. Those profits are important, but they will never be big enough by themselves to encourage the amount of idea creation that would be ideal for the economy. The market is a wonderfully powerful engine for economic growth, but it runs much faster when the government turbo-charges it with strong financial and institutional support for education, science, and the free dissemination of ideas. (p. 28)

Romer's emphasis on the role of government represents a very considerable modification of free-market ideas in their pure form. Again, however, a notable emphasis in this extended passage is that it is ideas controlled by producers that lead to profits. Consideration of how profitability might be achieved by designing better products and services for customers as a primary strategy is lacking.

The National System

Almost seventy years after Adam Smith published The Wealth of Nations, a German economist, Friedrich List, (1789–1846), completed his own major work, The National System of Political Economy, published in stages between 1841–4. List has remained little known in the English-speaking world, but his concepts have had continuing influence in his native Germany and continental Europe, subsequently percolating through to Japan and East Asia.

As a civil servant in the German state of Würtemburg, advocacy of reforms brought him into conflict with an authoritarian government and led to exile in the United States in 1825.

There he edited a German language newspaper, became an American citizen and eventually returned to Germany in 1834.

He was strongly influenced by observing the effects of British industrialization and its growing competitive power on Germany, which made it difficult for German manufacturers to compete from a position of comparative technical backwardness. List regarded the advocacy of free trade by British politicians as a means of ensuring continued economic expansion and political dominance.

List had two primary objections to Smith's ideas. Smith's focus on the individual led to a concept of the economy and society based on the principles of laissez-faire, with state intervention reduced to a minimum. Secondly,

List thought Smith's emphasis on the division of labour neglected wider questions of the levels of skill and motivation necessary in manufacture.

In contrast, by the mid-1820s, List (1827/1996) elaborated an alternative view emphasising the role of nation states as the social organization within which individuals functioned. Instead of the division of labour, he proposed the concept of "productive power," an umbrella term for the "deeper lying causes" that explain how a nation sustains its ability to produce in the context of a broader social concept of how economic wealth was created. This in turn led him to advocate a concept of the nation state actively intervening to ensure that productive powers were consistently developed and maintained for the benefit of the nation as a whole, which to some extent anticipates Romer's concept of government subvention of idea generation (CIO Insight, 2003).

He believed that only the nation state exercised effective political and economic power (List, Ingersoll, Liebig, & Larouche, 1827/1996). "The object of the economy of this body," meaning the nation state, "is not only wealth as in individual and cosmopolitical economy, but power and wealth, because national wealth is increased and secured by national power, as national power is increased and secured by national wealth. Its leading principles are therefore not only economical, but political too" (p. 31).

There was also a dimension of moral objection in List's critique of Smith's ideas. In addition to the separation of economic from social behaviour, List objected to the manner in which the concept of the division of labour led to a debasement of work. Instead he regarded skill and competence as essential in understanding economic achievement, and he anticipated on a national level the contemporary concept of intellectual capital to a remarkable degree. By 1827, he wrote of productive power essentially constituted by "the intellectual and social conditions of the individuals, which I call capital of mind" (List et al., 1827/1996, p. 63).

> The present state of the nations is the result of the accumulation of all discoveries, inventions, improvements, perfections, and exertions of all generations which have lived before us; they form the mental capital of the present human race, and every separate nation is productive only in the proportion in which it has known how to appropriate these attainments of former generations and to increase them by its own acquirements...
> (List, 1827/1966, p. 140)

This broader concept of productive powers, the mental capital of a nation, is generated not only by those who create value in exchange, but also "the instructors of youths and of adults, virtuosos, musicians, physicians, judges, and administrators" (List, 1827/1966, p. 140) who are also responsible for creating productive powers.

In addition, the influence on List of his period of residence in the United States as a political refugee cannot be ignored. He was strongly influenced by what he learned of ideas and efforts to protect the nascent industries of the young republic, particularly the work of Alexander Hamilton.

As early as 1783, Hamilton argued against free trade, advocating that the new republic should regulate imports, so that "injurious branches of commerce might be discouraged, favourable branches encouraged, [and] useful products and manufactures promoted" (Chernow, 2004, p. 183). Later, in a Report on Manufactures commissioned by the U.S. Congress and submitted in December, 1791, Hamilton, by this time Secretary of the Treasury in President Washington's administration, again recommended the promotion of manufacturing in the United States in much greater detail.

List (1827/1996) supported such ideas, arguing that each nation should seek to develop its productive powers in ways appropriate to its specific circumstances. He realized the changes wrought by industrialization meant that material resources, the capital of nature, were increasingly of less importance than the capital of mind in transforming those resources through invention. He saw this as a double-edged sword, capable of decimating existing industry if allowed to proliferate unchecked, but also of enhancing national productive power if carefully adapted by means of a protective national policy.

> By securing the home market to home manufacturers, not only the manufacturing power for the supply of our wants is for all times secured against foreign changes and events, but an ascendancy is thereby given to our manufacturing powers in competition with others, who do not enjoy this advantage in their own country. (List et al., 1827/1996, p. 103)

Above all, List argued that, in principle, an economy based on division of labour must also be socially divisive. In contrast, the concept of a national economy encompassed not only a division of commercial functions between individuals but also the union of powers in a common cause. Industry, society and culture were therefore viewed as indissolubly linked in List's vision of what an industrialized country could achieve. If not only protected but actively promoted by national policies, a beneficent cycle of improvement could lead to a constant enhancement of the achievements and potential of a country.

> In the manufacturing State the industry of the masses is enlightened by science, and the sciences and arts are supported by the industry of the masses. There scarcely exists a manufacturing business which has not relations to physics, mechanics, chemistry, mathematics, or to the art of design &c. No progress, no new discoveries and inventions, can be made in these sciences by which a hundred industries and processes could not be improved or altered. (List, 1841–4/1966, p. 145)

Unlike Karl Marx, List did not advocate the replacement of capitalist society. He regarded competition within an economy as a vital necessity for its effective functioning, but argued that the industries of some countries needed protection until they could compete internationally on equal footing. In short, he was suggesting an alternative way in which capitalism could function, with countries such as Japan, South Korea and Taiwan providing compelling illustrations.

Design from the standpoint of economic theory

The greatest problem in considering what economic theory explains about design, specifically or by implication, is in the context of Neo-Classicism, which in the Anglo-American world dominates both academic theory and applied economic practice. Neo-Classicism explains what exists and is not fundamentally concerned with what might be. Widespread criticism of it focuses on assumptions about the static nature of products and markets. If they are as constant as depicted in Neo-Classical theory, this at best reduces design to a trivial activity concerned with minor, superficial differentiation of unchanging commodities—a role, indeed, that it does frequently perform. At worst, it contradicts the whole validity of design.

In contrast, a central assumption of design practice is that it is innately concerned with change: designers' concepts become the products, communications, environments and systems of the future. Design, in other words, is about envisioning change.

An obsession with short-term financial profitability at the expense of on-going product and service development is also a consequence of Neo-Classical theory, with disastrous results evident in the current financial crisis. When General Motors went to plead for bail-out funds from the American Congress on December 5th, 2008, Micheline Maynard (2008) writing in the New York Times commented:

> G.M.'s biggest failing, reflected in a clear pattern over recent decades, has been its inability to strike a balance between those inside the company who pushed for innovation ahead of the curve, and the finance executives who worried more about returns on investment.

As soon as the possibility of change, development and innovation are admitted into economic models, however, the perspective shifts and it becomes much easier to relate design to economic theories. For example, the holistic nature of Friedrich List's (1841–4/1966) concepts of the role of state policy in promoting productive powers specifically acknowledges "the art of design" as one of the factors capable of profound influence in improving the manufacturing industry. The evolution of this idea has informed German industry and has been an integral element in its remarkably resilient performance despite political traumas and devastating military defeats.

The continuity of List's ideas was apparent in the early years of the twentieth century in the work of a liberal politician, Friedrich Naumann, who frequently wrote about the need to harness the potential of mechanization and to create new forms expressing the spirit of the time. In a book, Neudeutsche Wirtschaftspolitik, (New German Economic Policy) published in 1907, Naumann elaborated these ideas. In reviewing the book, Anton Jaumann (1907) observed that Germany's competitive position was characterized by possession of few natural resources and dependence on imports of raw materials that had to be paid for by manufactured exports. How could it then survive the intense levels of international competition?

> We must bring goods to the market that only we can manufacture. We cannot in the long run compete in cheap mass-production. Only quality is our deliverance. If we are able to deliver such excellent goods that can be imitated by no other people in the world and if these goods are so excellent that everyone wishes to buy them, then we have a winning hand. (Jaumann, 1907, p. 338)

Nothing, concluded Jaumann, injured the commercial reputation of a nation as much as the label, "cheap and nasty." Many countries have faced this problem, the latest being China, which is looking to generate an image of their products based on design and innovation.

The example of Germany also played a very important part in the modernization of Japan, where individualism has similarly played a less prominent role in the country's economic progress. There too, the role of state policy in initially establishing design competences and encouraging their application in Japanese industry and commerce has been a remarkable example of how, indeed, a government can encourage the development of productive powers. In the mid-1950s, there existed virtually no formally trained professional designers in Japan. As the result of policies introduced by the Ministry of International Trade and Industry (MITI), it was estimated that the country had 21,000 industrial designers alone by 1992. Their development has been an integral part of the success of Japanese products in international markets in the intervening period. Policies based on the Japanese model were also introduced in Korea and Taiwan and similarly have played an important role in their economic growth.

If List's (1841–4/1966) ideas have been important on a macro-economic level, other schools of theory also have implications for design in micro-economic terms. In this respect, the dynamic view of entrepreneurialism and change advocated by adherents of the Austrian school is particularly valuable. As Lachman (1976) points out, "All economic action is of course concerned with the future, the more or less distant future. But the future is to all of us unknowable, though not unimaginable" (p. 55). Designers also constantly face risk in the challenge of imagining what is as yet unknowable. Although generally silent about design in specific terms, the ideas of the Austrian school reverberate with implications that potentially open up a broader understanding of what the economic role of design can be.

Institutional theory also provides a contextual richness that similarly offers opportunities for a reconsideration of design's functions, raising important questions on the role of design in society, as generator of the specific forms of a culture, and the institutions that frame its practice. More specifically, theories such as Coase's (1998) on transaction costs offer enormous possibilities for discussion of how in such fields as information and communications, the role of design can powerfully enhance competitiveness.

New Growth Theory's inclusion of knowledge, both coded and tacit, as a factor in understanding how business can function also has intriguing possibilities. Of especial value is the argument that technological knowledge has built-in value based on its capacity to derive innovative ideas from practice. A question now raised is whether, or to what degree, design can be incorporated into this concept of knowledge. To some degree knowledge of technological options can open the door to designs contributing to the process of generating innovative ideas. Innovative ideas, of course, are by no means the sole perquisite of designers, but whatever the source, all will need translating into tangible form or definable process in terms acceptable to users, which is the particular skill and contribution of design—its role can be summarized as humanizing technology. There is no significant consideration of these factors in New Growth Theory which, for all its insights, remains embedded in the context of production. In that context, three clear areas of concern for designers can be stipulated:

- Their work must be capable through innovation on multiple levels of contributing to creating new economic value for a firm;
- Given the crucial role assigned to technology in New Growth Theory, an ability to understand technological opportunity and act upon it is required, otherwise designers remain visualisers of other's ideas or incremental improvers of existing products;
- They must function within institutional structures of various kinds that enable and constrain their endeavours. In other words, they are not independent spirits, but dependent on the view of design held by management or the cultural imperatives of an organization.

Nathan Rosenberg (1982), in examining the problems of technological innovation, points to "a frequent preoccupation with what is technologically spectacular rather than economically significant..." (p. 62) A parallel observation is possible about some problems of design innovation; in this case the preoccupation being with what is visually spectacular rather than economically significant.

The third strand of economic theory, institutional structures, impinges upon design in innumerable ways, even when design is not specifically considered as an element in their workings. For example, laws, such as those in the U.S. on product liability, or those in Germany on recycling packaging materials, or European legislation on recycling electrical and electronic products, profoundly affect design practice. Other factors, including the general cultural climate of a society, the way design is manifested in public and private institutions, whether and how design is taught at all levels of the educational system, and the immediate context of the firms in which or for which designers work, are just a few of the institutional influences that merit close consideration.

Specific attempts to explain design in an economic context have generally sought to justify it in terms of the numerical, quantitative values that dominate business processes. Since the main arena of activity for designers is the firm, however, a major emphasis in discussing the role of design needs to be at the microeconomic level and encompass a greater degree of qualitative factors. A consideration of the functions and processes at the level of the firm could reveal substantial contributions of design to innovation not generally considered in any economic theory.

A further level at which design research could be capable of articulating a role for design not currently articulated in any depth in economic theory is the context of use, of the role played by products, communications, environments, services and systems in the lives of people beyond the point at which most economic theory halts: the point-of-sale. It is in understanding this arena and its human problems, potential and challenges that design is of crucial significance in introducing change that is both meaningful in people's lives and simultaneously capable of creating sources of competitiveness for firms.

In other words, the next stage of work needs to elaborate concepts of economics through the prism of design theory and practice.

References

1   Anonymous (1996, September 28). Making waves: Is information technology different from earlier innovations? *The Economist*, 340 (7985), S7–S9.

2   Arthur, W. B. (1996, July-August). Increasing returns and the new world of business. Harvard Business Review, 74(4), 100–9.

3   Chernow, R. (2004). Alexander Hamilton. New York: The Penguin Press.

4   CIO Insight (2003, Febuary). Expert voice: Paul Romer on the new economy. CIO Insight, 1(23), 28.

5   Coase, R. (1998). The new institutional economics. The American Economic Review, 88(2), 72–4.

6   David, P. A. (1993). Knowledge, Property and the System Dynamics of Technological Change. In L. Summers & S. Shah (Eds.), *Proceedings of the World Bank Annual Conference on Development Economics 1992* (pp. 215–48). Washington, DC: International Bank for Reconstruction and Development.

7   Demsetz, H. (1977). The firm in economic theory: A quiet revolution. *The American Economic Review*, 87(2), 426–9.

8   Demsetz, H. (1997). The primacy of economics: An explanation of the comparative success of economics in the social sciences. *Economic Inquiry*, 35(1), 1–12.

9 Drucker, P. F. (1986). *Innovation and entrepreneurship: Practice and principles.* New York: Harper Row.

10 Friedman, M. (1962). *Capitalism and freedom.* Chicago: The University of Chicago Press.

11 Hayek, F. A. (1948). *Individualism and economic order.* Chicago: The University of Chicago Press.

12 *IPod.* (n.d.). Retrieved July 12, 2008, from http://en.wikipedia.org/wiki/IPod

13 Jaumann, A. (1907). Die Wirtschaftliche Bedeutung der Angewandte Kunst [The economic significance of German applied art]. *Innen-Dekoration, 18,* 338.

14 Klein, P., & Miller, E. (1996). Concepts of value, efficiency, and democracy in institutional economics. *Journal of Economic Issues,* 30(1), 267–77.

15 Lachmann, L. M. (1976). From Mises to Shackle: An essay on Austrian economics and the Kaleidic society. *Journal of Economic Literature,* 14(1), 54–62.

16 List, F. (1966). *The national system of political economy.* New York: Augustus M. Kelley.

17. List, F., Ingersoll, C. J., Liebig, M., & Larouche, L. H. (1996). *Outlines of American political economy in twelve letters to Charles J. Ingersoll.* Wiesbaden: Bottiger.

18. McCormick, K. (1997). An essay on the origin of the rational utility maximization hypothesis and a suggested modification. *Eastern Economic Journal,* 23(1), 17–30.

19. Menger, C. (1976). *Principles of economics.* (J. Dingwall & B. E. Hoselitz, Trans). New York: New York University Press. (Original work published 1871).

20 Micheline, M. (2008, December 6). At G.M., innovation sacrificed to profits. New York Times. p. B1.

21 Mises, L. von. (1949). *Human action: A treatise on economics.* San Francisco: Fox & Wilkes.

22 Nelson, R. H. (2001). *Economics as religion: From Samuelson to Chicago and beyond.* University Park, PA: The Pennsylvania University Press.

23 North, D. C. (1990). *Institutions, institutional change and economic performance.* Cambridge, MA: Cambridge University Press.

24 Polanyi, M. (1983). *The tacit dimension.* Gloucester, MA: Peter Smith.

25 Robinson, P. (1995, June). Paul Romer. *Forbes, 15,* 66–71.

26 Romer, P. M. (1992). Two strategies for economic development: Using ideas and producing ideas. In L. H. Summers (Ed.), *Proceedings of the World Bank Annual Conference on Development Economics* (pp. 63–92). Washington, DC: International Bank for Reconstruction and Development.

27 Rosenberg, N. (1982). Inside the black box: Technology and economics. New York: Cambridge University Press.

28 Schumpeter, J. A. (1942). *Capitalism, socialism and democracy.* New York: Harper.

29 Smith, A. (1937). *The wealth of nations.* New York: The Modern Library.

30 Simon, H. A. (1981). *The sciences of the artificial* (2nd ed.). Cambridge, MA: The MIT Press.

31 Veblen, T. (1990). *The instinct of workmanship and the state of the industrial arts*. New Brunswick, NJ: Transaction Publishers. (Original work published 1918).

32 Veblen, T. (1994). *The theory of the leisure class*. London: Penguin (Original work published 1899).

33 Wieser, F. von. (1891). The Austrian school and the theory of value. *Economic Journal, 1*, 108–21.

PART IV

Reflections

Notes on the Readings
in Parts IV and V

As indicated at the beginning of this book, the last four readings in many ways take up and echo the themes introduced in Part I (and in the introduction), though with the crucial difference that each represents a late reflection on these themes and on Heskett's own trajectory and work. This is especially true of reading #28, his last reflections on Hong Kong, and reading #29, 'On Writing', which complements and extends some of the biographical details given in the introduction.

But as suggested earlier, no-one who studies design can be satisfied with mere reflection. The question of practice, and thus of the future, looms perpetually and it does so here, particularly in the first of these reflections (#27) and in the very last text in the book, 'Can the Centre Hold?' (#30). The reflective stitching together of past, present and future, the project from which so much of Heskett's work began, seems a suitable way to round-out this volume.

27

Past, Present and Future in Design

How can we prepare to cope with what is not wholly apparent? Two immediate responses can be: an endless curiosity and openness to change, with the ability to retain as much flexibility as possible in thought and practice—in other words, a rapid response capability to new challenges; secondly, we can constantly seek to understand what is happening by tracing patterns from the past. The implications of these two responses are different. In any design organisation, the first is a practical objective that has managerial and organisational implications. The second is more philosophical in nature, although it also has practical implications. If it is a truism that the past never completely repeats itself, history nevertheless retains several virtues. It is the essential tool in explaining our present situation; it contains a fund of generic ideas about practice that illustrate some possibilities for emerging technologies; and it is also a valuable guide in understanding the nature and consequences of change and how to cope with it. If we examine the major stages through which design has evolved in the past, and particularly in the twentieth century, what signposts (and I stress the choice of term) are discernible about how it is likely to develop in the future. Predictions are inherently unreliable since the future has an awkward tendency to be different in fundamental respects from what we can today imagine. Hence the stress on signposts, a more indicative projection forward, together with the need for flexible adaptation to meet the unexpected. There is an innate paradox in basing concepts of the future on a study of the past. History is concerned with what is knowable and has the inestimable benefit of 20/20 hindsight, while prophecy expresses hopes and expectations about what is presently unknowable. Prediction easily become a projection of hopes and ideals, of what one wants to see happen. Despite such cautions,

First published as "Past, Present and Future in Design," *Design Indaba*, no. 4, 2003. By kind permission of Design Indaba.

however, the effort is vitally necessary. An inherent characteristic of design
is its innate concern with the future. Any designer, working in any situation
on any kind of project, is projecting concepts that become the tangible
reality of future daily life. Design without a sense of the future is therefore a
contradiction in terms. Yet design as we presently understand it, is also a
relatively recent concept. We need therefore to understand its origins and
influences. One of the confusions for any designer trying to explain their
contemporary and potential future role is the great diversity of how people
generally understand the term "design". The roots of this confusion go deep
into history and the pattern of evolution in the role of designers. Not only
have there been multiple changes through history in response to new
situations but the changes have not been sequential and end-on. In other
words, a new development does not entirely supplant the old, but becomes
layered upon it. The functions of the old may be diminished or marginalised,
but do not become entirely supplanted. Neither do the ideas associated with
them, which accounts in considerable measure for the confusion. For
example, there are still pockets of people living a hunting/gathering existence
and making objects from what is at hand in order to survive; rural,
agricultural communities based on craft traditions still exist; as do small
manufacturing workshops using hand work in serial production; in large
industries stylists are still common, while many consultant designers' work
has become global. Although I have never been to South Africa before I
would be most surprised if it is not possible to find multiple examples of this
kind of layering still in existence. Study of this diversity can yield some
important lessons in terms of generic patterns that still have often surprising
validity. For example, in rural craft practice it is typical that the objects used,
of all kinds, are traditional in nature, the expression of a community's
experience. Both makers and users understand this, and the emphasis is
therefore upon how objects can be adapted to the specific and particular
needs of users. In an age when we are again talking in design about
customisation, is there nothing we can learn from those generations of
practice? In another example, in the eighteenth century, the government of
King Louis XIV set out to make the French economy superior to all its
competitors by attracting the best craft talent in Europe and training the
most promising young people in their own country in design. The legacy
today is that France still has over 40% of the world's annual trade in luxury
goods. Is there no lesson here for modern governments in design policy?
There are, of course, also cautionary tales that can be drawn from the past.
The belief in the power of imagery that led to products in America developing
to a point where they lost contact with reality is one such—think of the
1950s automobiles with their fins and jet outlets that were unsafe and
uneconomic. The method used to design them, evolved by Harley Earl, who
became Vice-President for Styling for General Motors, remain for many
people the definitive forms of design practice: renderings rapidly provided
and defined the overall visual appearance of a proposed automobile, which,
once approved, would then be translated into full-sized clay models to work

out the final details before manufacturing specifications were drawn up. The interiors were an afterthought. In contrast, many independent consultant designers began to sound a warning about such procedures, most notably Donald Deskey, who in 1960 sounded a warning that overseas companies were taking a much more wide-ranging and long-range view of design and could deeply penetrate the American market. Large segments of American industry were subsequently decimated by imported products from countries such as Japan and Germany that paid greater attention to production quality with a more holistic approach to design. Some young contemporaries, however, did take up the ideas advocated by Deskey and Loewy with great intelligence. Richard Latham demonstrated the effectiveness of the concept of strategic design planning in consultant work over many years for several corporations, even to becoming a board member, including Rosenthal, Bang & Olufsen and Land's End. Jay Doblin, who began his career in Loewy's New York office, also developed methods to implement the concept in the practice he established in Chicago and in his teaching at the Institute of Design at Illinois Institute of Technology, that has the first post-graduate design course dedicated to design strategy and planning. The twentieth century therefore witnessed several important major changes in design and how it is practiced and regarded in. To what extent will these processes continue in the future? On one level, it may be that change will not be radical or substantial. For example, the design and production of an increasing number of consumer products is already diffused across much of the globe on the basis of standardised concepts of form and technology. As countries increasingly attempt to develop and modernize their economies, there will probably be a continued expansion of mass-production in China and its spread into new geographical regions, such as Eastern Europe and South America, together with efforts to use styling as a means of adding value to products. This will be particularly true of product sectors in which the concept of what a product is, and how it is made, remain relatively stable. For example, the concept of a vacuum cleaner or an electric iron has undergone little change since the introduction of electrical technology. Most electrical consumer products have in essence similarly changed little— basically they have become commodities. Where the production of such products is dependent primarily on cost and style factors there will probably be few changes in how design is used and an emphasis on adaptation to different geographical and cultural conditions. In the last two decades, however, it has also become increasingly clear that significant radical changes are taking place on many other levels: in technology, particular flexible manufacturing and information technology; in types of products; in markets; in the structure of business organisations. These are not incremental shifts, but powerful and often discontinuous changes of a fundamental and structural nature.

Given such patterns, there is clearly a need for new concepts and methods in design. The signs of change are too widespread. Sometimes they are manifest in a disjunction, as when old products begin to creak under the burden of new technology. Intractable problems are caused when extra functions are loaded on to existing products, without the consequences of the extension being fully understood. Telephones, for example, were originally a simple, monofunctional instrument, for the purposes of speaking and listening to another person at a distance. Today, in the revised form of cellphones they are becoming loaded with multiple functions—memories, message functions, answering facilities, redialing, and now cameras. Many of these functions are obscure and difficult to operate, requiring pages of explanations in booklets that purport to be instructional but are simply just confusing. Yet many manufacturers and designers still persist in treating telephones as a styling problem, ignoring the desperate need to reconsider and redesign them and how they are used as a complex interface problem, and as an element of a system. The role of designers similarly shifts: from visual form-giver seeking individual expression and differentiation, to designer as enabler—designing flexible systems on the basis of complex technologies that can be controlled by and adapted to user needs. Mass production and styling generated product concepts intended to be the final form in which they were used. A toaster, a radio, or an automobile were designed as a complete entity, to be used as defined and designed by the producer. In contrast, the products of modern digital technologies, for example, the laptops in widespread use today, are flexibly adaptable to users. This signals a changing emphasis: from visibility—differentiation through visual appearance—to usability, in terms defined by users. The key to this argument is the fact of complexity in many modern technologies and products. When a situation becomes complex, a single solution is unlikely to be relevant to more than a tiny proportion of potential users. The reverse side of complexity must therefore be flexibility in response: allowing users to adapt designs to their own purposes.

Many products using new technology have never made this conceptual leap to "user-centeredness"—a classic example being video tape recorder. The innate problems in operating them in terms appropriate to the flexible potential of the technology have still not been adequately addressed by designers and manufacturers. Another identifiable shift is towards the "dematerialization of products," as they merge into other structures, such as Automated Teller Machines (ATMs). These are generally integrated into buildings to provide a constant service in providing cash dispensing and other banking functions. The key to such products is the way they give access to a wider system. Again, they have an enabling function, but it is not the physical configuration of these machines that is decisive, rather the user interface—how information and services contained in the system are made comprehensible, accessible, relevant and pleasing to users—qualities they seriously lack. A common thread in all this is the emergence of systems in various forms as one of the critical dimensions in which designers and, in particular, design planners, must think. Examples are the concepts of "platforms" as the basis for global product lines in automobiles or washing machines, or the need to coordinate information systems in banking and financial services. Whether conceived as a product or service system, the trend is in considerable measure away from a single product as the primary source of value, to defining systems as coherent wholes with individual items positioned as adaptable elements of them. This does not mean supplanting design skills in visual terms—they still remain vitally important in detailed execution, but they also have to be understood in a wider context. The greatest current challenge of new technology, however, is in the possibilities of innovation, through design, to bring out entirely new products that have the capacity to create markets—in combining, for example, computers, cable television and telecommunications, which also presents incredibly complex problems of interface design. Computers, whether used at work or home, have already evolved into a personal, interactive technology of often considerable complexity. What are the additional problems of adding to such a combined device the present capabilities of telephone, fax, answering machine, and a whole spectrum of audio, video, printing and photographic functions? Unless such problems are addressed, and these devices are thought of systemically, the burdens of operating VCRs will seem minute.

Remarkable developments are also possible in the applications of computer chips to products that will push the concept of flexible adaptation into new dimensions. What will the consequences be, for example, of putting a computer chip and fuzzy logic programming into a chair, so that it can automatically adapt to the size, weight and posture of any person sitting in it without prior programming? Or of putting a similar chip into sports shoes so they immediately reconfigure to whether their user is running, jumping, or standing still on a variety of surfaces—sand, stones, or tarmac? Success in these and in many other respects will hinge on designing applications being understandable and immediately usable for a wide range of purposes. Such changes are also affecting designers' tools and working procedures. Just as the delicate calligraphic skills of medieval manuscript scribes were made obsolete when embodied in slugs of lead type, leading to the new design skill of typography, so more recent design skills are rapidly being embodied into computer software that makes them cheaper and more widely accessible. New skills and methods of organisation are emerging to replace the old. Yet concepts of designing are not always compatible with these new developments—the habits of old procedures do not easily or gracefully adapt to new demands. Theories of the role and purpose of design are in fact being radically redefined, most notably through what is called "human-centered design." This applies concepts of flexible manufacturing and information technology across a broad spectrum of industrial and commercial activity to focus more specifically on, and rapidly adapt to, the needs of users. The most fundamental need, and the greatest problem, in this process of adaptation to change, however, is at the level of corporate design policy, which generally needs to be radically reshaped to meet new conditions. Three levels of change can be identified: strategic design,

design management, and design practice. If used as an integral element of future strategic planning, design can potentially contribute to every aspect of corporate activity, improving both internal organisation and market effectiveness. A total, integrated approach to design can create concepts and prototypes that combine products, communications, environments and systems in new and powerful combinations, capable of reshaping what a company, or major program, can be. The implementation of such ideas, however, requires the coordination at the highest level of how design functions in every aspect of a manufacturers' business. If designers are to be equipped to operate in these new and highly demanding ways, design education will need to be radically changed. Teaching design as a form of art, with an emphasis on visual skills in executing other people's idea, and approach that is already widely obsolete, can hardly be considered appropriate as a means of educating a new type of designer. We live in an age in which change is widespread and fundamental, and design, being innately concerned with the future, cannot be exempt from its consequences. Practitioners who fail to comprehend that they cannot claim to be agents of change in a complex future, without design itself being significantly changed, will rapidly be marginalised. The designers that survive will do so by rapidly and creatively exploiting new techniques and methods appropriate to new situations and challenges. The consequences are likely to be profound. To break out of this pattern, it will be necessary to support design practice with a defined body of theory and methodology. This is often anathema to designers educated to what can be called the romantic "cowboy" concept of their practice: designers as the embodiment of true individualism, close to the essence of things, and ever riding off into creative wide, open spaces to perform deeds of heroic originality. In such a schema, systematic thinking and creativity are seen as irreconcilable opposites. There is an alternative view, however, which is sustained by the fact that many disciplines capable of routinely encouraging high creativity require exactly such a structure of knowledge and methodology—mathematics and music, to give two widely divergent examples. Such a concept would enable the best of current ideas and practice in design to be codified, effectively communicated and constantly improved. Research is at the heart of such a development. It needs to function both in terms of extending the field, probing the boundaries of future possibilities for design and its connections to other disciplines, and of being constantly tested and refined to provide a core of methodologies—as a platform to sustain high-level creativity. That is the heart of the argument here. If design follows this path, there is hope we can begin to grapple with the size and complexity of the problems facing us that desperately need humane solutions. The alternative is to defiantly cling to the dwindling consolations of the role described by George Nelson, with caustic wit, of designers as "exotic menials." One final lesson from history: if designers don't adapt to the challenge of the new, other emerging disciplines will.

28

Reflections on Design
and Hong Kong

This article is being written in June 2010, at a time when my contract with the Hong Kong Polytechnic University is coming to an end and I will return to the United Kingdom after twenty-two years absence, 16 in the United States and the last six in Hong Kong. A new chapter in my life beckons.

I've been asked to give a critical overview of developments in the field of design during my time in Hong Kong, with recommendations about what might be worthy of attention for future development. I should point out that my acquaintance with Hong Kong is not restricted to my six years of full-time employment here, but has been an on-going relationship since 1982, with many activities in other Asian countries, including a ten-year stint as consultant to Hirano & Associates, a leading Japanese design firm.

All that lay in the future, however, when in mid-1982 I received an invitation from the Council for National Academic Awards (CNAA) to be one of a party of five people to spend two weeks assessing the first proposals for a degree course in design at Hong Kong Polytechnic, as it was then known. The CNAA was an organization established by the UK government to award degrees and monitor standards at all institutions outside the university sector.

After flying into Kai Tak Airport on a bright, sunlit November day, I went for a long walk around Tsim Sha Tsui to try and get the flight out of my system. Where Harbour City and Ocean Centre now stand were dockyards for cargo ships and fishing boats. The streets leading off were filled with shops and restaurants, with colourful signs in Chinese calligraphy hanging overhead, and everywhere, the hustle and bustle of people going about their business. I was badly jet-lagged, but surfed a wave of adrenalin and

First published as "The Last Chapter" in *Hong Kong Creative Ecologies*, ed. Kai-Yin Lo, Hong Kong Design Center/Hong Kong Trade Development Council, 2010, pp. 208–13. By permission of Hong Kong Design Center.

excitement, and, like many another new arrival, was utterly captivated by the energy and dynamism that enveloped me.

The following two weeks of the visit presented a marked contrast in experience, between formal meetings at what was then called the Swire School of Design to discuss the design degree course proposals, and the outside context of Hong Kong and Chinese culture. Superficially, the school had a structure and organization derived very closely from the British model, and a large majority of the teaching staff were British expatriates or British-educated Hong Kong Chinese. The degree course proposals were familiar in their structure, concepts and terminology, so a round of tours of facilities, meetings with teachers and administrators, dialogue and questioning developed that fell into a pattern we knew well. There was an impression, however, that this administrative structure modelled on colonial and military procedures went its own way detached from its context.

Evidence of difference lay in the large number of students drooped fast asleep over books in the library and the fact that studios were open late into the night. Many students came from poor families and were the first in their family to enter higher education. Visits to student's homes in early examples of Hong Kong's public housing blocks revealed the small-scale environment in which families lived, 25 square meters for a family of four, and the need for students to have access to some kind of alternative space. Yet what was impressive was that Hong Kong was clearly providing opportunities for a population that was avidly seizing the educational potential for its younger generation.

Visits to manufacturing plants provided opportunities for discussions with potential employers of the Swire School's graduates and in this case it was noticeable that many business people thought of design as, at best, a middle-level skill giving a final gloss to a product concept. There was a lot of good technological competency from OEM (original equipment manufacturing) producers, but no sense of design being an economic driver for Hong Kong businesses.

Other meetings were arranged with the heads of design consultancies, the most prominent of which were expatriates, whose work seemed to be mainly for the larger overseas-owned service businesses, such as HSBC and Cathay Pacific, which appreciated their skills more than local manufacturers.

At that time the frontier with China was firmly sealed, but a one-day trip across the border to Shenzhen was arranged that turned out to be a highly organized propaganda exercise by CITS (China International Travel Service), *the* Chinese government tourist bureau. It included a trip to a reservoir where it was pointed out that this was Hong Kong's water supply and was controlled by China; there was an exhibition of Socialist realist painting of cheerful banality; at a school children in Young Pioneer uniforms performed with well-practiced and devastating charm; and we ended with a walkabout in the centre of Shenzhen accompanied by a guide who explained how the government had recently designated this fishing village of some

10,000 souls as a new Special Economic Zone. I doubt if any of us visitors had the slightest idea of what this implied.

At the end of two weeks the degree course was duly approved and a new phase for the Swire School began. For me, the time had been packed with intense, new experiences that were the beginning of a complete fascination with Asian life, culture and history.

That initial encounter came at a time when the role of design in any serious sense had a limited application in the Hong Kong economy that was still dominated by OEM manufacturing activities—producing according to contractual specifications for multinational brands. The second phase of my relationship with Hong Kong covered the next twenty years, during which I recurrently revisited on a frequent basis to advise, consult and report in various capacities. This period covered the decision by the British government to hand back Hong Kong to China, the reaction in the run-up to the handover on July 1, 1997, and the first decade of Hong Kong being officially part of the PRC.

The decade up to the handover was one of considerable uncertainty. Many design teachers at the Polytechnic, or the Polytechnic University as it was renamed in 1994, as well as many other design practitioners working in the Hong Kong economy, left to find posts overseas or took steps to obtain overseas passports as a precaution against possible residence restrictions.

Across the border, however, there were even more startling changes as China's leader, Deng Xiaoping, opened up the economy to the world by stimulating an astonishing expansion of manufacturing industry and associated services.

Many people used to ask me whether Hong Kong had changed very much after its "take-over" by China. My reply was always to point out that in fact, much of the Pearl River Delta region had already been taken over by Hong Kong. The figures on the numbers of people in the delta employed in factories owned by Hong Kong capital were huge and an indication of a major shift of manufacturing activity from the former colony to the mainland. Many of these companies investing in the mainland, however, kept their headquarters and key functions located in Hong Kong itself, where its stability, legal system and lack of widespread corruption were strong attractions. Design was one of the functions that generally remained located in Hong Kong and provided services that were either not yet available on the mainland or if they were available were not yet of an adequate standard. Despite frequent complaints from Chinese clients that the fees of Hong Kong designers were too high, there was, in particular, a boom in work for industrial designers and interior designers, the latter servicing the huge expansion of hotels and public buildings in China.

Although the handover in 1997 marked a fundamental change in Hong Kong's status, the process that ensued was marked as much by continuities as by major alterations. Apart from superficial change in icons and some imagery, the impression was of a government and administration otherwise continuing in much the same way as during the colonial period. Perhaps avoiding fundamental shocks and keeping change to a minimal level was one way in which *it* was intended to reassure the population of Hong Kong that life would continue much as normal. The uncertainty that was endemic before the handover soon dissipated.

An immediate and widespread response to the new status was an increase in historical references. The history of China has a richness and depth that few cultures can match. One response in Hong Kong has been to lay claim to "Chineseness" by using forms derived from history for modern clothing, furniture and artefacts, although these are often superficial copies without any understanding in depth about why the historical models evolved as they did. It is easy to copy the form, say, of a Ming horseshoe chair, but when allowed to sit in an original in a friend's home, what struck me was the incredible comfort of it. The discipline of ergonomics had another three centuries before it emerged, but the Ming furniture makers instinctively understood how to make a piece of furniture fit the human body in ways that still elude many modern copyists. Simply adapting a past form without any real awareness of the impulses that motivated it leads to pastiche.

What is needed if the past is to have value is what I would instead term an act of homage. This requires a more sophisticated understanding of history and its relation to the present: rather than simply copying past forms it means seeking to understand the principles underlying the processes of how forms emerged in the past and the cultural role they have signified over time. Understanding these principles and up-dating them in ways appropriate to the present, rather than just blindly adopting western practices, would require a genuine respect for the past and a determination to continue practices that have innate value.

It has taken time for people to begin to widely reflect on what the relationship of Hong Kong to China and the rest of the world could be or might be. There have been many sentiments expressed about the "return to the Motherland," but what does this really mean? What does the history of China signify for Hong Kong, which grew into an international city in the context of colonial rule and a capitalist economy? China's recent decades, in contrast, had been steered by the Communist Party of China through events such as the Great Leap Forward and the Cultural Revolution, which wiped out any historical sympathy or sensibility in several generations of Chinese. Hong Kong's form of capitalism has been widely extolled as a shining example of *laissez-faire* economics, but *in* the processes of building the human capital, the skills, methods and processes needed for the future, something more is needed from government policy than a brand image for Hong Kong or a focus on so-called creative industries, which may add some new texture to the city, but does not represent major economic development.

Culture is never static, but continually grows and evolves under the impact of both internal and external changes. Hong Kong's greatest challenges in the immediate future, it seems to me are twofold- The first is internal, to strengthen the identity and facilities of the city through projects that have a purpose beyond commercial profit; the second concerns the economic role of Hong Kong in the Pearl River Delta region.

On the first, internal, level I would make a comparison with a small country such as Denmark, which like Hong Kong has a similarly small population and lack of resources other than its people. Despite that, Denmark has built an enviable reputation for *the* role design plays in all aspects of life, economic, political, social and cultural. *The roots of the country's splendid design achievements are explained in terms of democratic principles and humanistic philosophy. Simply put, the Danes believe that society exists to benefit and engage everyone in it and design is a key tool in how government and society functions. Long-term planning is an* important element of the Danish approach.

It is difficult to point to similar vision and policies in Hong Kong. There is hope, however, that the West Kowloon Cultural District project provides an opportunity for a magnificent extension of the city on a prime harbour-front. An experienced and talented team is being assembled to tackle the challenge and complexity of this project, which will require a deep involvement in a guiding vision, not only from politicians, but the population as a whole. It could be a dramatic foundation stone for a new concept of design in public and social life.

In terms of the external context, economically, the future of Hong Kong needs to extend beyond the confines of the Special Administrative Region. The Pearl River Delta offers another potential new vision of stunning magnitude. It seems that the PRD is morphing into a huge interconnected region with a population of over 100 million people, comparable in size to Germany and Japan, and with a range of businesses and technologies that truly make it "the workshop of the world" for our age. The needs of the region are manifold, but among them is a profound need for businesses to shift away from thinking of design as a late decorative addition or as styling, to a level of thinking of design as a strategic tool, defining new scenarios and instead of copying what is already on the market, providing new products and services that people never knew they wanted or thought they could have. Hong Kong could be an engine of growth for the PRD, bringing entrepreneurial knowledge and advanced design methods and skills from around the world to bear on the immense potential represented by the delta region.

Hong Kong still has an edge in design capabilities over the mainland, but it would be foolish to assume that its leadership will not come under severe threat in the near future. If one examines the economic trajectory of Japan, Taiwan, Korea, and now China, there has been a top-down process of stimulating the growth of the necessary human capital to provide for the needs of the future. I think back to that first visit to the fishing village of Shenzhen in 1982 and compare it with what I see now—Shenzhen as the UNESCO World City of Design, 2009. The biggest question of all, for me, is whether Hong Kong's *laissez-faire* approach will be adequate to withstand the competitive threats it will face in the near future from its hinterland. Perhaps Hong Kong will only truly be reunited with the Motherland when it plays a dynamic role in the new reality discernible in the Pearl River Delta. That is not the end of the story, however, for beyond the PRD is the whole of China and Asia. It has been remarked by many commentators that Asia has survived the "financial tsunami" of recent years better than Europe or the Americas, and this is seen as a resurgence of economic strength in the region as a whole. Asia, I believe, is returning to the position it occupied for a thousand years before the Industrial Revolution of the mid-eighteenth century, as the technological and cultural hub of the world. If Hong Kong has the vision, there is huge opportunity beckoning on every level of activity and many more new chapters to be written.

29

On Writing

In accepting an invitation to speak at a conference, there is always a danger of letting oneself in for something that isn't quite what one originally imagined it to be. The brief for this session refers to "imagining and anticipating the audience, including finding the right information structure, tone and references." Well, I don't really have a clear answer to any of those points. This isn't an attempt to be belligerent, because all the things described there are important and require consideration. Its simply that the process of thinking about this presentation has involved me in considerable reflection on my experience of writing about design, and my reasons for doing so, and I realize it doesn't conveniently fit the neat structure of that description, its much more messy and ill-organized.

To begin with, I want to express my belief at the outset that no-one can write, just as no-one can design, without some sense of personal commitment and satisfaction. Not that what I write is in any way "art," in which my own criteria are paramount and it doesn't really matter what anyone else thinks. It does matter, and it matters profoundly, but there isn't a process that can be conveniently laid out. While I can also think of more objective justifications, the essential spring lies in my own experience and my drive in writing is intensely personal. Explaining this therefore requires a substantial component of autobiography.

The English educational system through which I progressed was reformed in 1944, just after I entered it. It divided children into two streams at the age of eleven on the basis of a range of examinations, thus opening the system to children's ability rather than parent's ability to pay, although the concept remained profoundly hierarchical. The top twenty percent or so went into grammar schools, which opened the route to university, college or entry into a profession; the other eighty percent were destined to be hewers and toilers.

A presentation given to the American Center for Design, Design History Conference, March 3rd, 1995. Previously unpublished.

I did well enough in the examinations to be sent to a grammar school, but had a rocky career. To some extent, this was due to coming from a poor family with no track record of education at this level and therefore not party to all the accepted assumptions of what was required. So I floundered. My other difficulty was that the grammar school emphasized traditional academic virtues, and it was assumed that any interest, or competence in, practical subjects such as art or metalwork, could only be a compensation for a lack of academic ability. It turned out eventually that I was good at both. This created problems: not only was I the scruffy kid from the projects but was challenging the accepted conventions of the system. When eventually I expressed a desire to go on to a college of art and design, the pressure from both school and family was intense. The arguments ran along these lines: if you go to art school, the only thing you can do to earn a living is commercial art (as it was then widely termed;) commercial art is not very well paid and is unstable as a career. There were also overtones, never exactly expressed, that it was an activity with a somewhat disreputable aura. The alternative pressure, the only sensible thing to do it was suggested, was to go to university, which everyone agreed opened the door to a well-paid, respectable career.

There was no discussion of personal fulfillment; that was a wild fancy considered irrelevant to the practical business of "getting on in the world."

So I eventually went to university on a full scholarship, to the London School of Economics, and studied economics, politics, philosophy and history, which I have to say was a marvelous experience and I have absolutely no regrets about the choice.

In my final year I specialized in economic geography, which included a component on the development and use of maps and diagrams that briefly gave me some indulgence in visual form that I really enjoyed. After graduating, this specialism led to a job in what was then called Town and Country Planning for a regional government authority. All new building development had to be approved by the authority, and I wanted to help create a better physical environment. After two years I left, however, finding that the work was really concerned with bureaucratic administration and local politics rather than any creative possibility.

After several temporary jobs, teaching as a stop-gap, I went to Australia and continued to teach in secondary schools – I was beginning to enjoy it on the basis of greater competence. After three years Down Under, I took a ship to India and spent three months travelling overland back to Europe. The visual impact of the countries and civilizations through which I travelled was profound.

So at the age of thirty I found myself back in England, looking for a job and not really knowing what to do. Life so far had been a crab-like progression, accumulating an interesting ragbag of experiences, but without discernible pattern. My dilemma was solved by a tiny advertisement, one inch high and one column wide, in an education journal, for someone to teach the social and economic background to art and design at what was then Coventry Polytechnic, now the University of Coventry. Reading it was one of those decisive moments of instinctive recognition that shape a life. I didn't quite know what it meant, but I knew with absolute certainty that it was for me. All I had to do was get the job, which, fortunately, I eventually did. That was twenty-seven years ago, and I have never wanted to work in any other context.

At this time, in 1967, all students on courses in design were required to study the History of Art, a provision inserted into degree regulations largely at the urging of Nikolaus Pevsner. He believed design education was low-level, in which he was largely right, but wrongly believed the compensation for the defect could be found in compulsory History of Art. The creation of my post at Coventry was the result of pressure by an enlightened Head of Design, by name of Giles Talbot-Kelly, who believed that something more than art history was necessary for design students, and with his encouragement, I soon began to argue that the social and economic background was manifested in designed artefacts, and so the possibility of design having its own theory and history. In 1970, Coventry held what I believe was the first conference on Design History anywhere, a small event of about twenty people but the start of a growing network in Britain.

For ten years, I worked at developing courses in design history and theory and also began to undertake research into design in Germany. Various people suggested my work should be published, but here another problem cropped up, that was also personal. I have always loved books and from an early age have been an avid reader, but the influence of school, with a heavy emphasis on the formalities of English grammar that I found a constant torture, created a real block and a belief that writing in any sustained sense was something beyond me. Of course, I wrote a lot of material for both personal and professional purposes, but always hesitantly, with a sense of inadequacy.

In 1977, however, an acquaintance who was on the editorial board of History Workshop, a journal with a very strong reputation, asked me to write an article that reviewed available work on German art and design in the Third Reich. I was pleased, since it was a very good journal, but also highly apprehensive at the prospect of revealing my incompetence in writing to the world.

History Workshop described itself as a journal of socialist history, and in keeping with its emphasis all articles were reviewed by a large group called the editorial collective. In terms of the brief for this session, however, there was no "imagining and anticipating the audience," rather I cringed from them. Preparing a paper to be submitted to this gathering of left-wing academic demi-gods was a long and painful process. Their reactions to my draft varied: one person, I recall, indignantly demanded to know why this subject was being considered at all, commenting, "The next thing I suppose is that we will be asked to take Afrikaner poetry seriously." More importantly, however, some very good historians for whom I had the utmost regard wrote supportive comments, saying it opened up discussion on a hitherto ignored subject, and making good suggestions for improving the article, which was accepted in revised form. When the issue containing my article in print arrived, it was a great moment. My first-born! But essentially, I was a parent who didn't know the facts of life.

The next major step came soon after, when the publishers Thames and Hudson wrote saying they wanted to add a book on the history of industrial design to their World of Art series, several people had recommended me, and would I be interested, etc. The idea of writing a book, a whole book, was simultaneously deliriously exciting and as frightening as hell. I had some misgivings about it being for an art series, but on the other hand, I'd long bemoaned the lack of a basic text for my students and the book would be inexpensive and widely available. The basic fact, however, was that here was one of the leading publishers in the field knocking unbidden at my door and there was no way I could turn them down. After talking and submitting a proposal, I signed a contract to deliver a text in ten months.

Thames and Hudson stipulated that the book should be both "academically respectable and accessible to a general audience." I later realized this specification was useless, but in fact wasted a huge amount of time trying to wrap my mind around it in order to get some idea of what the book should be, and what approach to adopt. Six months later, I was utterly disoriented and crazy with frustration, with no text and no idea of what to do. At a low point of desperation, however, I grasped at a straw: my audience was not some amorphous academic community or the equally vague general public, but very simply, my students. The sense of a real audience that I knew was a real breakthrough. The words began to roll, the book was basically written in four months, and the text was delivered on time. Another discovery in that process was the serendipitous nature of writing, something that remains a constant pleasure. As I got deeper into the material, new levels of understanding would explode in my mind as disparate ideas fused in new and fascinating combinations.

Thames and Hudson were pleased with the manuscript and I went off to London to meet the editors, very pleased with myself. A boozy lunch and lots of praise went to my head, and it was a jolt when in the afternoon I was delivered to a lady named Ann Coffelt, who was to be my sub-editor. She brought me down to earth with a mighty thump, making it very clear how much work there was still to do before publication. I returned home both chastened and hung over.

The sub-editing process at Thames and Hudson, however, is the point that I believe turned me into a writer. Ann Coffelt had a marvelous capacity to bring out abilities and insights that I suppose were dormant but had never seen the light of day, continually nudging me towards a level of expression that I could subsequently look at and sometimes wonder, "Is this really me." I got a lousy percentage from Thames and

Hudson for the book and have never earned very much from it, but have no regrets because what the experience taught was beyond price. I learnt an enormous amount in a short time about the craft of writing, of how to read critically and continually look for improvement in detail. I finally began to abandon my inhibitions and to really enjoy writing. It didn't become easy, it has never been that, but as earlier with teaching, confidence came with experience.

The most important lessons for me in these early stages, therefore, emerged from the processes of review and comment, of learning to take criticism as a possibility for improvement, which has continued to be a major theme of my work. Another example came last year when writing an essay on German design in the inter-war period for an inaugural publication of the Wolfsonian Museum in Miami Beach. I was under pressure, both personally and professionally at the time, and dashed off a text at great speed, that was delivered late. It was returned by Wendy Caplan, a curator at the museum and editor of the book, with a series of comments that took my text to pieces, accompanied by a covering letter, stating forthrightly that she knew I was capable of much better and wouldn't settle for anything but my best. It isn't always easy to take criticism, and some people give criticism in a manner that is difficult to accept. Wendy not only pointed out the real weaknesses in what I had written but phrased her devastating critique in a way that showed real sensitivity and made it easy to accept. The revised piece is good, I think, but wouldn't have been so without the tough critique of a really good editor.

Someone once wrote: "Criticism should be a divining rod for the discovery of hidden riches, not a birch rod for the castigation of offenders." Which is exactly right. The essential act of writing is a very individual, isolated activity, but the work that gives me most satisfaction has emerged from this process of review and comment.

The publication of Industrial Design in 1980 was also important in that it opened up all kinds of other opportunities for writing. There were many other lessons to be learnt. Getting involved on a more journalistic level, for example, with all the pressures for punchy lines and compressed arguments, called for a very different approach from writing books. The difference is somewhat parallel to that between working on a two-hour full-length movie for the big screen, and a one-minute commercial for television. Both have to tell a story, but in very different ways. Writing a column for ID magazine opened up another approach, with great emphasis on a personal point of view that had to be expressed and argued in 2000 words. Writing for journals in Japan, Germany, England or America each require a shift in cultural perspective and subtle adaptations to how and what one writes. Writing a review means putting into practice all that I've said earlier about the role of criticism.

Each form has distinct requirements that demand flexibility and adaptation. I can't give you the rules for each, however, because any piece of writing for me is a reiterative process of accumulating large amounts of information, of preliminary idea or statement, consideration, revision and reformulation, occasionally becoming complete transformation and starting all over again. Its hard, lonely work and no one else can do it for you, but modern technology is an important ally. In this process of groping towards the expression of an idea that makes sense, I repeatedly call down a litany of blessings on all who invented the Macintosh and made it easy for me to adjust, correct, "Save As" and cut and paste, all without the overflowing waste-paper baskets of my early efforts.

What does it all add up to? Throughout some seventeen years of writing in many formats there has been a common thread. Looking back, I realize that the rigid division of "academic" and "art" in my early education also divided me personally, making it difficult to achieve the integration that is such an important key to development. Asserting the vital role of design in all our lives can be justified from the point-of-view of social relevance, but once again, bridging that gap in both my life and work, is immensely important in personal terms.

This personal satisfaction, however, has to be balanced by an awareness of the possible effect of what is written. Occasionally, young people have told me that reading something of mine has given them a sense of purpose in following their desire to be a designer, which on one level is very gratifying. For example, a Taiwanese graduate student at the Institute of Design recently told me he decided to switch to design from engineering after reading Industrial Design. Yet if one's work can have that effect, it also imposes a huge responsibility, especially in an age as rapidly changing as ours, to continually monitor the accuracy or veracity of what one is writing.

Is there any advice I can give that might help aspirants in the audience? Simply this. If you have a burning point of view about something, anything: write; your head of department hates you: write; ten editors have rejected your previous efforts: write; your significant other is smoldering with resentment at being ignored: write. There are useful rules and tools that can be quickly learnt, but nothing can substitute for a sense of conviction in what you do. If you have the commitment and persistence, sooner or later, ideas and words will shape themselves in ways that not only express what you want to say, but will enlarge and enhance it.

An English acquaintance recently visited me in Chicago after stopping over for meetings in New York. When asked there about her next stop and mentioning visiting John Heskett, she told me a frequent reply was, "Oh, the writer." Her story took me aback, although to be honest, it was very flattering. It delights me because I also carry the memory of what was written long ago on one of my school reports: "He has some good ideas, but suffers from a poverty of expression." Maybe you will understand my belief that achievement in life is possible despite one's education.

PART V

Last Words

30

Can the Center Hold?

In being asked to write an article for the INDEX: anthology I find myself reflecting on the fact that my next birthday will be my 75th and as I grow older my conviction that the world needs radical change becomes more intense. It seems to me a matter of urgency that we, and by that I mean every living, conscious human being on the planet, recognize that we are engulfed in a huge, growing crisis on multiple levels that will not be easily resolved. In addition to a series of recent natural disasters of uncommon destructiveness, we have to cope, among other things, with widespread economic collapse, a distrust of politicians and political systems, insurrections and riots, civil wars and fundamentalism of many varieties, a flood of weaponry swilling around the world, and dwindling resources to meet the needs of an ageing population. By any standards, these are troubling times.

Surrounded by the bombardment of bad news that is the staple fare of the media, I think often of some frequently quoted lines from a poem, *The Second Coming,* by the Irish poet William Butler Yeats that remain powerfully appropriate to our situation:

Things fall apart; the centre cannot hold;
Mere anarchy is loosed upon the world,
The blood-dimmed tide is loosed, and everywhere
The ceremony of innocence is drowned;
The best lack all conviction, while the worst
Are full of passionate intensity.

It is difficult to maintain a positive stance in the face of all the daunting obstacles that lie ahead, but perhaps the worst dangers are those of feeling helpless and negative about our capacity, not just to survive, but to achieve a life for a greater number of people of sustainable well-being—a phrase coined by colleagues at the TU Delft.

"Can the Centre Hold," *Index*, Denmark, 2010. By permission of Index.

After a lifetime working in the field of design, I am still convinced of its enormous power to beneficially reshape the world of artifice we have created and inhabit. I've written elsewhere of my belief that design is a unique characteristic of what defines us as human beings, enabling us to create a world of artifice to meet our needs and give meaning to our lives. It therefore has a long evolution, going deep into the prehistory of humanity, but gradually emerging with an enhanced capacity to create tools and weapons, shelter and apparel, items for storage and transportation. Design, defined in these general terms has moved through many stages since the emergence of homo sapiens, but has been integral to the major stages through which modern life has emerged, such as: nomadism, rural settlement, early urbanization and craft industry, mercantile economies, mechanical industry, electrical industry, and, in our time, electronic industry. In each phase a new paradigm for design has emerged and, I would argue, a new phase is emerging now. Throughout all these phases, the levels of creative genius apparent in objects and structures of all kinds should be a continuing source of profound inspiration for us in the tasks that lie ahead.

This power of design, however, is neither unconditional nor universal. In suggesting that design is one of the major instruments available to us, I do not want to suggest that it is some kind of absolute or universal fix for all the difficulties confronting us. Entangled in the beliefs and practices of design are many convenient assumptions that need to be questioned and redefined. In much of design education, the educators who should be pioneering new models for their students' future are locked into mindsets that suggest they have still to come to terms with the nature of the dramatic shifts underway in our time.

Emphasizing the evolution of a personal style, of the individualistic emphasis on "the designer" and suggesting that all problems can be solve through the singular emphasis of "the design process," are all still frequently to be found in the teaching studios around the world that are still based on a master-apprentice relationship. The emphasis on design as a minor form of art that is still found in education, practice, business and the media acts as a barrier to the generation and acceptance of a body of knowledge and methodology that is vital to the contemporary development of new applications, such as systems work in teams; designs that rather than emphasizing "the designer," empower generations of users; and service design emphasizing interactivity, multiple technique and methods to solve a myriad problems.

A further obstacle to design lacking the capacity to fulfill its potential in the modern world is that the overwhelming majority of designers work in business or commercial contexts, most of them in middle-level posts where they carry out the orders of executives who are frequently from other disciplines. The predominance of commercial values and, in particular, the proposition that greed is good, that it is what fuels the working processes of markets, has left designers, and many others, without a voice to challenge this pigs-in-the-trough approach to how the business affairs of nations and companies should be conducted.

We are living in an age in which the dominance of mass-production is no longer total, but, instead, is being superseded by flexible, information technology that is accessible to ever-growing numbers of people around the planet and gives not only access, but, increasingly, a new and remarkable degree of control. It is this point that needs to be clearly understood in terms of its potential.

Mass production and all the other manifestations of the age of mass, such as mass media, mass communications, mass transport, mass education, mass marketing, mass advertising and mass consumption, were in effect controlled by producers, who sought to shape markets, with users as a passive constituency to be targeted for producers' benefit. The result of this can be seen in the way many parts of the world in under-developed and developing economies are still bereft of the basic necessities for a decent life.

It is into this gulf between the contrasting arenas of commercial control and poverty-stricken backwardness that INDEX: is seeking to develop a niche in which the best design ideas of our time are dedicated to the poor, the stricken, the oppressed and deprived of our world, who number still in hundreds of millions. Giving them not just relief from poverty and sickness, but using appropriate technology to give them a voice in decisions affecting their life and ensuring they are heard, giving them recognition and dignity for their achievements, and above all giving them a vision of a better life for their children. INDEX: rejects the tawdry banalities of celebrity design and its manipulative cycles of unnecessary change to focus instead on remedies for the wastage of crucial abilities that constitute a vital constituent of our future human capital. INDEX: does not pretend to have all the answers, but it does seek to ask some pertinent questions and it can support appropriate solutions. To work with INDEX: as I have the honour to do, is to feel hope and a sense of values and the conviction that no problem is insuperable. It brings together committed people on a basis of common endeavours that have compassion at their core, rather than greed, and so generates a conviction that something must be done and can be done to improve the lives of those who, through no fault of their own, are trapped in deprivation.

W. B. Yeats wrote that "the centre cannot hold." The old centres of power and influence are indeed increasingly under pressure. All is not decay and crumbling ruin, however, organisations such as INDEX: represent new centres of ideas and practice, vigorously asserting a focus on people and articulating values appropriate to how the new design of our time can serve their needs.

APPENDIX: A FIRST BIBLIOGRAPHY OF JOHN HESKETT'S PUBLISHED WORK

Note: The following is not definitive. It is based on a resume listing complied by John Heskett a few years before his death but this was incomplete. This represents my understanding of Heskett's published work as December 2015. The format follows that of the original.

Books: As single author

2011   *Works in China*, Joint author with Michael Young, privately published, Hong Kong.

2005   *A Very Short Introduction to Design*. Translated into Spanish, Swedish, Korean, Portuguese (Brazil), Japanese, Greek, Chinese, Turkish and Serbo-Croat. Oxford University Press, Oxford. This book is the second edition of *Toothpicks and Logos: Design in Everyday Life*, Oxford University Press, Oxford, 2002.

1989   *Philips: A Study of the Corporate Management of Design*. Trefoil Publications, London, and Rizzoli, New York.

1986   *Design in Germany 1870–1918*, Trefoil Press, London and Taplinger, New York.

1980   *Industrial Design*. Translated into Spanish, Portuguese, Japanese, Korean, Dutch and Italian. Thames & Hudson, London.

Books: Edited

2007   *Very Hong Kong* (a review of ten years of Hong Kong design since the handover to China), Hong Kong Design Centre and Hong Kong Trade Development Centre.

2004   *Design in Hong Kong*, Hong Kong Trade Development Council, Hong Kong.

Reports

2005   *Design In Asia: Review of national design policies and business use of design in China, South Korea and Taiwan.* Research report commissioned by the Design Council, UK as a contribution to Sir George Cox's report to the Chancellor of the Exchequer on the future of design in the United Kingdom.

2003   *Shaping the Future: Design for Hong Kong: Report of the Design Education Task Force.* Hong Kong Polytechnic University, Hong Kong.

Contributions to anthologies, conference proceedings, catalogues

2010   "A New Chapter," *Hong Kong: Creative Ecologies: The Shaping of a Design Culture*, ed. Kai-Yin Lo; Hong Kong Design Centre/ Hong Kong Trade Development Council, Hong Kong, pp. 208–13 (in Chinese, pp. 214–15).

2005   "Some Lessons of Design History," in *Designkompetanse— Utvkling, forskning og undervisning*, ed. Astrid Skjerven, Oslo: Akademisk Publishing, pp. 11–21.

2003   "Industrial Design in the United States," *Hall of Fame Companies, Searching for Excellence in Design: A Review of the Twentieth Century*, Peter Zec, on behalf of ICSID, ed. Essen: Reddot.

2003   "The Desire for the New: The Context of Brooks Stevens Career," *Industrial Strength Design: How Brooks Stevens Shaped Your World*, ed. Glenn Adamson, Milwaukee: Milwaukee Art Museum and Cambridge, MA, The MIT Press, pp. 1–8.

2002   "The Emergence of the Industrial Design Profession in the United States," *The Alliance of Art and Industry: Toledo Designs for a Modern America*, ed. Davira S. Taragin, Toledo: Toledo Museum of Art, pp. 67–81.

1998   "The Growth of Industrial Design in Japan," *Japan 2000: Architecture and Design for the Japanese Public*, ed. John Zukowsky, Chicago: Art Institute of Chicago and Prestel: London and Munich, pp. 82–93.

1998   "The Economic Role of Industrial Design," in Tevifk Balcioğlu
        (ed.), *The Role of Product Design in Post Industrial Society*,
        Middle East Technical University Press, METU-Kent Institute,
        Ankara, pp. 77–92.

1998   "Design function of a product," in *The Handbook of Technology
        Management*, Richard Dorf, ed., Boca Raton: CRC Press, section
        14.1, pp. 14.2–14.6.

1995   "Cultural Human Factors," *Design Innovation for Global
        Competition*, Sharon Poggenpohl ed., Institute of Design, IIT,
        Chicago, 1995, pp. 26–40.

1995   "Design in Inter-war Germany," *Designing Modernity: The
        Arts of Reform and Persuasion*, Wendy Kaplan, ed. Thames &
        Hudson and the Wolfsonian Foundation, London and New York,
        pp. 256–85.

1993   "Friction and inertia in industrial design," in *The Necessity of
        Friction*, ed. Nordal Akerman, The Swedish Institute for Future
        Studies and Heidelberg: Physica Verlag, pp. 291–308.

1993   "A Question of Image," in *High Speed Trains: Fast Tracks to the
        Future*, John Whitelegg, Staffan Hulten and Torbjorn Flink, ed.
        Hawes, Leading Edge.

1992   "Design and Business: The Challenge Ahead," in conference
        proceedings *Design: A Strategic Partnership with Business,*
        American Center for Design, Chicago, pp. 32–6.

1990   "Modernism and Archaism in Design in the Third Reich," in *The
        Nazification of Art*. Brandon Taylor and Wilfried van der Will,
        eds. Winchester Press, Winchester, pp. 110–27.

1990   "American Design in the 1950s," in *Raymond Loewy*, catalogue of
        an exhibition jointly organized by Internationales Design Zentrum,
        Berlin, the Stedelijk Museum, Amsterdam and the Centre Georges
        Pompidou, Paris. Prestel Verlag, Munich, pp. 115–22.

1988   "British Industrial Design since 1945," Boris Ford, ed., *The
        Cambridge Cultural History of Modern Britain*, Volume 9,
        Cambridge University Press, Cambridge, pp. 288–318.

1987   "Industrial Design" in Hazel Conway (ed.) *Design History: A
        Students Handbook*, Routledge, London, pp. 110–33.

1979   "Tubular Steel in German Industrial Design," in Barbie Campbell-
        Cole and Tim Benton (ed.), *Tubular Steel Furniture*, The Art
        Book Company, London, pp. 22–7.

1979   "Archaismus und Modernismus im Design im dritten Reich," in
        B.Hinz et al (eds.), *Die Dekoration der Gewalt: Kunst u. Medien
        im Faschismus*, Anabas Verlag, Giessen.

Articles

2010 "Can the Centre Hold?" *Index* (Denmark)

2008 "Creating economic value by design," *International Journal of Design*, 3(1), 71–84.

2005 "HK Design: Lo Stato Delle Cose/The State of Things," *Arbitare*, #450, May, pp. 182–92 (in Italian and English).

2003 "Past, Present, Future in Design," *Design Indaba*, #4, pp. 24–6.

2002-3 Review of Regina Lee Blaszczyk, *Imagining consumers: Design and Innovation from Wedgewood to Corning* in **Studies in the Decorative Arts**, Fall-Winter 2002-3, vol. X, no. 1, pp. 147–9.

2002 'Wo bleibt das Neue Design? Waiting for a New Design," *Form, The European Design Magazine*, # 185, September/October. pp. 92–8.

2002 "Past, Present and Future in Design for Industry," *Design Issues*, vol. 17, no. 1, Winter.

1999 "National Design Policy and Economic Change," *MD-Magazine* (Germany), August. In German and English, pp. 58–60.

1997 "Past, Present and Future in Design," *Cooper-Hewitt National Design Museum Magazine*. vol. 4, #3, Autumn, pp. 14–17.

1994 "Trends in Amerikanischen Design," *Special Design Supplement, Frankfurter Allgemeine Zeitung*, November 29, Frankfurt-am-Main, Germany.

1994 "Making Waves: Britain's new Design Council mandates a changing of the guards." in *International Design*. September/October, pp. 28–30.

1994 "An interview with John Heskett," *Design*, September, Seoul, Korea.

1994 "Re-designing Design," *Nikkei Design*, June, Tokyo.

1994 "Mr. Sunbeam: Ivar Jepson, 1903-1968," in *I.D.*, May/June.

1994 "Globalization - fact or fancy?," *I.D.*, March/April.

1994 "Eastern expansion," *I.D.*, January/February, pp. 26–8.

1993 "Creative destruction: the nature and consequences of change through design (effects of design innovation on business),"*I.D.*, September/October, pp. 28, 30.

1993 "The Future of Design," *Design Processes Newletter*, vol. 5, no. 1, Chicago, pp. 1–3, 5.

1993 Review of Arthur Pulos, *The American Design Adventure 1940-1975*, in *Science, Technology and Human Values*, vol. 18, no. 2, Spring, pp. 263–5.

1993   "Lessons abroad: what America can learn from Germany's integrated design policy," *I.D.*, May/June, pp. 34, 36.

1993   "Taking the Next Steps in Washington (A design policy for America?)," *I.D.*, March/April, pp. 30, 33.

1993   "Management theory in translation (what constitutes quality and the problems of how design can contribute to it)." *I.D.* January/February, pp. 30, 34.

1992   "The Business of design: American designers hit by a failing economy and pervasive corporate apathy," *I.D.*, November/December, pp. 68–73.

1992   "Do designers need public endorsement to contribute to a company's values?," *I.D.*, September/October, pp. 46–7.

1992   "GM's current woes reveal the price of corporate arrogance and amnesia," *I.D.* May/June, pp. 38, 40–1.

1992   "Commerce or Culture: Industrialization and Design," *American Center for Design Journal*, Vol. 6, no. 1, Chicago, pp. 14–33.

1992   "Putting bite into the bark: How RCA is using design as a strategic tool in its fight- back." *I.D.* March/April. [Japanese translation in *Nikkei Design*, May, pp. 126–31.]

1992   "Why don't American companies use design more intelligently?," *I.D.*, Jan/Feb, pp. 36, 38–9.

1991   "Product Integrity," *Design Processes Newsletter*, Institute of Design, IIT, Chicago. Re-published under the same title in *Innovation*, journal of the IDSA, Spring 1992, pp. 17–19.

1990   "Design and international markets." Introduction to conference proceedings, *Strategies in a Changing World,* American Center for Design, Chicago, October.

1989   "Integrating Design into Industry," *Design Processes Newsletter*, no. 2, vol. 3, pp. 1, 2–6; and 1990, no. 1, vol. 4. Chicago. [Hebrew translation in *Packaging and Design*, nos. 37–38, 1991. Tel-Aviv]

1989   "Design in the 1990s." *Industrielle Ontwerpen*. Rotterdam. December.

1989   "Philips featured in the Triad design project." *Industrielle Ontwerpen*. Rotterdam. November

1988   "Mud at the wall?" (design education in the UK). *Design*. October. London.

1988   "Design Economics." *AXIS*. June. Tokyo.

1984   "Made in Japan." (Interviews with top designers at Cannon, Honda, Japanese National Railways, and Matsushita) *I.D.* January/February.

1984   "Design und Kunsthandwerk unter Faschismus." *Kunstchronik*.
        no. 1.

1983   Review of *Consultant Design: The History and Practice of the
        Designer in Industry"* by Penny Sparke, and *The Industrial
        Designer and the Public* by Jonathan Woodham, Design History
        Society Newsletter, September 1983.

1981   "The Role of Design History in Design Courses," Design History
        Society Newsletter, no. 10, February 1981, pp. 35–40.

1980   "Modernism and Archaism in Design in the Third Reich,"
        Block 3, pp. 13–24.

1978   "Art and Design in Nazi Germany," *History Workshop Journal*,
        no. 6, pp. 139–53.

INDEX

Adler, cars   170
Adler, Jonathan   49, 51, 253
AEG   71, 154, 155, 164, 167
Aristotle   258
artifice and nature   76–7
Arts and Crafts Movement   36, 113,
      145–6

Banham, Reyner   4
Bauhaus   159, 160, 163, 167, 172
Beatrice Europe   192
Behrens, Peter   71, 143–4, 146
Berlin, S-Bahn design   150
Berry, Wendell   38
Blake, William   34
Blasscyck, Regina   126–30
Boulton, Mathew   28–9
Braun   71, 75, 191, 225, 234, 287
British Telecom   295–6

Canon   278
Caplan, Ralph   125
Carlyle, Thomas   181
Chandler, Alfred D.   127
change, processes of   76
China
    cuisine and cooking
            implements   84–8
    culture   237–8
    history, and design   343
    Pearl River Delta   241
    trade, shipping   96–7
    trade, Silk Road   95–6
China design   69–70
    Ming Dynasty chair   83–4
    reading #6   82–8
China design companies
    Founder Technology   246
    Huawei Technologies   244–5
    Konka Telecommunications   245–6

Lotusland Furniture   246
    UTOP design   247
China design education   248
Chinese design policy   237–51
    Beijing Industrial Design
          Center   239
    central government policy   238
    Guandong Industrial Design
          Association   241
    Guangzhow Industrial Design
          Promotion Association
          242–3
    Industrial Designers
          Association   241
    Shenzen Design Union   243
Cicero   75
Clark, T. J.   3–4
Coca-Cola   297
Cole, Henry   30–1, 32
Colgate-Palmolive   294
Colt, Samuel   106–7
Corning   126, 130
Cox report (UK Govt)   179, 237–51,
      252–67
    introduction to   226–7
craft   23, 27, 100, 105, 114, 147,
      164–5, 168–9, 173
    adaptation   121, 132, 164–5
    Arts and Crafts movement   23,
      35–6, 40–1, 113
    means   33, 100
    practices   26–7, 79, 98, 132, 335
    production   120–1
    in history   74–8
    skills   26, 68, 91, 101, 230
    tradition(al)   107, 109, 149, 161–2,
      164, 169, 335
    training   146–7, 335 (see also
      design education)
    values of   26, 272–3

craftsmanship 89, 129, 170–1
  and craft labour 26
  and Division of Labour 28–9
    in slavery 89, 97–9
    traditional 29–30
craftsmen (craftspeople) 26, 29,
        68–70, 93, 143–4, 147, 169,
        see also nomadic cultures
  as entrepreneurs 69
  Germany (*see* German design)
  guilds 68–70
  slaves, as craftspersons 98–101
creative destruction 80, 179, 271,
        273–4, 278, 283–5, 317, 362
Csikzentmihayi, Mihaly 75
culture and environment 77

Denmark 344
design, concept and capacity 5, 8,
        19–23
  basic/unique characteristic 20, 356
  competency 275
  confusions over the term "design",
        19–21, 118–19, 335
    art 49, 69 (*see also* history
        of design, tension with art
        history)
    definitions 21–2, 356 (*see also*
        history of design, layered &
        accumulative)
  distinction, between art and 255–6
  evolution of 77–82
  functions of 284, 338
  future, and 46, 267
  generic or species capacity 20–3,
        65, 82
    abstraction (as ablility) 75–6
    knowledge base, necessity
        for 65
  modern 159–60
  modernity and 164
  neo-classicism 43–4
  thinking 181–2
  user-centred 46, 79, 256, 265
        (*see also* design diagrams,
        user-centered design)
    customers 52, 70
    and users 47, 53
  value, and 42–3, 52–3, 181, 187,
        272–3, 280–1, 310–11, 316

Design Council (UK) 7, 14, 60,
        179, 230, 243, 252, 255, 260,
        264–6, 360
design diagrams
  context of design 264
  context of design practice 263
  context of production 52
  context of use 53
  design as research 258
  design as strategy 260
  designer as enabler 257
  designer as formgiver 256
  knowledge and complexity in
        designing 259
  levels of design practice 261
  process, complex model 51
  process, simple model 50
  user-centred design 256
  Value Chain 255
designers: roles
  anonymous 162
  as artists 37
  conscience 124–5 (*see also*
        design practice, critique of
        profession)
  economic thinking, and 47
  enabler 257–8, 337 (*see also* design
        diagrams, designer as enabler)
  formgiver 256, 258, 337 (*see also*
        design diagrams, designer as
        formgiver)
  organizations, roles in 260–2
        (*see also* design
        diagrams 262–4)
  originators 52
  researcher 258
  "star" 69, 137, 260, 265
  work in team 80
design history, *see* history of design
design: policy, national
  countries
    China (*see* reading #21 237–51)
    Design Council (UK) 7, 260,
        265–6
    Germany 46 (*see also* reading
        #20 233–6)
    Japan (*see* Japan, MITI)
    Nazi Germany, policy towards
        design 166, 169
    UK (*see* reading #22 252–67)

introduction to 224–8
objectives 229
    national competitiveness 231–2
review of issues 224–8, 229–30
design, practice
  bad design 20, 266
  business 11, 50–1, 72, 192,
    269–70
    approaches (see OEM, OBM....)
  concern, human factors 291–2
  contexts of design
    profession 263, 264
  critique, of profession
    as executant 124
    conscience 125, 356
  cultural factors in 293–302
    Japan's 136
  economics, and 42–56 (see also
    reading # 26 303–27)
    design standpoint on
      economics 49–56
    economic standpoint on
      design 7, 43–8
  education, educational,
    problems 55–6, 61, 182,
      232, 266, 339, 348, 356
    institutional influences 48
    managers 200–1
    planning 42, 262
    Policy (in Philips) 203
  problems
    of appropriation 21
    of range 21
    of studying 77
  reflective theory 258
  research, as 258–9
  roles across history 81–2, 130
    as agency 7
    as intermediary 128
  strategy, as 258 (and see below,
    re manufacturing)
  styling, critique 125 (and see
    Adler, Jonathan) 164, 185
  tacit knowledge and 47, 55, 258,
    271, 273, 319–20
Deskey, Donald 336
Detroit (car industry) 194–8
Diderot, Denis 74
Disneyland 298, 300
Division of labour/labour 28–9, 121

Doblin, Jay 125, 213, 275, 277, 336
Dresser, Christopher 31
Drucker, Peter 186–7, 196, 312
Dyson (UK) 231

economics of creative destruction 80,
    179, 271, 273–4, 278, 283–5,
    317, 362
economic standpoint on
    design 43–8, 324–7
economics (theory)
  Austrian theory 46, 270–2, 283–4,
    303, 310–12, 315, 325
  Institutional theory 48,
    312–16, 325
  National system 321–3
  Neo-classical models 43–4, 47, 54,
    170, 269, 280, 304–11, 324
    critique of neo-classical
      theory 43–4
  New Growth Theory 47, 316–21,
    324, 326
  quantitative, problem 54
  users (in economic theory) 53
economists
  Coase, Ronald 314
  David, Paul 319
  Hayek, Friedrich von 46, 270,
    311–12
  List, Ferdinand 44, 312–13
  Menger, Carl 46, 272, 310
  Mises, Ludwig 311
  Nelson, Richard 48
  North, Douglas 315
  Polyani, Michael 320
  Reich, Robert 233
  Romer, Paul 317–21
  Rosenberg, Nathan 49
  Schumpeter, Joseph 80, 274,
    284–5, 316–17 (see also
    creative destruction)
  Smith, Adam 27–8, 307, 321
    Wealth of Nations 28
  Veblen, Thorstein 271, 273,
    313–14
  Weiser, Theodore von 272
Electrolux 295
electronic technology 78–9
ERCO lighting 130, 222, 235
  Maack, Klaus-Jürgen 191

Fallan, Kjetl   13 n.i
Feyerabend, Paul   279
Focke-Wulf   156
Fokker, Anthony   153
Ford, Henry   54–5, 114, 154, 184
Ford motor company   54–5, 184,
        187, 192
France, Merchantilist tradition and
        luxury goods   129, 144, 230

Gandhi, Mahatma   32
Geidion, Siegfried   2
General Electric   205
General Motors (GM)   38, 183–8,
        225–6
    Sloan, Alfred   183
Germany, design   6, 35–6, 44–5, 130,
        156–7 (see also readings #11,
        #12, #13)
    design 1870–1918   62–3, 140–51
    design education c.1900   146–7
    design in German press   234, 236
    design policy   233–6
    Deutsche Industrie Normen
        (DIN)   162
    Deutsche Normen Auschuss
        (DNA)   162
    Handwerke   164
    Jugendstil   142
    Ministry of Economics   235
    navy, design for   149
    Nazi period: design in (see Nazi
        Germany, design in)
    Reichkuratorium für
        Wirtschaftlichkeit
        (RKW)   163
Gillette   286
Grand Rapids, furniture
        industry   111–12
Grange, Kenneth   117
Great Exhibition, Crystal Palace,
        1851   30, 105, 108

Halberstam, David   54–5
Hamilton, Richard   4
Harley, Earl   184
Heskett, John
    art and Design in Nazi
        Germany, Heskett on   6, 11,
        13, 62–3, 364

biography   1–2, 5–7, 17, 178,
        340–1, 346–50
books
    Crafts, Commerce, Industry   7–8,
        10, 12, 59–60, 74, 89
    Design: A Very Short
        Introduction   6, 17, 268
    Design in Germany
        1870–1918   6, 62
    Industrial Design   5, 60, 69,
        114, 349–50
    Toothpicks & Logos   6, 268
corporate design policies, Heskett
        on 177–8 and see readings
        #14–#18
critical perspective on   11
design History, in context of   2–3,
        4–5
design Management Institute,
        and   6
Hong Kong, and   340–5
involvement in design policy   7, 178
journalism
    I-D: International
        Design   10–11, 178
    move towards economics   7
    national design policies, Heskett
        on   178–9 (see also section
        (III) B. readings #19–#22)
    UK Design Council, work with   7,
        178–9, 230, 260, 265
    in USA, 1989–2004
        American Center for
            Design   178
        Institute of Design, IIT, and   6,
            42, 178–9, 275, 336, 351
    writings, range of   10–12
Hirano, Takao & Associates   133, 137
history, role of   80, 130
history of design
    early development of the
        field   3–6, 348
    layered & accumulative   24, 335
    vs. linear and sequential   66
    relation design history and the
        past   88
    tension with art history   3–4,
        23, 66
    viewed in evolutionary
        perspective   65

History Workshop Journal   62, 348
Hobsbawm, Eric   61
Holden (Australia)   185
Honda   135–6
Hong Kong   294, *see also* reading
        #28   340–5
Hong Kong, design strategies in
        business   215–23, *see also*
        Manufacturing
Hong Kong Polytechnic University
        (Swire School of Design)   61,
        215, 341–2
Humanscale   257

I:D, International Design   6, 11–12,
        42, 178–9, 185, 189, 237,
        283, 303
IDSA (Industrial Designers Society of
        America)   123, 178
Index (Denmark)   355–7
industrialization   24–41, 61, 71, 101,
        120, 131, 164, 321, 323
Industrial revolution   24–5, 29, 61, 70,
        120, 283
innovation, by design   48–9, 51–2,
        107, 200, 261, 271, 274,
        283–6, 309, 317
    innovative   23, 47, 70, 227,
        277, 326
Institute of Design, IIT (Illinois Institute
        of Technology)   61, 133,
        179, 336

Japan, history
    1850s–1930s   131
    evolution, industrial
        design   134, 138
    retro-design   137
Japan, MITI (Ministry of
        International Trade and
        Industry)   46, 132–3, 136,
        230, 325
Japan, Olympic Games 1964   134, 154
Japan Industrial Designers
        Association   132
Jaumann, Anton   44
Jefferson, Thomas   106
Jepson, Ivar   12
Jordan, Chuck (GM)   196
Junkers   156

Knoll   157
Kodak   110
    Brownie Camera   110

Latham, Richard   125
Lawrence, D. H.   30
Lowey, Raymond   336
LSE (London School Economics)   1,
        17, 181, 191, 269–70, 347
Lukács, Georg   3–4, 8

McCormick, Cyrus   108
McDonalds   300
McKinsey, value-chain   254–5
making, generic human capacity   67
    history of   74 (*see also* reading
        #7   89–103)
    separation, from design   70
Mannesmann   152–3
manufacturing strategies (Hong Kong),
        see also reading #18   215–23,
        #28   340–5
    OBM (Own Brand Manufacturing)
        220–2
    ODM (Original Design
        Manufacturing)   218–20
    OEM (Original Equipment
        Manufacturing)   217–18
    OSM(Original Strategic
        Management)   222–3
Marlboro   294
mass production   71, 128, 275, 375
    and flexible production   79–80
    and futures   78
Matsushita Electric   117
Merton, Jubal   26
Montgomery Ward   112
Morris, William   34, 111
Mr. Coffee   193–4
Munich   148
Muthesius, Hermann   44, 144–6

Naumann, Friedrich   44
Nazi Germany, design in   119,
        157, 165–73
    crafts in Nazi Germany   165,
        167–8, 170–1
    Deutsche Arbeitsfront (DA) German
        Labour Front   167
    Deutsche Werenkunde   171

domestic design   170
Four Year Plan 1936   167–8, 171
'Good Form'   161
interpretations of design
      in   159–61
policy towards design   166, 169
relations to Weimar period   172
'Strength through Joy'   120
use of aluminium   168
Nelson, George   304
Nike   257
Nissan   137, 193
nomadic cultures
      (and design)   89–94
   steppe tribes   92

objects, role of in life   27, 32,
      74–5, 92–3
   manifest creative ability   81, 356
OBM (Own Brand
      Manufacturing)   220–2
ODM (Original Design
      Manufacturing)   218–20
OEM (Original Equipment
      Manufacturing)   217–18
Oldsmobile   114, 193
Olivetti, Camillo   191
OSM (Original Strategic
      Management)   222–3
Owen, Robert   321

Papanek, Victor   2
past, source of value, see reading
      #27   334–9, 343
past present relations   66
Paul, Bruno   142, 147
Paxton, Joseph   30
Pearl River Delta   241, 247, 276,
      342, 344
Pentagram   117
Pevsner, Nikolaus   2, 4, 69
Phillips   117, 195–203, 268
   Blaich, Robert   195–203
Pick, Frank   191
Poelzig, Hans   146
Poggenpohl, Sharon Helmer   181–2
Popper, Karl   279
Porsche, Ferdinand   119
Porter, Michael   256

product Development and design,
      strategies   134–6, 164, 177,
      181, 245, 260–1, 278, 281, 286
products
   changing conceptions of   336–7
   quality, importance of   29 (see also
      reading #24   287–91, 230)
Pulos, Arthur   123–5

RCA (Radio Corporation America),
      case study of design as a
      strategic tool, see also reading
      #17   204–13
Redgrave, Richard   31
Remington, Philo   110
Remington Typewriter   110
Riemerschmid, Richard   143, 149
Royko, Mike   193
Ruskin, John   32–3, 35, 39, 111
Rykwert, Joseph   3

St. Louis exhibition, 1904   144–5
Sakai, Naoki   137
Salt, Titus   31
Schmacher, E. F.   39
Schmidt, Karl   148
Schumpeter, Joseph   80, 274,
      284–5, 316–17
Schweik (Good Soldier)   161
Sears Roebuck   112
Siemens   161, 234
Simon, Herbert   4, 76, 270–1, 304
Singer, Isaac   109
Singer Sewing Machine   109
slavery   97–102
slaves, as artisans   98–102
   craftsmanship   99–101
   sweetgrass baskets   100
Sloan, Alfred   38, 184–6, 193
Sony   280
   Walkman   285
Stam, Mart   155
Stempel, Robert   193
Sturt, Georg   26

tacit knowledge   47, 55, 258, 262,
      271, 273, 319, 326
Thonet   157, 167
3M   222, 286

Toyota   135, 277
Tubular Steel (Germany,
        1900–1940)   152–7
Tupperware   285
Turin exhibition 1902   144
typewriter, development of, USA   110

United Kingdom, Design Council, *see*
        design policy
United Kingdom, trade deficit in
        manufactured goods   280
Utilitarianism   32

Velde, Van der   147
vernacular tradition in design   121–2
Volkswagen   119–20, 161, 298

Wagenfeld, William   161
Watt, James   29
Wedgewood, Joseph   29, 126–7
Weimar   147, 160, 166
Werenkunde   157
Werkbund (Germany)   35, 235
Wheelwright's Shop
        (George Sturt)   26
Whitney, Eli   106, 115
Woolworth, F. W.   127
Wright, Frank Lloyd   112–13

Yamaha   135
Yeats, W. B.   355

Zara   277